COLERIDGE'S ASSERTION OF RELIGION

COLERIDGE'S ASSERTION OF RELIGION

ESSAYS ON THE *OPUS MAXIMUM*

Edited by

J<small>EFFREY</small> W. B<small>ARBEAU</small>

PEETERS
LEUVEN – PARIS – DUDLEY, MA
2006

Library of Congress Cataloging-in-Publication Data

Coleridge's assertion of religion : essays on the Opus Maximum / edited by Jeffrey W. Barbeau.
       p. cm. -- (Studies in philosophical theology; 33)
       Includes bibliographical references and index.
       ISBN 90-429-1787-3 (alk. paper)
       1. Coleridge, Samuel Taylor, 1772-1834--Religion. 2. Religion in literature.
       3. Coleridge, Samuel Taylor, 1772-1834--Opus Maximum. 4. Coleridge, Samuel
       Taylor, 1772-1834--Criticism and interpretation. I. Barbeau, Jeffrey W. II. Series.

PR4487.R4C66 2006
821.7--dc22

                                                                            2006043999

© 2006 - Peeters, Bondgenotenlaan 153, 3000 Leuven, Belgium.

ISBN-10 90-429-1787-3
ISBN-13 9789042917873
D. 2006/0602/77

In Memoriam

The Rev. Prof. Colin E. Gunton (1941-2003)

TABLE OF CONTENTS

PREFACE

The eminent Victorian philosopher John Stuart Mill once remarked that S. T. Coleridge's contribution as a poet had been given rightful praise by the mid-nineteenth century: "The healthier taste, and more intelligent canons of poetic criticism, which he was himself mainly instrumental in diffusing, have at length assigned to him his proper rank, as one among the great, and (if we look to the powers shown rather than to the amount of actual achievement) among the greatest, names in our literature." By contrast, according to Mill, Coleridge's place as an intellectual remained almost wholly without assessment: "But as a philosopher, the class of thinkers has scarcely yet arisen by whom he is to be judged... This time has not yet come for Coleridge."[1] The completion of the momentous critical edition, *The Collected Works of Samuel Taylor Coleridge* (*CC*), and, perhaps most notably, the publication of Coleridge's unfinished *Opus Maximum*, the "great work" in which Coleridge hoped to demonstrate the philosophical vitality of the Christian religion, have the potential to rewrite the appraisal of Coleridge that has taken place since Mill. Left to J. H. Green at Coleridge's death, the fragmentary remains of the *opus* were the source of considerable speculation during the nineteenth century. In the twentieth century, renewed interest in the unpublished remains of the *opus* led to the collection of the fragments by several libraries. Still, the fragments remained inaccessible to all but those few scholars willing and able to examine the *opus* remains in manuscript. The completion of the *Collected Coleridge* has now made the whole of Coleridge's wide-ranging writings — from his major publications to a vast array of previously unpublished notebook entries — accessible to all. The essays in this volume are the first collection of scholarship on the published *Opus Maximum*.

The foundation for this collection of essays lies in two events worth recounting. Shortly after the release of the *Opus Maximum*, volume 15 of the *CC*, Douglas Hedley suggested that we jointly lead a post-graduate seminar on the *Opus Maximum* at the Faculty of Divinity of the University of Cambridge. The seminar was held weekly and included both post-graduate students and University faculty members. Each week a short portion of the text was introduced and then scrutinized by those attending

---

[1] John Stuart Mill, *On Bentham & Coleridge* (New York: Harper, 1950), 103-4.

the seminar. The second event was the capstone of the seminar: a one-day reading workshop, entitled "S. T. Coleridge and the *Opus Maximum*," held at Clare College, Cambridge. The reading workshop was designed to expand the participation of the original seminar and to introduce members of the University and abroad to the *opus* by actively engaging participants with a series of short papers and extensive discussion of the text. Five scholars produced 30-40 minute papers. Each paper was followed by over an hour of discussion of a related excerpt of the text. At the conclusion of the event, it was decided that a volume would be produced that not only included revised versions of the papers given during the reading workshop, but, expanding the scope of scholarly engagement once again, also incorporated additional essays by members of the broader Coleridge community who were unable to participate in the seminar and conference. This volume is thereby the fruit of a series of intense, informed, and collegial reading workshops in which the text of the *Opus Maximum* has been scrutinized, digested, and analyzed by an international assemblage of Coleridge specialists.

This text consists of thirteen contiguous essays on distinct facets of Coleridge's thought as developed in the *Opus Maximum*. The first chapter ("The Quest for System: An Introduction to Coleridge's Lifelong Project") is a biographical and historical introduction to Coleridge's persistent hope to write a *magnum opus*. There, I compare Coleridge's many attempts to outline his projected *magnum opus* and set the text within the philosophical context of other contemporary efforts to complete a universal account of religion.

If the many accounts of Coleridge's *magnum opus* name what Coleridge had planned to write, Daniel W. Hardy's essay ("Harmony and Mutual Implication in the *Opus Maximum*") sets the tone of the volume by explaining what he believes Coleridge actually achieved. Hardy proposes that Coleridge's achievement lies in his method of discovering the center of all things in God, a prominent theme in several essays. Through an examination of prose and poetry alike, including the *Rime of the Ancient Mariner* and the *Treatise on Method*, Hardy maintains that a system of "mutual implication" finding its reference point in God drives Coleridge's philosophical theology and marks an important contribution to the history of ideas.

The harmony that Hardy perceives in Coleridge's system gains a complementary corroboration in Luke S. H. Wright's essay ("*On the Divine Ideas*: The Systematic Theology of Samuel Taylor Coleridge"). Although the now-published form of the *magnum opus*, the *Opus Maximum*, joins a series of manuscript fragments of the projected work into a single volume, Wright proposes that the *Opus Maximum* — properly arranged — nonetheless contains a "logically progressive," systematic theology. Wright maintains that a reordering of the existing fragments reveals sixteen consecutive chapters of a complete and cogent — though not wholly expanded — constructive theology.

The apparent fragmentariness of the *Opus Maximum* will long be a source of discussion among those who study Coleridge. While Hardy approaches Coleridge's fragmentary *Opus* by means of "mutual implication" and Wright through the lens of theological system, Murray J. Evans's essay ("Reading 'Will' in Coleridge's *Opus Maximum*: The Rhetoric of Transition and Repetition") assesses the unifying features of the manuscripts through an examination of rhetoric. Evans proposes the metaphor of "unfolded summary" as a means of conceptualizing Coleridge's philosophical argument and rhetoric of repetition in the *Opus Maximum*.

As with Evans, rhetoric drives James Vigus's suggestion ("'With his garland and his singing robes about him': The Persistence of the Literary in the *Opus Maximum*") that the *Opus Maximum* is "deliberately unliterary." With particular attention to *The Friend* and *Biographia Literaria*, Vigus attends to Coleridge's pursuit of truth in the *Opus Maximum* through the identification of a connected rhetorical style that re-envisions the long-held myth of a "divided" Coleridge. Moreover, Vigus examines the rhetorical function of authoritative quotation in the *Opus Maximum* to provide insight into Coleridge's quest for a unifying philosophy.

The division Vigus contends with — particularly between poetry and prose — provides Graham Davidson ("Duty and Power: Conflicts of the Will in Coleridge's Creation of the Self") with a framework for exploring Coleridge's theoretical and practical visions of love. Davidson maintains, with marked attention to "Fragment 1" and Coleridge's striking description of the relationship between the mother and child, that Coleridge's statements on the rational human will fail to conform to his explorations of the morally responsible self.

Next, Scott Masson argues ("Repeating the Act of the Infinite in the Finite: Theological Anthropology in Coleridge's *Opus Maximum*") that the responsible self and consciousness form the basis of Coleridge's development of anthropology in the *Opus Maximum*. Masson's essay challenges the identification of Coleridge as a Romantic by turning to the *Biographia Literaria* and the role of the Imagination; he thereby highlights how Coleridge's philosophical claims were grounded, for example, on theological discussions of conscience and revelation.

Indeed, the connection that Masson makes between theology and anthropology indicates the central place of conscience in Coleridge's writings. In the essay that follows ("Science and the Depersonalization of the Divine: Pantheism, Unitarianism, and the Limits of Natural Theology"), I place Coleridge's turn to conscience in the context of his prominent dismissal of William Paley's natural theology. I examine a key passage of "Fragment 2" of the *Opus Maximum* in order to show how Coleridge's response to scientific rationalism illuminates his attempt to distance himself from the atheism he perceived in both pantheism and, surprisingly, Unitarianism.

The complexities of pantheism and monotheism also provide a framework for Alan P. R. Gregory's essay ("'That I may be here': Human Persons and Divine Personeity in the *Opus Maximum*"). Gregory explores the Trinitarian theology that Coleridge turned to shortly after 1800 and describes how Trinitarian relationality supplies the ground for personality and an ontology for a distinction between "persons" and "things." Notably, Gregory's account of personality draws forth a renewed consideration of the relationship between Reason and revelation.

Pantheism provides an important point of reference in any discussion of Coleridge's philosophical theology. Yet Douglas Hedley's contribution ("Philosophia Trinitatis: Coleridge, Pantheism, and a Christian Cabbala") helpfully reminds us to distinguish between disparate forms of Neoplatonism. Hedley offers a striking critique to McFarland's oft-discussed thesis accounting for Coleridge's contact with the "Pantheist tradition." Hedley, focusing especially on "Fragment 3" of the *Opus Maximum*, maintains that Coleridge's invective against pantheism ought to be set in the broader context of the Romantic-idealist reception of Spinoza and a mediating cabbalist tradition.

Coleridge's interest in Neoplatonism provides Karen McLean ("Individuality, Unity, and Distinction: Plotinian Concepts in the *Opus Maximum*"), too, with an opportunity to discuss vital parallels between Coleridge and Plotinus. McLean considers how Coleridge has adopted and modified aspects of Plotinian philosophy in his development of an account of individuality vis-à-vis God. McLean suggests that, for Coleridge, true personality is grounded in God, even while a distinction between the Divine and the human remains.

One common thread throughout these essays is the role of the "Logos." In the penultimate essay of this volume, Nicholas Reid ("The Logosophia: How the Logos Acts as Unifying Principle in Coleridge's Thought") demonstrates how the Logos draws together a series of concepts in Coleridgean thought. Through an examination of a series of themes — alterity, form, image, and language, for example — Reid proposes that far more of Coleridge's projected *magnum opus* is available than has customarily been recognized.

The concluding essay of the volume ("Coleridge's *Magnum Opus* and His *Opus Maximum*") is written from the unique standpoint of one of the original scholars involved in the publication of the *Collected Coleridge*: John Beer. Beer's essay looks back at Coleridge's projected *magnum opus* and looks ahead to the future of Coleridge studies in light of the completion of Princeton's *Collected Coleridge* edition. His reflections on the gradual completion of the edition and the particular difficulties associated with the publication of the *Opus Maximum* serve as a guide to the larger, perennial themes facing Coleridge studies. In all, it is hoped that this diverse but unified set of essays on Coleridge's *Opus Maximum* stimulates fresh engagement in the intellectual vision of a fascinating thinker, whose time, perhaps, has finally come.

The text is dedicated to the memory of the Rev. Prof. Colin E. Gunton (1941-2003). Gunton had long been a friend of the Coleridgean community. He was also among the first individuals asked to present at the one day conference that served as the foundation of this volume. Gunton was asked to participate because, like so many of Coleridge's greatest followers, his work in philosophy and theology relied on insights drawn from the great Sage of Highgate, while never slavishly duplicating it. Notably, Gunton's monumental 1992 Bampton Lectures, *The One, the Three and the Many: God, Creation and the Culture of Modernity*, refers to Coleridge as "that most comprehensive of Anglican minds and the presiding genius of this book."[2] Gunton was unable to participate in the conference due to a prior engagement and, further, he tragically passed away before the workshop ever assembled. Yet, as Stephen Holmes wrote of Gunton in *The Guardian* (June 3, 2003), he was "[o]ne of the most distinctive and powerful voices in British theology." Reflecting on the legacy of Gunton in directly influencing so many in this generation, Holmes suggested, "He would not be pleased with the comparison, but, arguably, not since John Henry Newman has an English theologian generated such a school of followers."[3] If the publication of the *Opus Maximum* and the completion of the *Collected Coleridge* signifies the

---

[2] Colin E. Gunton, *The One, the Three and the Many: God, Creation and the Culture of Modernity*, The Bampton Lectures, 1992 (Cambridge: Cambridge University Press, 1993), 15.

[3] Stephen R. Holmes, "The Rev Prof Colin Gunton," *The Guardian* (June 3, 2003).

opportunity for Coleridge to re-enter the ongoing dialogue in philosophy, theology, and the full range of contemporary thought, Gunton surely ranks among the most prominent thinkers to have actively participated in that process. In this way, Gunton stands alongside many of Coleridge's greatest disciples.

Clearly, the formation of this volume is the fruit of the efforts of many contributors, and if the debts of each contributor to this volume were mentioned here, this Preface would swell immensely. My own work has been aided by many. Chiefly, it was Douglas Hedley who first encouraged me to pursue the *Opus Maximum*, and it was his idea that we form the weekly seminar as well as the one-day conference. He has not formally edited these pages, but his influence abounds. I also wish to thank the contributors of this volume for their efforts to bring this project to completion. They consistently responded to my requests thoughtfully and willingly, and this volume is the fruit of their labor. Members of the original seminar, including Daniel Hardy, Camille Wingo, James Vigus, Sita Narasimhan and Maggi Dawn, among others, helped develop an enriching and challenging environment of critical analysis. Thanks are also due to Graham Davidson, who offered numerous, insightful comments on an earlier draft of my introductory essay, "The Quest for System"; Steven Studebaker; Wayne Coppins; Harvey Shoolman; Nicholas Halmi; J. Robert Barth, S.J.; Dean Roger Greeves and the Fellows of Clare College; Catherine Pickstock; Rosalind Paul; the Center for Advanced Religious and Theological Studies (CARTS) and the Faculty of Divinity of the University of Cambridge, where I was a Visiting Fellow during my academic year in England. John Beer graciously read and commented on the whole volume while preparing his concluding essay; of course, any editorial errors that remain are my own. Peeters Publishers and the editors of the series have been generous throughout. Finally, scholarship is almost always pursued with the support and care of friends and family too numerous to mention. Above all, I thank my wife Amber and our young children for willingly relocating across the Atlantic to pursue Coleridge and, all the while, offering me their endless love. We ventured for only a short time, but gained more than we could ever have imagined.

Jeffrey W. Barbeau

EDITORIAL NOTE

Throughout this volume, standard abbreviations have been used for the *Collected Works of Samuel Taylor Coleridge* (gen. ed. Kathleen Coburn; Bollingen Series, 75) (*CC*). Additionally, readers should note that since the primary document of this volume, the *Opus Maximum*, contains many insertions and deletions (as a transcription of a dictated text), all manuscript corrections and related marks, unless otherwise noted, have been silently edited throughout the volume.

AR	*Aids to Reflection*. Ed. John B. Beer. Vol. 9 of *CC*. Princeton: Princeton University Press, 1993.
BL	*Biographia Literaria*. Eds. James Engell and W. Jackson Bate. Vol. 7 of *CC*. 2 parts. Princeton: Princeton University Press, 1983.
C&S	*On the Constitution of the Church and State*. Ed. John Colmer. Vol. 10 of *CC*. Princeton: Princeton University Press, 1976.
CL	*The Collected Letters of Samuel Taylor Coleridge*. Ed. Earl Leslie Griggs. 6 vols. Oxford: Clarendon Press, 1956-71.
CM	*Marginalia*. Eds. H. J. Jackson and George Whalley. Vol. 12 of *CC*. 6 parts. Princeton: Princeton University Press, 1980-2001.
CN	*The Notebooks of Samuel Taylor Coleridge*. Eds. Kathleen Coburn, Merton Christensen, and Anthony John Harding. Bollingen Series L. 5 vols. Princeton: Princeton University Press, 1957-2002.
Friend	*The Friend*. Ed. Barbara E. Rooke. Vol. 4 of *CC*. 2 parts. Princeton: Princeton University Press, 1969.
Lects 1795	*Lectures 1795: On Politics and Religion*. Eds. Lewis Patton and Peter Mann. Vol. 1 of *CC*. Princeton: Princeton University Press, 1971.
Lects 1808-1819	*Lectures 1808-1819: On Literature*. Ed. Reginald A. Foakes. Vol. 5 of *CC*. 2 parts. Princeton: Princeton University Press, 1987.

Lects 1818-1819	*Lectures 1818-1819: On the History of Philosophy.* Ed. J. R. de J. Jackson. Vol. 8 of *CC*. 2 parts. Princeton: Princeton University Press, 2000.
Logic	*Logic*. Ed. J. R. de J. Jackson. Vol. 13 of *CC*. Princeton: Princeton University Press, 1981.
LS	*Lay Sermons*. Ed. R. J. White. Vol. 6 of *CC*. Princeton: Princeton University Press, 1972.
Op Max	*Opus Maximum*. Ed. Thomas McFarland, with the assistance of Nicholas Halmi. Vol. 15 of *CC*. Princeton: Princeton University Press, 2002.
PW	*Poetical Works*. Ed. J. C. C. Mays. Vol. 16 of *CC*. 3 vols. in 6 parts. Princeton: Princeton University Press, 2001.
SW&F	*Shorter Works and Fragments*. Eds. H. J. Jackson and J. R. de. J. Jackson. Vol. 11 of *CC*. 2 parts. Princeton: Princeton University Press, 1995.
TT	*Table Talk*. Ed. Carl Woodring. Vol. 14 of *CC*. 2 parts. Princeton: Princeton University Press, 1990.
Watchman	*The Watchman*. Ed. Lewis Patton. Vol. 2 of *CC*. Princeton: Princeton University Press, 1970.

THE QUEST FOR SYSTEM: AN INTRODUCTION TO COLERIDGE'S LIFELONG PROJECT

By Jeffrey W. Barbeau

Friend and confidant of Samuel Taylor Coleridge, Joseph Henry Green once wrote that "[t]he truth is that Coleridge was remarkable amidst even what might have been deemed the wildest flights of fancy, for an ever watchful logic, closeness of reasoning, & continuity of mind."[1] In conversation, whether for the first time or after many occasions, Coleridge struck all, says Green, with "the total impression left on his mind" of "a *man of genius*."[2] But for all of Coleridge's deipnosophistic skill, his lifelong dream of completing a monumental work of prose, his *magnum opus*, never materialized. Alternately denominated throughout his lifetime as "the great work," "Logosophia," "Assertion of Religion," *magnum opus* and the *Opus Maximum*, Coleridge's *opus* was a topic of frequent discussion and allusions to the plan pepper his published writings, private notebooks, and personal correspondence.[3] Consistently, Coleridge wished to develop a complete system drawing on the history of ideas — including philosophy, theology, history, and natural science — towards a robust and formidable defense of the Christian faith. However, despite endless planning and seemingly interminable preparatory studies, at Coleridge's death the "great work" remained incomplete and the task of publishing or reworking the manuscript fragments of the *magnum opus* into a serviceable form fell on Joseph Henry Green, one of Coleridge's amanuenses. Yet Green's publication of Coleridge's manuscripts also never occurred and the text remained unpublished until 2002. In this introductory essay, I introduce Coleridge's lifelong project, its historical and

---

[1] Joseph Henry Green, "Introduction to the Philosophical Remains of S. T. Coleridge," in *SW&F*, II, 1527.

[2] *SW&F*, II, 1526.

[3] Bate calls the nomenclature unfortunate and confusing, but notes that the connection between the "over-all ambition" of the *magnum opus* and the "comparatively restricted work that actually exists" can be justified in so far as the "hope of a synthesis of arts, sciences, [and] philosophy, through religion" appears in a "more concentrated" form in the *Opus Maximum* (Walter Jackson Bate, *Coleridge*, Masters of World Literature [London: Macmillan, 1968], 182, 212).

philosophical context, and delineate the relative consistency of the disparate expositions of the planned work. Moreover, I set the stage for an informed analysis — a process that begins in this volume and will continue for years to come — of the now published remains known as the *Opus Maximum*.

The History of the Projected *Magnum Opus*

The relationship between Coleridge and his writings has continued to engage the imagination of readers. What is most perplexing about the *magnum opus* is the simple fact that it was never completed. The puzzlement of the student of Coleridge is magnified, however, when one begins to examine the various attempts to outline distinct segments of the work over the course of his life. Although the extant manuscripts of the *Opus Maximum* appear to have been written during the final full decade of his life — the productive 1820s — Coleridge's earliest plans to complete a great work can be traced years before the appearance of *Lyrical Ballads*. Savor the thought for a moment. Imagine the significance of a project that predates much of Coleridge's most well-known work. Consider the magnitude of a project that Coleridge envisioned as his true legacy while yet a young man in his twenties. Now consider the fact that the earliest conceptions contain the heart of what remained an unfinished dream some thirty years later. For all of the scholarly debates about Coleridge's consistency or inconsistency, fragmentation amidst unity, and shifting philosophical allegiances as well as theological and political wrangling, in the projected contents of the *opus* we have a single narrative of a life devoted to the search for a system of truth.

Of course, the attempt to compose a philosophic system of truth was not exclusive to Coleridge. One major impetus for Coleridge's proclivity for system stems from Immanuel Kant. Kant's *Critique of Pure Reason* describes system as "the unity of the manifold modes of knowledge under one idea."[4] System implied not the expression of a single, isolated proposition, then, but rather involved the structure of the whole of knowledge: "not only is each system articulated in accordance with an idea, but they are one and all organically united in a system of human knowledge, as members of one whole, and so as admitting of an architectonic of all

---

[4] Immanuel Kant, *Critique of Pure Reason*, trans. Norman Kemp Smith (New York: St. Martin's, 1965), 653 (A832; B860).

human knowledge, which, at the present time, in view of the great amount of material that has been collected, or which can be obtained from the ruins of ancient systems, is not only possible, but would not indeed be difficult."[5] To those who followed Kant, including Fichte, Schelling, and Hegel, philosophical system seemed a genuine possibility. Fichte suggested that "all propositions in [philosophy] hang together in a single basic proposition and unite themselves in it into a whole."[6] Schelling's *System of Transcendental Idealism* (made famous in England through Coleridge's plagiarisms in the *Biographia Literaria*), likewise, sought a comprehensive expression of knowledge, "to discover a system in human knowledge, to determine the principle whereby all individual knowing is determined."[7] Yet, what Fichte and Schelling had only partially approximated, explains one commentator, Hegel "resolved to do" in his *Encyclopedia*: "They had spoken of 'system' without making a really rigorous and comprehensive attempt to construct a system in such a way that it would be clear where anything they had written had its place in the system."[8] Notably, while Coleridge was enthralled at various times with Kant, Fichte, and Schelling each, he was curiously unimpressed with Hegel and appears to have paid him little notice.[9]

Yet, despite Coleridge's philosophical differences with each of these German proponents of "system," he shared a common concern that was equally rooted in the wider Christian intellectual tradition. On one hand, Coleridge's conception of the *opus* certainly relies on the desire to bring the whole into view; thus, in one prospectus for a course of lectures on the history of philosophy, for example, Coleridge reflects on the manner in which philosophy reduces "a common object... to harmony of impression and total result."[10] Coleridge's notion of the *magnum opus* comprises far more than the foremost achievement of a life's work, it is also a "philosophical work that defends in extended rational argument the

---

[5] Kant, *Critique of Pure Reason*, 655 (A835; B863).

[6] Quoted in *Op Max*, lxxvii.

[7] Michael Vater, "Introduction," in F. W. J. Schelling, *System of Transcendental Idealism* (1800), trans. Peter Heath (Charlottesville: University Press of Virginia, 1978), xx.

[8] Walter Kaufmann, *Hegel: Reinterpretation, Texts, and Commentary* (New York: Doubleday, 1965), 242.

[9] The editorial comment prefacing Coleridge's marginalia on Hegel's *Logic* is telling: "In view of the apparently Hegelian colour of some of C's terms and logical schemata the evidence of a cursory and unsympathetic reading — seen in the small number of marginalia (some 928 pages of text remain unannotated), the unopened gatherings, and the terse dismissive remark... is striking" (*CM*, II, 988).

[10] *Lects 1818–1819*, I, 5.

concept of ultimate meaning in human life." McFarland suggests that the planned *opus* needed to satisfy two fundamental requirements: "First, there must be an *assertion* of Christianity or some other doctrine of ultimate meaning, [and] second, there must be a *defence* against alternate possibilities."[11] Defined in this sense, McFarland links Coleridge's *magnum opus* to the tradition of Aquinas and Ficino as well as Joseph Butler and Andrew Ramsay. Arguably the most important of all Christian "systems" was that formed by the Cambridge Platonist Ralph Cudworth. Cudworth's massive opus, *The True Intellectual System of the Universe* — an abiding interest of Coleridge's from the 1790s onwards — countered every form of "atheism" and magisterially concluded that "there is one only necessary existent, the Cause of all other things; and this an absolutely perfect Being, infinitely good, wise, and powerful."[12]

    In light of this, it should not come as a surprise that even as a young man, Coleridge entertained the idea of developing a complete system of his own. The earliest plan for the *opus* appears as early as 1796 while Coleridge was embroiled in the difficulties of publishing his own political miscellany, *The Watchman*.[13] Worried about the excessive costs of publishing and mounting trouble at home, Coleridge wrote to his good friend Thomas Poole in May 1796, pondering the possibilities for his future. Two options lay before him. On one hand, he might become a Dissenting (Unitarian) parson. But the idea was distasteful since

---

[11] *Op Max*, clix–clx. McFarland points to the first fragment as direct textual evidence: "The main purpose of this digressive chapter has been to preclude offence in one class of readers, and the opportunity of flattering their unbelief in another, and misunderstanding in all… Thus will the one main object of the present work be justified and the true spirit of the following chapters be recognised, that, namely, of invalidating the most plausible objections of infidels, those which are built on the uncertainties and chasms occasioned by the loss or corruption of documents and outward testimony, by a proportional diminution of their necessity, which can alone be effected by establishing and increasing the anterior probability" (*Op Max*, 16).

[12] Ralph Cudworth, *The True Intellectual System of the Universe* (London, 1820; reprint: Elibron Classics, 2003), IV.1, 213.

[13] Writing from Bristol for Dissenters and political liberals, Coleridge's *Watchman* boasted the advocacy of truth and used a prominent passage of Scripture from the Gospel of John as a motto: "That all may know the truth; and that the truth may make us free" (John 8:32). But the tone of Coleridge's political dissent lacked the mature quiescence that could have sheltered him from distrust. In the March 9, 1796 issue of the *Watchman*, Coleridge denounced the practice of national fasts in a satirical piece that turned the levity of an ecclesiastical matter on its head. Coleridge mocks the notion of fasting, when the poor "can afford nothing but bread and cheese on Christmas days" (*Watchman*, 54). More troubling than Coleridge's topic, however, was the ill-advised choice of Isaiah 16:11 as a headnote: "Wherefore my Bowels shall sound like an Harp." Coleridge later reminisced that the jocular selection cost him nearly five hundred of his subscribers.

"[p]reaching for Hire is not right" when the temptation to continue teaching what one has come to disbelieve in later years seemed a bitter prospect. Alternatively, Coleridge proposed an idea that forms one of the earliest plans parallel to the vision of the *magnum opus*. He contemplated a trip to Germany where he could learn the language "with tolerable fluency" and return with cheap editions of works not only in the sciences but especially the works of great German philosophers and theologians including Spinoza, Semler, Michaelis, and "the great German metaphysician" Immanuel Kant. Upon his return, Coleridge envisioned a school of eight young men whom he could *"perfect"* in three areas of study:

1. Man as Animal: including the complete knowledge of Anatomy, Chemistry, Mechanics, & Optics. —
2. Man as an *Intellectual* Being: including the ancient Metaphysics, the systems of Locke & Hartley, — of the Scotch Philosophers — & the new Kantian [system].
3. Man as a Religious Being: including an historic summary of all Religions & the arguments for and against Natural and Revealed Religion. Then proceeding from the individual to the aggregate of Individuals & disregarding all chronology except that of mind I should perfect them 1. in the History of Savage Tribes. 2. of semi-barbarous nations… Gracious Heaven! that a scheme so big with advantage to this Kingdom, therefore to Europe, therefore to the World should be demolishable by one monosyllable from a Bookseller's Mouth!"[14]

The plan, by his own admission, was "impracticable," but it is a telling portrait of his intellectual optimism nonetheless. The essential elements of what might have become the *opus* were all in place. The student trained in scientific, intellectual, and spiritual fields would be fully equipped for public service in government and could benefit, ultimately, the whole world.

The story of the gradual demise of the *Watchman* and the account of Coleridge's plan to develop a school illustrates two themes that recur in the history of the *opus*. First, Coleridge's devotion to truth is paramount. There is a persistent dedication in Coleridge's writings to the importance of the quest regardless of the difficulties encountered. Secondly, the *Watchman* account immediately brings to the fore his longing to grasp a

---

[14] *CL*, I, 209. It is intriguing to consider how many of Coleridge's published and unpublished prose writings fall under these three categories.

sense of the whole. Still, Coleridge's visionary schemes, as taught or composed, knew no limits and may legitimately be criticized as impracticable.

One friend who seems to have intuitively known the value of Coleridge's quest was Charles Lamb. In a letter of January 10, 1797, Lamb asked Coleridge if he intended to complete an extended work on "the Evidences of Natural & Revealed Religion." Lamb may have in mind the essays collected as *Lectures 1795: On Politics and Religion.* In these Bristol lectures, Coleridge had not only attempted to garner funds for his pantisocracy scheme with Southey, but had likewise attempted to preach his vision of truth by distinguishing between the Christian and the so-called Infidel.[15] Lamb's interest in the projected expansion of the lectures is important. He asks, "Have you let the intention go? Or are you doing any thing towards it?"[16] Lamb's curiosity suggests to us that the project was neither casual nor merely intimated. Rather, the planned work on religion appears to be something that Coleridge had talked about and ruminated over for some time.[17] It is also an early indication that Coleridge's friends were aware of the difficulties he had in following through on his plans. Lamb's prodding words signal another part of this story: the interest of others in Coleridge's constructive dream. Coleridge, the talker, had already built up a pronounced expectation among his contemporaries.

What seemed "impracticable" in 1796 was not wholly without merit in 1799. Writing to Josiah Wedgwood on May 21, Coleridge recounted his travels in Germany: he had learned to speak the language, despite his hideous pronunciation; he could read German well; he had studied the sciences, including physiology and anatomy; and he had gathered collections for various histories, including a life of Lessing. In sum, he had worked assiduously, "harder than, I trust in God Almighty, I shall ever have occasion to work again."[18] Moreover, in addition to these studies,

---

[15] *Lects 1795*, 189.

[16] Quoted in, *Op Max*, xci.

[17] McFarland suggests that "Coleridge seems to have broached the possibility of the *magnum opus* in conversation before he did so in writing... it would seem safe to conclude that Coleridge was talking about plans for the *magnum opus* in the previous year" (*Op Max*, xci).

[18] *CL*, I, 518–19; for more on Coleridge's study of German literature and language "within the cultural context of its production," see Maximiliaan van Woudenberg, "Coleridge's Literary Studies at Göttingen in 1799: Reconsidering the Library Borrowings from the University of Göttingen," *The Coleridge Bulletin* n.s. 21 (2003): 66–80.

Coleridge purchased a sizeable collection of books, chiefly on meta-physics, with one goal in mind: "with a view to the one work, to which I hope to dedicate in silence the prime of my life."

Two years later, writing to Thomas Poole in March 1801, Coleridge's interest in a great work is increasingly apparent. He reports that "the most intense study," most importantly of Immanuel Kant, has led to an extri-cation of notions of time and space as well as to overthrowing the Hartleian Necessitarianism of his youth.[19] Surprisingly, in words not unlike his earlier discomfort over preaching for hire, Coleridge laments his poetic commitments. "Christabel," ideally, would be published imme-diately in order to free himself from his commitments to his publisher Longman. Instead of poetic compositions, Coleridge hopes to devote him-self to writing on philosophical themes in his continued quest for truth: "it seemed to me a Suicide of my very soul to divert my attention from Truths so important, which came to me almost as a revelation / Likewise, I cannot express to you, dear Friend of my heart! — the loathing, which I once or twice felt, when I attempted to write, merely for the Bookseller, without any sense of the moral utility of what I was writing."[20] Coleridge bemoans the thought of publishing a popular collection of travels drawn from his time in Germany "merely to *amuse* people" and thereby expos-ing himself to the sarcasm of his critics. Instead, Coleridge intends to propose a book on Locke, Hobbes, and Hume as a "*Pioneer* to my greater work." The letter provides a remarkable insight into the fabled division between Coleridge as poet and thinker: Coleridge turned to metaphysics not from an alleged loss of poetic power, but due, in part, to a rather sober rejection of the demands of the popular press.[21] Subsequently, Coleridge's description of this pioneering project will be incorporated within the larger framework of the *magnum opus*.

Among the most interesting notebooks related to the projected *magnum opus*, one entry from March 1803 stands out in particular. Here, Coleridge jots down a list of some ten or more projects, several of which contribute

---

[19] In one letter to Poole on February 13, 1801, Coleridge mentions his reading habits, "I turn at times half reluctantly from Leibnitz or Kant…," and notes that "[s]ince I have been at Keswick, I have read a great deal / and my Reading has furnished me with many reasons for being exceedingly suspicious of *supposed Discoveries* [e.g. "the supposed Dis-covery of the Law of Association by Hobbes"] in Metaphysics" (*CL*, II, 675–76).

[20] *CL*, II, 707.

[21] Mays has recently suggested that the "customary explanation of Coleridge's decline from poetry into metaphysics, which he himself helped to promulgate, is a circuitous fic-tion" (*PW*, I.1, xcvii).

to our own reconstruction of the developing contents of the *magnum opus*:[22]

> On Man, and the probable Destiny of the Human Race. —
>
> *My last & great* work — always had in mind.

Coleridge explains that this is the "work which I should wish to leave behind me." The most important aspect of this list is Coleridge's association of the work "On Man" and on the "Destiny of the Human Race" with the great work. Subsequent conceptions of the *magnum opus* diminish this overtly anthropological feature, but remarkably it reappears in 1825 and later outlines of the project.

One striking disparity between the 1803 account of the *opus* and subsequent plans is Coleridge's nascent interest in the doctrine of the Trinity. In the 1795 lectures on religion, Coleridge had rejected the doctrine of the Trinity, in Priestleyan fashion, as an absurdity. By 1805 Coleridge had made a resolute philosophical decision in favor of Trinitarian doctrine. In 1814, nearly ten years later, Coleridge articulates his philosophical commitment to Trinitarianism in the planned *magnum opus* by calling it his "Logosophia." He suggests that his most important hours of the day, in the morning, are devoted to "my most important Work" whose title is "Christianity the one true Philosophy — or 5 Treatises on the Logos, or communicative Intelligence, Natural, Human and Divine."[23] Coleridge explains that the central purpose of his work on the Logos is to provide a philosophical defense of the Thirty-Nine Articles of the Church of England. The first treatise is called "Logos propaideuticos — or the science of systematic Thinking in ordinary life" and seems to be a version of the projected work on Logic. The second treatise, "Logos architechtonicus" is an attempt to apply the constructive process to metaphysics and natural theology. The third treatise, Logos theanthropos, or "the divine Logos incarnate" is designed to provide a commentary on the

---

[22] *CN*, I, 1646. Coleridge specifically mentions a "History of Logic," a "History of Metaphysics in Germany" and a work devoted to "Revolutionary Minds." Notably, one letter to William Godwin in June of that year provides an extended exposition of the proposed contents of a work of logic aiding "the Senate, the Pulpit, & our Law courts" (*CL*, II, 948; June 4, 1803).

[23] *CL*, III, 533; September 12, 1814.

Gospel of St. John especially in the light of Paul's doctrine of "preaching Christ alone, & him Crucified." The fourth treatise, "Logos Agonistes" is a life of Spinoza that brings to the fore Coleridge's persistent concern for pantheism. The fifth treatise, "Logos alogos" or "logos illogicus," is devoted to a discussion of modern Unitarianism with reference to its causes and effects. Humbly, Coleridge explains that the second treatise will be largely unintelligible to "the great majority even of well-educated Readers." As for originality, his work will "have that at all events from the first page to the last."

This detailed description of Coleridge's *magnum opus* is repeated in two nearly identical explanations of the project in letters written near the close of 1815. In September 1815, Coleridge writes to John May, a wealthy wine merchant, about the status of his writings. He explains that the manuscript for the forthcoming *Biographia Literaria* as well as his collection of poems, *Sibylline Leaves*, are both with his printer John Gutch in Bristol. Moreover, Coleridge's tragedy, *Zapolya*, is in the final stages of preparation for publication. But his mind is on another writing, even in the midst of one of the most fruitful periods of writing in his entire life: the great work. The work that drove all the rest was entitled, at this stage, the "LOGOSOPHIA: or on the LOGOS, divine and human, in six Treatises."[24] It had occupied some twelve years of his life already, which places the project's inception at the November 1803 notebook exposition, and provided the impetus (at least on the surface) for other, financially-driven enterprises: "My highest object in writing for the stage is to obtain the means of devoting myself, *a whole and undistracted man*, to the bringing forth a work, for which I have all the materials collected & ready for use."[25]

The contents of the proposed work largely mirror the earlier September 1814 description, but contain several important distinctions. Notably, first of all, Coleridge's plan for a history of philosophy precedes the whole. In 1801,

---

[24] *CL*, IV, 589.

[25] *CL*, IV, 589. Mays's recent contribution to our understanding of Coleridge and theater helps to elucidate the tenor of Coleridge's favor of metaphysics and his corresponding disdain for the "drudgery" (shared by many of his contemporaries) of the stage: "in Coleridge's lifetime, the theatre became less respectable; or, what amounts to the same thing, society became respectable in ways which found the stage immoral and cheapening. This was in part a reality: the theatre in the early 1800s was patronised less by the aristocracy and theatres were reported to be thronged with prostitutes. It was in part a fiction encouraged by Methodism, the cult of nature and solitary feelings, indeed any number of elevated attitudes. Not until mid-century, under Victoria's patronage, did theatre become properly respectable again" (*PW*, I.1, clxiii).

Locke, Hobbes, and Hume appeared not as solitary figures, but rather as a part of a larger portrait of the history of philosophy from Aristotle to Kant. In September 1815, Coleridge's attention seems drawn particularly to Germany, almost to the exclusion of the rest — if such a singular emphasis is possible in Coleridge. Yet, in the September description, these two emphases are drawn together in their most explicit form to this point: "The first, or preliminary treatise contains a philosophical History of Philosophy and it's [*sic*] revolutions from Pythagoras to Plato & to Aristotle — from Aristotle to Lord Bacon, including the scholastic metaphysicians of what are *called* the dark ages — from Bacon to Des Cartes and Locke — and from Locke to the revival of the eldest Philosophy, which I call *dynamic* or constructive as opposed to the material and mechanical systems still predominant."[26] Rather than recording history for an antiquarian purpose, Coleridge's vision of system incorporates the whole of philosophy for a dynamic or constructive end. It is a distinctive feature of the age, as one commentator has observed: rather than tracing the history of philosophy as mere genealogy, "it is possible to select the significant advances towards an end that has been achieved and to reject as false starts the initiatives that did not contribute... [Coleridge] hoped to learn from past wisdom truths that his contemporaries had forgotten, and he was to attempt to awaken them to their blindness by showing the persuasiveness of their neglected predecessors."[27] The September 1815 account also synthesizes other prior interests in the grand Logosophia. It contains a description further articulating his devotion to logic, "the science of connected reasoning," and re-introduces a key phrase worth noting: "applied practically to the purposes of ordinary life, the Senate, Pulpit, Bar, &c." Moreover, the formerly undefined interest in Spinoza, Bruno and Boehme is now explicitly linked to an explication of Pantheists and Mystics (and George Fox is added to the list). As before, Coleridge reasserts his interest in a defense of Christianity and expresses his hope "to submit the work to some one or more learned and dignified Divines of the Church of England, the defence of whose articles I have most at heart, next to that of the Gospel

---

[26] *CL*, IV, 589. Subsequent occurrences of Coleridge's practice of substituting "it's" for "its" will not be noted.

[27] *Lects 1818–1819*, I, xliii. J. R. de J. Jackson continues, noting that "[i]n one respect he differed from almost all his significant contemporaries among the philosophical historians and philosophers of Germany; he was as intensely concerned with the social implications of religion and its history as he was with philosophy itself, and not merely interested in religion as an influence or as an element that mingled from time to time with philosophy. For Coleridge religion and philosophy were both indispensable and he looked forward to a time when they might become united" (xliii).

Truth, which in all but some inessential and comparatively trifling points I sincerely believe coincident with our Articles & Liturgy."[28]

The third major description of the *magnum opus* in just over a year repeats the two prior entries extensively. Although only writing ten days after suggesting that his project began some twelve years prior, he now alleges that he has been "collecting the materials for the last 15 years almost incessantly."[29] Conspicuously, Coleridge mentions the investigation of "Toleration" as an element of his history of philosophy and, as before, the treatise on logic is related "to the purposes of real Life — the Bar, the [Pul]pit, the Senate, & rational Conversation."[30] The third and fourth sections on the transcendental philosophy and the Gospel of St. John appear, in many ways, as the centerpiece of the whole. In fact, the third treatise, the constructive or transcendental philosophy, is "introductory" to the commentary on John and "the object of both," according to Coleridge, is "to prove, that Christianity is true Philosophy, & of course that all true Philosophy is Christianity."[31] Coleridge estimates that the whole will comprise around 1200 pages in two large octavo volumes.

In early 1819, Coleridge relates to Southey that he has made "regular and considerable progress" on the *opus* ("we have already compassed a good handsome Volume") by dictating to Green "4 and oftener five hours twice a week."[32] Six years later, in 1821, Coleridge remains devoted to the pursuit of truth and the completion of his *opus*, increasingly referred to as his "Assertion of Religion."[33] In July 1821, Coleridge avers to Thomas Poole that a bright future remains for his work: "I have little *pleasant* to say except that I am advancing regularly and steadily toward the completion of my Opus Magnum on Revelation & Christianity, the Reservoir of my Reflections & Reading for 25 years past — and in health not painfully worse."[34] Writing to Thomas Allsop two months later,

---

[28] *CL*, IV, 590.

[29] *CL*, IV, 591. Despite the difference in chronology, Coleridge's memory in this letter is not entirely inaccurate since his letter in March 1801 contains an early account of the project.

[30] *CL*, IV, 592; October 7, 1815.

[31] *CL*, IV, 592.

[32] *CL*, IV, 917. Notably, the *Opus Maximum* "Fragments 1–4" have been dated by Halmi to this period (1819–23).

[33] For further insight into Coleridge's conception of the *opus* as the "Assertion of Religion," see the manuscript fragment and editorial note for the "Outline of the 'Assertion of Religion'" (*SW&F*, II, 905–6).

[34] *CL*, V, 160; July 1821. The dating of his efforts, "25 years past," now places the commencement of work on the *opus* around 1796.

Coleridge's description of the project is less exacting than the entries of 1814 and 1815. The project is referred to as the "greater Work" and described as a project "in assertion of the ideal truth & the *a priori* probability and a posteriori internal and external evidence of the historic truth of the Christian Religion."[35] This description lacks the divisions of constructive philosophy, biblical commentary, and anti-Unitarian polemics, but still elaborates on a consistent vision of Christianity as the true philosophy. Absent from this letter is a discussion of the history of philosophy, though surely the publication of the *Biographia Literaria* and his delivery of the "Lectures on the History of Philosophy" in 1818 and 1819 had served as a means of satisfying the desire, or perhaps need, to explore these pivotal ideas. More importantly, Coleridge's *Logic* is described quite distinctly as its own work and one that he hopes to publish should suitable and equitable terms be arranged. The departure in 1821 from earlier portraits of the *magnum opus* certainly raises important questions that need to be addressed about the nature of the project and the potentially erosive effect of Coleridge's prior publications such as the *Biographia Literaria*. For now, I think we should be careful not to privilege these early descriptions to the detriment of his later visions and, furthermore, to oversimplify the extent of Coleridge's intellectual intentions.

With that in mind, it is striking to note how drastically changed Coleridge's description of his great work may appear to some by 1825. In May, the same month as the appearance of *Aids to Reflection*, Coleridge wrote to John Taylor Coleridge, his nephew, with the first third of the volume for his perusal. It is a religious book, Coleridge explains, and few will purchase it except those who "purchase it *as* a religious book."[36] But *Aids*, no matter how full and ready an account of his thoughts it may be (Coleridge remarks, "no one hereafter can with justice complain that I have disclosed my sentiments only in flashes and fragments"), leaves two things wanting. First, there are six disquisitions, "ready for the Press," that contain a supplement to *Aids*: faith, the Eucharist, the philosophy of prayer, the prophetic character of the Old Testament, the church, and the right and the superstitious use and estimation of the Sacred Scriptures. The disquisition on the church appeared in his lifetime as *On the Constitution of the Church and State* (1829) while that on the right use of Scripture was only privately circulated until

---

[35] *CL*, V, 177.
[36] *CL*, V, 443; May 8, 1825.

its posthumous publication by Henry Nelson Coleridge as *Confessions of an Inquiring Spirit* (1840). Moreover, while *Aids to Reflection* only touched on the Trinity "in a *negative* way," as a means of "exposing the causes of it's rejection and in removing (what by experience I know to be) the ordinary obstacles to it's belief,"[37] it remained to establish the doctrine on positive grounds. This positive establishment of the idea, God, as well as an exposition of Creation and Evil as distinguished from original sin, remained for his "larger Work." Already finished, however, is the first division of the work: "the *Philosophy* of the Christian Creed, or Christianity true in *Idea*." The second division, Christianity true in *fact*, is a demonstration of the historical veracity of the faith. The final division, Christianity true in *act*, explores moral and spiritual truth. *Aids to Reflection* and the supplemental disquisitions are a complete "*System* of internal evidences" and leave no "essential Article of Faith" untouched.

If the publication of the *Biographia Literaria*, the *Lay Sermons*, and the republication of *The Friend* did not dilute Coleridge's interest in publishing a "great work" by the beginning of the 1820s, it is no surprise that *Aids to Reflection*, with its aphoristic pursuit of truth, could not diminish the hope of a lifetime either. Writing to John Hookham Frere in January 1826 with hopes of securing a sinecure from Lord Liverpool, Coleridge again mentions the *opus* and his desire to see its completion. He calls the *opus*, along with *Aids to Reflection* and a proposed publication of *Logic*, "the fruits of a laborious life, if hard thinking and hard reading are labor."[38] The *opus*, compared to *Aids*, is that "far larger work, my Opus Maximum containing the sum and system of my philosophy and Faith on reason & revelation, the life of Nature and the history of Man, of which the MSS *materials* are complete, and somewhat more than a third of the Work reduced to form, and in a *publishable* state..."[39] Both Coleridge's testimony and the dating of the extant manuscripts suggest that some portion of the project had been committed to paper. Two features characterize Coleridge's conception of the *opus* at this moment: the emphasis on Reason and revelation, largely consistent with the 1825 trajectory on the philosophy of the Christian creed, and the conspicuous reappearance of Coleridge's interest in the history of Man (the first seminal insight noted in 1796). The notion of "Man" seems to have encompassed not only an interest in anthropology and the development of races but also notions of

---

[37] *CL*, V, 444.
[38] *CL*, VI, 539.
[39] *CL*, VI, 539–40.

human will and the self.[40] Separate from the account of the *opus*, yet once again closely linked in his own mind, is a form of his long-projected *Logic*: "a complete volume in which the main *Results* of the preceding are given in a dramatic and popular form, entitled Travels in Body and Mind, or the Sceptic's Pilgrimage to the Temple of Truth."[41] "Travels" as noted here is strikingly similar to *Logic*, which, as early as 1803, is directed towards those preparing for "the Bar, the Pulpit or the Senate" and ultimately "furnishes the key, and contains the preliminaries to all my other works."[42] If these three are completed — *Aids*, *opus*, and "Travels," — and "if [it] please God to prolong my life," then Coleridge intends to prepare his lectures on Shakespeare, Milton, Dante, and Cervantes for publication. But, even then, Coleridge is certain that his *opus* will be the continued object of his attention, "being assured by my past experience that no month will pass without some addition to my Opus Maximum on which I chiefly rely for the proof that I have not lived or laboured in vain."[43]

Nearly two years later, writing in November 1827 to Joseph Blanco White, Coleridge's great hope of completing the *opus* slowly wanes even as he oozes vainglory. Coleridge recounts a dream at once reminiscent of Aquinas' wakeful declaration, "all I have done is but straw": "as I awoke last night, or… succeeded at length in awakening myself out of a terrific fantastic Dream, which would have required tenfold the imagination of a Dante to have constructed in the waking state, I could not but thank God on my knees for the lesson of Humility I had received, exclaiming, O vanity!"[44] Coleridge writes of his *opus* with a sense of near-completion, while aware of his current inability to express all that appears necessary. Perhaps he only wishes to impress White, it is difficult to determine. But he does write with assurance that much of the *opus* is complete and nearly ready for publication should he only be able to obtain the resources to complete it and thereby fill the needs of a nation rather than its appetite: "it will be hard for me to effect under my present necessity of scribbling

---

[40] The twofold nature of Coleridge's interest in "man" is apparent, for example, in one fragment of a course of lectures, *SW&F*, II, 1399ff.

[41] Notably, Snyder proposed that the manuscript fragment entitled "On Reason" in *SW&F* (BM MS Egerton 2801 ff 37–42) "may well be a portion of the proposed 'Travels in Mind and Body'" (Alice D. Snyder, *Coleridge on Logic and Learning, with Selections from the Unpublished Manuscripts* [New York: Yale University Press, 1929], 153). The editors explain that "[i]t has not been possible to confirm this conjecture" (*SW&F*, I, 565); if Snyder is correct, then the ms. is peripherally connected to the projected *opus*.

[42] *CL*, VI, 540.

[43] *CL*, VI, 541.

[44] *CL*, VI, 714–15; November 28, 1827.

what the Public *like*, instead of giving what the mind of the country *wants*. God's will be done!"[45] The whole consists of six parts or works but will be published as "three large volumes" or "three several Works" that contain "all my researches and reflections concerning God, Nature, and Man" and, as before, "you will not wonder that I name it my OPUS MAXIMUM, the Harvesting of my Life's Labours."[46] Moreover, with reference to his indescribable dream, Coleridge sardonically remarks that he has recently announced himself to a friend, "as the author of a SYSTEM of Philosophy on Nature, History, Reason, Revelation; on the Eternal, and on the Generations of the Heaven and the Earth, and [yet] I am unable to solve the problem of my own Dreams!"[47] In this way, while the letter is too inexact to provide a close comparison with the detailed explanations of the *opus* that one finds in other letters and notebooks, it is clear that a triadic conception of the whole exists, focusing — like so many of his philosophical contemporaries — on the three primary divisions that command our attention: God, Nature, and Man.

What surely seemed a nearly complete project when presented to White, however, could not be so confidently described by one of Coleridge's most-trusted intellectual companions: Joseph Henry Green. Writing just two months later, Coleridge laments not only the state of his seemingly ever-declining health, but the state of his *opus*. Pathetically, Coleridge shares his fading hopes to complete his lifelong work: "I have no wish to have my life prolonged but what is involved in the wish to complete the views, I have taken, of Life as beginning in separation from Nature and ending in Union with God, and to reduce to an *intelligible* if not artistical form the results of my religious, biblical and ecclesiastical Lucubrations."[48] The work is composed of the same vital elements as before, including quite explicitly God and Nature. Throughout, human Life is presupposed and the postscript to the letter makes explicit Coleridge's continued interest in and speculation about the "Phaenomenon of the Races." Notably, the religious element is pronounced and while the historical-philosophical dimensions that seemed to dominate in earlier conceptions of the *opus* seem to have fallen into the background, it is clear

---

[45] *CL*, VI, 714.

[46] *CL*, VI, 714. The six works are left unexplained by Coleridge. Rather than a recollection of some earlier pattern, however, the notebook entry of May 1828, to be discussed shortly, is a more likely account of the six parts of Coleridge's proposed system (see *CN*, V, 5868).

[47] *CL*, VI, 715.

[48] *CL*, VI, 722–23; January 25, 1828.

that these elements are all of one philosophical-theological system and could not, piecemeal, be broken from the whole for Coleridge. His last wish is only that he completes what he most assuredly believes to be a divinely-imparted gift: "I have no other fear of Dying than that of being seized with the stolen goods on me."

Perhaps the most exhilarating and, simultaneously, unsettling of Coleridge's numerous plans for the *opus* appears in a May 24, 1828 note-book entry. The entry is an extraordinary account of Coleridge's intellectual ambitions and remains worthy of study in its own right. Here Coleridge places "on record" the six principal divisions of the Coleridgean or "Ēstē-sĕān or Ēsstĕcēan Methodology, or Philosophy of Epochs and Methods" to which he had likely referred in November 1827 while writing to Joseph Blanco White.[49] The first part, composed of three sub-divisions, begins with an account of things Divine and follows a movement from a settled state (stasis), through the fall (apostasies), to the redemptive scheme.[50] The whole, then, "Commences with the Absolute actuality, essentially causative of all Reality" and includes discussion of "the Tetractys, and Tri-unity" as well as "The Will to actualize the eternal possibility." The first section concludes, notably, with "The divine Condescension — scheme of Redemption."[51]

In part two Coleridge's attention turns to Nature and commences with five primary divisions including the birth of time and nature by the polarization of chaos, polar forces, forms of nature as inorganic, vegetable life, and philo-sophic astrology. The remaining divisions draw out the relationship between nature and humanity: "Animal life from the *Polyp* to the primæval Man — Ends with the physiological, & the rational Grounds for the Assumption, that Man is not in the state, in which the original Family must have been both constituted and circumstanced: or a Fall of Man shewn to be a necessary Postulate of *Science*..."[52] All of these divisions promote Coleridge's cen-tral goal in this second part, along with the third: to enunciate the Idea "that Life begins in detachment from Nature and ends in unition with God."

The third part flows out of the second insofar as Coleridge's attention turns from Nature to the human person. Coleridge's account of this section of the work includes an extended introduction on revelation and the claim that Christianity is the only true religion: "Religion *implies*

---

[49] *CN*, V, 5868.

[50] Coleridge leaves the final stage unidentified. However, the same pattern is employed in the introductory creed of *Confessions of an Inquiring Spirit*, where this section is identified as metastasis-anastasis or "of the change of the state and the rising again" (*SW&F*, II, 1119).

[51] *CN*, V, 5868.

[52] *CN*, V, 5868.

Revelation... Religion and Revelation are synonymous Terms and Revealed Religion a Pleonasm." Coleridge devotes the bulk of the third part to the human condition and the Divine plan of Redemption. Notably, Coleridge's longstanding interest in races is given voice in this section of the Estesean Methodology. In particular, the races are considered in reference to the Mosaic account of the Fall, Noachic generations, and the subsequent redemption; throughout, Coleridge's descriptions evoke a nascent sociality as the foundation of all life.

The fourth part of the planned work, in many ways, culminates in the explication of what has been a pivotal feature of each of the previous sections: the role of the Redeemer. Coleridge constructs, in outline, the foundation of a Christian philosophical scheme of knowledge on the twofold offices of Christ: revelation and Reason. Coleridge sees in the prophetic writings of the Old Testament a "line of march" and progressive unfolding of the Divine "Redemptorial Scheme": even in the midst of "apparently retrograde movements, the Victory of the Redeemer in the Defeat of the Men, the Success in the Failure, the Constancy in the Folly and Fickleness." Likewise, this redemptive scheme is clarified through Reason and thereby requires an account of the progressive "conversion of the Idea of the Redeemer into the expectation of a Messiah": "goes back to Egypt and traces the course of Paganism, Greek Art, Science, Philosophy & Roman Realization and Fixture of Greek Ideas, with the History of the Jews from Ezra to John the Baptist — composing the substance of my Course of Lectures in the History of Philosophy — shewing the completion of the Cycle of Philosophy just before the Coming of Christ." The section concludes with an account of the incarnation of the Logos in Jesus and the purpose and mission of the life of Jesus.

The fifth part takes up the questions first raised in Coleridge's work on Scripture, known as *Confessions of an Inquiring Spirit*. In reality, far more than an account of the nature of Scripture, however, it is a full, critical commentary and history of the Bible: "It will be a real History of the Bible — not a flat new-working of the Bible History — the great object to restore the Bible to it's due place in the Love & Veneration of Christians by at once establishing its Homopneumaty yet asserting it's Humanities." At first glance, the extended treatment of Scripture in this account of the *opus* may appeared disconnected from the prior divisions, yet throughout even those sections there exists a strong devotion to biblical comment and analysis in the extended 1828 plan.

The final section Coleridge delineates in the 1828 account of the *opus* is substantially that material found in the 1829 *On the Constitution of the*

Church and State. Still, his notebook account has the potential to progress beyond that which found publication in his own lifetime. It provides the philosophy and "a philosophic Abstract of the History of the Visible Church & of Christendom from the Apostles to the present times." Moreover, it delineates Coleridge's now famous distinction between the Church of England as an estate of the realm (*enclesia*) and the function of ministers as members of the broader Church of Christ (*ecclesia*).

In sum, the whole is a massive project, but not one that Coleridge deems impossible.[53] Still, in order to construct an entire system, Coleridge needed to marshal all his intellectual energy to the task. Moreover, the plan reflects his burgeoning concern to demonstrate the need for redemption, yet maintains the central features of even the earliest accounts of the *opus*: "If the completion of this Great Work, the Main Labor of my Life, would be to the Glory of God in the advancement of the Truth in Christ, may God grant me Space and grace to write Finis on it's last leaf."[54]

For some time Coleridge maintains an urgent desire to complete his life work. In many ways, the work epitomizes the significance of his life. Writing in June 1831, Coleridge suggests to William Sotheby that two things alone remain in his life: "my two remaining Prayers, the one conditional, namely, if it should be for the advantage of my Fellowmen — the other, unconditional, are — that He who has hitherto sustained my life, may yet enable me to put the last hand to the works, so near their completion! and 'not to forsake me in my old age, now I am grey headed — until I have shewn his truth unto this generation, and the breadth, depth, and exceeding Goodness of his Laws, Ways, and Dispensations to them that are yet for to come.' *Psalm 71. v. 16* [18]. — The other is — to die in the faith in which I have lived, laying hold of the promises of mercy in Christ, the trust in *his* perfect righteousness prevailing over the sense of my own unworthiness."[55]

Less than a year before his death, however, the project remained unfinished and Coleridge's hopes were fading. It is likely for this reason that Coleridge extended an invitation to John Sterling, a kindred spirit who had read his works with sympathy, asking for the help he and Green would need to complete a life's aspiration: "Many a fond dream have I amused myself with, of your residing near me or in the same house, and of preparing with your & Mr. Green's assistance, my whole system for the Press, as far as it exists in writing, in any *systematic*

---

[53] This, despite McFarland's claim to the contrary (*Op Max*, c).
[54] *CN*, V, 5868.
[55] *CL*, VI, 866; June 3, 1831.

form…"[56] The "system" contains three primary parts in this late account. The first is called "the Propyleum, On the Power and Use of Words" and is yet another version of *Logic*. The system also contains "the Methodus et Epochae, or the Disqui[si]tion on God, Nature, and Man." Coleridge equates the whole with his "Dynamic Philosophy" and adds a section, largely by Green, "on the application of the Ideas, as the *Transcendents* of the Truths, Duties, Affections &c in the Human Mind."[57] If these were published, Coleridge assures Sterling he "should then have no objection to print my MSS Papers on the positive Theology — from Adam to Abraham — to Moses — the Prophets — Christ — and Christendom. — But this is a Dream!" Despite this, Coleridge also expresses his desire to set aside two months in order to prepare a metrical translation of the biblical Apocalypse, the Book of Revelation, "with an introduction on the Use & interpretation of Scriptures — a Prophecy &c — and a *perpetual* illustration, as the Germans say." At this late stage, when thoughts of his own epitaph similarly weighed his mind, the prospect of not completing a project that "could not be compressed in less than three Octavo Volumes" seemed an ever-increasing reality.[58]

The project, despite extensive dictation and even amidst these final efforts, never fully materialized.

Interpreting the *Opus*

Two questions emerge from this historical and biographical overview. The first centers on a judgment: amidst all of Coleridge's attempts to

---

[56] *CL*, VI, 966–67; October 29, 1833. Green's role in the *Opus* is marked in the 1820s. On August 22, 1830, Coleridge wrote a note reflective of Green's positive contribution to Coleridge's life; he spent the evening "with my dear Friend, J. H. G., pleasurably, I know, to *us*, and I trust, not unprofitably for others. It it [*sic*] is most delightful to observe the continual and progressive expansion, comprehension, and productivity of my friend's intellect. Well! may I look forward with delight to the conjunction of our names, and with a pardonable pride of heart indulge my fancy in the conceit, that the System of evolving all the truths and central facts of moral & physical Science, all the constitutive principles of the Fine Arts, and all … spiritual verities of Religion, out of One Postulate, to which no man can refuse his assent but by a perverse exercise of the very power, the existence of which he denies — that this bold, but at all events meritorious Attempt may be known to the World under the name of the Chloroesteesian Philosophy or connected Disquisitions concerning God, Nature and Man by J. H. Green, and S. T. Coleridge" (*CN*, V, 6410).
[57] *CL*, VI, 967.
[58] One 1832–33 account of the *Opus* — alternately called "Epochs and Methods" and "God, Nature and man: a System of Theosophy, Physiogony, and Anthropology" — calls for seven volumes.

enunciate a plan for the *magnum opus* in private letters, notebooks, and even published works, what features most distinctly characterize the aims and goals of this lifelong dream? The second question flows naturally from the first: what, in fact, does the published *Opus Maximum* accomplish? Both questions will be the subject of dialogue for years to come.

Reconstructing the Plan

The history traced in the first part of this essay clearly brings to the fore a number of key themes and emphases that Coleridge persistently discussed as vital to his attempt to develop a complete philosophical system, the Logosophia. Although numerous other entries could be incorporated into this chronological account, Tables 1-4 trace many of the major descriptions of the planned *opus* as examined in this essay. Notably, at points, the distinctions between categories are far more fluid than the tables may suggest; yet, it allows us to better perceive the subtly distinguished categories that he explicated in defining his system.

Table 1

	May 1796[59]	March 1801[60]	November 1803[61]
A.	On Man		On Man
B.	On Locke, Hartley, and Philosophers	On Locke, Hobbes, and Hume — from Aristotle to Kant	History of Metaphysics in Germany
C.			History of Logic
D.			Revolutionary Minds
E.			On Bruno, Boehme, and Spinoza
F.			
G.			
H.			
I.			
J.			

[59] *CL*, I, 209.
[60] *CL*, II, 707.
[61] *CN*, I, 1646. Coleridge projects each as independent works.

Table 2

	September 1814[62]	September 1815[63]	October 1815[64]
A.			
B.		History of Philosophy	History of Philosophy
C.	Science of Systematic Thinking	On Logic with attention to Senate, Bar, and Pulpit	On Logic
D.			
E.	On Spinoza	On Pantheists and Mysticism	On Mystics and Pantheists
F.	Constructive Philosophy	Constructive Philosophy	Transcendental Philosophy
G.	Commentary on St. John	Commentary on St. John	Commentary on St. John
H.	On Unitarianism	On Unitarianism	On Unitarianism
I.			
J.			

Table 3

	September 1821[65]	May 1825[66]	January 1826[67]
A.			On History of Man
B.			
C.	On Logic		Travels in Body and Mind [on Logic], mention of Senate, Bar, and Pulpit
D.			
E.			
F.	Constructive Philosophy	Philosophy of the Christian Creed [Six Disquisitions, including] "On the Scriptures"	On Reason & Revelation and Life of Nature
G.			
H.			
I.		[Six Disquisitions, including] "On the Church"	
J.			

---

[62] *CL*, III, 533.

[63] *CL*, IV, 588.

[64] *CL*, IV, 590.

[65] *CL*, V, 177. Coleridge projects each as independent works.

[66] *CL*, V, 443.

[67] *CL*, VI, 539. Coleridge projects *Travels* as an independent work resultant from the *opus*; the division between "reason and revelation" and "the history of man" is rooted in Coleridge's explanation but ultimately artificial in this schema.

Table 4

	January 1828[68]	May 1828[69]	October 1833[70]
A.	Man and Races	On Man and Races	On Man (with God and Nature)
B.		History of Philosophy	
C.			On Words
D.			
E.			
F.	On Life and Nature	On God and Nature	God and Nature (with On Man)
G.		Commentary on the Bible, with respect to "On the Scriptures"	Translation of Apocalypse, with respect to "On the Scriptures"
H.			
I.		"On the Church"	
J.			J. H. Green on Ideas

When visually prepared, the consistency is striking. Still, one cannot ignore the shifts, expansions, and other changes that take place over time.

Coleridge's concentration on "man" is perhaps the least recognized element of the projected *opus* (Row A), though some recent research has shed considerable light on this pivotal aspect of Coleridge's thought.[71] "On Man" appears both in the earliest entries in the 1790s as well as the latest in the 1830s. Notably, his speculative interest in the development of races, particularly in association with the biblical narrative, appears consistently.[72] Indeed, much of what appears projected in Coleridge's "constructive philosophy" is concerned distinctly with the human person, for example, the will, as well (Row F). In fact, the division between the

---

[68] *CL*, VI, 722.

[69] *CN*, V, 5868.

[70] *CL*, VI, 967. Coleridge projects the translation of the Apocalypse as an independent work. The topics "On Man" and "God and Nature" are two parts of a singular portion of the projected work.

[71] Most notably, Mary Anne Perkins, *Coleridge's Philosophy: The Logos as Unifying Principle* (Oxford: Clarendon Press, 1994), esp. ch. 4, "Logos: The Human Principle."

[72] See, for example, *SW&F*, II, 1384–86; with Green, *SW&F*, II, 1387–416.

two, especially in later accounts, is nearly arbitrary. The 1833 proposal to Sterling of "the Methodus et Epochae" exemplifies the synthetic quality of Coleridge's philosophical disquisitions on "God, Nature, and Man."[73]

By contrast, few will be surprised to note the regular attention to Coleridge's interest in the history of philosophy (Row B). This seems to be not only a matter of historical interest, but a form of intellectual justification to the broader community. As noted, in July 1821 the history drops out of Coleridge's account of the *opus* — though not permanently — and it is likely that his work in the *Biographia* as well as the "Lectures on the History of Philosophy" in 1818 and 1819 brought a sense of accomplishment that temporarily mollified this urge to state the division as a projected part of the *opus*. As previously highlighted, Coleridge's interest in the history of philosophy is rooted in an "attempt to awaken them to their blindness by showing the persuasiveness of their neglected predecessors."[74] Certainly, it is a similar drive for contextualizing and furthering his own philosophy that propels his interest in "revolutionary minds" (Row D) and the mystics (Row E).

Coleridge's incorporation of *Logic* merits further consideration (Row C). Though a number of studies have examined Coleridge's concern for the use of words and the "science of systematic thinking," the secondary literature probably does not reflect the interest in these matters that Coleridge himself maintained. The repeated reference to a work useful in preparation for "the Bar, the Pulpit or the Senate" ought not be overlooked. Late in his life the work is frequently, though not always, discussed as a composition independent of the *opus*.[75] Here we meet the synthetic quality of Coleridge's plans, thoughtfully expressed in one notebook entry:

I

Aids to Reflection, in the
Discipline of the Understanding
and in the Conduct of Life.

II

Aids to Discourse in Writing
and Speaking: a Practical
Treatise on the power, use, and

---

[73] *CL*, VI, 967.

[74] *Lects 1818–1819*, xliii.

[75] *Op Max*, ccxxii–ccxxix; see Jackson's similar assessment, *Logic*, xl–xli; cf. *CL*, VI, 967.

Logical Management of WORDS; with
an analysis of the Constitution and
Limits of the *Human Understanding* —
intended principally, as a Preparation
for the Senate, the Pulpit and the Bar.

III
Aids to BELIEF for the
attainment of stedfast Convictions from
Insight: or the
Faith and Philosophy
of S. T. C. systematically evolved.[76]

In the next entry, Coleridge delineates the three as Common Sense, Logic, and Faith & Reason; the symbiotic interrelation within the triad is paramount to the Coleridgean method: "Common Sense may exist without FORMAL Logic, and Logic without the ultimate Truths of Reason; but Logic cannot exist without Common Sense, nor Reason without both."[77] In this light, it is no surprise that Coleridge once claimed that such a work ultimately "furnishes the key, and contains the preliminaries to all my other works."[78]

Increasingly, however, Coleridge's plans for the *opus* take on a distinctly Christian tone as the years passed. It is for this reason that "Logosophia" became a fitting denomination for the *opus* in the years following his re-conversion to Trinitarianism, shortly after the turn of the century. A Platonic and Trinitarian vision of philosophy brought the language of the Logos to the fore, even as later years made the explicitly redemptive qualities of Christ the seminal expression of alterity. As early as 1814, Coleridge's plans for the *opus* incorporate biblical commentary into his work, particularly the Gospel of John, with its Logos Christology and spirituality (Row G). Looking back in the *Biographia*, Coleridge recalls how, "[f]or a very long time indeed I could not reconcile personality with infinity; and my head was with Spinoza, though my whole heart remained with Paul and John."[79] Years later, writing on John 3 in his notebooks in 1830, Coleridge rapturously declares his devotion to the Gospel of John: "I cannot

[76] *CN*, V, 5969; February–March 1829.

[77] *CN*, V, 5970.

[78] *CL*, VI, 540.

[79] *BL*, I, 210. In one 1829 entry, Coleridge suggests that one division of the *opus* would include a refutation of the German biblical critic Eichhorn: "If it please God, I purpose in the division of my great Work that treats of Paul, to translate the principal §§phs. Of Eichhorn's Einleitung, & to answer them §§p by §§ph — or rather to expose their futility" (*CN*, V, 6056).

describe the awe, with which the depth of the philosophic truth in almost every verse of this divine Gospel impresses me."[80] Coleridge's desire to complete a biblical commentary — at least on John — was so vital that it prompted "a desire to live, I should not otherwise feel —."[81]

Similarly, by the 1820s, the role of the church in society is understood as a prominent aspect of Coleridge's true philosophy (Row I). Writing in one proposed account for his "*System* of Thought on God, Nature, and Man" in September 1833, Coleridge suggests a section on the church at the close of the first division: "I should be anxious to give, as an appendix, My Reasons for being by free preference a Member of the Reformed Church of England, as presently in it's Articles, Liturgy, and intended Constitution and Organization, the purest form of a Christian Church in union with the National Church or Clerisy of a Christianized Country."[82] In fact, though ultimately assigned to Green, his 1833 plan to examine the "application of the Ideas, as the *Transcendents* of the Truths, Duties, Affections &c in the Human Mind" (Row J) are closely related to the Idea of the church first formally enunciated in *On the Constitution of the Church and State*.

There is no denying a shift in interest and concern in the thinker even amidst a stability and constancy of thought. Seamus Perry has recently commented on the appearance of the final volume of notebook entries, "[t]he Coleridge of volume five is… really quite different to the Coleridge of volume one."[83] Much the same could be said of Coleridge's *magnum opus*: the *opus* of the 1830s is really quite different than the *opus* of the 1790s. One explanation for this difference, offered by McFarland, is quite

---

[80] *CN*, V, 6495. The verse under consideration, one that "contains a germ, out of which the whole Tree of Christian Truth with all it's healing fruits might be *evolved*!," is John 3:18, "He that believeth on him is not condemned: but he that believeth not is condemned already, because he hath not believed in the name of the only begotten Son of God."

[81] On December 23, 1830, Coleridge read John 15 and wrote, "The desire to complete a commentary on John's Gospel which I yet cannot publish but as subsequent to the first Division, at least, of the Chloro-esteesian Philosophy — often prompts a desire to live, I should not otherwise feel —." The weight of this Gospel for his entire philosophical system of the Logos remained impervious: "How strongly throughout this divine Gospel & how beautifully in the first nine verses, is the great idea confirmed of Christ, as the Base, Ground, or Antecedent Unity of our proper Humanity…" (*CN*, V, 6583).

[82] *CN*, V, 6737.

[83] Seamus Perry, Review of *The Notebooks of Samuel Taylor Coleridge Vol. 5: 1827–1834*, ed. Kathleen Coburn and Anthony John Harding, *Wordsworth Circle* 34 (2003): 182.

simply that the accounts of the project shifted in relation to the publication of various aspects of the project: "The transformations of its projected contents were in the main simply correlatives of the fact that
Coleridge began publishing in separate form various constituents of the
whole scheme, with the result that the fragmentary remainder known as
Opus Maximum is merely the unpublished residue of his total project."[84]
On this basis, for McFarland, the *magnum opus* can be equated with three
other works — *Aids to Reflection, The Philosophical Lectures*, and *Theory of Life* — that form "a kind of tripod that supports Coleridge's chief
aspirations in the systematic outline of natural, philosophical, and theological understandings he wished to set forth; the three works, taken
together, serve as an alternative statement of the *magnum opus*."[85] There
can be no doubt that McFarland has pointed out a decisive trait of
Coleridge's plans for the *opus*. For example, following the publication of
the *Biographia*, which deals with Bruno and the mystics as projected of
the *opus*, Coleridge's distinct emphasis on mystics and pantheists subsides
in later accounts of the plan. Similarly, although the anti-Unitarian critique remains in the emphasis on Christ in later accounts, the brief mention at the close of the *Biographia* and, more substantially, the argument
of *Aids to Reflection* appear to have diffused the need for heavy critique.[86]

Even so, McFarland's *opus* thesis fails to do justice to the fullness of
Coleridge's vision. After the publication of some works such as
Biographia or *Aids to Reflection*, Coleridge continues to insist on his
desire to write a fuller work. For instance, although he had completed
his lectures on philosophy a decade earlier, the long 1828 notebook entry
still suggests that the project remains to be fulfilled in the *opus*. Similarly,

---

[84] *Op Max*, xcvii. McFarland often writes notes that appear to substantiate this claim;
for example, in "Fragment 1," McFarland suggests that a passage that also appears in *Aids
to Reflection* has been drawn *from* the *Opus*: "The lifting of this passage out of the *Op
Max* to make an Aphorism in *Aids to Reflection* provides a revealing example of the tendency, noted in the Prolegomena, for C to drain off the *magnum opus* in the interests of
works that did see publication" (*Op Max*, 56n.160). However, McFarland quickly draws
in this hypothesis stating, "[o]n the other hand, he frequently quoted or paraphrased his
own works in the *Op Max*, e.g. the *Essay on Faith*."
[85] *Op Max*, cxcvii; McFarland repeats the claim later, stating "the three works, taken
together, virtually present an alternate version of the *magnum opus* itself" (ccvii).
[86] *BL*, II, 245–46; *AR, passim*; Douglas Hedley has effectively argued that the context
of *Aids* is the Trinitarian-Unitarian controversy of the early nineteenth century (Douglas
Hedley, *Coleridge, Philosophy and Religion: Aids to Reflection and the Mirror of the
Spirit* [Cambridge: Cambridge University Press, 2000], 14). In ch. 8 ("Science and the
Depersonalization of the Divine"), I argue that anti-Unitarianism propels a latent argument
in "Fragment 2" of the *Opus Maximum* as well.

the letters that became known as *Confessions of an Inquiring Spirit* are treated by Coleridge in the same entry as if they were merely a prefatory work written as a prelude to that part of the *opus* devoted to biblical commentary. Equally important is the realization, as the chart visually reveals, that McFarland's proposed "tripod" simply cannot bear the weight of Coleridge's plans. The three may be partially fulfilled if one privileges the middle years ("the most satisfactory descriptions of the content of the *magnum opus*"),[87] but any effort to press this claim would ignore Coleridge's own insistence for nearly twenty years that the *opus* remained incomplete. Any proposed alternative statements would invariably exclude other published works that Coleridge not only envisions as prefatory to the *opus* — such as parts of *The Friend* that are incorporated[88] — but also unpublished compositions that are especially integral to the content of the *Opus Maximum* — such as the *Essay on Faith*, which is quoted at length in fragments "1" and "2."[89] One must also question why the descriptions of the *opus* in the middle years ought to be privileged above later versions. McFarland regards the 1828 version as the "least reliable" because "it was produced at a moment when Coleridge, realizing that time was running out, had virtually ceased work on the *magnum opus*; one suspects that the plan became more grandiose in inverse ratio to its likelihood of fulfillment."[90] Certainly the plan is more detailed than earlier accounts, but hardly any more extensive than Coleridge's March 1803 plan for more than *ten separate works*. While remaining surprisingly consistent, the only significant alteration is the pronounced theological content and extended contact with biblical material. Rather than a disfigurement of an earlier vision, these later accounts are perhaps better regarded as legitimate, extended developments of a persistent quest for system: a complete "Assertion of Religion."

Publishing the Opus Maximum

Despite these criticisms, I do believe that McFarland rightly concludes that "what exists of the *magnum opus* is both more extensive and far

---

[87] *Op Max*, xcviii.

[88] For example, Coleridge's *The Friend* often figures prominently in the text of "Fragment 1" (*Op Max*, 43); consider, too, Coleridge's recommendation of both *The Friend* and the first *Lay Sermon* later in the same fragment (60); for other efforts to incorporate prior works, see, for example, *Op Max*, 89.

[89] See *Op Max*, 72ff.

[90] *Op Max*, c.

more consequent than legend would have it."[91] Left to Green at Coleridge's death in July 1834, the shattered hopes and fragmentary remains of a life's labor remained unpublished. Perhaps left uninspired with the passing of the Sage of Highgate, Green was unable to bring together the manuscripts in a publishable form. Green's own work, published in 1865 as *Spiritual Philosophy: Founded on the Teaching of the Late Samuel Taylor Coleridge*, never managed to stir the imagination of his readers in the manner of his mentor.[92]

Nearly a century after Coleridge's death, unpublished manuscripts long associated with the planned *opus* came under critical scrutiny for at least two distinct reasons: the critique of "system" and the state of Coleridge's *opus* manuscripts. Quite simply, the persistent philosophical effort to express the whole in system was accounted a failure. The disparate encyclopedic efforts of Hegel and Novalis were impeded by the strictures of reality itself.[93] Coleridgean patterns of connectional thinking, polarity and system-building fell out of favor, as well, in the face of the modern scientific deluge of information. The twentieth century rejected the claims of system in favor of analytic and existential philosophies that embraced incompleteness as consubstantial with true existence.[94] Yet, ironically (for Coleridge), the apparent failure of system-building has led to a persistent identification of Romanticism with fragmentation — but incompleteness was never Coleridge's goal.

For those able to overcome the rising philosophical critique of system, the unfortunate state of the *opus* manuscripts compounded the problem. Alice D. Snyder noted the masses of unpublished research left by

---

[91] *Op Max*, cv.

[92] Joseph Henry Green, *Spiritual Philosophy: Founded on the Teaching of the Late Samuel Taylor Coleridge* (London: Macmillan, 1865).

[93] McFarland notes that "[b]oth the *magnum opus* and the *Enzyklopädie* found it difficult to cast their systematic nets around the Leviathan of reality" (*Op Max*, clxxxi). Ferris suggests that Hegel and Novalis "exemplify two attempts to overcome what became a central difficulty in the legacy of Enlightenment thought and its encyclopedic project: how to avoid a merely representational and therefore incomplete system of knowledge or science" (David S. Ferris, "The Question of a Science: Encyclopedistic Romanticism," *Wordsworth Circle* 35 [2004]: 4; see also, Tilottama Rajan, "Philosophy as Encyclopedia: Hegel, Schelling, and the Organization of Knowledge," *Wordsworth Circle* 35 [2004]: 6–11).

[94] See *Op Max*, clviii; McFarland's extended case for Romantic fragmentation maintains that "incompleteness, fragmentation, and ruin — the diasparactive triad — constitute the deepest underlying truth of Romanticism's experience of reality" (Thomas McFarland, *Romanticism and the Forms of Ruin: Wordsworth, Coleridge, and Modalities of Fragmentation* [Princeton: Princeton University Press, 1981], 338 and *passim*).

Coleridge and questioned the suitability of his *Logic* and the *opus* manuscript fragments for publication in any generation. On this basis, Snyder concurred with Green's earlier judgment against publishing the manuscripts independently: "I do not wish to reverse the verdict. I am sure, for example, that it would not redound either to the enlightenment of a twentieth century public or to the credit of Coleridge to foist on the world in their entirety the masses of unorganized, unfocused material..."[95] Shortly thereafter, John H. Muirhead's landmark study, *Coleridge as Philosopher* (1930) concurred with Snyder's decision against publishing more than distinct parts of *Logic* and other manuscripts, stating "[i]t is manifestly incomplete, and bears marks of illiteracy on every page." But Muirhead's interest in Coleridge's attempt at a complete philosophical system is equally apparent and, on this basis, he invokes a less restrictive guide to manuscript publishing. He states that "[t]he study of philosophy in England and America has advanced in vain during the present generation if the student may not be trusted to select the ore and leave the dross in the work of its pioneers."[96] More importantly, after affirming that the manuscripts now present in the *CC* as fragments "1," "2," and "4" are "undoubtedly" part of the *opus* as well as the Huntington Library manuscript "On the Divine Ideas" ("Fragment 3"), Muirhead postulates the existence of other fragments and laments the state of the *opus*: "It is possible, perhaps even probable, that other parts of the MS. of the *Opus Maximum* survive, and may still be found. Sufficient has been quoted from those which we have to show how far, on the subjects dealt with, they supersede all that is derivable from other sources. As compared with anything we have in the published works they show a mastery of the implications of his own fundamental principles, and a command of his materials that makes their fragmentary character all the more deplorable."[97] Unlike Snyder, Muirhead's assessment of the fragments is notably optimistic.

Years later, James D. Boulger raised the fragmentary remains of the *opus* to the level of a seemingly complete work. It is on this basis that

---

[95] Snyder, *Coleridge on Logic and Learning*, vii. Yet, citing the abiding value of these texts to Coleridge scholars, Snyder provides a series of topical excerpts in her book. Among the themes she highlights are "The Child's Arithmetic," "The National Schools," "Atomism and Philosophy," "Scientific Assumptions," "The Formal Sciences and the Platonic Dialectic," and "The Discovery of Truth" (Snyder, *Coleridge on Logic and Learning*, 127–35).

[96] John H. Muirhead, *Coleridge as Philosopher* (London: George Allen & Unwin, 1930), 268.

[97] Muirhead, *Coleridge as Philosopher*, 269.

Boulger shifted the language describing the *opus* to that of a substantial and authoritative text vying with that of prose works published in Coleridge's lifetime: "The challenge of the 'Idea of God,' sketched in the *Biographia* and hinted and assumed in *Aids* and elsewhere, Coleridge finally faced in the late Notebooks and Opus Maximum."[98] Later, Boulger's language seems wholly unfettered by the fragmentary and seemingly desultory quality of the materials that Snyder thought better left unpublished save a few seminal passages; he writes with assurance: "The personality of the Absolute Will is proved in the Opus Maximum by the means sketched briefly in *The Friend* and *Biographia Literaria.*"[99]

The pivotal moment in the posthumous life of the *opus* came with Kathleen Coburn's decision to publish the manuscript fragments in an independent volume of the monumental *Collected Coleridge*. Though other, more prominent works in manuscript form had been assigned to the *Shorter Works and Fragments* volume in the collection — most notably Coleridge's influential *Confessions of an Inquiring Spirit* — the decision to place the *Opus Maximum* on its own solidified the formerly nebulous state of the great work. McFarland later surmised, "Kathleen Coburn very much wanted a contextualized edition, her hope, I believe, being to raise her beloved Coleridge from his limbo of fragmentation to the rank of an accepted figure in the annals of philosophical history."[100] McFarland, too, came under some scrutiny in his attempt to stabilize what Snyder had called "the masses of unorganized, unfocused material."[101] In one article, quoting from his own projected "Introduction" to the *CC* edition, McFarland highlighted the need for and legitimacy of re-paragraphing and punctuating the manuscripts, since the current form was largely generated by Coleridge's amanuensis Joseph Henry Green. The appropriate solution, for McFarland, lay in the hands of an editor: "Coleridge's arguments tend to be abstract and difficult. They need to appear with the subtle qualifications with which he conceived them. With Green's punctuation, the flow of words at times emerges as something perilously close to gibberish. But with careful attention, Coleridge's own voice can sometimes almost be heard, with the half-stops and stops, and above all, the

---

[98] James D. Boulger, *Coleridge as Religious Thinker* (New Haven: Yale University Press, 1961), 126.
[99] Boulger, *Coleridge as Religious Thinker*, 130.
[100] Thomas McFarland, "*Opus Maximum*," *Wordsworth Circle* 27 (1996): 61. McFarland notes the often vastly divergent opinions in the Coleridgean community surrounding the decision to publish the *Opus* independently.
[101] Snyder, *Coleridge*, vii.

parenthetical qualification, that Green did not reproduce. The attempt of
the editorial re-punctuation and re-paragraphing here undertaken is, as
far as possible, to let that voice be heard."[102] McFarland fully realized the
implications of his approach ("Such statements are of course in their very
nature invitations to controversy"),[103] but the matter proved so divisive
that the publishers enlisted Nicholas Halmi as an assistant to the editor,
as noted on the title page of the published *Opus Maximum*, with the
responsibility of "revising the texts" according to the principles of the
CC. In the statement of "Editorial Practice," written by Halmi, the difficulties encountered by countless others — Green, Snyder, and McFarland
— are fully apparent: "To present only a 'reading text,' from which all
the untidiness of the manuscripts is discreetly expunged, would be false
to the nature of the text; but to present only a 'diplomatic text,' in which
all that untidiness is scrupulously translated from handwritten to printed
form, would be a severe trial to the reader — and one that could still not
claim the degree of textual fidelity that a photographic facsimile of the
manuscripts would offer. The present edition, therefore, is intended as
compromise between editorial intrusiveness and restraint. But no attempt
is made, for example, to fashion main clauses for sentences consisting
entirely of subordinate and relative clauses."[104] In this way, the published
text of the *Opus Maximum* attempts to maintain a balance between the
desire to efficiently format a full-length writing project along the lines of
the projected *magnum opus* and the requisite ethic to preserve the fragmentariness that the appearance of a solitary volume — the *Opus Maximum* — might otherwise level. In effect, the Princeton edition managed
to tame the leviathan that no other — certainly not Coleridge — could
harness.

In sum, the story of Coleridge's lifelong dream to produce a "great
work" reveals Coleridge's participation in the post-Kantian hope to
express "the manifold modes of knowledge under one idea." Deeply con-
versant with prior attempts at philosophical system — including not only
Fichte and Schelling but English divines from Cudworth to Butler —
Samuel Taylor Coleridge hoped to complete a philosophical defense and
assertion of Christianity as true religion. The sundry outlines of the *magnum opus* suggest at once the development of an immense project requiring the highest levels of perspicuity and continuity. Now, at last, the

---

[102] McFarland, "*Opus Maximum*," 63.
[103] McFarland, "*Opus Maximum*," 63.
[104] *Op Max*, xvii.

publication of the *Opus Maximum* allows scholars to begin to answer the question that could only be posed in prior generations: "What do we actually have in the *Opus Maximum*?" The essays in this volume mark a commencement of the discussion that will transpire in the years to come.

HARMONY AND MUTUAL IMPLICATION IN THE *OPUS MAXIMUM*

By Daniel W. Hardy

I can readily believe that in the sum of existing things there are more invisible beings than visible. 1. But who will explain this great family to us — their ranks, their relationships, their differences, and their respective duties? [What do they do, and where do they live?] 2. Man's intelligence has always sought knowledge of these matters, but has never attained it. Meanwhile, I do not deny that it pleases me sometimes to contemplate in my mind, as in a picture, the idea of a greater and better world; lest the mind, grown used to dealing with the small matters of everyday life, should dwindle and be submerged in petty thoughts. Nevertheless we should be vigilant of truth and keep a sense of proportion, so that we may discriminate between things certain and things uncertain, daylight and darkness.

> Epigraph to *The Rime of the Ancient Mariner* (1817) from Thomas
> Burnet's *Archaeologie Philosophicae*[1]

Introduction: "The Sum of Existing Things"

That epigraph chosen by Coleridge for *The Rime of the Ancient Mariner* summarizes the dilemma he faced in his work. He knew, or had some intimation of, the scope of reality. And he realized that the credibility of his Christian faith rested on the possibility of explaining "this great family." Here I shall try to trace some of the key features of his attempt to do so.

First, however, we need to acknowledge the benefits and difficulties his "explaining" creates for those who now attempt to read him. On the one hand, close study of his writings can be continually rewarding. With the agnosticism and unconcern for moral goodness that pervade so much

---

[1] From Thomas Burnet's *Archaeologie Philosophicae* (1692, Trans. Derek Roper) in *Coleridge's Verse: A Selection*, ed. William Empson & David Pirie (London: Faber and Faber, 1972), 119. The words in brackets were added by Coleridge; cf. *PW*, I.1, 371n.

philosophical, cosmological, anthropological, and social study today, it can be highly illuminating to engage with someone whose frame of reference for "this great family" includes both the material and social worlds with the Divine, understood both in themselves and as interpenetrating in Reason and moral will.

On the other hand, it is often such features of his writing that people either ignore or resist. Why? One reason is that questions of the sort Coleridge persisted in pursuing are simply set aside in the attempt to manage the complexities of life today. When the conditions of life are formed by such complex and changing cultural, commercial, legal, and governmental factors as they are today, "the mind [grows] used to dealing with the small matters of everyday life": people tend to concentrate on finding their way through the conditions that immediately affect them; and the sorts of questions with which Coleridge was concerned are pushed into the background. Even if readers are ready to face these questions, Coleridge pursues them with such unremitting intensity of attention, thought, and expression as to make them difficult for all but the most patient and careful.

There are still other and more fundamental challenges. For one thing, Coleridge was primarily concerned with "explaining this great family," the "order of things" from the most concrete to the most ultimate, with their moral implications. Sadly, nowadays it is rare for people to seek to find — and respond morally to — the "order of things" in this full sense, and to do so with genuine commitment to pursue its depths. For another, in his search for the "order of things," Coleridge conducted a continuous dialogue with current thought and practice in all domains, from the sciences of the day to the most profoundly religious. Though it occasionally led him astray, this practice was laudable: he always endeavored to engage with expert views, and this prevented him from developing a self-referential view of "a greater and better world." But it makes his writing difficult for those unfamiliar with the debates of his time.

These challenges can cause difficulties for even the most capable interpreters of Coleridge, who often subtly — even if unintentionally — underrate him. As they concentrate on this or that feature of his personality or achievement, and attempt to do justice to that particular aspect, they may easily fail to appreciate its significance when viewed within the wider frame of reference — natural, human, and Divine — within which he intended it to be seen. The overarching plan and intentions of his work are overlooked, to such an extent that most people are unaware of what they were, or why he held to them with such passionate determination.

Briefly stated, his intentions were to *discover the order of all things in relation to their source in God*, and thus to *recover what it is for them to be formed in their fullness by reference to the purposes of God*. For him, this task was self-involving — to use a more recent term — but also more: we are always implicated in the matters under consideration, not only cognitively but volitionally, and we are always to be measured by the highest criterion, the purposes of God. For Coleridge, this meant passionate and unremitting participation at every level, from the most minute to the most universal. After all, the task was to establish the entire span of knowledge and moral agency in relation to the Logos and Spirit in God, which were both accessible to human beings and yet beyond proof. "I also hold, that this Truth, the hardest to demonstrate, is the one which of all others least needs to be demonstrated; that though there may be no conclusive demonstrations of a good, wise, living, and personal God, there are so many convincing reasons for it, within and without — a grain of sand sufficing, and a whole universe at hand to echo the decision! — that for every mind not devoid of all reason, and desperately conscience-proof, the Truth which it is the least possible to prove, it is little less than impossible not to believe! only indeed just so much short of impossible, as to leave some room for the will and moral election, and thereby to keep it a truth of Religion, and the possible subject of a Commandment."[2]

Estimating Coleridge's achievement in this wide-ranging task is the purpose of this essay, and it requires that we risk the attempt to outline, even if only briefly, some of the major aspects of his work. Along the way, we should be able to ascertain some of the distinctive features of his position, and some unexpected implications will appear which show that Coleridge has a more significant place in philosophy and theology than he is usually allowed.

Can Man's Intelligence Know?
The Difficulties of Coleridge's Context

Coleridge lived in a time when the conceivability of such an undertaking, establishing the entire span of knowledge and moral agency in relation to the Logos and Spirit in God, was under threat; and this challenge has persisted, and grown, ever since. Since at least the seventeenth century the hitherto preferred ontological and epistemological scheme for

---

[2] *AR*, 186.

reality, idealism in the broad sense, had been under continuous pressure. Some today would say that it has now altogether collapsed, or at least completely outlived its usefulness, and has been — or soon will be — displaced, if not by fragmentation into special domains with their own self-justifying practices, then by linguistic or semiotic approaches.[3]

Of course, the idealism that survived in Coleridge's time was not simply a "standard" one; it had been developed in various ways to meet the challenges already evident. And, highly creative as he was, he himself redeveloped it. If his own creativity did not demand it, circumstances required it. The theology, philosophy, and science of his day already raised immensely difficult problems, and the intelligibility and defensibility of Christian belief were regularly challenged. There were what he considered particular kinds of naïve fragmentation: of sense-derived knowledge (cf. empiricism) from the certainties of reason (cf. Cartesianism), of cognition from moral striving (cf. Hume), of history from truth (cf. Lessing), of noumenal from phenomenal knowledge (cf. Kant), etc. As if all this was not enough, scientific discovery and its application in emerging industry and commerce were advancing rapidly, promoting a practical commitment to utilitarianism with little attention to the philosophical implications or moral consequences.

Given his intention to order all things in relation to God, he found all these positions problematic. But the way forward he proposed was not, on the whole, to deny their legitimacy in their appropriate sphere, so much as to find their limitations and knit them together in what might be called an idealist scientific and theological encyclopaedia. He sought therefore to find the *mutual implication* of all things — and the methods by which they were to be understood — with the finding of truth and goodness in God. It is this special way of proceeding with which we will be largely concerned here.

Enlarging the Intelligence

Coleridge's plans were no less wide than they were lofty, and he found that he never knew enough to be finished. Not only this, knowledge and

---

[3] Something like this fragmentation is found in those accounts of Coleridge that, as we have just seen, fail to see the significance of aspects of his work within the frame of reference he was actually employing.

practice were also advancing rapidly, and he was fully aware of their *historical contingency*: he saw new discoveries, as "no mere supplementary Postscript to former works" but as affecting "the whole theory and consequent arrangement of the Art or Science to which they belong."[4] The *Opus Maximum*, like Coleridge's other writings (the *Lay Sermons* and *On the Constitution of the Church and State*, for example), shows the marks of its origins early in the industrial revolution, when the application of evolving scientific knowledge to machines for the manufacture of goods for commerce were accompanied by, and further enhanced, utilitarian attitudes.

On the one hand, rapid developments in the "mixed" and "experimental" sciences continued, and, through his friendship with a wide range of those involved, Coleridge was in close touch with them. There was active conversation and controversy about the significance of what was being found, and Coleridge took part in the argument, especially at places where key issues were at stake. On the other hand, the early years of the nineteenth century saw remarkable theoretical discussions about *how all* cohered. Kant's critical idealism passed *via* Fichte into a full-blown spiritual phenomenology that required spiritual enlightenment; and Schelling attempted to encompass natural scientific research within philosophy. New discoveries in magnetism and electricity led Schelling, like Coleridge, to see nature as dynamic processes based on polarities of attraction and repulsion, and then later to elevate the aesthetic faculty to unify all other faculties. Coleridge was not only familiar with this discussion, but figured in the network by which it was transferred to England and *via* James Marsh to New England and the Transcendentalists.[5] This is not to suggest that he simply copied Schelling, for his own plan was developed along less coercively systematic lines.

Of particular importance was the question of how there might be harmony or unity within and between theoretical and practical sciences, the matter of "connected reason" or "relational ideas." What was their relationship? The situation cried out for a substantial answer, and Coleridge attempted to provide it, though not of course along utilitarian lines. The circumstances bred a far-reaching project, to manifest the unity of knowledge — "one harmonious body of knowledge" — in both theory and practice. But the *basis* of the unity Coleridge found was different.

---

[4] *SW&F*, I, 587 ("Encyclopaedia Metropolitana").
[5] Cf. Randall Collins, *The Sociology of Philosophies: A Global Theory of Intellectual Change* (Cambridge: Harvard University Press, 1998), 630–33.

The issue for Coleridge was how realities *are constituted* and, while remaining fully themselves, are also *mutually implicated*, that is fully related to each other both proximately and also ultimately by reference to God. That issue surfaces frequently throughout his writing and in many different forms; and his responses to it remain important. The full range of Coleridge's engagement with it appears in his *Opus Maximum*. In many ways the most difficult of Coleridge's work to appreciate, and not only because "the fragmentary remainder known as the *Opus Maximum* is merely the unpublished residue of his total project,"[6] it is demanding because it is often not easy to see what is going on, analytically or constructively.

For one thing, like Coleridge's other writings, it attempts a range of topics often unknown to readers today, and the kinds of conclusions it reaches are also unfamiliar to those who now engage with it. As regards topics, it combines Coleridge's lifelong concern for the theoretical and practical aspects of the sciences, philosophy, and religion with methodological and specifically Christian ones, where other discussions tend always to fragment such matters and to sidestep those that are more difficult. What is still more difficult to see is how Coleridge actively explores the deep ways in which all these are related, how they are *mutually implicated* by reference to what they are and may yet be.

Contemplating a Better World: Improving the Mind and Heart

These matters do not appear only in the *Opus Maximum* or in his explicitly philosophical and theological writings, and one accessible way of appreciating their importance is in his poetry.

> Farewell, farewell! but this I tell
> To thee, thou Wedding-Guest!
> He prayeth well, who loveth well
> Both man and bird and beast.
>
> He prayeth best, who loveth best
> All things both great and small;
> For the dear God who loveth us,
> He made and loveth all.[7]

---

[6] McFarland, "Prolegomena," in *Op Max*, xcvii.

[7] *The Rime of the Ancient Mariner* in *PW*, I.1, 419 (lines 610–17). Apart from commas, the text was the same in the revision of 1834 as in 1798.

Both the scope and intensity of Coleridge's overall concerns are captured in these stanzas of *The Rime of the Ancient Mariner*: the *quality of prayer*, and therefore direct relatedness to God by a human being, is directly linked to *genuine love for all things*: the one requires the other. It is especially interesting that — as prayer deepens, moving from "well" to "best" — the scope of the love required widens from the animate to all things, and becomes macroscopic and microscopic, reaching to "great and small." Hence attentiveness and love, first for "man and bird and beast" and then for "all things both great and small," are necessarily *implicated* first in praying well and then in praying best. Most important of all, the quality of prayer is not simply sustained by love, but by the God who made and loves us and all, to whom prayer is directed: the One who "made and loveth all" informs and shapes the love of the one who prays for "all things both great and small." The movement is a complex one:

1. the *scope* or *extensity* widens from all that is animate ("man and bird and beast") to include everything ("all things both great and small"),
2. the *intensity of love* increases from "well" to "best,"
3. correlatively, the *intensity of prayer* increases from "well" to "best," and
4. even with *maximum extensity* (1) the *greatest intensity of prayer* (relationship to God) (2) becomes actual not because of human capacity but because God made and loves both us (acknowledged in calling God "dear") and all things,
5. accordingly, prayer includes not only loving attentiveness but also the reasoning of that which is made by God.

Changing the mood and reversing the sequence shows the meaning: "You, *dear* God, loveth us and made and loveth all: only in acknowledging both who you are and what you did and do, do we best pray, love, and know all things."

Here in poetic fashion, therefore, we see the *implicateness* between "man and bird and beast" that arises in loving them all, then the *implicateness* found between "all things both great and small" in loving and knowing them all, and how these hinge on active prayer to the dear God "who loveth us, [who] made and loveth all." There is a matter of great significance here, for dealing with the full scope of existing things — their "*extensity*" — in all their actual differentiation and complexity happens only with full attention to the *intensity* of God's identity in God's creation of, and love for, the world. Ironically, we can *know* the world in all its complexity (extensity) only insofar as we are most attentive to the God that God is (intensity), because the one is made actual by the other,

and we can *live* satisfactorily in the one only insofar as we are attentive
to the love that God is.

These two, how to know and how to do, need always to be kept in
mind in reading Coleridge. In Coleridge's time, adequately acknowledging the full scope and complexity of the world, and the relations by which
"all things" cohered, while yet finding how they were ordered in relation
to God, was a pressing issue for science, philosophy, and religion. Likewise, how to *do* was an enormously pressing issue for one beset by opium
addiction:

> ... You have no conception of what my sufferings have been, forced to
> struggle and struggle in order not to desire a death for which I am not pre-
> pared. — I have scarcely known what sleep is, but like a leopard in its den
> have been drawn up and down the room by extreme pain, and restlessness,
> worse than pain itself.
>
> O how I have prayed even to loud agony only to be able to pray! O how
> I have felt the impossibility of any real *good will* not born anew from the
> Word and the Spirit! O I have seen far, far deeper and clearer than I ever
> saw before the ground of pernicious errors! O I have seen, I have felt that
> the worst offences are those against our own souls! That our souls are infi-
> nite in depth, and therefore our sins are infinite, and redeemable only by an
> infinitely higher infinity; that of the love of God in Christ Jesus... O God
> save me — save me from myself...[8]

Broadly speaking, these were the topics with which Coleridge was repeatedly concerned, and with which he was to be preoccupied in his long-
planned *magnum opus*.

Explaining the Great Family: The *Opus Maximum*

These large issues are deeply embedded in the *Opus Maximum* as we
now have it: broadly speaking the tracing of all proximate relations to
their ultimate relation to God. There is good evidence — internal and
external — as to Coleridge's intentions. Externally, there is good cumulative evidence for these in the many plans he offered for what was to be
his major work, even if the fragments of the *Opus Maximum* as now published fit uncertainly with them. In which plan does this or that fragment
figure? Strictly speaking, we do not know. But the outline plans were
clear enough. Internally, if we can but see, there are many indications as

---

[8] *CL*, III, 463 (to Thomas Roberts, *c*. December 19, 1813).

to the wider and deeper intentions he had. We will need to look at them later. First, let us recall his plans.

In 1814, five years before the time to which the earliest fragment ("Fragment 4") is assigned — *c.* 1819 — he proposed a work titled "Christianity the one true Philosophy — or 5 Treatises on the Logos, or communicative Intelligence, Natural, Human, and Divine: — to which is prefixed a prefatory Essay on the Laws & Limits of Toleration & Liberality illustrated by fragments of *Auto*-biography —."[9] It was already clear that he intended a discussion of what might called "relational ideas" in nature and man, as implying — or implied by — Divine self-communication in the *Logos*, which he found in the Gospel of St. John, by comparison with the other Gospels the only one "for the Church Universal of all ages."[10]

In 1815, Coleridge projected a developed form of the same thing, *Logos* as *wisdom*, which he found in John's Gospel. This *Logos* was the

> Eternal Wisdom and all-sufficing Beatitude... contained in that all-perfect Idea, in which the Supreme Spirit contemplateth itself and the plenitude of its infinity... the beloved Son, in whom the Father is indeed well pleased.[11]

Coleridge intended to trace this, and where necessary correct it, in the whole realm of philosophy, the logic of reality both practical and transcendental, and theology. The work was to be a "Logosophia, or on the Logos human & Divine, in six Treatises" on: the philosophy of the history of philosophy; the "science of connected reasoning" (logic) as "applied to the purposes of real Life"; "the Science of Premises or transcendental Philosophy" ("*intellectual geometry*"); a commentary on John's Gospel; pantheism and mysticism; and "the causes and consequences of Unitarianism."[12]

In his 1817 plan for the *Encyclopaedia Metropolitana*, which was to be arranged not arbitrarily (e.g. alphabetically) but in accordance with "a correct Philosophical Method," the *range of topics and their intended links* (what I have called their "mutual implications") are still more fully evident,[13] especially how the *pure sciences* are linked with the *mixed* and *applied sciences*, with the *fine arts* as the intermediate link, "in which both the matter and form are wholly from, in and for the mind," and how

---

[9] *CL*, III, 533 (to Daniel Stuart; September 12, 1814); cf. *BL*, I, 136n.
[10] *CM*, I, 447.
[11] *AR*, 312.
[12] *CL*, IV, 591–92 (to Daniel Stuart; October 7, 1815).
[13] See Editor's Note, *CL*, IV, 723–24.

all these are present in the reality of historical life.[14] In the 1818 plan, there were four related divisions, which we can abridge as follows:

I. *Pure Sciences*: the formal — universal grammar and philology; logic, particular and universal (the forms of conceptions and their combinations); mathematics or the forms and constructions of figure and number; metaphysics or the universal principles and conditions of experience (determining the reality of speculative knowledge), and morals as the principles and conditions of the coincidence of the individual will with the universal Reason, determining the reality of practical knowledge, and theology or the union of both in their application to God as supreme reality.

II. *Mixed Sciences* (mechanics, hydrostatics, pneumatics, optics, astronomy), and *Applied Sciences*
    1. Experimental Philosophy: magnetism, electricity, light, heat, colour, meteorology.
    2. The Fine Arts: poetry (introduced by psychology), painting, music, sculpture, architecture.
    3. The Useful Arts: agriculture (introduced by political economy), commerce, manufactures.
    4. Natural History: physiology in the widest sense; inanimate (chrystallography, geology, mineralogy); insentient (phytonomy, botany); animate (zoology).
    5. Application of Natural History: in anatomy, surgery, material medica, pharmacy, medicine.

III. *The Biographical and Historical*: biography chronologically arranged, interspersed with introductory chapters of natural history, political geography and chronology, and accompanied with correspondent maps and charts[15] and

IV. *Miscellaneous and Lexicographical*: alphabetical, miscellaneous, and supplemental, including a gazetteer and a philosophical and etymological lexicon of the English language, with citations ordered by age, yet with every attention to the independent beauty or value of the sentences chosen which is consistent with the higher ends of a clear insight into the original and acquired meaning of every word.

The Index.[16]

---

[14] *SW&F*, I, 576ff.

[15] History shown in its *reality*, that is "in their truly philosophical form" (*SW&F*, I, 586).

[16] Cf. *SW&F*, I, 686–87.

The order and contents of this encyclopaedia deserve close attention: the whole compass of reality — as spoken, thought, practiced, and implied — was to be included: language, logic, thought, mathematics, metaphysics, morality, and theology, united with the sciences, applications, natural history, "arts" and medicine, all of them necessary for understanding historical reality. All of these — *pure thought in its relation to reality, morality and God as found in the theoretical and practical sciences, historical and socio-political reality as seen in its truth,* and *Christian belief and practice* — appeared consistently in Coleridge's plans thereafter.

In all these plans, Coleridge intended to show the integral relation of all these, the reciprocal relation within and between the first two, while the third or "Biographical and Historical part" would "teach the same truths by example, that have [previously] evolved."[17] Wherever seen, therefore, Coleridge's concern was with the entire *span* of knowledge and reality as then or prospectively available, seen both formally and in concrete actuality, and its *integration for the human mind in an ongoing teleological dynamic*, ultimately by reference to the *Logos*. What distinguished him from others was not only this but also his active engagement with all that it might involve, from the most detailed and concrete current investigation and theorizing to the exploration of its ultimate reference in God. All these engagements are present in the *Opus Maximum*.

Vigilant of Truth and Keeping a Sense of Proportion

One way of describing Coleridge's endeavor is to say that it embraced the span of everything — its full extensity — while seeking the relatedness of all things according to the character of each. So we might expect him to be concerned with the composition or constitution of each thing, whether inanimate or animate, or indeed spiritual. And since there is no point when each in its individuality is not also related to others, or their relationship is not conditioned by their particularities, we might equally expect him to try to find the ways in which these relationships occur, whether they are fixed or variable, and what is their quality. It is very important to note that this is already to "summarize" their relatedness, to *move toward notions of their coherence*, and to start on the way to what might be their *ultimate coherence*, a coherence

---

[17] *CL*, IV, 724 (headnote to no. 1054).

that would be found in their origins and fulfillment. While Coleridge is concerned with "everything," with "extensity" as we call it, he is no less concerned with how things are together, and how they implicate each other in such a way as to counterbalance sheer extensity by "intensity."

Such considerations require a lot of delving into the origins, proximate relations, and ultimate coherence of things cosmic, human, social, etc. As Coleridge undertook this, if he was to be responsive to current discussions, he would have to engage with current scientific, artistic, and philosophical views in the development of his work, while retaining his own perspective.

Even if not obvious to those of a utilitarian cast of mind, those who juxtaposed theories and/or practices in order to achieve a quantitatively conceived good for society, it was clear enough that the relation between them would have to be *intrinsic* to the things related. Any view of the relation between things that was *external* to them (as we might say) or depended on "modes of *arrangement*" (as Coleridge said)[18] was simply inadequate. For this reason, his concern with the intricacies of the world in every respect — the manifoldness of its extensity, as I call it — was not simply out of curiosity, but in order to place himself in a position to see them *as themselves*.

The way forward, Coleridge thought, was to describe or explain them more adequately, not externally or by their (mechanical) arrangement, but by reaching the active or "energetic" "inward principle of whatever is requisite for the reality of a thing, as *existent*," as distinct from "the *essence*, or essential property [which] signifies the inner principle of all that appertains to the *possibility* of a thing."[19] This "energetic" inward principle is the concern of the "science of DYNAMICS." Insofar as it is universalized in any phenomenon, doing so *attributes* to that some *efficient law in nature*, whose *subjective correlate* is called an "IDEA." In this, Coleridge could find support in the views of his distinguished friend and chemist Humphry Davy: "who would not be ambitious of becoming acquainted with the most profound secrets of nature, of ascertaining her hidden operations, and of exhibiting to men that system of knowledge which relates so intimately to their own physical and moral constitution?"[20]

---

[18] *CL*, II, 727 (to Humphry Davy; May 4, 1801).
[19] *Friend*, I, 467*.
[20] *Collected Works of Humphry Davy*, ed. John Davy, 9 vols. (New York: Johnson Reprint Corporation, 1972), II, 320.

Before proceeding, we should take note that an Idea for Coleridge is neither abstracted nor generalized from the phenomenon, but is *attributed* to it. The relations thus found were found by the human mind, and *real* as such. Methodologically, the counterpart was Coleridge's differentiation of the Understanding from the Reason. Sensations and their accompanying "conceptions," as analyzed by John Locke, were the terrain of the *Understanding* by which experience was organized. This enabled the observer to apprehend by forming conceptions. *Reason*, however, was where the observer formed explanations, in what is called *abduction*, and achieved fuller description by means of ideas. "Reason depends on the slow and gradual apprehension of broad, abstract patterns of the value, the meaning, and the end goal of a thing rather than its number, weight, or dimensions."[21]

Discriminating Between Things Certain and Things Uncertain: Humanity

One of Coleridge's suppositions was that people *were* normally concerned with how things are *methodically* related: "What is it that first strikes us, and strikes us at once in a man of education, and which, among educated men, so instantly distinguishes the man of superior mind? Not always the weight or novelty of his remarks, nor always the interest of the facts which he communicates... The true cause of the impression made on us is, that his mind is *methodical*. We perceive this, in the unpremeditated and evidently habitual arrangement of his words, flowing spontaneously and necessarily from the clearness of the leading idea; from which distinctness of mental vision, when men are fully accustomed to it, they obtain a habit of foreseeing at the beginning of every sentence how it is to end, and how all its parts may be brought out in the best and most orderly succession."[22] It is striking that he speaks of the *methodical mind* as evidenced in "*distinctness of mental vision*" and in the *arrangement of words* "flowing spontaneously and necessarily from the clearness of the leading idea." So method could be found in literature or art as well as more formal exposition. Coleridge sought method in *all relations*, because all things were *mutually implicated*.

---

[21] Pamela Edwards, *The Statesman's Science* (New York: Columbia University Press, 2004), 35.

[22] *SW&F*, I, 638 ("Treatise on Method" [1818]).

Drawing upon the Greek notion of method as meaning a way, path, or transit, the method he looked for was a step-by-step transition in which there was a progressive unifying by an act of the mind, and the demand placed on the mind was proportionate to the range or extensity of the sphere increased: "the wider the sphere... the more comprehensive and commanding must be the initiative: and if we would discover an *universal Method* by which every step in our progress through the whole circle of art and science should be directed, it is absolutely necessary that we should seek it in the very interior and central essence of the human intellect."[23] Coleridge outlined this "essence" in dynamic terms:

> Man is a finient being, an intelligence, which by power of his Will dat sibi finem [gives himself a limit], *determines* the relations of his own being & of that being to Nature, and the relations of nature & of what is above nature as far as these have relation to his being. The question is here with regard to the relations of his own being.
>
> The Ground of Man's nature is the Will in a form of Reason. It is this which gives the Totality, One-ness, and it is the various metamorphoses, degradations, and varying relations of the Will, which determine the particular energies, functions & acts of his existence...
>
> Now according to this in man there is a higher nature of which the function is designated as *Spirit* and a lower nature or animal life of which the function manifests itself as *Spontaneity*[,] the lowest form of a true life. But man as a finite being occupying the place between the transcendent life & the animal life, appears in a twofold character of a particular intellect and a particular will, which we present in the Understanding or *Judgement,* and in the *Affection* as the Will in a relatively passive form.[24]

Following one trajectory from lowest to highest, it is the influence of the Spirit on *human Understanding*, therefore, that acts upon and raises animal life from *sensation* and spontaneity in turn to *Instinct, judgment* and the *Lumen rationale*, progressively producing the capacity to see things in their fullest relations. Following the other trajectory from lowest to highest, the influence of the same Spirit on *volition* lifts it from sheer spontaneous *volition* to *appetite* and then directs it by *affection* and *love*. The co-presence of these two trajectories brings growth, acting to produce *individuality*, *genius*, and *integrity*. So the Spirit is what raises in the human intellect the capacity for Reason, and in the will the capacity for love, the two together making it possible to think — and enact — things in their fullest relations. Without that, human apprehension remains cognitively and volitionally at lesser levels, and will be incapable of the

---

[23] *SW&F*, I, 630 ("Treatise on Method" [1818]).
[24] *SW&F*, II, 1385–86 ("Schema of the *total Man*").

higher levels of reason and love needed for wider spheres: the levels of instinct and judgment (a self-conscious act of uniting or relativizing) will fall short of Reason (the *Lumen Rationale*), and the levels of appetite and affection (the craving for being or having) will fall short of the passion of Love.

Such a "Schema of the *total Man*" explains the disastrous effects of being caught in sensory awareness uninformed by judgment or Reason, and in spontaneous will undirected by any higher appetite or affection. We find that also in the *Rime of the Ancient Mariner*, as the mariner arbitrarily shoots the albatross, bringing about death and a "rotting" sea and ship. Likewise it explains the pivotal importance of the sight of beauty in the water snakes, and the good will in "blessing them unawares," and their capacity to bring new life.

> O happy living things! no tongue
> Their beauty might declare:
> A spring of love gushed from my heart,
> And I blessed them unaware:
> Sure my kind saint took pity on me,
> And I bless'd them unaware.
>
> *The spell begins to break.*
>
> The self-same moment I could pray;
> And from my neck so free
> The Albatross fell off, and sank
> Like lead into the sea.[25]

Surprisingly, there is a great deal in common between this "rotting sea" and the chaos of which Coleridge speaks elsewhere, and between the cause of the one — blindness and spontaneous, arbitrary killing — and the cause of the other — "habitual submission of the understanding to mere events and images, as such, without any attempt to classify and arrange them."[26]

---

[25] *PW*, I.1, 393, 395 (lines 282–91).

[26] Seeking for kinds of relations in the *order of things*, Coleridge distinguishes between two principal ones, the relation between things by which a thing *must be*, which he identifies as the relation of *Law* (the establishment of a rule to which things must *necessarily* conform) and the relation of *Theory*, in which observation suggests an arrangement for the purpose of *understanding* and sometimes control. The latter, with their corresponding Method, reaches beyond "things only" to their relations and their directed use for good, such as are found in the "scientific arts." The former views relations of things as necessarily existent, "predetermined by a truth in the mind itself"; it relies on higher possibilities of judgment. And these are closely linked to "the relation of Law... in its absolute perfection conceivable only of God, that Supreme Light, and Living Law, 'in whom we

All things, in us, and about us, are a chaos, without Method: and so long as the mind is entirely passive, so long as there is an habitual submission of the understanding to mere events and images, as such, without any attempt to classify and arrange them, so long the chaos must continue. There may be transition, but there can never be progress; there may be sensation, but there cannot be thought: for the total absence of Method renders thinking impracticable; as we find that partial defects of Method proportionately render thinking a trouble and a fatigue. But as soon as the mind becomes accustomed to contemplate, not *things* only, but likewise *relations* of things, there is immediate need of some path or way of transit from one to the other of the things related; — there must be some law of agreement or of contrast between them; there must be some mode of comparison; in short, there must be Method.[27]

Darkness and Light

Pivotal to the highest view of relations between things, or to the highest love for things, was the presence of the Logos and Spirit of God by which all things, and their relations, were constituted. This was not "external" either to human beings or to the created, but was the inner source by which Reason and love were attracted to see and do. But, interestingly, these conclusions were not simply introduced by Coleridge by *fiat*. The most important part of "Fragment 4" shows him struggling over "the history of the Cosmogony": "The truth I seem to myself to have mastered, but I shrink from the difficulty of explication."[28] The struggle arises from two sources, it seems: the seriousness of his engagement both with the Bible (especially the Book of Genesis and the Gospel of John) and also the conclusions of current science, the two here superimposed on each other; and his attempt to reach a coordinated explanation of what is the case in the universe. His line of argument, which is difficult in the extreme, merits careful consideration. While it deserves line-by-line analysis, I shall have to deal with it more summarily.

First, Coleridge contemplates the primal state of the earth just after the ("lucific") act of light-giving. In a fashion not unlike the great twentieth-century theologian Karl Barth much later, who traced sin and evil to the resistance of Nothingness (*das Nichtige*) to the creative act of God,

---

live and move, and have our being'" (Acts 17:28 var.). Between these two, there is clear difference, but the latter should lead to the former.

[27] *SW&F*, I, 631 ("Treatise on Method" [1818]).

[28] *Op Max*, 324.

Coleridge finds the "matter of light" deficient ("pravity") and, in its self-seeking, "apostate": it only "is" or "acts" by *rejecting* the light: "By the rejection of Light, I mean only that the tendency produced by this lucific influence may, from the pravity of the agent (material), viz. by the original apostatic self-seeking, become a nisus to division without that distinction which necessarily implies a community, or the existence of another in the self, as another and yet equal to self. This would, of course, produce, in consequence of Light, a contrariety to Light. Not less real than mere indistinction, it would be a virtual rejection of Light, as particularity devoid of Distinctiveness."[29] From the rejection of Light arises *division*, or at least an inherent tendency to it, not the more positive *distinction* (which implies continuity or community), which would allow inherent (internal) relation to another ("the existence of another in the self, as another and yet equal to self"). That division would in itself be a "virtual rejection of Light, as particularity devoid of Distinctiveness." *Accordingly*, it lacks the distinctiveness proper to any created thing. Even without following Coleridge's argument into parallels with science, we see here a carefully-thought development of John 1:9–10 ("That was the true Light, which lighteth every man that cometh into the world. He was in the world, and the world was made by him, and the world knew him not"). It is a statement about the internal dividedness of creation, not only of human beings (for example, "the good I would, I do not" [Rom. 7:19], spoken of by Paul). So, even while the Light is admitted, resistance to the Light robs creation of the true distinctiveness-in-community of its parts, and leaves it chaos, deprived of all but the "hybrid offspring" of Light as division.

If, however, the initial condition of the cosmos was positive indistinction or fluidity — absence of particularity, or distinguishability — Coleridge continues, "we must conceive a number of intermediate gradations between these… [from] fluid [to] solidescent, then oscillative, and lastly separated." So, "the epoch under which we exist must be regarded as a part or diminuendo of the oscillation, and the separation…

a necessary gradation, a state in which the light shall be not so absorbed as to exclude a partial result — the contractive tendency, for instance — and on the other hand a state in which the contractive, being disarmed by the dilative — in chemical language, the oxygen by the hydrogen — Light shall be virtually rejected, i.e. admitted but not received, and all this still imperfectly, as being states of a not yet wholly ceased oscillation, so viz. that the

---

[29] *Op Max*, 324–25.

transmission of light may still be accompanied by a reflection of the same, and the reflection of light be rarely, or in the first conception never, so perfect but that, in its lower form at least, it shall have been received not, indeed, as Light, or the power of distinction, but as the hybrid offspring of Light as division, or the tendency to Division, by contraction with the various results which complicate balances and counteractions will necessarily bring into existence.[30]

So the cosmos as we find it, in Scripture or science, is complex in its evolution. Coleridge's view is not far from the notion of a pulsating cosmos found in some twentieth-century science.

Polar Oppositions and Being Drawn to the True Center

In more summary fashion, Coleridge describes the actual universe, from darkness "as the positive ⚹ and possible basis of Light," or in other words actual indistinction as potential multeity, like the indistinctive as "faces of the waters."[31] It is this that Light (*verbum lucificum*) actualizes as multeity-with-continuity, which in turn has a retroactive effect on the indistinct.

Through this, what Coleridge emphasizes is the "true" polar opposition between the self-referential cosmos ("apostatic" in the sense that it commits apostasy) and the "redemptive spirit and Word." Methodologically, the counterpart of this self-referential cosmos is "the idolatry of the senses, the consequence of which is the passion for death, and the reward a dead palsy of intellectual life, and choosing darkness for light, turns the light itself into darkness and science into a pompous sepulchre of truth."[32] What moves beyond this polar opposition is a relation between the creaturely Self and the Divine Word where the Will is "patient" — here a form of action — with a "preparatory impregnation" "effected by an act of Free-grace, an overflowing of the Love in the descent of the Spirit."

In the most striking terms, Coleridge "counts" the movements he has found:

I.   Abduction from the Self, as manifesting the being drawn toward the true center, as ⚹, the self-seeking or tendency to the false and fantastic centre in the opposite direction. These are realized Poles, and manifested in the Creature = Vis centrifuga ⚹ Vis centripetalis.

---

[30] *Op Max*, 325.
[31] *Op Max*, 326.
[32] *Op Max*, 326.

II.   The actualized Indistinction ♓ Multeity. Offspring in the Creature or the realized Poles. Attraction ad extra. Appropriative Attraction, or Astringency, as ♓ separative Self-projection, or Volatility.

III. The influx from the Light, with the Spirit[,] as ♓ by the creaturely: Conjunction: Offspring or realized Poles, Particularization, Contraction as ♓ Omneity, Dilation.[33]

At this point, after traversing the history of cosmogony, we reach Coleridge's most distinctive achievement, "the being drawn toward the true center" of all, the Logos and the Spirit, in continuity with but distinct from (♓) the polar opposites of self-seeking and attraction to falsity. In II, this movement is found in the creaturely: (chaotic) indistinction and multeity are actualized in reality as polar opposites, and they too are attracted *ad extra*, but in order to appropriate it or separately to live in a volatile self-projection. Broadly speaking, this is a description of the fundamental distortion of human beings, whereby they react badly to the "center" beyond them. In III, the coming of the Light with the Spirit, as distinct from but in continuity with (♓) the creaturely, are transformatively conjoined to the creaturely, both in particularity (Christ) and in its dilation into universality (the Holy Spirit). In these few sentences, therefore, we find a compressed statement of the whole scheme of creation and salvation. In other words, the *source and end* to which, in the "Schema of the Whole Man," we saw Coleridge tracing the movement by which human beings were illuminated in Reason and directed in love is also the "true center of all" upon which all else depends.

The *movement of attraction* is identified by Coleridge by using a term known in some philosophical circles, chiefly those of modern pragmatism, as "abduction." Logically this is often seen as the postulating of a possible explanation, a "third" form of reasoning beyond — but resourcing — induction and deduction. Here in Coleridge, an ancestor of modern pragmatism, however, we find that abduction is *"the being drawn toward the true center"* of all, the Logos and the Spirit. A second difference from the usual logical use is that this "being drawn" incorporates both ontological and temporal elements of the created world, including differentiation and continuity, and also the enduring and the progressive, as mutually complementary. A third is that it is applicable both to the individual (as in *Aids to Reflection*) and also to society (as in *On the Constitution of the Church and State*), as that which serves

---

[33] *Op Max*, 327–28.

"both for the permanence and the progressive advance of whatever...
constitute the public weal."[34]

In that "being drawn," human beings are most truly enabled to affirm
themselves and the order of all things, as they are illuminated in Reason
and directed in love toward "all things both great and small, for the dear
God who loveth us, He made and loveth all." This "abduction" is indeed
a maximal insight, a fitting conclusion, both methodological and realis-
tic, to Coleridge's lifelong pursuit of the mutual implication of all things
in the Logos and the Spirit.

[34] *C&S*, 53.

ON THE DIVINE IDEAS: THE SYSTEMATIC THEOLOGY OF SAMUEL TAYLOR COLERIDGE

By LUKE S. H. WRIGHT

Introduction: The Received Text

For most of his mature working life, certainly for the last two decades of his life, Samuel Taylor Coleridge spoke repeatedly, in both his letters and his table talk, of constructing a substantial work that would demonstrate Christianity as "the one true philosophy." His own daughter, Sara, in a letter written to her friend Mrs. Plummer in October 1834 (some two months following her father's death) makes clear that she believed this to be the primary focus of her father's work:

> We feel happy, too, in the conviction, that his writings will be widely influ-
> ential for good purposes. All his views may not be adopted, and the effect
> of his posthumous works must be impaired by their fragmentary condition;
> but I think there is reason to believe, that what he has left behind him will
> introduce a new and more improving mode of thinking... it is not to be
> expected that speculations which demand so much effort of mind and such
> continuous attention, to be fully understood, can ever be *immediately* pop-
> ular... Heraud, in his brilliant oration on the death of my father, delivered
> at the Russell Institution, observes that religion and philosophy were first
> reconciled — first brought into permanent and indissoluble union in the
> divine works of Coleridge; and I believe the opinion expressed by this gen-
> tleman, that my father's metaphysical theology will prove a benefit to the
> world, is shared by many persons of refined and searching intellect both in
> this country and in America, where he has some enthusiastic admirers; and
> it is confidently predicted by numbers that this will be more and more felt
> and acknowledged in course of time.[1]

Sara's discussion serves well as an introduction to the heart of this article, which argues that Coleridge's *Opus Maximum* is a cogent metaphysical theology built on a vitalist model.[2] Her prophetic comment that
the posthumous works' "fragmentary condition," which demand "so
much effort of mind and such continuous attention," will keep them from

---

[1] Sara Coleridge, *Memoir and Letters of Sara Coleridge*, ed. Edith Coleridge (London: Henry S. King, 1873), I, 113–14.
[2] See below for a precise definition of "vitalism" as used in this article.

becoming immediately popular is also astute — though it is difficult to
believe that she would have envisioned that it would take nearly 170 years
for an edition of his metaphysical theology to emerge. Nor is it likely
that Sara could have foreseen that after that time there would still be
questions surrounding the ordering of the fragments themselves. How
could she if she was among persons who knew Coleridge's own intentions of the order (which have been lost)?

It is widely believed by Coleridge scholars (it would not be an exag-
geration to say that it is agreed) that Coleridge failed in the attempt to produce a work that portrayed Christianity as the one true philosophy in any
recognizable form. That, characteristically, though he made a number of
attempts to create such a system, he became distracted with other projects
(ranging from *Aids to Reflection* to *Logic*, *On the Constitution of
the Church and State*, etc.) and left only a group of fragmentary and either
truncated or aborted attempts to construct this system — these are the
"Fragments" published in the volume of the *Collected Coleridge* titled
Opus Maximum. In fact this view is accurate for only one of the four
fragments ("Fragment 4," the earliest). Fragments "1," "2," and "3"
contain a systematic theology in sixteen, logically progressive chapters,
which, though it may not be polished nor constitute the entire extent to
which Coleridge hoped to expand the work eventually, is certainly cogent,
detailed, and "complete" as it stands. At the very least the received text
as we have it is a "finished" draft of the first volume of a work that
Coleridge *might* have intended to expand into other volumes — though
it ought to be noted that Coleridge produced no multi-volume work. The
work is titled *On the Divine Ideas*.

Redacting the Fragments

The cogency of the work can only be seen and understood when the fragments are redacted differently from the order in which Tom McFarland
believes they were drafted. Even Nicholas Halmi respectfully points out
that there are questions about the order of writing:[3] "[the fragments] are
presented in the order preferred by the senior editor, although it is not the
order of composition, insofar as that can be determined from physical
evidence (e.g. watermarks) and textual evidence (e.g. borrowings from

---

[3] The ordering is a live issue as Murray J. Evans has pointed out in his article in
The Coleridge Bulletin ("The Divine Ideas in Coleridge's *Opus Maximum*," *The Coleridge
Bulletin* n.s. 22 [2003]: 39–47).

Coleridge's other writings). Although none of the manuscripts can be dated with precision, Fragments 1–4 were dictated mostly [*sic*] likely between 1819 and 1823, while the holograph Preface was written no earlier than 1828 and more likely in 1832."[4] It is the premise of this article that the proper order in which the fragments should be read, the order in which *Coleridge* intended them to be read is: 3, 1, 2. This view is not only supported by both higher and lower literary criticism (not to mention good historical methodology), but by the logical progression of the theological system, which takes the premise of "Fragment 3," God understood as the Absolute Will, uses it as the central hermeneutic by which the entire system is to be constructed and examined, and then progresses through consequent philosophical and theological issues and doctrines.

What emerges in the final four chapters of the work when viewed in this order, in other words approximately the second half of "Fragment 2," is an *a priori* vitalist system of philosophy that is centered on the Absolute Will (equated to God and scripturally grounded in the Hebraic concept of the Elohim) as the vital animating element of the system through the eternal expression of the Primary act of the Divine Will: the "I AM." Overlapping and interlaced with this discussion (and pursued in the first five chapters of the work as well) is a philosophical theology that presents the Trinity as the one and only logically possible form that the Divine could take. Chapters VIII through XIII are a focused presentation of Coleridge's theological anthropology, or Doctrine of Man, with chapter XIII providing the bridge from the discussion of humankind to the discussion of humanity as a part of nature, and introducing the discussion of Coleridge's vitalist system of philosophy. All the chapters are continually referent to the concept of God as the Absolute Will. In other words, the system presents Christianity as a philosophy, and Trinitarian Christianity founded on the concept of Absolute Will as the one possible "True Philosophy."

In fact, though, there is not as much divergence between this redaction of the fragments and that of McFarland as there might appear to be on the surface. There is complete agreement that "Fragment 4" is the earliest and that "Fragment 2" follows directly from "Fragment 1." Indeed, the range of dates that he and Halmi give for the composition of "Fragment 3" (1822–1823) is consistent with the possibility of placing it before "Fragment 1," which is dated as being written between 1820–1823. Furthermore, McFarland and Halmi hang their dating of "probably 1822–3"[5]

---

[4] Halmi, *Op Max*, xx.
[5] *Op Max*, 214.

solely on speculative evidence: the assumption that a comment on the *Memoirs* of Thomas Halyburton, written in Coleridge's own hand, from a separate notebook, which they argue indicates that this comment was written on July 29, 1822. Halmi remarked in 1997 that on the inside of the front cover is written the addresses of Ralph Wedgwood, Thomas Monkhouse, and John Watson (by Coleridge), and that these were written "probably between Dec 1820 and Jan 1821."[6] Why would Coleridge write the addresses of three friends on the inside cover of a notebook that he was not to use for a further two years? The anecdotal evidence is contradictory.[7]

In short, this cross-referencing to the separate notebook[8] is probably too threadbare a piece of evidence to overwhelm: 1. the logical progression of the three fragments; 2. the classically Coleridgean introduction to the entire project, which the first two paragraphs of "Fragment 3" constitute; 3. the fact that "Fragment 3" begins with a title, "ON THE DIVINE IDEAS," written entirely in capital letters; and 4. the fact that "Fragment 3" consists of two chapters, the second of which discusses the impossibility of demonstrating the existence of God through scientific methodology (see below), while "Fragment 1" begins "Chapter III" and the second sentence of the first paragraph reads: "We have spoken of *Science*, of *Sciences*, in the severest sense of the word, viz. those superstructures of the pure intellect in which the speculative necessity reigns throughout and exclusively, the act itself of reasoning and imagining being the only practical ingredient, or that alone in which any reference is made to the Will, and even in this to the Will in that sense only in which it remains utterly undetermined..."[9] This is a perfect description of the lion's share of the content of the second chapter of "Fragment 3." In other words, the "lost" two chapters of "Fragment 1" are in fact "Fragment 3."[10]

"Fragment 4" does not fit *into* the system; it is an inchoate, or embryonic, version of the philosophical positions and ontological presentations of Christian doctrines that exist in the sixteen chapters of *On the Divine Ideas* (from here throughout that title refers to the work as a whole and

---

[6] *Op Max*, 214.

[7] The only surviving letter written to any of the three men between 1820–1825 is a letter written to Thomas Monkhouse on June 24, 1820.

[8] *CN*, IV, 4909.

[9] *Op Max*, 5.

[10] Note: even if "Fragment 3" was written in August of 1822, "Fragment 1" could still have been written in the later months of that year and subsequent months of 1823.

not simply to "Fragment 3"). It indeed is a fragment. "Fragment 4" is best understood as analogous to a detailed and focused notebook in which Coleridge worked out unpolished sections of his system that he gave a proper finish to in the received form of *On the Divine Ideas*. Hence it is not surprising that McFarland found analogous, or overlapping, material with the discussion undertaken in the second chapter of "Fragment 3": but it was misguided of him to suggest that it should be viewed as the completion of that chapter (and oddly inconsistent with the editors' simultaneous argument that "Fragment 4" was the earliest fragment of the work). Part of the problem may be that McFarland ordered the fragments without properly dating them, a task that was left to Halmi, and because of this the published order is not synchronic with the dates of composition.

Because of its fragmentary nature (and because the force of this article is to argue that a coherent and logically cogent system exists in the received text of fragments "3," "2," and "1," and that "Fragment 4" was a forerunner to them), textual exegesis of "Fragment 4" will not take place in this article. "Fragment 4" may be informative when viewed as a "foregoer" or "pathfinder": drafts of arguments that he would polish in the work itself (or even, given a most sympathetic reading, as subsidiary commentary on the system by Coleridge — which is difficult to square with it being the earliest composed notebook); but, it is informative *only* in a subsidiary fashion. To give two examples: 1. the attack on mechanistic philosophy is indeed informative as a stronger, more snide, and less-polished presentation of Coleridge's views on mechanism (it may even be a truer presentation of his feelings),[11] and 2. his discussion of pneumatology and his linking of it to basic chemistry (metallurgy) may make even clearer his intention of uniting God with Nature in a vitalist system of theology.[12] Neither of these passages, however, is as elegant or, more importantly, as logically tight as the presentation that each of these subjects receives in the received text of *On the Divine Ideas*. *On the Divine Ideas* was written over a period of time: much in the same way as Coleridge compiled virtually all of his published works over the space of at least two years.[13]

---

[11] *Op Max*, 295–96.

[12] *Op Max*, 320.

[13] Halmi was given a task that many would argue is simply not possible: assigning specific dates for the composition of Coleridge's fragments (a task that was made all the more complicated in that he was forced to accept a previously decided upon order in which the fragments would be printed [by McFarland]). Still, even taking into account the fact that

The work as we hold it (the received text of "Fragments 1–3") is complete, if not "finished" (or to use a more literary term "revised"): the argument that Coleridge himself considered it so is reinforced by the fact that he wrote a "Preface" to it. (Hegel, for instance, famously wrote the preface to his *Phenomenology of Spirit* last: only after he had completed the work.) Coleridge's "Preface," though, is problematic. Far from being a summary of the work, it is extremely short and, characteristically of Coleridge, cryptic in the best light. The "Preface," while establishing one point (that Coleridge believed he had a finished system), creates other subsidiary confusions that draw one away from the yield of its composition. In it he wrote that his "System is divided into three unequal parts, each of which forms an independent Work — the whole comprised in five Volumes. Two of these, and the larger part of the third, are prepared for the press — and of the remainder the materials & principal contents exist in Sybilline MSS."[14] It appears that McFarland took this statement in the "Preface" to be referent in the micro scale to the unpublished works only constituting the *Opus Maximum*: in this case it becomes clear why he chose to have the narrow interpretation that the first three fragments were the "[t]wo... and the larger part of the third" prepared for the press, and that "Fragment 4" was the "Sybilline" manuscripts holding further unfinished promise, rather than seeing the earliest fragment as a draft of the work. But, there are other options: if one examines the statement from the "Preface" on the macro scale: *On the Divine Ideas* might constitute "the larger part of the third [volume]," or *Confessions of an Inquiring*

Halmi gives a range of dates for each of the fragments, his stated evidence is not beyond question. Though I agree with the view that this fragment is the earliest of the four, Halmi's methodology and reasons for dating "Fragment 4" as the earliest are unconvincing (which is not insignificantly relevant to the reliability of the dating of "Fragment 3"). For a second time Halmi has used the similarity of a passage of the text with material in a single manuscript entry in a separate bound notebook (*CN*, IV, 4775–76) and relied entirely on the dating of this separate entry by Kathleen Coburn (Coburn's dates themselves are not beyond question). In other words, Halmi relies on threadbare evidence to assign the fragment the date of 1819. The attempt to buttress this date by suggesting that "[a] reference on f 8 to 'the growth of a tulip in 1819' suggests that year as the *terminus a quo* of the fragment's composition" (*Op Max*, 291) is, frankly, specious because the entire sentence reads "[t]he assumed priority, therefore, would at best be but an historical accident, with no more causative connection than the age <birth> of George the Third <in 1750> to the growth of a tulip in 1819" (295). The third argument that "[t]he list of chemical symbols on ff 193–4 is very similar to one in a notebook entry of June 1819" (291) is also less than overwhelming. In short, the evidence that Halmi relies on for dating the fragments is less than entirely convincing or historically reliable, and, as has been demonstrated above, at times contradictory.
14 *Op Max*, 4.

Spirit might constitute that larger part of the third volume (the inclusion of the latter part of the work within the greater system being supported by the fact that an inchoate version of the "Pentad of Operative Christianity" appears at the bottom of the page on which the "Preface" is written). If either of these is the case, I suspect that the two published parts are *On the Constitution of the Church and State* and the *Lay Sermons* — the former of which was published about the time the "Preface" was written (depending on when the "Preface" actually was written in the same year).[15] Even if *On the Divine Ideas* was only the "prophetic (Sybilline) manuscripts," or equally possibly if McFarland was correct and Coleridge referred only to the unpublished materials now known as "Fragments 1–4," the "Preface" still makes it clear that Coleridge considered his system of "Deo, Homine et Naturâ" to exist.[16] The point is not esoteric decoding of, and speculation on, what Coleridge meant by his "five volumes"; the point is that in 1828/32 he believed he had a cogent system and wrote a "Preface" to it. The force of the "Preface" is that at the end of his life *Coleridge* considered his system of "Deo, Homine et Naturâ" to exist, as, apparently, did his daughter Sara, her family, and her father's companions. In any of the above possibilities, *On the Divine Ideas* constitutes the philosophical theology, the ontology.

On the Divine Ideas has been identified as a "vitalist" project, and it is important to clarify both what is generally understood by the term in philosophical circles, and then what is specifically meant when it is used within this article in reference to Coleridge. It would be difficult to find a more concise or uncontroversial definition than that provided by the *Routledge Encyclopedia of Philosophy*:

> Vitalists hold that living organisms are fundamentally different from non-living entities because they contain some non-physical element or are governed by different principles than are inanimate things. In its simplest form, vitalism holds that living entities contain some fluid, or a distinctive "spirit." In more sophisticated forms, the vital spirit becomes a substance infusing bodies and giving life to them or vitalism becomes the view that there is a distinctive organization among things. Vitalist positions can be traced back to antiquity... Vitalism is best understood, however, in the context of the emergence of modern science during the sixteenth and seventeenth centuries. Mechanistic explanations of natural phenomena were extended to biological systems... Vitalism developed as a contrast to this mechanistic view. Over the next three centuries, numerous figures opposed the extension

---

[15] I suspect this because the works discuss "The Christian Nature of Society" and "The Christian's Actions in Society," respectively.

[16] *Op Max*, 4 ("God, Man and Nature").

of Cartesian mechanism to biology, arguing that matter could not explain movement, perception, development or life.[17]

Coleridge integrated a vitalist natural philosophy into his systematic theology in order to create an ontology that used God (defined as the Absolute Will) as the "spirit" that animated the living. The mechanism that he was opposing was utilitarian in its ethics and static in its metaphysics: a stance that removed the participation of the Divine from the immediacy of action and the permeation of the now. The mechanistic system most particularly in vogue at the time *On the Divine Ideas* was written was that of Paley — though within this work Coleridge was not necessarily attacking Paley specifically, he was attacking the sterility of utilitarianism and mechanism generally (and thus certainly Paley by implication):[18] "The scheme of pure mechanism, which under all disguises, tempting or repulsive, christian [*sic*] or infidel, forms the groundwork of these systems of modern moral and political philosophy, political economy, and education, which by manufacturing mind out of sense and sense out of sensation, which reduces all form to shape and all shape to impression from without, leads... to its own confutation and, scorpionlike, destroys itself, while the tail turning round in its tortures, infixes the poisoned sting in its head — inevitably leads to it, I say, if only it be forced by a stern logic into all its consequences."[19] What Coleridge conceived was a system in which each action is a manifestation of the particular will and each act of will is a manifestation of the Absolute Will: God becomes the indwelling ground of all will and as such the indwelling ground of each conscious act, the animating principle of each moment of life; this is coupled with this individual's faculty of Reason as the *Imago Dei*. "What then is the ground of this coincidence between reason and experience? between the laws of the sensible world and the ideas of the pure intellect? The only answer is that both have their ultimate ground, and are ultimately identified in, a supersensual essence, the principle of existence in all essences and of the essences in all existence, or the Supreme Reason that constitutes the objects which it contemplates and then by the powers thus constituted, viz. the divine Ideas, gives being to the whole phaenomenal universe... and it needs only remind the reader

[17] *Routledge Encyclopedia of Philosophy*, gen. ed. Edward Craig (London: Routledge, 1998), IX, 639–40.
[18] For the most thorough treatment of Coleridge's attack on Paley, see Douglas Hedley, *Coleridge, Philosophy and Religion: Aids to Reflection and the Mirror of the Spirit* (Cambridge: Cambridge University Press, 2000).
[19] *Op Max,* 145–46.

that the original postulate... was that of a responsible Will from which the reality of a Will generally became demonstrable."[20]

The intellectual sources of Coleridge's use of the will as the focus of his system remains an unsettled question: the cynic might answer "the Christian tradition of rational thought." That cynic's answer is likely to be as close to the truth as any other, though it is also unlikely that Schelling's captivation with the subject of the will can be discounted as a constructive influence. Schelling's concentration on the subject of the will began with his discussion of it in *On Human Freedom*, published in 1809 (a particular work the conclusions of which Coleridge vehemently disagreed with), and from that point on the subject of the will remained in the center of Schelling's philosophy.[21] It is also equally unlikely that Schopenhauer's exhaustive and idealistic discussion of the will as the center of encountered reality (both in *The Fourfold Root* and *The World as Will and Representation*) was not an influence in some form, though there is less forensic bibliographical evidence to demonstrate this influence than there is with Schelling. Where he made it his own is by moving from the philosophical realm to pure theology by equating the Absolute Will with the Elohim: the Hebraic concept of animating and eternal breath of God married to the concept of the creative "I AM" (in the Gospel of Mark, the *ego eimi*). "This perfect union of personeity and the absolute Will is, the reader will have already noticed, strongly marked in the Mosaic History, here quoted only as the most ancient documents of the human mind. When the sublime writer is speaking of the supreme Will, he is named Elohim, i.e. the self-existent, the strengths or all strengths or efficient powers contained in one unoriginated, the Origin and perpetuation of all. But the yet higher revelation he reserves for the Jehovah himself, 'I am,' and as the consequence of this, 'I am the Lord thy God.'"[22] His vitalist system was not a system of science but rather a system of theology, and from the very beginning of the work Coleridge made clear that he was writing a "Theology." The word "Theology" appears eleven times in the two chapters of "Fragment 3."

---

[20] *Op Max*, 163–64.

[21] Coleridge makes mention of Schelling during his discussion of the economic Trinity at the very end of "Fragment 2" (the very end of chapter XVI). There he warns readers against understanding any concept of succession in the term "becomes" (when referent to the idea that will of the Father "becomes" the will of the Son) as "in the recent writings of Schelling and his followers, as often as they attempt to clothe the skeleton of the Spinozistic pantheism and breathe a life thereinto" (*Op Max*, 204–5).

[22] *Op Max*, 164–65.

Within the scope of an essay of this length it is clearly impossible comprehensively to discuss the entirety of the text of all three fragments. The only comprehensible way to seek to demonstrate how the text of *On the Divine Ideas* fits together as a united system is to set out a précis of each of the sixteen chapters, with absolutely minimal commentary, and only after this is done to use quotations drawn from throughout the text to allow Coleridge to make his own argument. In other words, only once the reader has a picture of the system in his or her mind can exegesis of the text be made to support the interpretation.

The System Presented: The Sixteen Chapters and their Content

In the following sixteen précis, the skeleton of Coleridge's argument in each chapter is illustrated, and the page numbers of each of the chapters in the *Opus Maximum* (*CC*) are given at the outset. Any title that Coleridge gave the chapter is printed in quotation marks. Coleridge only numbered the chapters contained in "Fragment 1," though he titled five of the eight chapters contained in "Fragment 2." Chapters I and II are the text of the notebook termed "Fragment 3"; chapters III–VIII are the text of the notebook termed "Fragment 1," and chapters IX through XVI are the text of the notebook termed "Fragment 2."

Chapter I: pp. 215–47,[23] "ON THE DIVINE IDEAS."[24] Coleridge's cosmology followed by his cosmogony; the Divine is the Absolute Will; as individual will differentiates itself from Absolute Will the ontological fall takes place; the Absolute Will is protected from the charge of being the origin of evil because the differentiation of the particular existed in the Absolute Will only "in potentiality."

Chapter II: pp. 248–90 (no title). The necessity of viewing evil thus originated as the differentiation of particular will demonstrated (a position clearly heir to and structurally influenced by Kant's discussion of Radical Evil differentiated from Natural Evil in *Religion Within the Limits of Reason Alone*);[25] possible alternative cosmologies to his own shown

---

[23] Throughout this section the page numbers following the chapter number indicate the pages in the *Opus Maximum* (*CC*).

[24] Written in a substantially larger hand than the lines that follow it — centered, and underlined in the Holograph — this title is more substantially emphasized than other chapter titles: suggesting that it is the title of the entire work.

[25] Later in the work, in chapter VI (contained in "Fragment 1"), Coleridge wrote "faith (faith, which is used here in the same sense as Kant uses the Will, as the ground of all

to be false; the complete originality of the Trinity as a Christian doctrine demonstrated and all *apparent* precursors to the Christian Trinity (particular the Plotinian) dismissed as influences. The second half of the chapter concentrates on the eradication of the possibility of giving a scientific proof of the existence of God: this is refuted on the grounds that science exists in the realm of the Understanding, rather than the Reason, and hence includes a presupposition in all of its postulates and proofs.

Chapter III: pp. 5–11 (numbered by Coleridge but not titled). The incapacity of a scientific proof of God reiterated, married with the concept of the Will (both Absolute and particular) and the necessary consequence of moral responsibility demonstrated. The consequent reality and essential difference of moral Good and Evil delineated.

Chapter IV: pp. 12–16 (numbered by Coleridge but not titled). The purity of the faculty of Reason as an attribute of the Divine and the inextricable nature of its tie to this antecedent element (the Absolute Will or God) re-emphasized. This is the point in the work where Coleridge formally dismisses *a posterori* evidence on a *purely philosophical* level: discussing the actual being of a responsible will.

Chapter V: pp. 16–24 (numbered by Coleridge but not titled). The actual being of particular wills discussed, and examined as separate from the Absolute Will. This is the beginning of Coleridge's theological anthropology or Doctrine of Man.

Chapter VI: pp. 24–48 (numbered by Coleridge but not titled). Continuation of the theological anthropology: the concepts of self love, sensuality, pleasure and pain are discussed. The self that loves is decisively differentiated from "self love." In the second half of the chapter, the concept of the self is married with the concepts of the will and moral responsibility (in other words the discussion undertaken in chapters III and IV is joined with the discussion of chapters V and VI).

Chapter VII: pp. 48–57 (numbered by Coleridge but not titled). A reprise of all the discussion that has taken place to this point: a gathering and clarifying of his discussion of the human condition in the encountered creation: a shift back into a philosophical theology from a purely theological discussion: this chapter ends with a long quotation from Jeremy Taylor.

Chapter VIII: pp. 57–79, "FAITH and CONSCIENCE."[26] This chapter ties the concepts of self-consciousness to the concept of the will, and

---

particular acts of willing) is a *total* act of the soul: it is the *whole* state of the mind, or it is not at all!" (*Op Max*, 43).

[26] The chapter is both numbered and titled by Coleridge.

then the particular will to the Divine Absolute Will. Coleridge argues that
the concept of the "I" or the "Self" can only be self identified or differentiated from the world around it through the will: "Man... knows
himself to be because he is a man, but he is a man because God is and
hath so willed it. It is the great 'I am' only, who is because he affirmeth
himself to be..."[27] This chapter also begins Coleridge's project of building a vitalist system of natural philosophy by formally differentiating his
philosophy from the "mechanico-corpuscular system."[28] This, he makes
clear, is because in his system Reason (rather than the Understanding)
supplies the only guiding light to the conscience, and Reason is a projection of the Divine Will.

Chapter IX: pp. 80–96 (neither numbered nor titled by Coleridge).
Coleridge's doctrine of the *Imago Dei*. The image of God is in human
Reason as the synthesis of the concepts of identity and the absolute: in
fidelity to the Absolute Will through informed actions (specific acts of the
particular will) in accordance with the Absolute Will. When Reason is
usurped by the Understanding, the personal will rebels against the
Absolute Will and the acting individual descends into the level of the
sensuous. Faith is the obedience of the individual will to Reason; therefore it is fidelity to both God and oneself.[29]

Chapter X: pp. 96–119, "On the existential reality of the Idea of the
Supreme Being, i.e. of God" (titled but not numbered by Coleridge).
Coleridge delineates an apophatic (*via negativa*) approach to defining the
attributes of the Deity. On the surface this chapter seems a disappointing
"gearing down" from his discussion of the will in the preceding chapter.
There appears to be a break in logical flow, but this is not the case.
The hermeneutic of apophaticism becomes the key to distinguishing
the idea of "personeity" (distinguishing the *particular* from the *absolute*:
the individual will from the Divine Will). This hermeneutic is how
Coleridge will effect the incorporation of the vitalist philosophy in chapters XIV and XV into his theological system.

Chapter XI: pp. 119–27, "Of the Origin of the Idea of God in the Mind
of Man" (titled but not numbered by Coleridge). Coleridge argues that
the origin of the idea of God begins with love: the love of a parent by a

---

[27] *Op Max*, 67.

[28] *Op Max*, 73.

[29] It is arguable but far from certain that Coleridge was drawing at least the shadow of
a doctrine of the atonement through the heavy emphasis on faith as fidelity to both the
Divine Will and the particular will and the identification of Reason (the guide by which
the particular will must act to be faithful) as the synthesis of the individual and the absolute.

child. Originally the child is conscious of only one self in the relationship: the parent; the parent is comprehended as all that is other than the
infant. The love for the parent is "elevated to the universal Parent."
Important in this short chapter are the opening paragraphs that place
humanity in the context of an all evolving natural system, which is the
first time that the subject of Nature is introduced (clearly Coleridge was
familiar with the theories of Erasmus Darwin).

Chapter XII: pp. 127–33, "On the present general education of man in
relation to the Idea of God" (titled but not numbered by Coleridge).
A short chapter expanding the idea that the apophatic approach to the idea
of God can be demonstrated in the development of self-consciousness in
a child. Coleridge argues that it is only in the absence of the presence of
the mother that the idea of a self, which was developed by the child to conceive of the mother, is applied to the child as the periods of absence of the
mother from its presence are increased.

Chapter XIII: pp. 133–50 (neither numbered nor titled by Coleridge).
The philosophical argument of the chapter is twofold. It first expands the
development of the child still further from mere self-consciousness into
the concept of "personeity" (the natural progression of the Reason in the
child). Secondly it discusses the "artificial education" of the mind: the
development and cultivation of the Understanding. Coleridge argues that
it is through this process of artificial education that the *idea* of life is
translated into the concept of "power." This discussion of the Understanding and of the artificial education is how Coleridge begins to draw
his vitalism together (using the idea of life) and where he begins a frontal
assault on mechanistic philosophy (145).

Chapter XIV: pp. 150–66 (neither numbered nor titled by Coleridge).
The vitalist system of created nature is expanded: its vital element identified as the indwelling of the Divine Will. Coleridge demonstrates its
scriptural grounding and distinguishes himself from deism and pantheism;
he uses the concept of the will to join Reason and experience through the
"Divine Ideas" (163–64). The Absolute Will is the source of the idea of
personeity; it is unified with history in the Mosaic History (returning to
the scriptural focus of the chapter). The Will is identified as the *Elohim*:
the spirit of God.

Chapter XV: pp. 166–77 (neither numbered nor titled by Coleridge).
On pages 166–67, the vitalist philosophy is linked back (and riveted to)
the hermeneutic of apophaticism. The approach allows Coleridge the ability to leave everything that cannot be identified and defined as the vital
element — Absolute Will. If a thing can be defined it has a personeity,

or a being without personeity (as in plant life); therefore a thing that can be defined is either an individual will with moral responsibility or it is a definable part of nature perceivable through the sensuous impulses. Everything else is God: the Absolute Will animates all as the *Elohim* through the act of pure will contained in the originating "I AM."

Chapter XVI: pp. 177–213, "Ideas flowing out of the Divine Personeity" (titled but not numbered by Coleridge). Coleridge's Christology and his discussion of the personeity of the Holy Spirit. Human responsibility for the fallen nature is explained and the Divine ideas are identified as the three persons of the Trinity. The theological system comes full circle, having traveled through a discussion of both the nature and fallen state of the human and his place in the overall creation constituted by Nature, and is knitted back into its starting point: the Divine Ideas.

Textual Exegesis Of The System

One of two central premises of *On the Divine Ideas* is that what is absolutely true is eternal (be it the Divine Being or the mathematical fact that in every triangle the sum of the angles is 180 degrees), and that these truths can only be arrived at by the Reason. The second of the central premises of Coleridge's systematic theology is that God is Absolute Will. As he does elsewhere, Coleridge distinguishes Reason from Understanding. The distinction is probably more simple, though no less substantial, than Coleridge presents it as being: Reason provides knowledge that can only be gained *a priori*, while the Understanding only provides knowledge that can be gained *a posteriori*. The Understanding is dependent upon the senses and human perception and therefore cannot provide knowledge of truths that are eternal. A discussion of the Divine or its attributes can only be undertaken through the Reason.

A substantial section of the first paragraph of the first chapter is quoted in several sections below. The reason that such a substantial section of the text of this first paragraph has been quoted is to demonstrate that it is proleptic of Coleridge's full system: not merely a part of it.[30] This indicates that Coleridge had a fairly complete idea of what he intended to write when he began. What may at first appear to be apostrophe when

---

[30] The word "hitherto" appears twice in the paragraph; in the context in which Coleridge uses it, "hitherto" implies "before the philosophy of Samuel Taylor Coleridge" (a statement that he was not too modest to make) rather than "earlier in the work."

reading the first sentence is actually a merely prolix way of stating that throughout the system his discussion of the Divine Will takes place on an *a priori* path:

> I cannot commence this subject more fitly than by disclaiming all wish and attempt of gratifying a speculative refinement in myself, or an idle + presumptuous curiosity in others. I leave the heavenly hierarchy with all their distinctions "Thrones, Dominations, Princedoms Virtues Powers." Names Fervours, Energies, with the long et cetera of the Cabbalists and degenerated Platonists to the admirers of the false Dionysius, and the obscure students of Cornelius Agrippa. All pretence, all approach to particularize on such a subject involves its own confutation: for it is the applications of the understanding through the medium of the fancy to truths of which the reason exclusively is both the substance beheld + the eye-beholding or had the evident contradiction implied in the attempt failed in preventing it the fearful abuses, the degrading idolatrous superstitions, which have resulted from its application to that beautiful yet awful article of the Christian faith, the unbroken unity of the triumphant with the militant church, or communion of Saints, form too palpable a warning not to have deterred me even from motives of common morality. [31]

It is not unimportant to remark upon the fact that this passage is characteristic of many of Coleridge's introductory passages in his published works in that it is more literary and circumlocutive than practical. To demonstrate that these traits are characteristic, the reader has only to examine the opening passages of, for instance, any of the issues of *The Friend* or *The Watchman*, either of the *Lay Sermons*, *On the Constitution of the Church and State*, or the *Biographia Literaria* — or for that matter any other published work of Coleridge's. But what is more important still, is that this is the *only* chapter of *any* of the fragments that contains a general introduction; *all* the other chapters are referent to an antecedent discussion.[32] If one accepts the order of the fragments as they are printed within the *Opus Maximum*, then one must account for this substantial break in tone and rhetoric; there is no reason to believe that Coleridge would have broken his rhetorical practice within the work to introduce a subject that he had already treated at length throughout "Fragment 1" and "Fragment 2" (will and God as the Absolute Will). This passage was meant to be the first sentences of a work.

---

[31] Whenever quoting "Fragment 3," my own transcription of the holograph is used; the page numbers in the *Op Max* (*CC*) where the McFarland/Halmi transcription appears are provided following (here, *Op Max*, 216–17).

[32] See below for a discussion of the antecedent references, especially in the outset of "Fragment 1."

In the next sentence he identifies his project: "In what I am about to deliver I have but one end in view, that of presenting an intelligible though not comprehensible idea of the possibility of that which in some sense or other is, yet is not God nor One with God."[33] In other words: intelligible to the Reason but not comprehensible to the Understanding. Later in the same paragraph Coleridge makes a subtle but clear indication that he is creating a vitalist system of philosophy: "freed from the phænomena of time + space + seen in the depth of real being no longer therefore a nature, namely a That which is not but which is for ever only about to be, reveals itself to the pure reason as the actual immanence... Are we struck at beholding the cope of heaven imaged in a dew-drop? The least of the animalcula to which that dew drop is an ocean presents an infinite problem, of which the omnipresent is the only solution... the philosophy of nature can remain philosophy only by rising above nature, and by abstracting from nature..."[34] In the second paragraph of the work he moves on to a discussion of the encountered world and the Divine Will as the means of creation (or as he puts it "causative of reality"):

> The Will, the absolute Will, is that which is essentially causative of reality, essentially + absolutely that is boundless from without + from within. This is our first principle, this is the position, contained in the postulate of the reality of Will at all, Difficult we have never attempted to conceal from ourselves, is it to master this first idea nor could it be otherwise, in as much as an insight into its truth is not possible and we are perforce constrained to the only succedaneum, the sense of the necessary falsehood of the contrary. We affirm it not because we comprehend the affirmation, but because we clearly comprehend the absurdity of the denial. But in this affirmation it is involved that what is essentially causative of all possible reality must be causative if its own reality. It is not the cause of all reality because it is causative of its own but it is necessarily causative of its own reality because it is essentially causative of all possible reality. These however are so far one, that the act being absolute and infinite, *such must the reality be consequently the absolute will itself realized must in its own reality include the plentitude of all that is real as far as it is absolutely real, that is as far as the reality is actual + not merely possible.*[35]

On these two principles hang his entire theological system.

The concept of the will and God as the Absolute Will permeate fragments "1" and "2." During the discussion of Reason as the *Imago Dei* in Chapter IX, for instance, Coleridge maintained that "[i]f there be that in

---

[33] My transcription; *Op Max*, 216.
[34] My transcription; *Op Max*, 217–18.
[35] My transcription (italics mine); *Op Max*, 220–21.

man, which is one with the universal reason, it cannot but coincide with or be congruous with, the absolute Will."[36] Or again later in "Fragment 2": "In Man the will as Will first appears, enough for him that he hath a Will at all; for this is the condition of his responsibility of his humanity. In the possession of a responsible Will his creator has placed him, with all means and aidances to boot, to its growth and evolution. With these, in the possession of a Free-Will he is to place himself — that he may be in the divine humanity even as the divine humanity, that 'God may be all in all.'"[37] And it is this free will, the ability to choose to act rationally in accordance with the Divine Will, for instance self sacrificially or altruistically, to proceed on the basis of Reason rather than the Understanding, that demarcates Man as separate from the remainder of creation, which also contains the vital animating power of the Divine Will. Coleridge makes clear that will is only free will when it is willed using Reason. An important passage at the beginning of chapter XV makes that clear: "still less dare we predicate personality of the single beast or plant. Why not? Of a fox, for instance? Here equally as in a man there is a unity of life in an organized whole. Equally with man the fox is found to possess vital power, instinct, perception, memory, recognition; and as far as we mean by 'understanding' the faculty of adapting means to ends according to varying circumstances, it is most undeniable that the fox possess understanding."[38] So the fox possesses Understanding, but not Reason. As Coleridge argued, "we withhold the name of person from the higher order of animals [because they do not possess] Reason and the responsible Will."[39] For Coleridge the will is inseparable from personeity: "That of a Will, personeity is an essential attribute, we have cleared from all objections."[40] It is from the perspective of personeity that Coleridge will build his own presentation of an economic[41] Trinity: "this divine reciprocation in and by which the Father attributeth his self to another, and the Son beholdeth and knoweth himself in the Father, is not and cannot be contemplated otherwise than as an act — as an act, therefore of the divine Will, which is one in both and therefore an act..."[42]

---

[36] *Op Max*, 88.

[37] *Op Max*, 144.

[38] *Op Max*, 166–67.

[39] *Op Max*, 167.

[40] *Op Max*, 195.

[41] "Economic" is used in its patristic meaning: merely indicating a Trinity that has intellectual commerce between the three persons.

[42] *Op Max*, 205.

Throughout the entire text of fragments "1" and "2," throughout every doctrine from the procession of the Son from the Father, to the concept of freedom in humanity, to the distinction of Man from beast: the reference point is always the will, and reference is always made to the Absolute or Divine Will. The premise that Coleridge laid down in his first chapter runs through the entire work functioning not unlike a rhetorical spine. God as the Absolute Will is never far from the surface of any discussion Coleridge undertakes.

So having seen that the premises that Coleridge outlined in the first sentences of "Fragment 3" both permeate and bind the sixteen chapters as a whole, there remains to treat one subject that could produce a possible counterargument to this view: the question of internal antecedent references within the fragments. Perhaps the clearest example comes in the second paragraph of chapter XV: "If we are to speak of the reason not as it is one with the Will — that is, not of the absolute Will, which is one with the Supreme Reason, but of the Reason in its relations to the finite and responsible Will — the reply is obvious: it has been clearly demonstrated in a former chapter, in our disquisition on the nature of Faith and Conscience, that Reason is incompatible with individuality, or *peculiar* possession."[43] This is a clear reference to a chapter of "Fragment 1," which Coleridge both numbered and named, and it is a perfectly accurate reference to the contents of that chapter[44] and specifically to Coleridge's statement: "REASON implies an insight into the necessity and universality of relations, and may be defined [as] the power of drawing universal and necessary conclusions from individual forms or facts, ex.gr. from any three-cornered object or outline we conclude that in all triangles the two sides conjointly are necessarily greater than the third."[45] So there is a clear reference from "Fragment 2" to "Fragment 1," which is indisputable.

There is one case in which antecedent reference could be used to argue against ordering the fragments "3," "1," "2."[46] This is the antecedent

---

[43] *Op Max*, 167.

[44] See *Op Max*, 72–77.

[45] *Op Max*, 77.

[46] There, could be an argument made for the current ordering of the fragments based on the fact that within the final five pages of chapter XVI (*Op Max*, 208–13), the term "The Divine Ideas" is used several times, and that a discussion of Plotinus is promised (and one takes place, though at insubstantial length) in the first chapter of "Fragment 3." This argument has its own flaws, and may be based on a misunderstanding: the use of the term "The Divine Ideas" is a grand conclusion to the work as a whole. Coleridge has concluded with a discussion of Christology within his view of the Trinity, the point from which he began, and in doing so brings his argument full circle to come to a conclusion with his title.

reference in the second paragraph of chapter III. The clear transition of subject matter between the final chapter of "Fragment 3" and the first chapter of "Fragment 1" has already been discussed. That subject is the nature of science as a practice of the Understanding and hence science's inability to demonstrate the existence of God. The following antecedent reference from the beginning of "Fragment 1," however, must be sourced: "It has likewise been shown that the power of withholding and, indirectly at least, of refusing our assent to the necessary foundation of an intellectual superstructure forms the essential difference between the moral and sciential systems. The assent having been given, this difference ceases, and moral positions both may and ought to be treated as sciences subject to the same universal logic as those of number and measure."[47] This reference matches the transition between the two chapters of "Fragment 3." The first is in large part concerned with theodicy and the existence of evil within the world in which God operates as an animating principle in the form of the Absolute Will. It is therefore a discussion of moral issues. Between pages 236 and 250 of "Fragment 3," the issue of how moral evil can arise is the focus of Coleridge's argument. In Coleridge's system (like Kant's) evil is moral evil: a rebellion against the Divine Will, which we come to know through Reason. Coleridge's point throughout "Fragment 3" is that any proof of the existence of God must be made *a priori* and that science as a method dependant upon the faculty of Understanding cannot demonstrate the existence of God because it would rely upon *a posterori* observations. All the above quotation is arguing is that Coleridge has previously demonstrated that an *a priori* (or moral) demonstration of the existence of God is the live option: an interpretation that is reinforced by the final sentence of this very short chapter: "In one concluding sentence: there are several positions, each of which might be legitimately assumed and each of which might stand on its own grounds as a postulate of humanity, and à fortiori, therefore, of every code of religion and morality. But the one assumption, the one postulate, in which all the rest may assume a scientific form, and which granted we may coercively deduce even those which we might allowably have assumed, is the Existence of the *Will*, which a moment's reflexion will convince us is the same as *Moral Responsibility*, and that again with the reality and essential difference of moral *Good* and *Evil*."[48] The chapter is unquestionably, and specifically, referent to the subjects immediately

[47] *Op Max*, 6.
[48] *Op Max*, 11.

previously discussed in the first two chapters; Coleridge has simply introduced the term "moral" in opposition to "scientific."[49]

On the Divine Ideas is a systematic theology beginning with the chapter of that name and its internal references demonstrate this.

Some Concluding Thoughts

What does this systematic theology of Coleridge's yield for the contemporary period? One answer might be to breathe new life into the concept
of vitalism. In a climate that is increasingly dominated by either one of the
two binary opposites of scientific reductionism or a remorselessly uncriti-
cal acceptance of the received text of the Christian biblical literature (which
Coleridge would have termed "bibliolatry"), a hermeneutic that 1. uses the
human faculty of Reason as the basis for differentiating Man from higher
animals, 2. acknowledges that higher animals do possess the faculty of the
Understanding, and 3. sees God as the Absolute Will indwelling *all* animated creation as the Elohim (or the primordial "I AM" from which all particular acts of will descend) *might* present a viable "Third Way" between
these two poles. Vitalism fell from favor because it was used as a principle of natural philosophy or science: vitalist scientists sought to use the philosophy to explain nature. Perhaps rational Christian theologians who have
no wish to deny demonstrated truths of science could use Coleridge's vitalist model of will to put God back into encountered reality. It seems to me
that this was what Coleridge was attempting to do: poach the hermeneutic
of vitalism from the natural philosophers and scientists and make it his
own as a theologian. Coleridge's vitalism may well provide a way to allow
God to permeate creation as described by twenty-first-century science.
There is something that rings with a beautiful truth in Coleridge's focus on
God as the Absolute Will; it seems to have a penetrating accuracy.

---

[49] There are, however, several cases of antecedent references that support the proposed
ordering: these are the references in fragments "1" and "2" to the "historical portion of
the work," which assume that it has already been presented. These are referent to chapter
I of "Fragment 3": Coleridge's discussion of the history of philosophy and the history of
the Trinity. One has to look no further than the first two paragraphs of "Fragment 3" to
see Coleridge's use of the word "History" (*Op Max*, 218 ff.). This is the only portion of
the received text that attempts anything near a comprehensive approach to the history of
philosophy.

READING "WILL" IN COLERIDGE'S *OPUS MAXIMUM*: THE RHETORIC OF TRANSITION AND REPETITION

By Murray J. Evans

The publication of the *Opus Maximum*, thanks to Princeton University Press and editors Thomas McFarland and Nicholas Halmi, makes this erstwhile mysterious and largely unread text available for more general perusal. What will also now become clear is how much of the text is often difficult to read. Part of this difficulty is peculiar to the *Opus Maximum* and its edition. That the fragments of the *Opus Maximum* were drafts, not yet ready for publication,[1] is clear in numerous ways. Victoria College Library MS 29, part iii — McFarland's "Fragment 1" — opens at "Chapter III," not "I."[2] While some chapter titles are helpful and chapter lengths relatively digestible, others, such as the long one on the Trinity concluding "Fragment 2," do not always contain self-evident continuous argument. Aside from fragments "1" and "2," moreover, the sequence of fragments according to their contents is not clear.[3] Furthermore, if one moves from the *bon mots* of the *Opus Maximum*, still only infrequently cited in secondary sources, to the contexts of those excerpts, there is the shock of trying to follow Coleridge's argument, a shock that editorial emphases in the Bollingen edition — and even a summary of the

---

[1] *Op Max*, xvii.

[2] The principal manuscripts of the *Opus Maximum* are the three volumes of Victoria College Library MS 29, parts i, ii, and iii, labeled "Fragments" "4," "2," and "1," respectively; Henry E. Huntington Library MS HM 8195 ("On the Divine Ideas"), labeled "Fragment 3"; and MS New York Public Library (Berg Collection), labeled "Proposed Preface." Halmi cautions that McFarland's preferred sequence of fragments is probably not the chronological one (*Op Max*, xx). Before McFarland's parlance of numbered fragments and their sequence becomes commonplace for Coleridgeans, my own extensive work on Middle English romance manuscripts, as well as the manuscripts of the *Opus Maximum*, leads me to be cautious of how the editorial labels of textual scholars can cause to disappear important features of texts that subsequent scholars encounter only in modern edition (see for example Evans, "The Explicits and Narrative Division in the Winchester MS.: A Critique of Vinaver's Malory," *Philological Quarterly* 58 [1979]: 263–81, particularly 263–64 and 279–80). I will therefore often refer to these texts by their manuscript names as a way of keeping various hermeneutic options open.

[3] I assume in this essay that Huntington 8195, "On the Divine Ideas" ("Fragment 3"), follows MS 29, parts iii and ii (fragments "1" and "2"); see also, note 20 below.

Opus Maximum's arguments — will only partially alleviate.[4] Apart from the peculiarities of the *Opus*, this difficulty is, of course, familiar to readers of other Coleridge texts, such as the *Biographia Literaria*. Heather Jackson acutely locates the challenge in Coleridge's "art of suppressed or concealed transition," his freer adaptation of the rhetorical figure *transitio* "that explicitly signals the passing from one subject to another." Jackson believes that a dearth of scholarly attention to transition needs to be remedied, since it is the technique by which Coleridge's "method" is manifested. With a focus on one of Coleridge's letters, Jackson suggests that for Coleridge transitions "belong not to the literal content of a text but to its conceptual structure, not to its diction but to its syntax, not to its parts but to the unarticulated relationship between the parts."[5] In this essay, I wish further to address this scholarly gap identified by Jackson, anatomizing in some detail the method of Coleridge's rhetoric in some key passages in the *Opus Maximum*, themselves different kinds of transitions in which repetition of various forms also plays a part.

Coleridge's Postulate of the Will

I begin with a particularly recondite example of such unarticulated "syntax" of parts, occurring in the opening chapter of Victoria College Library MS 29, part iii (McFarland's "Fragment 1"), at the end of which Coleridge proposes his first "postulate." McFarland is surely correct when he mentions in his notes to this conclusion that "the Existence of the *Will*" is for Coleridge "the foundation of everything else." He calls this context an "initial complex" that "will bear the burden of the entire elaboration of the *Op Max*," since it is intrinsic to Coleridge's reasoned rejection of pantheism and "goes hand in hand with the doctrine of the Trinity, which the progress of the *Op Max* is also moving to extricate."[6]

---

[4] McFarland's long "Prolegomena" to the *CC* edition frame the *Opus Maximum* as the extant portion of Coleridge's grandly conceived and unfinished total project, the *magnum opus*, and the residue of material hived off into publications like *Aids to Reflection*. As a result, the arguments of the edited texts themselves receive relatively little attention in his introduction and the force of many of his notes, recording cognate passages elsewhere in the Coleridge canon, is often centrifugal, away from understanding the challenges of immediate context; see also Murray J. Evans, review of *Op Max* in *European Romantic Review* 14 (2003): 493–96.
[5] H. J. Jackson, "Coleridge's Lessons in Transition: The 'Logic' of the 'Wildest Odes,'" in *Lessons in Romanticism: A Critical Companion*, ed. Thomas Pfau and Robert F. Gleckner (Durham: Duke University Press, 1998), 217, 214, 218–20.
[6] *Op Max*, 11n.14 and 15.

I propose a related, but alternative metaphor to McFarland's of bearing burdens or extrication: the unfolded summary, which does, and does not, illuminate what follows and which is only one version of a larger and varied rhetoric of repetition throughout the *Opus Maximum*.

Elinor Shaffer argues that Coleridge, covertly in chapter 12 of *Biographia Literaria* and more openly in the *Opus Maximum*, adapts the idea of the "postulate of philosophy," a key term in late eighteenth-century moral and aesthetic philosophy, in its attempt to construct philosophy from primary intuitions. Kant believed only mathematicians could make such constructions, but Schelling thought otherwise. Just as the pre-existence of a circle in the mind cannot be proved from experience, but can be demonstrated in our experience by drawing the circle, so the validity of moral axioms can be demonstrated, in "a kind of practical proof," by fulfilling them in action. Furthermore, for Schelling philosophy too "is an activity which creates the validity of its own postulates; it is not a body of theoretical knowledge." The "cultivated ability" of philosophers has as its objects "the activities of the mind itself"; such intuitions are demonstrated empirically by the work of art. Shaffer cites Coleridge's definition of his first postulate, from the opening chapters of MS 29, part iii; she only suggests, but does not elaborate, that Coleridge adapts Schelling's arguments in the *Opus Maximum*.[7] While the *Opus Maximum*'s Chapter III is a case of such adaptation, Shaffer's hint of an overt use of the postulate also deserves detailed attention in its own right.

In the opening of "Chapter III" of "Fragment 1," for example, Coleridge appears to be rehearsing some of Schelling's argument on postulates in science: "In every science something is assumed, the proof of which is prior to the science itself, whether supplied by some other science or consisting of some fact, the certainty or validity of which is of common acknowledgement, or lastly of some idea or conception without which the science itself would be impossible and the denial of which implies the logical falsity of the whole, and consequently stamps the very act of commencing it in detail with the character of absurdity."[8] In science then, Coleridge continues, necessity rules in the postulate, with little scope for application of the human will. In other words, in geometry we assent to acts of imagination regarding classes of lines necessarily: once we decide what a circle is and draw it, we cannot withhold our

---

[7] Elinor S. Shaffer, "The 'Postulates in Philosophy' in the *Biographia Literaria*," *Comparative Literature Studies* 7 (1970): 304, 307, and *passim*.

[8] *Op Max*, 5.

assent from, or imagine anything contrary to these acts, without absurdity. There is no opposite to their necessity.[9]

Coleridge then embeds this postulate of scientific systems in a contrast with that of moral systems, in which there must be, to begin with, "the power of withholding... assent,"[10] the possibility of an opposite. This becomes a repetition of technique, which pervades the chapter. The technique is a version of what Shaffer regards as Coleridge's manner of handling opposites, "his characteristically moderate, semi-dialectical method of progressive redefinition: by multiplying slighter gradations between the two terms, they are made to approach each other.[11] In this more complex case, Coleridge entertains a nexus of opposites in search of middle terms, a use of transition between two terms to generate a third. On his way to enunciating a third category of postulates, then, Coleridge suggests that we may take for granted a fact — i.e. "an assertion respecting particulars or individuals" as contrasted with "universal truths or positions." From a fact "once taken for granted" can follow deductions and conclusions as "a logical truth." (A long digression on usage of "fact" follows.) Even if we assume an absurdity, an absurd syllogism could *logically* follow from it: in effect, we assume an "if" as a prefix to any such assumption: "Thus all stones think; but a flint is a stone; therefore a flint thinks." Now, Coleridge continues, if moral truths are to be not only equal, but also superior to scientific ones, we need an opposite to both "hypothetical positions or those grounded on facts" — Coleridge has now named his third category of postulate — and "the unconditional necessary" of the scientific position.[12]

Coleridge's quest for a middle position between these two poles takes us on a dialectical dance, in which the moral postulate would possess some of each position's characteristics. It would have the force of affirmations of science, their universality and their necessity, but in order for the two not to be identical, this necessity in the moral would not be unconditional: there would remain, as for hypothetical positions, the "possibility of affirming the contrary." Like hypothetical positions, the moral would possess contingency for the mind, but again with a difference. Such contingency exists for hypothetical positions even when

---

[9] *Op Max*, 5–6.
[10] *Op Max*, 6.
[11] Elinor S. Shaffer, "Coleridge's Revolution in the Standard of Taste," *Journal of Aesthetics and Art Criticism* 28 (1969): 214.
[12] *Op Max*, 6–8.

"removed by the establishment of the fact" (as in absurd syllogisms); but
for the moral, "the necessity must remain in the mind while the contingency is retained in the fact." A clarifying example, again from language
usage, follows. The conditional necessity of "you must do that" is different from the contingency of affirming "mere facts." That sheep in a
particular field are white is verifiable, but there is no imperative that they
must be white. In contrast, we tell someone "to abstain from any given
act of baseness or ingratitude with the same fullness of conviction," no
matter which way the person chooses to respond. Here, then, while there
is "no more contingency" than in mathematics, the contingency in the
moral, to be distinct from the scientific, "must not be wholly divided
from the position itself," must be unlike the case where the ideal properties of an arch are not contingent on their exact realization in this or that
actual arch.[13] Therefore the moral position must be real, "even independently of its application." *And* "its necessity must not only remain" when
"refused or subverted" in fact. The "denial of the position must be itself
a reality and a realizing act [also] in addition to and even independent of
the contingency of the accordance or discordance of the fact connected
therewith."[14] Such a discursive mouthful needs an example, which follows. An extended dialogue labels someone's refusal to help a sick parent as more than hateful and less than bestial — another triad emerging
— indeed as a rejection of obligation, of "the principles of reason." To
"transgress but still to acknowledge" is "the riddle of humanity[,]... the
mystery of the world," but to "transgress and disown" is fiendish.[15] What
is contingent in the mathematical — a real arch approximates more or less
its idea properties — in the moral has, beyond the failure to be human,
the superadded result of beginning to be devilish. Coleridge thus defines
his moral postulate by a dialectic that generally combines selective similarities and differences from scientific and hypothetical ones, but does
this particularly by repeated mediations of opposite terms. This technique
of dialectical repetition, whose abiding principle elsewhere in the *Opus
Maximum* Coleridge calls "the logic of Trichotomy" or "the Tetractic"[16],
is recurrently present in the work. The benefits of this method are

[13] *Op Max*, 8–9.
[14] The denial of the position, in other words, must exceed the "hypothetical" or fac-
tual realization (or not) of an ideal arch in an actual one. This topic becomes a major point
in Huntington Library HM 8195 ("Fragment 3"); see, for example, *Op Max*, 225–26,
236–38.
[15] *Op Max*, 9–10.
[16] *Op Max*, 254.

twofold: to generate non-pre-existing middle terms constructed from existing opposites and to provide forward momentum in constructing an argument.[17] The short-term liability of the method is residual or co-existing unclarity. In context, there remains the air of the penny not yet quite dropping. Coleridge's only partial remedy is further repetitions of the same kind, that will unfold new (as yet latent) intermediate terms and examples in this discourse of "pregnant Indistinction."[18]

Coleridge says as much in the conclusion to this chapter, although he is naming the unfolding to come, rather than at present calling attention to its method: "In this imagined conversation we have insensibly developed the first and most general forms of morality and of religion."[19] This new note of religious postulates, Coleridge develops through another repetition — a convoluted, over eleven-line summary of the preceding argument concerning moral postulates — reviewing the selective kinship of moral, hypothetical (now apparently called "empirical"), and scientific positions; but returning to the new note, that these moral actions by their empirical-like "reality and realizing power contain the substance and form the first general conception of religion." In other words, we know the first postulate of religion from the moral actions informed by it. If we were to "recapitulate the code and creed given in the first chapter,"[20] we would know "what the assumptions and the postulates are" according to the following now familiar conditions of their necessity, distinguishable from scientific and hypothetical positions, some of which Coleridge now rehearses again. Typically, this repetition again cumulates in another new note implicit in the previous anecdotes of the sheep and the arch. The *necessity* of the moral/religious postulate "arises out of and is commensurate with human nature itself, the sole condition being the retention of

---

[17] See also below, on "positive proof."

[18] *CL*, IV, 807 (January 12, 1818). The phrase is used of the Prothesis, discussed further below in relation to Coleridge's use of Pythagoras.

[19] *Op Max*, 10.

[20] It is more than tempting to think that Coleridge meant Victoria College Library MS 28 ("Appendix A" in *Op Max*), the first notebook of which contains a first chapter and the beginning of "Chapter 2d." The first chapter lists a creed: "These doctrines, etc., as common to all christians [*sic*], collectively constitute the CHRISTIAN RELIGION, the following being the sum..." (*Op Max*, 348). There is also a recapitulation of a Christian creed in "Chapter VII" of MS 29 part iii, with the recurring link back: "These articles constituting the common creed of christendom have been stated in our first chapter, and may be thus compressed..." (*Op Max*, 53). Is MS 28's first notebook the first two missing chapters preceding "Chapter III," which opens the extent MS 29 part iii ("Fragment 1"), where my essay begins?

humanity." Its *contingency* lies in the fact that humans may be "dishumanized" by their own acts. These facts are "the very ground and efficient cause" of the "supremacy" of the moral/religious postulate over other sorts. It differs from the scientific, then, not by subtraction but "by addition... of the same power in a higher dignity, namely by adding goodness to truth while it realizes truth by goodness, enlightens goodness by truth and transubstantiates, as it were, truth and goodness each into the nature of the other."[21] Evidently, the "truth" of scientific positions is of the same kind as the moral/religious, but the latter super-adds goodness and commingles truth and goodness. The religious discourse of transubstantiation here is no coincidence, given the passage's use of the epithets of truth and goodness that Coleridge also applies to members of his preferred formulation of the Trinity, the Tetractys.[22] The passage thus foreshadows, again by unfolded summary, both MS 29's culminating elaboration of the Tetractys, and also its central discussion of conscience and faith, at the end of "Fragment 1" and beginning of "Fragment 2" in the *CC*, an expansion of Coleridge's *Essay on Faith*.[23] What is more, this passage on truth and goodness enacts in little the repeated dialectic of much of the chapter, whereby one term and an other are counterpointed, combined, and reconstituted in unfolding argument, each repetition gathering strength before the addition of a new term into the just achieved synthesis.

The chapter closes in an attempt to summarize "[i]n one concluding sentence." There are "several positions, each of which might be legitimately assumed and each of which might stand on its own grounds as a postulate of humanity, and à fortiori, therefore, of every code of religion and morality." Only one of these candidates stands out, however, upon closer inspection, as surpassing the merely scientific or the penultimate: "But the one assumption, the one postulate, in which all the rest may assume a scientific form, and which granted we may coercively deduce

---

[21] *Op Max*, 11.

[22] See, for example, *SW&F*, II, 1510. For mention of the Tetractys in the *Opus Maximum*, see *Op Max*, 209–10.

[23] *Op Max*, 192–213 and 57–96. Much material on conscience precedes the latter: see *Op Max*, 21–48, 55–57. In the introduction to the *Essay on Faith*, in *SW&F*, II, 833, cites J. Robert Barth, S.J., *Coleridge and Christian Doctrine* (Cambridge, Massachusetts: Harvard University Press, 1969), 29n.38, who suggests that the *Essay* is a "somewhat amplified" version of the *Opus Maximum* version. On a closer examination, the *Opus Maximum* version proves to be markedly longer, also taking into account the material written on verso leaves (*Op Max*, 61–67; foliation from the original manuscript silently rationalized by Nicholas Halmi).

even those which we might allowably have assumed, is the Existence of
the *Will*, which a moment's reflexion will convince us is the same as
Moral Responsibility, and that again with the reality and essential difference of moral *Good* and *Evil*."[24] It is unlikely that "a moment's reflexion" will suffice for many of us to understand the triple equivalence of
will with moral responsibility and "the reality and essential difference of
moral *Good* and *Evil*" in this statement. Coleridge will take most of the
extant *Opus Maximum* to unfold this summary. But evidently Coleridge
can understand this equivalence; and I think that many of "us" following his arguments through the *Opus Maximum* can eventually, thus
informed, in a "moment's reflexion" come to understand it. That this
might prove to be the case arises from two central qualities about the
"point" of the *Opus Maximum* and the force of Coleridge's repetition in
it. All other possible postulates, he says, "assume a scientific form" in
relation to this primary "postulate of humanity"; since all others, moreover, are "coercively deduced" from it, they are both contained in it and
follow by unavoidable necessity. Secondly, this postulate of the Will "is
the same as *Moral Responsibility*" and "the reality and essential difference of moral *Good* and *Evil*." The same reality or postulate can be
named variously. These two dynamics — of all-in-one (or all-derived-
from-one) and "this-is-this-is-this" — have further implications for repetition, which I will turn to shortly.

Coleridgeans have not failed to notice the importance of this,
Coleridge's statement of the postulate of the Will. Besides Shaffer's
already noted mention of it, Boulger cites it in a wider-ranging discussion of Coleridge on conscience.[25] There is clearly a useful portability of
the definition without close reference to its context. The advantage of
also being aware of that context is seeing how the definition arises progressively in Coleridge's rhetoric, constituted out of the "transubstantiation" of successive couplings of terms. And this method of argument,
and not just the content of the definition, is extremely useful for reading
other difficult passages in the *Opus Maximum*.[26]

---

[24] *Op Max*, 11. This postulate he picks up again in the opening of Chapter V as "the
actual being of a *responsible Will*" (*Op Max*, 17), with a reference back to this chapter.

[25] James D. Boulger, *Coleridge As Religious Thinker* (New Haven: Yale University
Press, 1961), 122–23.

[26] For example, Murray J. Evans, "The Method of Coleridge's Argument on the Trinity in the Opus Maximum," a paper presented at the Coleridge Summer Conference 2000,
at Cannington College, Somerset, UK, July 20–26. A version of this paper will appear in
my book-length study of the *Opus Maximum*.

Will and Absolute Will

Coleridge's rhetoric on his first postulate is not always so complex, however. After the next, somewhat digressive chapter labelled "Chapter IV,"[27] Chapter V returns expressly to the matter of Chapter III: "At the close of the last chapter but one, we had agreed to reduce the postulates and assumptions... to the one great and inclusive postulate and moral axiom — the actual being of a *responsible Will*. À fortiori, therefore, the actual being of WILL in genere."[28] His definition of will to follow is more logically accessible, on the whole. He encapsulates Will simply as "the *power* of *originating* a *state*." In order to arrive at this definition, and admittedly more indirectly, Coleridge uses negative definition: he speaks of collating a number of "negatives" — Coleridge's "will" is, for example, neither instinct nor appetite — so as to yield "the only positive which will present itself." Next, he indicates the implications of this "verbal definition" of Will, once granted; they are, in effect, a continuation of negative definition (as the presence of negatives in the following citations confirm). Will so defined must be real and not merely conceivable, "[f]or if it be that which can absolutely begin a state or mode of being, it is evidently not the result or aggregate of a composition." Similarly, it must also be "incapable of explication or explanation"; it can have no antecedent, or else it would be a "consequent." Not only must it be "unique" and not subject to comparison; it also "cannot be an object of conception." In the language of the Schoolmen, it "may be known, but cannot be understood."[29] Coleridge intimates that he will later consider Will "in its absolute sense and not as now, under the predicate of responsibility, or the Will in the finite and creaturely." This is not a present, but a future, or predicted transition — to which I will return below. For the rhetorical purposes of this immediate chapter, Chapter V, negative definition of Will yields a positive that subsequently rules out other meanings of the word by default: "All that words and outward reasoning can effect is first to state an instance which is supposed to exemplify and thus expected to convey the direct, proper, and exclusive meaning, which as in the case of all terms representing simple truths or acts of knowlege [*sic*]

---

[27] Chapter IV addresses the difference between the statements, "such a truth may be known as truth by the light of reason" and "the same truth was discovered, or might have been discovered, by men by means of their reason exclusively" (*Op Max*, 12).

[28] *Op Max*, 16–17.

[29] *Op Max*, 17–18.

is insusceptible of any [other] definition or periphrasis."[30] While negative definition thus sophisticates the rhetoric of this extended definition
of Will, it is nowhere near as complex as Coleridge's dialectic in Chapter III.[31]

Neither is another example of a definition of Will later in the next and
last part of MS 29, in a chapter entitled "Chapter [no number inserted]
On the existential reality of the Idea of the Supreme Being, i.e. of God."[32]
Overall, the rhetoric here again differs from that in Chapter III, since it
is annunciatory rather than dialectical. We may divide the chapter into
three parts. The first third of the chapter is peppered with authorities:
Proclus, Simonides, Plato, Iamblichus, *Liber XXIV philosophorum*, Spinoza (planned as an insertion), Milton, Wordsworth, Pythagoras (by inference), Hesiod, Aristophanes, Luther, Vico, and Aristotle.[33] One example,
from Luther, will suffice: "Most cordially do I agree with this mighty
minister of truth: without that inward revelation by which we know ourselves responsible and thus know what no understanding can reach, the
reality of a Will. In vain should we endeavour to make up the notion of
a divinity out of any materials which the senses can convey, or the world
afford. So general, however, is the prepossession to the contrary that it
becomes more than merely expedient not to rest in an assertion if we cannot demonstrate by reason the existence of God, yet by reason itself to
demonstrate its indemonstrability."[34] This and the many other authorities reiterate the impossibility of proving God from the senses.[35] The last
third of the chapter, as I have argued elsewhere, similarly denies that the
argument from design can prove the existence of God unless the idea of
God is already present in the hearer's mind.[36] Both these sections argue
that sense data cannot (as pantheists claim) yield us the idea of God or
Absolute Will. Here a rhetoric of repetition proceeds straightforwardly by
argument from authority and assertion, respectively.

---

[30] *Op Max*, 19, 21.

[31] In predicting a transition to come, the chapter is itself a kind of negative transition,
a "time out" regarding content that might have been, but will not appear for a while.

[32] *Op Max*, 96–119.

[33] *Op Max*, 96–104 and pertinent notes.

[34] *Op Max*, 102.

[35] That the Reason can only demonstrate the idea of God as indemonstrable in effect
predicts more negative proof to follow, in "On the Divine Ideas" (*Op Max*, 273–90),
where Coleridge will argue that all competing views of God are flawed; see also Murray
J. Evans, "The Divine Ideas in Coleridge's *Opus Maximum*: The Rhetoric of the Indemonstrable," *The Coleridge Bulletin* n.s. 22 (2003): 43–44.

[36] Evans, "Divine Ideas," 45.

This straightforwardness and topic also hold for the middle part of the chapter, which is a very close counterpart to a note Coleridge had added to several copies of *The Friend*.[37] That Coleridge regards the passage as a key one for the *Opus Maximum* itself is evident from his framing of it: "[s]o important, indeed, does this appear to me that I present the final result of my reasoning at the commencement, so that no false alarm may render the enquirer disinclined to undertake the investigation, or make him hold with an unsteady hand the clue which, unfolding as it runs, is to trace the path through the obscure labyrinth into broad light and champaign."[38] And shortly thereafter, Coleridge introduces the key passage thus: "The concluding truth, which that the reader may see distinct in the clear light of his own understanding and possess in his own right, I would fain have him to accompany me through the whole process, is this."[39] I cite the passage only selectively:

> the dialectic intellect, by the exertion of its own powers exclusively, is sufficient to establish the general affirmation of a supreme reality, of an absolute being, but this is all — for here the power of the scientific reason stops; it is utterly incapable of communicating insight, or conviction, concerning the existence or a world different from Deity... the inevitable result of all *consequent* Reasoning, in which the Speculative intellect refuses to acknowledge a higher or deeper ground than it can itself supply, is — and from Zeno the Eleatic to Spinoza ever has been — Pantheism...[,] practical Atheism;... All Speculative Disquisition must begin with postulates, that derive their legitimacy, substance, and sanction from the *Conscience*: and from whichever of the two points the Reason may start, from the things that are seen to the One Invisible, or from the idea of the absolute One to the things that are seen, it will find a Chasm, which the *Moral* Being only, which the Spirit and Religion of man alone can fill up.[40]

The passage confirms that the moment forecast by Coleridge in Chapter III has come — when he considers Will in its "absolute" and not "finite" sense."[41] Apparently the "Speculative intellect," the "scientific reason," has followed the postulate of the Will only so far; now, as the opening of this chapter makes authoritatively clear, he must turn to the Absolute Will, which Reason can only prove indemonstrable. The portion of the quotation — "All Speculative Disquisition must begin with postulates, that derive their legitimacy, substance, and sanction from the *Conscience*"

---

[37] *Friend*, I, 522n.1.
[38] *Op Max*, 102–3.
[39] *Op Max*, 104.
[40] *Op Max*, 104, 106–7.
[41] *Op Max*, 19.

— is an apt summary of the argument so far, from the definition of Will
in Chapter III, through what is principally a discussion of conscience and
faith, including the expanded version of the *Essay on Faith*. What mainly
follows this quotation and chapter is two long movements that end
MS 29: the first, on how the development of children can be perverted
to construct yet more followers of the mechanical philosophy, and the
second, a long extrapolation of the Trinity from the postulate of the
Absolute Will.[42] These two movements are Coleridge's way of "filling
up" that "Chasm" between things and the Absolute. Indeed the two succeeding movements address Coleridge's two directions for "Speculative
Disquisition." His look at child development, suggesting a kind of trinity of mother, child, and God,[43] argues inductively from "the things that
are seen to the One Invisible";[44] and the subsequent extrapolation of the
Trinity, also extending beyond MS 29 into Huntington 8195 ("Fragment
3"), proceeds deductively "from the idea of the absolute One" to the
Tetractys — Absolute Will, Father, Son, Spirit — as the basis of "the
things that are seen." The former explores the "Spirit... of man" in the
child, the second, the "Religion of man." So here Coleridge's summary
appears as "clue... through the obscure labyrinth into broad light."[45] Here
is *transitio* in its traditional sense, then: in Janus fashion, the chapter
looks backward and forward. Unlike Chapter III, it does not "unfold";
it recapitulates and forecasts. The repetition of topic in the three sections
of the chapter reinforces its main point.

Repetition and Divine Prothesis

One clue to this repetition, and to the repetition of similar passages here
and in the note to *The Friend*, is a subsequent passage in MS 29 reaf-
firming the centrality of the postulate of the Will or as we have already
seen, its cognate, the idea of God. The passage defines, and even enacts,

[42] *Op Max*, 119–50, 150–213.
[43] "The child on the knee of its mother and gazing upward to her countenance marks
her eyes averted heavenward, while yet it feels the tender pressure of her embrace, and
learns to pray in the mother's prayers... That which the mother is to her child, a someone
unseen and yet ever present, is to all" (*Op Max*, 126). For a different formulation, see also
McFarland: "Coleridge's extrapolation of the dyadic origin of self in the mother-child
relationship served his needs in the attempt to validate the three-personed God of Christianity — that is to say, a dyadic relationship of God and Christ, with the Holy Ghost as
the binding principle" (*Op Max*, cxxxiii).
[44] *Op Max*, 107.
[45] *Op Max*, 103.

the ideology of repetition in the *Opus Maximum* at large, perhaps in Coleridge's philosophy in general. It begins with the metaphor of the circle as the shape of an argument always deriving from and depending on its initial assumption. As in natural science, so also "in grammar and in logic we ... still find one such circle assumed as the staple of the chain, rightly assumed and legitimately demanded as the only means of letting all the links that constitute the chain follow each other in one intelligible line of dependency... We must yield to one argument in a circle at our starting point as the only way of precluding it ever afterwards, and in every other case."[46] Coleridge then lists a number of discourses in which a sense of the postulate recurs. First, in grammar "we begin with the verb substantive, with that which is the identity of being and action, of the noun and the verb; and we regard the noun and verb as the positive and negative poles of this identity, the Thesis and Antithesis." Coleridge distinguishes this identity, "that which is both in one," from three kinds of synthesis in the discourse of chemistry: "synthesis by juxtaposition or mechanical commixture of the two constituents,... synthesis by the uniform solution of the one in the other (as, for instance, salt in water)," and "synthesis as a tertium aliquid engendered by the introsusception of the one element in the other, i.e. by proper chemical combination (as, for instance, carbonate of lime from lime and carbonic acid)." In contrast, he repeats, identity "can be no otherwise explained than as one containing in itself the ground and power of two as their radical antecedent." His next illustration, from geometry, is of "a point producing itself into a bi-polar line, when we contemplate the same as anterior to this production and as still containing its two poles, or opposites in unevolved coinherence." Coleridge next turns to biblical discourse, first from the Old Testament. Given the aptness of the verb substantive for expressing "the act by which we are[,]... we at once see the propriety with which the Hebrew Legislator named that coinherence of act and being which is the ground and external power of the universe, of all things, and of all acts, and yet not included in nor the same with the sum total of these, the Absolute I AM."[47] Before continuing with this passage, the relationships and logic of these discourses require some scrutiny.

The logic of the passage is evidently Pythagorean, what Coleridge adapted to comprise identity (or prothesis), thesis, antithesis, indifference

---

[46] *Op Max*, 187–88. This is a rewording of the opening of Chapter III (*Op Max*, 5), discussed above.

[47] Exodus 3:14; *Op Max*, 188.

(not mentioned explicitly in the passage), and synthesis — what he calls "the five most general Forms or Preconceptions of Constructive Logic." This is the Pythagorean logic *relatively* taken." "Taken *absolutely*,"[48] i.e. with reference to the Divine Prothesis, the foundation of Pythagoras's "grand system of the deity" was "the monas; not as the one, but as that which without any numbers and perfectly distinct from numbers was yet the ground, and, by its will, the cause of all numbers; and in the manifestation of the godhead he represented it by the famous triad three."[49] Accordingly, "One and *the One* must be carefully distinguished. The Monad is Prothetic — one Thetic, / one Antithetic = 2 / one Synthetic = 3."[50] Elsewhere Coleridge adds: "in numbers considered philosophically there was a perpetual reference to an unity that was yet infinite, and yet that in each number there was an integral or individual that still contained in its nature something progressive that went beyond it."[51] So the grammatical, chemical, geometrical and biblical/theological discourses of the passage in the *Opus Maximum* all sound alike logically. They share the sense of, are versions of, that prothetic "co-inherence of act and being" characteristic of the "Absolute I AM" — Coleridge's version of the Pythagorean Monas — as the "ground" of "all things, and of all acts," but not coincident with "the sum total" of those acts.[52] This definition obviously privileges theological discourse in relation to the others.[53] Later in the *Opus Maximum*, Coleridge will call these other, dependent discourses, not "proofs," but "a series of exemplifications of the same truth, as if a man should demonstrate the essential properties of a triangle in a vast succession of diagrams, and in all imaginable varieties of size, and colour, and relative position: each would have the force of all."[54]

That these exemplifications repeatedly affirm the centrality of the Absolute I AM is rhetorically emphasized by how the argument of our passage repeatedly circles back to the identity or prothesis: "the verb substantive,... that which is the identity of being and action... We say the

---

[48] *AR*, 180–82; here Coleridge also terms the five "Forms" a "Pentad."

[49] *Lects 1818–1819*, I, 79.

[50] *CM*, V, 231.

[51] *Lects 1818–1819*, I, 77–78.

[52] *Op Max*, 188.

[53] On the Pythagorean resonances of Coleridge on the Trinity, see the end of MS 29 (e.g., *Op Max*, 209–10); see also Tim Milnes, *Knowledge and Indifference in English Prose* (Cambridge: Cambridge University Press, 2003), 204–07, which addresses (for different purposes) some material similar to mine, in *AR* (175, 180–81) but not in the *Opus Maximum*.

[54] *Op Max*, 271.

Identity of these... Neither, I say, of these forms of synthesis are identity... the Absolute I AM." On the face of it, the Prothesis cannot be
repeated, since it is the informing basis of all other truths; it is prior to
repetition, i.e. numbers of any kind. This would appear to run counter to
the broader sense of "exemplifications of the same truth" the passage is
heading for. So does the continuation of the passage in an allusion to the
Gospel of John[55] apparently collapsing variety back into a unity: "The
first great truth, which may be with philosophical propriety called the
light that lighteth every man that cometh into the world — the first great
truth, which all men hold implicitly and which it is the highest object and
duty of education to render explicit, is comprized in the term 'GOD.'"[56]
But Coleridge then reverses his field and asserts that the "term 'GOD'...
unfolded (explicitum) is equivalent" to a series of propositions, which I
quote in Coleridge's words, with added enumeration:

I. "God is self existent and a pure spirit."
II. But in this, its highest acceptation, a spirit means 1st, a substance
    impassive, that is, a substance having the nature and perfection of
    an act, and 2dly, an act substantial, that is, an act having a ground in
    itself and being its own principle of permanence.
III. We express, therefore, one and the same meaning whether we say
    in the words of scripture, "God is a Spirit,"
IV. or with the School Divines, "Deus est actus purissimus," or "God
    is a most pure act."
V. Now if we join the two positions of self-existence and Spirit, there
    arises that unique idea which can belong but to one subject and can
    therefore be elucidated by no analogy, that the Fathers and the
    School Divines have struggled to express by the terms
    "αυτοπατηρ" and "causa sui,"
VI. but which is both more sublimely and more adequately conveyed in the
    Hebrew words "I am in that I am," or rather in the literal translation
    of the words, "That which I will to be I shall be." For the future, which
    here involves à fortiori the past and the present, is used as the fittest
    symbol of an eternal act, to God an all-comprehending present, and to
    every finite being a future in which nothing past is wanting or left
    behind.
VII. This sublime enunciation might be paraphrased thus, "The whole
    host of heaven and earth, from the mote in the sunbeam to the

---

[55] John 1:9.
[56] *Op Max*, 188.

archangel before the throne of glory, owe their existence to a Will not their own, but my own Will is the ground and sufficient cause of my own existence. What I will to be I eternally am, and my Will is the being in which all that move and live, live and move and *have* their being."[57]

All these propositions, then, are equivalent to the word or idea, God. In other words, "unfold" the term "God" and all these propositions, all these modes of discourse (the scholastic, the biblical, etc.) appear.[58] They are imbedded in the word; *they* are the repetitions of the same implicit idea. The prothesis, the idea of God, then, does not itself repeat, but is present in all. This is the ideology of the passage. But its "prothetic rhetoric" also enacts this ideology, repeats in varying guises what otherwise can only be defined negatively, as we have previously seen in Coleridge's definition of the Will in Chapter V — not an instinct, not an appetite, and so on. The repetition in prothetic rhetoric, however, evidently lacks the progressive forward motion associated with Pythagorean number above: "in each number there was an integral or individual, that still contained in its nature something progressive." This is the system-building of the dialectical rhetoric of Chapter III, whereby the dialectical friction between scientific and moral postulates yields two other kinds, the hypothetical or empirical, and the religious. This system-building Coleridge also calls positive proof.[59]

It is difficult to overestimate the ideological importance of the Divine Prothesis, unfolded by illustration and demonstrated by systematic elaboration, in Coleridge's discourse in the *Opus Maximum* and at large. That much of the contents of the citation above are also repeated elsewhere in

---

[57] *Op Max*, 189. Under II, I have inserted the words "impassive, that is, a substance," erroneously omitted in *Op Max*.

[58] *CL*, IV, 807 (January 12, 1818) calls the Prothesis "pregnant Indistinction."

[59] For example, in *SW&F*, I, 787, in seeking the first principle for a philosophical system, it is necessary to "ascertain the negative character of the *Principle*... as the condition, under which alone a methodical System was possible": not a form, abstraction, generalization, fact or contained whole. "These were the necessary *negative* characters of our Desideratum. The *positive* character and proof... could only be found in the actual production of the System out of this first Principle — and... the Faith in its truth would strengthen and deepen in proportion to the experience of its pregnancy." This statement, dated 1818 by the editors, obviously informs the *Opus Maximum* as I have been discussing it. Not surprisingly, "the Principle desiderated would be found in Will absolutely taken." Further on negative and positive proof, see also *CN*, IV, 4656 (1820), also discussed below; *Op Max*, 253–54, 273–74; and Evans, "The Divine Ideas," especially 46–47. A partial version of *Op Max*, 253–54, appears in *SW&F*, II, 1034–35.

the *Opus Maximum* and the Coleridge canon underscores this ideological importance.[60] In her book *Delicate Subjects*, Julie Ellison has suggested that such repetition in Coleridge's prose, of the pentad and the "Ancient of Days" passage for example, "functions as a rhetorical gesture" to deliver "the sensation of visionary power," perhaps "a kind of 'key'"; but if not, "at least" an encoding of desire for the feminine displaced onto God and onto system. My argument underlines that there is no "at least" or "if not" about the centrality of the Prothesis, the pentad not yet unfolded, in Coleridge's system and rhetoric.[61] Coleridge's articulation of how to present the key in argument and how readers are to grasp it, is not entirely clear, however.

Will and Absolute Will, Once More

Again, Coleridge seems to have predicted, in Chapter V, a transition from arguing from the postulate of the finite Will to arguing from the idea of the Absolute Will; and we have already marked that transition in the later chapter entitled "On the existential reality of the Idea of the Supreme Being, i.e. of God."[62] Returning for a closer look at Chapter V will somewhat trouble the distinction, however. First, Coleridge suggests that he could there have *started* with the Absolute Will as a postulate, "a kind of intellectual promissory note,"[63] rather than as an idea in the higher sense: "Had we purposed in this Place to have treated of the absolute Will, we must have propounded it under the above verbal definition as an idea, the acknowledgment or acceptance of which would have been

---

[60] For more on the idea of God as discussed in Huntington 8195, "On the Divine Ideas" ("Fragment 3"), see Evans, "The Divine Ideas." For repetition of the content and even wording of this passage, see also *Op Max* 72–73, 80–83, and 253–54; *CN*, IV, 4644 (March 1820), and *AR*, 178*.

[61] Julie Ellison, *Delicate Subjects: Romanticism, Gender, and the Ethics of Understanding* (Ithaca: Cornell University Press, 1990), 212–13. On the gender issue, I argue in two papers that Ellison's argument (176, 200–204) is seriously compromised by a misreading of *Friend*, I, 106, and of the array of Shakespearean characters in the first "Essay on Method" (*Friend*, I, 448–57): "The Coleridgean Sublime: A Reassessment Based on the *Opus Maximum*," presented at "Placing Romanticism: Sites, Borders, Forms": The 2003 Conference of the North American Society for the Study of Romanticism, Fordham University, New York City, August 1–5, 2003; and "Coleridge, the Anti-Feminist?," presented at the Conference of the Linguistic Circle of Manitoba and North Dakota, Winnipeg, October 24–25, 1996.

[62] *Op Max*, 96–119.

[63] The phrase is McFarland's (*Coleridge and the Pantheist Tradition*, 29), used there in another context.

recommended by a scientific interest only, namely by a demonstration
that without such an idea as the ground or inceptive position, a system of
Philosophy and therefore a consistent Philosophy of any kind, as distinct
from mere history and empirical classification, would be impossible, and
the very attempt absurd."[64] Here "idea" is qualified to sound like "postulate" ("by a scientific interest only"). Indeed, the passage is largely a
rewording of the opening of Chapter III, the beginning of Coleridge's
argument on postulates: "In every science something is assumed,... some
idea or conception without which the science itself would be impossible
and the denial of which implies the logical falsity of the whole, and consequently stamps the very act of commencing it in detail with the character of absurdity."[65] Then Coleridge corrects this impression. Short of
the "enquirer" having "mastered the idea so as to know its truth by its
own evidence... the position is not indeed an idea at all but a notion, or
like the letters expressing unknown quantities in algebra, a something
conceded in expectation of a distinct significance which is to be hereafter procured."[66] (This instability of "idea" will recur in what follows.)
Coleridge seems to be suggesting that the principle of the Absolute Will
can be taken "scientifically" by some readers as a starting-point, on speculation, or by others who will know its truth without proof, as an idea.
(We may call these "Plan A" and "Plan B," respectively.) Indeed,
"[w]ith him... who possesses the idea we have only to proceed with the
involved and consequent truths in order to determine by the fact itself
whether a Philosophy can be constructed thereon." For the one who has
the idea, in other words, positive proof or the construction of a systematic philosophy is a kind of authentication; Coleridge then repeats: "But
the success, i.e. the existence of such a Philosophy, is the sufficient and
only proof of its possibility."[67] Next Coleridge falls back to "Plan A":
"Here, however, we begin not with an idea in this high and pure sense
of the term but with the postulate of a fact and the assumption of a truth
as a necessary consequence of the fact." This fact is "the existence of
conscious responsibility," the postulate of the Will already defined. But
here Coleridge adds more mysteriously: "of its existence every conscious
and rational Being must himself be the judge, the consciousness being the
only organ by which it can be directly known. But the consciousness of

[64] *Op Max*, 19.
[65] *Op Max*, 5.
[66] *Op Max*, 19–20.
[67] *Op Max*, 20.

a conscience is itself conscience."[68] This statement Coleridge will unpack in the succeeding section on conscience including the *Opus Maximum's* version of the *Essay on Faith*, particularly on the "act" of "becoming conscious of a conscience."[69] But even in context, the present plan for his discourse hovers, not only between Plan A and Plan B, but also between those two definitions of "idea," two apparent versions of Plan A: between "the postulate of a fact" and the reality or "fact" of the "existence of conscious responsibility," what he also calls "simple truths or acts of knowlege [*sic*]." The postulate of a fact he has already presented as the assumed starting point for tentative argument; the reality or fact itself is apprehended by "direct knowledge," by "consciousness of a conscience." This latter sounds already very much like Plan B, possessing the idea. But finally Coleridge returns to the purer Plan A, in which "words and outward reasoning" can only go so far as to define conscience verbally and exclusively,[70] just as we have seen him do with Will previously in this same chapter.

To what extent, then, does the distinction between the postulate of the Will and the idea of the Absolute Prothesis hold for Coleridge? In the context of our discussion, this also amounts to the broader question: to what extent do his distinctions in general hold?[71] Coleridge's practice here suggests two conclusions simultaneously. His distinctions stand as positions of argument — in Chapter III, the scientific postulate and the moral one. But then they may also be altered in the search for new middle terms — also in Chapter III, the hypothetical and the religious. This mobility of terms is akin to Steven Knapp's discussion of various other Coleridgean pairings, such as fancy and imagination, allegory and symbol. On the one hand, Knapp comments on "the oddest feature of Coleridgean distinctions in general... their almost deliberate implausibility — as if they were designed to collapse under the weight of Coleridge's own examples." On the other, much of Knapp's discussion addresses how such distinctions also need one another so as not to collapse: "Just as the symbol needed to be saved from literal identity by the

---

[68] *Op Max*, 20–21.

[69] *Op Max*, 72.

[70] *Op Max*, 21.

[71] Given the paradigmatic nature of both Will and Prothesis for Coleridge, a question concerning their distinction will logically imply the question about all other distinctions. Similarly, early in Huntington 8195 ("Fragment 3"), Coleridge takes the definition of Divine Ideas (particularly the Idea of God that much of the treatise is preoccupied with) to inform whatever "conception... we attach to *Idea*" in general (*Op Max,* 223).

persistence of allegorical difference, so the imagination must be saved
by fancy from its own potential violence."[72] Coleridge's immediate
rhetorical need for the distinction between postulate and idea is one of
audience: those who "possess the idea" can move on to positive proof
immediately, to the arising system of philosophy that, à la Schelling, can
prove its own premises; while the uncommitted can try out the postulate
and, as negative proof eliminates opposing definitions, see where things
lead. But this distinction itself does not hold throughout the *Opus Maximum*. We have already seen the system-building of positive proof in
Chapter III in connection with the postulate, not the idea. Even in the cli-
mactic elaboration of the Trinity in MS 29 (near the end of "Fragment
2"), where we might expect Coleridge to emphasize the idea of the
Absolute Will and let the more tentative rhetoric drop, he does not entirely
do so. Still he mentions that as in "formal science," we may investigate
later the "reality... correspondent to the formula"; for the present, we
must "proceed as if we substantiated [in this case] Alterity itself."[73] Then,
shortly after, he insists that we must contemplate the idea alone, "every
where bearing evidence to its own reality" rather than being misled by
analogies. But next, he reminds his readers that he has been discussing
"truth in the idea" all along — for those "who admit, or at least are willing to assume, the legitimacy of ideas, as far as the possible truth of any
assumption is concerned."[74] Plan A, Plan B, Plan A-B — this combination and newly generated ones will greatly sophisticate the dialectical
rhetoric of Coleridge's argument for the Trinity beyond its beginnings in
Chapter III.[75]

The persistence of both "plans" thus relates, I believe, to Coleridge's
desire to take his readers with him, and his uncertainty as to what moment
each reader will seize to move from postulate to idea, from entertaining
Coleridge's argument to possessing it. In an ideologically cognate passage
in the notebooks, Coleridge names this moment indeterminately in a
sequence that by this point in my argument will be familiar to us. A "system of Philosophy and philosophic Science must *begin with* — a Verity...
negatively definable as being neither a particular fact, nor... a generalization, nor an abstraction." Reduced "to a verbal proposition," such a

---

[72] Steven Knapp, *Personification and the Sublime: Milton to Coleridge* (Cambridge: Harvard University Press, 1985), 39, 30.
[73] *Op Max*, 196.
[74] *Op Max*, 196, 198.
[75] See Evans, "The Method of Coleridge's Argument on the Trinity."

truth must be *"unquestionable"* so as to begin argument somewhere and must be "an *assumption* by force of its negative definition." "In this assumption an Idea must arise" — but Coleridge adds no specification as to when. From this idea emerges successively the positive proof of a constructed system and, as soon as possible, parallels in experience, but as illustrations of "the Idea" rather than strict proofs, all in order to demonstrate the "the *universality* of the Truth, namely, that it is at once real and ideal."[76] While this articulation conveys no certainty as to when the idea might arise in the assumption, then, it still prioritizes the assumption or postulate in terms of sequence. Coleridge's rhetoric in the *Opus Maximum* does not bear this plan out. Instead, his rhetoric proves to be more flexible than his schemata for its orderly unfolding, including his own announced plans in Chapter V of the *Opus*.

Conclusion

In conclusion, I have explored four contexts of the *Opus Maximum*, arguably comprising different kinds of rhetoric of transition and repetition. In Chapter III of MS 29, part iii ("Fragment 1"), we have seen a dialectical rhetoric in which repeated transition between two terms generates a third, and so on. In retrospect, we can see this method as what Coleridge calls positive proof, the systematic elaboration of a philosophy from the idea. His starting from the postulate of the will, and not the idea of Absolute Will, will not prevent that subsequent ambiguity of postulate and idea just discussed. As transition, I have called this opening chapter unfolded summary: much of what follows in the *Opus Maximum* is implicit in its conclusions. Two chapters later in Chapter V, a more assertive rhetoric of repeated negative proof is not itself transition but apparently predicts a transition to come, where tentative argument from the postulate will yield to positive proof. This apparent transition comes in the chapter on "the Idea... of God," where there is a more direct rhetoric of repeated assertion concerning the indemonstrability of the idea of God, the "clue... through the obscure labyrinth" of Coleridge's ensuing argument; here transition is typically Janus-like in its recapitulation of past material and anticipation of the major movements of argument to follow. Finally in MS 29, part ii ("Fragment 2"), there is what I have

---

[76] *CN*, IV, 4656 (1820).

called "prothetic rhetoric," the repetition of different discourses or illustrations of the Prothesis as unfoldings of the term "GOD." Such repetition thus enacts, rather than merely asserts, the centrality of the "I AM"
in Coleridge's ideology. The repetition of similar material elsewhere in
the *Opus Maximum* and in the Coleridge canon not only re-emphasizes
its ideological importance but also suggests an additional mode of transition, a sort of "landing-place"[77] or recurrent return to the prothesis
implicit in much unfolding, and as yet unfolded, argument. This particular sense of landing-place holds more generally for each of these passages. They each stand out from their contexts as turns, or predicted turns
in the text. They also provide reference points for how to read different
kinds of transitions and repetitions elsewhere in this collection of difficult texts. In particular, the wavering distinction between postulate and
idea, and the related cross-overs of associated rhetorics of positive and
negative proof also provide a helpful primer for sometimes puzzling, and
increasingly sophisticated argument elsewhere in the *Opus Maximum*, in
the last folios of MS 29 on the Divine Tetractys, for example.

It may seem curious to conclude that Coleridge likely also meant his
readers to receive pleasure from these rhetorical elements in the *Opus
Maximum*, judging by his earlier comments in his lecture of April 1, 1808
on Shakespeare. Drama, he says, shares in the "universal Principle of the
Fine Arts" by offering "delight... from that balance and antithesis of
feelings and thoughts," just as we delight in art-in-nature and nature-in-
art; indeed the principle applies to painting and music. Then Coleridge
generalizes even further into territory familiar to readers of our passages
in the *Opus Maximum*: "one great Principle is common to all, a principle which probably is the condition of all consciousness, without which
we should feel & imagine only by discontinuous Moments, & be plants
or animals instead of men — I mean, that ever-varying Balance — or
Balancing — of Images, Notions, or Feelings... conceived as in opposition to each other — in short, the perception of Identity & Contrariety —
the least degree of which constitutes *Likeness* — the greatest, absolute

---

[77] Cf. *Friend*, I, 148–49. Coleridge suggests three kinds of landing places in a stair-case
as "forms of the outward senses" to be translated by readers "into their intellectual analogies": the first, with "grand or shewy plants"; the second, an "extensive prospect" through
a "stately window" with colour-tinted "side panes"; and the last, a command of "the
whole spiral ascent... as if it merely *used* the ground on which it rested." While this
description suggests the virtuosic, the multi-faceted prospective, and the uncanny overview
as three rhetorical modes of transition, I take Coleridge's own practice in *The Friend* to
be expansive, thus giving me license in using the term here.

Difference — but the infinite gradations between these two from all the Play & all the Interest of our Intellectual & Moral Being."[78] The impulse of this pleasure and perception is teleological and although Coleridge does not here name the end, we know it from the *Opus Maximum* as the Divine Prothesis. The above passage continues: "till it lead us to a Feeling & an Object more aweful, than it seems to me compatible with even the present Subject to utter aloud, tho' most desirous to suggest it — for there alone are all things at once different and the same — there alone, as the principle of all things, does distinction exist unaided by division / Will, and Reason, Succession of Time & unmoving Eternity, infinite Change and ineffable Rest."[79] In its play on likeness and difference, emanating from "the principle of all things," Coleridge's rhetoric of repetition in the *Opus Maximum* is also meant to awaken in us pleasure and awe. In the words of the adage, God is in the detail.[80]

---

[78] *Lects 1808–1819*, I, 83–84.

[79] *Lects 1808–1819*, I, 84–85.

[80] I am grateful to the University of Winnipeg for generous financial support of research and travel related to the writing of this essay.

"WITH HIS GARLAND AND HIS SINGING ROBES ABOUT HIM": THE PERSISTENCE OF THE LITERARY IN THE *OPUS MAXIMUM*

By James Vigus

The urge has always been strong to divide Coleridge. Despite admiring his "spirit of universal research," Thomas De Quincey wrote of "the separate merits of Samuel Taylor Coleridge. Coleridge as a poet — Coleridge as a philosopher."[1] Wordsworth, reminiscing after Coleridge's death, regretted that metaphysics had "captivated [his] taste," to the detriment of his poetic mastery.[2] And it remains normal to summarize him along these lines: Thomas McFarland, for one, insists on "the immensely more urgent role, in his intellectual economy, of philosophy and theology rather than of literature and poetry."[3] Coleridge himself was admittedly the first to contrast his shaping spirit of Imagination from his abstruse research, and some such bifurcation is inevitable and necessary. But if this division has its uses, it is also reductive insofar as it often implies that Coleridge's interests changed radically around 1818: that the writer who is studied in departments of English Literature may thereafter be transferred wholesale to Theology. As De Quincey implied, we must divide Coleridge because he spans every discipline, and "where is the man who shall be equal to these things?"[4] Further, of Coleridge's texts, the *Opus Maximum* is the most theologically and philosophically complex, and therefore the most liable to be read in isolation from the earlier, canonically literary work. Compared with *The Friend*, whose title-page advertises "literary amusements interspersed," the *Opus Maximum* is dense, locally concatenated despite its fragmentary design, and lacking in the quotations of poetry and poetic prose hitherto so

---

[1] Thomas De Quincey, "Death of a German Great Man," in *The Works of Thomas De Quincey* (London: Pickering and Chatto, 2000–2003), 3:115; De Quincey, "Coleridge and Opium Eating," *Works*, 15:105.

[2] Reported by Robert Percival Graves writing to Felicia Hemans, August 12, 1834, quoted in Juliet Barker, *Wordsworth: A Life in Letters* (London, 2002), 227–28.

[3] Thomas McFarland, "Aspects of Coleridge's Distinction Between Reason and Understanding," in *Coleridge's Visionary Languages*, eds. Tim Fulford and Morton D. Paley (Cambridge: D. S. Brewer, 1993), 167.

[4] De Quincey, *Works*, 15:106.

characteristic of Coleridge. Its subjects are theological: the will, conscience, and the Divine Ideas. It might therefore seem appropriate to place it in a different category from Coleridge's earlier work, and assume a radical division between the two.

I wish to argue against that assumption. I share, that is, Graham Davidson's premise that Coleridge's "work is in principle an entity with a developing vision and life of its own, that his poetic, critical, philosophical, political, and theological writings are related as parts to a whole."[5] Accordingly this essay attempts to distinguish rather than divide the *Opus Maximum* from earlier works, especially the 1818 *Friend* and *Biographia Literaria*. I show that three preoccupations persist between those works and the *Opus Maximum*. First, the question of how to communicate truth; second, the philosophical and cultural problem that the *Biographia* names the despotism of the eye, and the *Opus Maximum* the lust of the eye; and third, the symbiosis of conscience and consciousness in Coleridge's thought. I devote one section to each of these preoccupations, considering each time how Coleridge invokes his favorite non-scriptural writers at key moments in the *Opus Maximum*. Albeit sparingly, he uses them as exemplars or authorities.

My first section contrasts the *Opus Maximum* with *The Friend* stylistically. I argue that Coleridge's essays "On the Communication of Truth" and "On Method" express an ideal of stylistic purity, or "sincerity," which he cannot in fact fulfill in *The Friend*, because of anxiety about the reaction of his readership. But the *Opus Maximum*, produced under special circumstances exempt from such anxiety, approaches that ideal: its style is deliberately "unliterary," minimizing rhetorical attractiveness generally and quotation in particular. However, overt rhetoric and quotation are not eliminated, since for Coleridge not all thoughts can be expressed in the a priori, logical mode. Sometimes in the *Opus Maximum* Coleridge *does* write "with his garland and his singing robes about him," as I discuss in my second section. There I suggest that the *Opus Maximum* strives for a mode of the sublime whereby a priori reasoning persistently approaches the inexpressible, the limit of language: at these points Coleridge — justifiably — raises his rhetorical intensity and employs poetic quotations. In particular, quotations of Wordsworth (negatively) and Milton (positively) constitute a warning about the despotism of the eye, which is inimical to the sublime. Milton has an especially

---

[5] Graham Davidson, *Coleridge's Career* (Basingstoke: Macmillan, 1990), 1.

"authoritative" status in the text, and I speculate that Milton even functions as a model for Coleridge's whole project. Coleridge reserves his greatest fanfare, though, for Shakespeare. As I explain in my brief third section, Coleridge uses the evil character of Shakespeare's Iago as a negative illustration of the symbiosis of conscience and consciousness. This symbiosis was also asserted in the "Essays on Method," where another Shakespearean character (Hamlet) was comparably used as a negative example. Murray J. Evans has noted that "frequent allusion to and citation from *The Friend* is a significant presence" in the *Opus Maximum*.[6] I would go further: the *Opus Maximum* cannot be properly understood without reference to the earlier, "literary" work.

The Communication of Truth

For Coleridge an appropriate writing style was paramount. "Great indeed are the difficulties of a true philosophy," he noted at around the time he was working on the *Opus Maximum*: "not merely those of attaining truth or the intellectual vision… but the difficulties of communicating the truth when attained."[7] This concern was longstanding: the latter phrase recalls the essays "On the Communication of Truth" in *The Friend*. According to these essays, conscience dictates that a writer or speaker must intend to communicate "an *adequate* notion of the thing spoken of, when this is practicable," and when not practicable, "at all events a *right* notion, or none at all."[8] It may be impracticable to convey an adequate notion because "unfit auditors," those unprepared, necessarily misunderstand truth nakedly presented. Mere verbal truth, a notion that evokes the scriptural opposition between letter and spirit, can therefore produce an effect of falsehood when addressed to the wrong audience. In Coleridge's view most contemporary writing is addressed to the wrong audience, the abstract "reading public,"[9] which in Coleridge's polemic is a lowest common denominator. The popular style is French, epigrammatic, "asthmatic" because of its short sentences. Its "brisk and breathless periods"

---

[6] Murray J. Evans, review of *Opus Maximum*, ed. Thomas McFarland, *European Romantic Review* 14 (2003): 495.
[7] *CN*, IV, 4774; 1820–21.
[8] *Friend*, I, 43.
[9] *Friend*, I, 21; cf. *BL*, I, 59: "the multitudinous PUBLIC, shaped into personal unity by the magic of abstraction, sits nominal despot on the throne of criticism."

offer momentary entertainment and flattery to the consumer, but ener-
vate the soul. By contrast Coleridge defines his own style as modeled on
seventeenth-century writers such as Hooker, Bacon, Milton and Jeremy
Taylor, whose "stately" architectural prose with its "difficult evolutions"
challenges for a thoughtful, attentive response.[10]

There are two contexts for these strictures on style. The first is the general shift in the center of intellectual power during the eighteenth century,
from the universities to London. The seventeenth-century writers whom
Coleridge admired had pursued academic debate within a prestigious university context in which a highly technical philosophical vocabulary and
common currency of classical learning were the norm: this milieu produced unapologetically learned prose addressed to learned men. In the
eighteenth century, however, the universities lost their currency, and London, with its salon culture, attracted writers who might hitherto have
worked in Oxford or Cambridge. The coffee-houses of London demanded
a wittier, more popular writing style, typified by *The Spectator*. Coleridge,
who in *On the Constitution of the Church and State* elaborated his theory of the clerisy, or learned class, deplored the change. He looked both
to Germany, whose flourishing university culture had produced work of
the technical complexity of Kant, and nostalgically back to seventeenth-
century England, when philosophers had vigorously debated metaphysical subjects with their peers.[11]

For the second context is the personal one of anxiety: Coleridge
despises and fears the undiscriminating "reading public." He feels
morally obliged to "guard against the herd of promiscuous readers."[12]
This defensiveness informs the peculiar twofold function of *The Friend*'s
foundational essays. On the one hand Coleridge tries to encourage fit
readers though few to trust in his sincerity as an intellectual guide. On the
other he tries actively to deter unfit readers from reading on. This delicate balancing-act results in a browbeating tone, a symptom of what Lucy
Newlyn has aptly termed the "anxiety of reception."[13] Thus Coleridge

---

[10] *Friend*, I, 20. For a critique of the "explicitly gendered tenor" of this section of *The
Friend*, see Lucy Newlyn, *Reading, Writing and Romanticism* (Oxford: Oxford University Press, 2000), 55–61.

[11] See Douglas Hedley, *Coleridge, Philosophy and Religion: Aids to Reflection and the
Mirror of the Spirit* (Cambridge: Cambridge University Press, 2000), chapter 6, esp.
272–79.

[12] *Friend*, I, 51.

[13] Newlyn sees "elitist defensiveness" in Coleridge's later prose style (*Reading, Writing
and Romanticism*, 87). Coleridge's complex sensitivities to audience-response are increasingly acknowledged: for a view of his "need" for friendship "projected upon the reading

twice protests his own sincerity[14] and repeatedly praises sincerity in the abstract. The concept of sincerity in fact seems to be linked with his ideal of prose style. "The whole faculties of man must be exerted in order to noble energies; and he who is not earnestly sincere, lives in but half his being, self-mutilated, self-paralysed."[15] Sincerity thus denotes wholeness, which a connected, seventeenth-century prose style would embody. Coleridge told a correspondent: "I must write to you in *sincerity* — i.e. sine cerâ, without *wax*, entire, unrivetted."[16] De Quincey, perhaps the most subtly attentive of all Coleridge's readers, borrowed the Coleridgean term "non-sequacious" to describe the epigrammatic prose style of Hazlitt, which he detested. De Quincey linked the non-sequacious style firmly to insincerity: one of Hazlitt's chief vices, he claims, is "the habit of trite quotation," a vice because "it is at war with sincerity… to express one's thoughts by another man's words." De Quincey again quotes (somewhat paradoxically) Coleridge's judgment of this practice as "mouth-diarrhoea." "It argues a state of indolent ease inconsistent with the pressure of strong fermenting thoughts," insists De Quincey, "before we can be at leisure for idle or chance quotations."[17] This is a polemically extreme view, but as De Quincey's mention of Coleridge implies, it is one with which Coleridge would have agreed — in those contexts in which strong fermenting thoughts may be allowed full rein.

The Friend is not such a context: although indulgently scolding the seventeenth-century masters for their excessive partiality to quotation,[18] *The Friend* quotes extensively, for both aesthetic and instructional effect. Nor indeed is *The Friend* a notably "sequacious" work in other respects. As a concession to a popular audience, Coleridge offers "literary amusements interspersed."[19] Passages of dense argument, always prefaced by

public" in *The Friend*, see Sophie Thomas, "Aids to Friendship: Coleridge and the Inscription of *The Friend*," *European Romantic Review* 14 (2003): 432. On "Coleridge's Anxiety" as a dominant aspect of his mind, see Thomas McFarland, *Romanticism and the Forms of Ruin: Wordsworth, Coleridge, and the Modalities of Fragmentation* (Princeton: Princeton University Press, 1981), 104–36.

[14] *Friend*, I, 19, 39.
[15] *Friend*, I, 41.
[16] *CL*, IV, 546; March 7, 1815.
[17] "Final Memorials of Charles Lamb," *Works*, 16:378. De Quincey ridicules the "asthmatic infirmity of humming and hawing" in bad prose (379): given so many Coleridgean allusions in this passage one might assume that the idea of asthma is drawn from *The Friend*.
[18] *Friend*, I, 52.
[19] *Friend*, I, 1.

exhortations to attention, are relatively few throughout the work. In fact
The Friend sometimes substitutes the quotation of an "authority" for the
lengthy reasoning that would be required to prove a point. Arguing in
the "Essays on Method" that an intuition of the Divine Idea must precede scientific investigation, Coleridge says that he "cannot enter on the
proof of this assertion," and instead cites Plato's approval, and Aristotle's
testimony to Plato's position.[20] Further on he quotes an authority in favor
of quoting authorities.[21] Would the criteria I have just drawn out suggest
that this was an *insincere* procedure?

Clearly not, but it does reflect Coleridge's anxious awareness of his
audience, whom he regarded as liable to dismiss purely logical writing
as "metaphysical jargon."[22] In a work intended for wide circulation, he
believes, he cannot treat every subject with logical "adequacy," so must
sometimes make do with a merely "right" notion, communicable through
"the *sweet Baits* of Literature."[23] My point is that were Coleridge instead
to have the sense of an ideally responsive audience, his theory of the
communication of truth would make it a matter of sincerity or conscience
to write as connectedly as possible, with maximum syntactical complexity to provoke maximum thought, and minimal use of the persuasive
power of rhetoric and quotation. This is precisely the case with the *Opus
Maximum*. When he dictated the manuscript, Coleridge was no longer
constrained by the financial necessity of publication. Publication was
intended but indefinitely deferred. Rather than declaim to the anonymous
hydra-headed reading public, he was able to speak as it were privately to
amanuenses and chiefly "my friend and enlightened Pupil, Mr. Green."[24]
This means that the *Opus Maximum*, attractively, lacks the reader-bait-
ing casuistry of *The Friend*, or "letter to a friend" to supply the place of
a missing transcendental deduction as in chapter thirteen of *Biographia
Literaria*. Instead, authorial addresses to the reader are respectful and
non-disruptive: the reader is quietly presumed to be a "professed
enquirer";[25] an "earnest enquirer" aware of reading a difficult work
addressed to "the speculative intellect."[26] Appealing to "the inward experience of our readers" the author awaits rather than demands a congenial

[20] *Friend*, I, 460–61.
[21] *Friend*, I, 488.
[22] *Friend*, I, 26.
[23] *Friend*, I, 23.
[24] *CL*, V, 28; March 30, 1820.
[25] *Op Max*, 22.
[26] *Op Max*, 241.

response. Again, at a difficult point the reader is counseled "not to be impatient with himself or us" if he does not at once understand.[27]

Correspondingly the *Opus Maximum* handles "authorities" very differently from *The Friend*. Whereas the latter uses authorities, as in the example of Plato and Aristotle just quoted, as a kind of shorthand to establish positions that by implication would otherwise require extended argument, the *Opus Maximum* is committed to arguing fully. Citations of authority are therefore seldom permitted to disturb Coleridge's own connected, authoritative voice. It is also significant that when Coleridge occasionally does invoke an "authority," he chooses Milton or Shakespeare — never Scripture. The few quotations of Scripture are defended explicitly as being "fit expressions" only, not authorities.[28] The surface reason for this is that the *Opus Maximum* aims to prove the "evidence à priori" of Christian doctrines, a procedure of pure Reason which renders revelatory confirmations strictly unnecessary.[29] The subtext is clear from a work Coleridge composed around the same period, *Confessions of an Inquiring Spirit*. He fears that to rely on Scripture as authority is to imply the popular but disastrous notion that the Bible was dictated by a "superhuman... Ventriloquist."[30] (Since no-one believed that the works of Milton and Shakespeare were divinely dictated, less caution was required in citing them.) Although the ventriloquistic doctrine of infallibility appears reverential to Scripture, it actually devalues it by extinguishing the congenial humanity that the prophets share with their readers. Scripture being not above human Reason but intimately involved with it, Coleridge believes he can serve it best by sustained use of his own Reason. His avoidance of scriptural props, then, represents an attempt both to accord Scripture its appropriate value and to preserve the sense of argumentative connection throughout the work.

That sense of argumentative connection raises a further point of comparison with *The Friend*. That *The Friend*'s "Essays on Method" are offered as both the basis of and introduction to Coleridge's future philosophical and theological writings suggests their importance to the endeavor of the *Opus Maximum*. Attacking schemes of arbitrary classification, the "Essays" argue that true scientific method proceeds by "progressive transition" from an initiative Idea in the mind. The initiative

---

[27] *Op Max*, 222.

[28] *Op Max*, 88; cf. 200–201.

[29] *Op Max*, 16.

[30] *Confessions of an Inquiring Spirit*, in *SW&F*, II, 1111–71; 1136. On the doctrine of infallibility as "the popular Belief," 1149; see also, J. Robert Barth, S.J., *Coleridge and Christian Doctrine* (Cambridge: Harvard University Press, 1969), 53–71.

Idea, based in the Reason, is the ground of the discursive work of the
Understanding. The affinity with the stylistic ideal of connectedness discussed above is clear: good writing like good thinking springs organically from germinal power within, as opposed to having its form mechan-
ically imposed from without. However, the ground or initiative Idea being
a truth of Reason, it is by definition incomprehensible, that is indemonstrable by the language of the Understanding. The final "Essay on
Method" appears to engage with this problem; but it actually offers a
polemic against commercialism, an abrupt transition to the well-known
passage recommending a meditation on "EXISTENCE, in and by itself, as
the mere act of existing," and a series of rhetorical exclamations and
questions designed to provoke contemplation of the burden of the mystery. Coleridge himself later regretted the lack of method in this essay's
prose.[31] As Evans writes, "his discourse is more lyrical than persuasive,"[32] the "intuition of absolute existence" being conveyed in unconnected language and without consistent terminology. This rhetorical confusion seems due to Coleridge's anxiety about readers' capacity and
appetite for sequacious reasoning, and consequent reliance on elision and
quotation of authorities at key points. Evans' excellent article contrasts the
corresponding section of the *Opus Maximum*, the concluding pages of
"On the Divine Ideas."[33] There, far from eliding, Coleridge argues fully
and with repetition. Free from publication-anxiety, Coleridge can use
extended argument, gradually demonstrating that contra Paley, no science
of God is possible. Whereas in the final essay on method Coleridge had
invoked the argument from design for its persuasive power, in "On the
Divine Ideas" he shows its inadequacy: for the senses to discern proofs
of Divine order in the world, the mind must already have a prior Idea of
the Divine. This argument is in fact repeated from a passage in "Fragment
2" in which Coleridge anticipates the shock a devout reader might feel
at learning that the Supreme Being is indemonstrable, but promises a new
source of faith thereby, since "to demonstrate a thing is to establish its
antecedent, and thus to construct the thing anew; that what is... first, can
have no antecedent, and what is absolutely One... no construction."[34]

The following directly linked claim also appears throughout the work:
"An Idea is not simply knowledge or perception as distinguished from the

---

[31] *Friend*, I, 514, 511n.3.
[32] Murray J. Evans, "The Divine Ideas in Coleridge's *Opus Maximum*: The Rhetoric
of the Indemonstrable," *The Coleridge Bulletin*, n.s. 22 (2003): 41.
[33] *Op Max*, 264–90.
[34] *Op Max*, 103.

thing perceived: it is a realizing knowledge, a knowledge causative of its own reality."[35] Ideal truth is known to be so by its own light: again, it cannot be *demonstrated*. David Vallins finds the interest in Coleridge's approach to such "philosophically insoluble problems" to "lie primarily in the circular process by which... Coleridge strives to express an intuition which itself arises primarily from that quest for expression... Coleridge's ideas of God and the processes of the human intellect are consistently characterized by an emphasis on their inexpressibleness which can only arise from a continual confrontation with the limits of language."[36] That the liminal confrontation is continual is important: Coleridge's use of repetition, of what McFarland calls a "circumvolving argument," is crucial to the power of the *Opus Maximum*.[37]

The work's circumvolutions might seem to counteract the claim I have made for the *Opus Maximum* as fulfilling *The Friend*'s ideal of connected discourse. It seems to me nevertheless defensible. Because Coleridge's foundational Ideas are indemonstrable, normal logical language, the language of proof, is necessarily inadequate to describe them: a different kind of discourse, what we might call rhetoric, is requisite. As Ernesto Grassi argues: "To prove [*apo-deiknumi*] means to *show* something to be something, on the basis of something... Apodictic, demonstrative speech... establishes the definition of a phenomenon by tracing it back to ultimate principles, or *archai*." Coleridge highlights the same "etymological sense of the word '*demonstrate*'" as showing, referring back to a prior basis.[38] The archai, or bases, themselves cannot be the object of logical, demonstrative speech, continues Grassi — otherwise they would no longer be themselves the first assertions. Archai "cannot have an apodictic, demonstrative character and structure but are thoroughly *indicative*." They "cannot have a rational but only a rhetorical character"; rhetoric is not, on this definition, "the technique of an exterior persuasion; it is rather the speech which is the basis of the rational thought."[39]

The ideal of a connected style, I have argued, would suggest a minimum of quotation, and particularly the avoidance of the quotation of

[35] *Op Max*, 223.

[36] David Vallins, *Coleridge and the Psychology of Romanticism: Feeling and Thought* (Basingstoke: Macmillan, 2000), 142.

[37] *Op Max*, 291n.1. On rhetorical tradition in relation to this point, see Wayne C. Anderson, "'Perpetual Affirmations, Unexplained': The Rhetoric of Reiteration in Coleridge, Carlyle, and Emerson," *Quarterly Journal of Speech* 71 (1985): 37–51.

[38] *Op Max*, 264.

[39] Ernesto Grassi, *Rhetoric as Philosophy: The Humanist Tradition* (University Park: Pennsylvania State University Press, 1980), 18–21; cf. *Op Max*, 264–65.

Scripture as authority. Yet clusters of other writers including Shakespeare, Milton, and Wordsworth, do appear in the work as examples or authorities, punctuating the connected flow of logical language. The very infrequency of such clusters of quotations lends them special interest. Kant, himself an important presence in the *Opus Maximum*, would have considered their use intolerably heteronomous in a work of pure reasoning. But I think they are explicable in terms of the problem just described, that for Coleridge (as for Grassi) no language can articulate the ground of demonstrated truths. All that can be communicated instead is a sense of the sublime, summoned indirectly by rhetorical repetition and judicious quotation.

The Despotism of the Eye: The Ideal of Milton

It is however important to Coleridge not to quote as he often does in *The Friend* for aesthetic delight. The first quotation of Shakespeare in "Fragment 1" is prefaced by an apologetic appeal not to pleasure but edification: "If in the present work we may without impropriety refer to the work of an author, next to Holy Writ, the most instructive…"[40] Indeed the "literary" quotations in the *Opus Maximum* nearly always seem to carry an admonitory purpose. If poetic quotation can evoke sublime indemonstrability, it is vital for Coleridge that this should not equate to substituting pictures for purely intelligible thoughts. The *Opus Maximum* mounts a sustained attack on "the LUST OF THE EYE,"[41] what in the *Biographia* was referred to more secularly as the "despotism of the eye."[42] It was after all constantly axiomatic for Coleridge that "the Eye is of all the Senses the least *reflective*, the most superficial" and that "Slavery of the Mind to the Eye" was dreadfully prevalent in contemporary philosophy, which reduces the conceivable within the bounds of the picturable.[43] If religion is a reverencing of the invisible,[44] of the Idea which cannot be demonstrated or *shown*, an empirical philosophy which reduces all Ideas in the mind to antecedent sense-impressions is necessarily irreligious. Since post-1688 culture has moved so strongly in this

---

[40] *Op Max*, 33–34.
[41] *Op Max*, 85.
[42] *BL*, I, 107.
[43] *CM*, III, 1036; quotation in *Philosophical Lectures*, ed. Kathleen Coburn (London: Pilot Press, 1949), 434; *BL*, I, 288.
[44] *Op Max*, 127; *Friend*, I, 440.

direction, "the habit of relieving" conceptual thought "by illustrations" is ingrained and requires effort to be "suspended."[45] The quotations I wish to examine thus constitute warnings against thinking in picture-language and in favor of the discipline of contemplating pure Ideas.

Quotation is scarce throughout "Fragment 1" and the *Essay on Faith*, which opens "Fragment 2." The first significant cluster of quotations occurs in the chapter "On the existential reality of the Idea of the Supreme Being." This is not surprising: it is precisely this reality that is inaccessible to logical language. So the chapter opens with a quotation from Proclus exhorting "a quiet... of imagining" and inward stillness.[46] To apprehend the Divine Idea requires "the negation of the senses": here Coleridge quotes Milton's phrase "darkness visible" — axiomatically sublime in the Romantic period — to suggest this turning inward. Plato and Luther and Simonides are summoned as witnesses to the profound difficulty of conceiving the infinite, against a naive *Spectator*-reader who can see nothing easier than to combine our notions of infinite power, infinite wisdom and infinite goodness; such satire against the simplifications of periodicals had not been possible to *The Friend*.[47] There follow brief quotations of Wordsworth, Aristophanes and Swedenborg. Then Coleridge considers the view opposite to his own, and so begins his first attack on the argument from design, as I cited above. Coleridge's rhetoric intensifies as he admits the "chill, and the shock" likely to be occasioned by the rejection of an argument for God's existence so natural, traditional, and beautiful.[48] The design argument is however engaged with the world of the senses and so tantamount in speculative terms (albeit not necessarily in the heart of the believer) to pantheism and hence irreligion, Coleridge insists. To demonstrate his own sympathy for the reverence for nature which pantheism can accompany he admits his own experience of being "lulled by these dreams," quoting a relevant nature-worshipping passage from his play *Remorse*. Most striking is the quotation of Wordsworth as an example of an ardent mind shrinking from the personal attributes of the deity, and substituting "a sense sublime/ Of something far more deeply interfused... A motion and a spirit..."[49] The imagination of Wordsworth is here identified as falling into the trap that "To

---

[45] *Op Max*, 197.
[46] *Op Max*, 96.
[47] *Op Max*, 99–100.
[48] *Op Max*, 108.
[49] *Op Max*, 113–14, quoting "Tintern Abbey" (lines 93ff.).

deduce a Deity wholly from Nature is in the result to substitute an Apotheosis of Nature for Deity."[50] Criticizing Wordsworth in a letter around this time Coleridge wrote further of "the vague misty, rather than mystic, Confusion of God with the World & the accompanying Nature-worship."[51] The "sense sublime" of "Tintern Abbey" is in the context of Coleridge's present argument dangerously delusive because it is a false sublime, arising from contemplation not of the ineffability of an Idea, but of visual phenomena.

The true sublime on the other hand is exemplified by Milton.[52] Coleridge's reverence for Milton is such that he twice even cites Milton as an "authority" for certain terms — "Arbitrement," and "discursive or intuitive" — a usage he cannot make of Scripture.[53] To invoke the sublimity of the mind's inward turn, he quotes Milton's "darkness visible," as just noted. The most substantial employment of Milton occurs in the parallel section to the chapter "On the existential reality of the Idea of the Supreme Being," the chapter "Ideas flowing out of the Divine Personeity."[54] Here Coleridge alludes again to Proclus' injunction to silence and stillness, in order to allow the still small voice to be heard which alone — without examples derived from the senses — can speak to the soul of the Divine light.[55] This light must mysteriously "divide itself from the darkness, on which a spirit higher than the individual soul hath descended and made pregnant; and as a birth, and the first day of a new creation, doth the soul contemplate it that doth indeed contemplate it." The vital echo is of the opening of *Paradise Lost*: "Thou from the first/ Wast present, and with mighty wings outspread/ Dove-like satst brooding on the vast Abyss/ And mad'st it pregnant."[56] Since Milton's

---

[50] *Op Max*, 118.

[51] *CL*, V, 95; August 8, 1820.

[52] Cf. Milton's "true sublime" distinguished from the "false sublime" of Erasmus Darwin, see *Lects 1808–1819*, I, 401.

[53] *Op Max*, 80, 86.

[54] *Op Max*, 177–213.

[55] *Op Max*, 197. The abrupt shift in metaphor from sound to light is characteristic of the Coleridgean sublime; cf. the line, "A light in sound, a sound-like power in light" added to "The Eolian Harp" in *Sybilline Leaves* in 1817 (*PW*, I.1, 233).

[56] *Op Max*, 197–98n.348, but I quote from *Paradise Lost*, ed. Alastair Fowler (New York: Longman, 1998), I, 19–22. The allusion to Milton is key, but a larger background of mysticism is also detectable. Meister Eckhart wrote in terms similar to the passage just quoted, that to "work an inward work" one must "hide himself from all images and forms." The New Birth is "accomplished in Man when he... keeps himself in silence, stillness and peace... letting God work and speak." Quoted in Evelyn Underhill, *Mysticism: A Study in the Nature and Development of Man's Spiritual Consciousness* (London,

addressee is the Holy Spirit it appears that Coleridge, via Milton, is equating the "Divine light" of an Idea with the Holy Spirit. Given that *Paradise Lost* in particular responds to (even exploits) the impossibility of describing that which is indescribable because it "surmounts the reach/ Of human sense," Milton provides perfect support for Coleridge here.[57] In a lecture Coleridge described Milton's technique as the substitution of "a grand feeling of the unimaginable for a mere image."[58] If the above-quoted "Tintern Abbey" passage represents for Coleridge a vicious clinging to the palpable, resulting in pantheism, the opening of *Paradise Lost* represents the corresponding virtue, "the sublime possibility of an entirely internal kind of poetic creativity,"[59] reflecting and encouraging a true apprehension of the Divine.

The paragraph continues Miltonically: "These words, though authorized and sanctioned by the greatest, wisest and best of the human race, will, I am but too well aware, appear to the many 'the flights of a poet soaring in the high season of his fancies, with his garland and his singing robes about him, yet even for those that consent to sit below in the cool element of prose amongst readers of no empyreal conceit,' it must appear evident on the least actual reflection that if ideas differ in kind from images, abstractions, and generalizations, and are diverse and more than these, nothing less can be declared of them."[60] Coleridge's reference to "the flights of a poet...," left unidentified by the editor, is actually a misquotation of Milton, who writes in *The Reason of Church Government*: "For although a Poet soaring in the high region of his fancies with his garland and singing robes about him might without apology speak more of himself than I mean to do, yet for me sitting here below in the cool element of prose, a mortall thing among many readers of no Empyreall conceit, to venture and divulge unusual things of my selfe, I shall petition to the gentler sort, it may not be envy to me."[61] This source substantiates McFarland's conjecture that "the greatest, wisest, and best of

---

1911, 1930), 319. The whole section of this chapter, on "Quiet," is relevant to Coleridge's procedure.

[57] *Paradise Lost*, V, 571–72.

[58] *Lects 1808–1891*, I, 311; see also, Coleridge's criticisms of illustrations of *Paradise Lost*: Robert Woof, Howard J. M. Hanley and Stephen Hebron, *Paradise Lost: The Poem and Its Illustrators* (Grasmere: The Wordsworth Trust, 2004), 34.

[59] Seamus Perry, *Coleridge and the Uses of Division* (Oxford: Clarendon Press, 1999), 214.

[60] *Op Max*, 197–98.

[61] *The Prose of John Milton*, ed. J. Max Patrick, *et al.* (Garden City, NY: Anchor Books, 1967), 107–8. In keeping with the predominantly "unliterary" nature of the *Opus*

the human race" refers at least primarily to Milton. Certainly, for Coleridge, sublime *"Ideality"*[62] is not merely an attribute of *Paradise Lost*: it is inherent in the being of the author himself. (As early as 1797 he wrote of Milton as a model for ambitious writers: "observe the march of Milton — his severe application, his laborious polish, his deep metaphysical researches, his prayers to God before he began his great poem...")[63] Further, the choice of a quotation from a passage in which Milton writes so much about himself and his ambition suggests Miltonic self-fashioning on Coleridge's part.

That Milton is a key exemplar and in particular an exemplar *against* the pantheistic aspect of Wordsworth aligns the *Opus Maximum* with *Biographia Literaria*. In *Biographia* Coleridge isolates several characteristic faults of Wordsworth's poetry, two of which involve over-enthusiastic engagement with the natural world. Firstly, Coleridge attacks Wordsworth's *"matter-of-fact-ness,"* one aspect of which is his tendency to describe objects with "laborious minuteness."[64] Secondly, he reproves Wordsworth for "thoughts and images too great for the subject," or *"mental* bombast."[65] Illustrating the latter criticism, Coleridge objects to Wordsworth's lines in "Daffodils": "They flash upon that inward eye,/

Maximum, however, Coleridge alters the substance of the quotation. Milton elevates poetry as the highest form of writing, claiming that the prose writer is also and essentially a poet; whereas Coleridge's meaning is that only the vulgar would regard his argument as the mere flights of a poet. This downgrading of poetry may be reflected in the alteration of a word: in *The Friend* (I, 44) Coleridge had misquoted the same passage (also left unidentified by the editor), but with the word: "...the high *reason* of his fancies..." (though n.2 mentions that in two manuscripts the word is *"region"* — as indeed appears in Thomas Birch's 1738 edition of Milton's prose, which Coleridge annotated in 1808). To change this in *Op Max* to *"season"* might suggest a desire to avoid linking Reason with poetic Fancy (italics mine). If Coleridge was dictating from memory, it is understandable that he might make a slip — but the slip could be Freudian. Significantly, the quotation of this passage in *The Friend* occurs in an essay in "On the Communication of Truth," in the context of the anxiety about readers I discussed earlier. Coleridge definitely associated Milton with the cultivation of "fit audience... though few" (*Paradise Lost*, VII, 31).

[62] *Lects 1808–1819*, I, 145. Perry links the term *"Ideality"* to Coleridge's celebration of "an inward creativity free from any dependence on external things or outward sense" (Perry, *Coleridge and the Uses of Division*, 215).

[63] *CL*, I, 320; early April 1797. McFarland, *Romanticism and the Forms of Ruin*, 238–54, discusses the contrasting role of Milton in the poetry of Wordsworth and Coleridge. McFarland characterizes Coleridge's relation to Milton as one of Bloomian anxiety, which induced a "false sublime" in certain of Coleridge's own poems. In these terms the more convincing sublime of the *Opus Maximum* might be seen as a stronger response to Milton than that evinced by the younger Coleridge.

[64] *BL*, II, 126.

[65] *BL*, II, 136.

Which is the bliss of solitude!" on the ground that the *inward* eye ought to have a worthier occupation than to behold images of flowers; otherwise, "in what words shall we describe the joy of retrospection, when the images and virtuous actions of a whole well-spent life, pass before that conscience which is indeed the *inward* eye: which is indeed '*the bliss of solitude*'?"[66] In contrast to Wordsworth's occasional confusion of inward with corporeal eye Coleridge cites Milton, who speaks to the Imagination instead of to the Fancy, presenting ideals rather than particulars, "*creation rather than painting*."[67]

In the *Opus Maximum* Coleridge further contrasts Milton with what he designates pantheistic poetry, that of the *Bhagavad-Gita*. He stigmatizes the work by reversing the praise of Milton just quoted: like "all Indian poetry" it attempts to "image the unimageable, not by symbols but by a jumble of Images helped out by words of number — a delirious *fancy* excludes all unifying *Imagination*."[68] The *Bhagavad-Gita* offers a false sublime, based not on the evocation of infinity but rather the unfortunately concrete evocation of a large number of large things. The translator's comparison of the work to Milton draws Coleridge's retort: "Milton!!... if there be one character of genius predominant in Milton it is this, that he never passes off bigness for greatness. Children never can make things big enough, and exactly so it is with the poets of India."[69] Coleridge indeed links "Brahman Theology" to atheism by quoting from Milton's *Samson Agonistes* on the absurdity of atheists: he would have expected that regarding Brahman sensual pantheism, "... of such doctrine never was there school,/ But the heart of the fool," were it not that such a religion does actually exist.[70] Coleridge's censure of the Sanskrit poem has an interesting parallel in Hegel, who contrasted the "affirmative sublime," pantheistic and to be found in Indian poetry, with the "negative sublime," an apprehension of the Absolute in which "the appearance falls short of the content." The "negative sublime" is negative with regard to the particular, and is to be found in Hebrew poetry such as the Psalms: "While therefore we found in the imagination of substantiality and its pantheism an infinite *enlargement*, here we have to marvel at the force of *elevation* of the mind which abandons everything in order to

[66] *BL*, II, 136–37.
[67] *BL*, II, 128.
[68] *Op Max*, 394 ("Appendix C").
[69] *Op Max*, 281.
[70] *Op Max*, 276.

declare the exclusive power of God."[71] This applies nicely to Coleridge's contrast between the *Bhagavad-Gita* and Milton. Moreover, it points to Coleridge's increasing preference for Hebrew poetry, a development of taste he may have been conscious of sharing with Milton himself.[72]

Coleridge quotes a passage from the *Bhagavad-Gita* as a focus for his objections. Enumerating the many and mighty attributes of the Supreme Being — an affirmative procedure very different from Coleridge's negative theology — this passage praises his "light immeasurable," said to be "like the ardent fire or glorius [*sic*?] Sun."[73] Perhaps it was partly this simile, unphilosophical as Coleridge would doubtless regard it, which provoked his irritation. For earlier in "Fragment 3," having circled back yet again to the theme of the indemonstrability of Ideas, Coleridge uses the sun as a symbol for the Trinity: something entirely different for Coleridge than a vague comparison between divinity and light.[74] The symbol of the sun can aid apprehension of how it is possible for the Eternal Will to diffuse itself into multiple wills, yet without diminution. Again, having reached the sublime limit of language, Coleridge turns to poetic quotation, accompanied by a warning about the despotism of the eye: specifically the "peril" of contemplating the symbol "in the spirit of the corpuscular system." The main quotation is a stanza of Henry More, and More is again quoted in the footnote. More, a prolific member of the seventeenth-century learned class Coleridge admired, provides apposite support here, being a Trinitarian who opposed the "corpuscular" philosophy of his day. Yet Coleridge's quotation of the homely verse of More also exemplifies the "unliterary" nature of the *Opus Maximum*: at a moment of such sublimity, Coleridge might have been expected instead to quote from the beginning of *Paradise Lost*, Book III: "Hail, Holy light…" Coleridge's vocabulary suggests that he did have Milton's invocation in mind. For he explains the symbol with deliberate convolution as follows: "Not more impossible is it to conceive the sun, the tri-unity

---

[71] G. W. F. Hegel, *Aesthetics: Lectures on Fine Art*, trans. T. M. Knox, 2 vols. (Oxford: Clarendon Press, 1975), I, 375 (II.ii.3), quoted in Stephen Bygrave, *Coleridge and the Self: Romantic Egotism* (London: Macmillan, 1986), 59.

[72] See, e.g., the encomium on Hebrew songs in the late work *Paradise Regained*, IV, 334–60, in *Milton: Complete Shorter Poems*, ed. John Carey (London: Longman, 1997), 498–99. Coleridge quotes part of this passage in *LS*, 8.

[73] *Op Max*, 279.

[74] In *LS* Coleridge explains, "by a symbol I mean, not a metaphor or allegory or any other figure of speech or form of fancy, but an actual and essential part of that, the whole of which it represents" (79; cf. 30, 73).

of the focus lux et lumen, to be in all its splendour and yet rayless than to conceive the spiritual sun without its effluence, the essentially causative Will without its co-eternal products."[75] The co-eternal products, here figured as the rays of the sun, are the second and third persons of the Trinity. Milton writes of "the *eternal co-eternal* beam"; and "Bright *effluence* of bright essence increate" (emphases mine): so there is at least a verbal echo. Why did Coleridge not refer explicitly to this passage, which he elsewhere implied to be one of the most sublime in *Paradise Lost*?[76] Probably it was a matter of theological scrupulosity — it is unclear whether Milton's lines bear a Trinitarian interpretation or not.[77] I suspect Coleridge's omission of the quotation despite partial recollection of it hints that he doubted Milton's orthodoxy with regard to the Trinity. This interpretation may be supported by the fact that in a notebook entry of 1825 Coleridge expresses dismay at the Arianism of Milton's newly discovered treatise, *De Doctrina Christiana*.[78]

Whatever Coleridge's view on this, however, it is clear that he summons Milton at crucial moments in the *Opus Maximum*. As I have already suggested, this may best be seen in the light of Coleridge's self-identification with Milton in earlier writing. The presence of Milton both explicit and implicit in *Biographia Literaria* is well documented, and extends beyond the Wordsworth criticism I cited above.[79] An allusive self-identification with Milton appears in particular in the notorious "letter from a friend" of chapter 13: in comparing Coleridge's theory of Imagination to "the fragments of the winding steps of an old ruined tower," the "friend" alludes (as Nigel Leask points out) to the ruined tower of Babylon, and hence to the ruin of Coleridge's own early faith in the ability of humankind to join forces to build a mighty republic. The biblical

---

[75] *Op Max*, 244–45.

[76] *Lects 1808–1819*, II, 428.

[77] For a critical summary, see Fowler, ed., *Paradise Lost*, 165–66.

[78] *CN*, IV, 5240; cf. 5262. *De Doctrina Christiana* was discovered in 1823 and published in a translation by C. R. Sumner (Cambridge, 1825). Much as Coleridge apparently feared, the British and Foreign Unitarian Association seized on it, publishing anti-Trinitarian extracts in *John Milton's Last Thoughts on the Trinity*, ed. Harriet Martineau (London, 1828).

[79] On Coleridge's discussion of Milton, excellent is Perry, *Coleridge and the Uses of Division*, chapter 5, esp. 209–33. On Coleridge's self-identification with Milton in the service of anti-Wordsworth argument, see Raimonda Modiano, "Coleridge and Milton: The Case Against Wordsworth in the *Biographia Literaria*," in Frederick Burwick, ed., *Coleridge's Biographia Literaria: Text and Meaning* (Columbus: Ohio State University Press, 1989), 150–70, where however that "case" seems to me overstated.

allusion simultaneously recalls the disappointed Milton's appeal in 1660 to English citizens in *The Ready and Easy Way to Establish a Free Commonwealth*, as the republican ideals for which Milton had fought were inexorably crumbling: what has happened, asks Milton, to "this goodly Tower of Commonwealth, which the *English* boasted they would build to overshadow Kings, and be another *Rome* in the West?"[80]

Accordingly Coleridge's retirement from the literary, political, and personal fray to his fit audience, though few, in Highgate in a sense parallels that of Milton after 1660, writing *Paradise Lost* in hiding in a now-hostile London. So at least it seemed to Coleridge when he wrote a note on *Paradise Lost* around 1818 or 1819, with an eye on his own situation: notwithstanding "an apparently unhappy choice in marriage," insists Coleridge poignantly, Milton's poetry shows him truly "susceptible of domestic enjoyments." Milton "was, as every truly great poet has been, a good man; but finding it impossible to realize his own aspirations, either in religion or politics, or society, he gave up his heart to the living spirit and light within him, and avenged himself on the world by enriching it with this record of his own transcendent ideal."[81] There is much of that spirit in Coleridge's later work, and the *Opus Maximum* has real parallels with *Paradise Lost*. Both works were written by dictation; both have free will as a central theme;[82] both are written in a style of extreme and unconventional complexity; both record a vision of hope in the face of overwhelming disappointment. The parallels should not be labored, of course, given the formal contrast: *Paradise Lost* is poetry, the *Opus Maximum* prose, and a prose mostly resistant to the sweet baits of literature. Yet the general similarities between Coleridge and Milton did strike a contemporary: De Quincey comments that like Milton, "Coleridge, also, is a poet; Coleridge, also, was mixed up with the fervent politics of his age — an age how memorably reflecting the revolutionary agitations of Milton's age; Coleridge, also, was an extensive and brilliant scholar."[83] And when Coleridge expressed his hope that the *Opus Maximum* would bring him, "[f]ame in the noblest sense of the word," he invoked Milton

---

[80] Quoted in Leask, *The Politics of Imagination in Coleridge's Critical Thought* (Basingstoke: Macmillan, 1988), 133.

[81] Quoted in David Vallins, ed., *Coleridge's Writings. Volume 5, On the Sublime* (New York: Palgrave, 2003), 96.

[82] Coleridge emphasized this in his readings of *Paradise Lost*: in opposition to Calvinism "Milton asserted the will, but declared for the enslavement of the will out of an act of the will itself" (*Lects 1808–1819*, II, 426).

[83] De Quincey, *Works*, 15:106.

again — this time the passage on fame in *Lycidas*.[84] Since in this passage the noblest kind of fame is said to be "fame in heaven," Coleridge's allusion discloses the truly epic or Miltonic scale of his ambition. Finally, it is curious that Coleridge saw Milton as enriching the world by "avenging himself" on it through *Paradise Lost*, given the weight of polemic in the *Opus Maximum* against "the prejudices of a rude and barbarous age": the phrase "barbarous age" echoing the prefix to *Paradise Lost*.[85]

The Symbiosis of Conscience and Consciousness: Shakespeare as Exemplar

I have suggested that Milton functions as an authority for Coleridge not only locally but even for the whole enterprise of the *Opus Maximum*. Locally, Milton exemplifies ideality, sublime detachment from the senses; taken whole, he exemplifies the power to construct a great work in the face of disillusionment. Yet Coleridge introduces one writer even more grandiloquently, as "an author, next to Holy Writ, the most instructive…"[86] This is Shakespeare. Coleridge's one substantial citation of Shakespeare addresses a moral topic central to his work, and in doing so briefly revisits his earlier Shakespeare criticism: conscience and its relation to consciousness. The opening assertion in "Fragment 1" is that there exists a responsible Will, defined as "the *power* of *originating* a *state*."[87] Every human being, on reflection, is necessarily conscious of this power, a power evidently lacked by animals, which equates to admitting that unlike animals we possess "conscious responsibility." However much mechanical philosophers might try to argue against the existence of conscience, the inward testimony is inescapable. "[T]he consciousness of a conscience is itself conscience."[88] The symbiosis of conscience and consciousness intimated here is vital throughout "Fragment 1" and indeed the whole work: Coleridge goes forth to argue in "Fragment 2" that since moral responsibility is the defining feature of humanity, conscience is in fact logically prior to consciousness. Our Will means that we are conscious (even if we refuse to admit the fact) of having free choice as to

---

[84] *CL*, V, 28 (March 30, 1820), to Thomas Allsop, referring to *Lycidas*, lines 64–84 (*Milton: Complete Shorter Poems*, 247–49).
[85] *Op Max*, 115 and n.135.
[86] *Op Max*, 33–34.
[87] *Op Max*, 18.
[88] *Op Max*, 21.

whether or not we obey Reason, which dictates to us the moral law or
Divine Will. Insofar as our finite Will strays from the Divine Will, our
conscience is a "bad" conscience. The reference to Shakespeare forms
part of Coleridge's refutation of the opposite view, namely that all actions
originate in "motives," that rather than possessing free will we are continually driven by outside forces, and behave altruistically only as a means
to a pleasurable end — the self-satisfaction of having a good conscience.
This is intuitively false, claims Coleridge: instead of looking to isolated
and exterior motives to explain a person's actions, we should ask instead
what a person habitually seeks, "thence deducing the state of the Will."[89]

So far Coleridge's argument is thoroughly Kantian.[90] However where
Kant attempts a priori reasoning exclusively, avoiding the "heteronomous" use of examples, Coleridge conveys the sublimity of the
moral law through a literary citation. He invokes Shakespeare as the
author next to Holy Writ most instructive: he claims that one must perceive the truth of the existence of the responsible will and concomitant
superfluity of "motives" in order, "to understand (I might say Shakespeare generally, but more particularly) the character of Iago, who is represented as now assigning one and now another and again a third motive
for his conduct, each a different motive and all alike the mere fictions of
his own restless nature, distempered by a keen sense of his own intellectual superiority and a vicious habit of assigning the precedence or primacy
to the intellectual instead of the moral, and haunted by the love of exerting power on those especially who are his superiors in moral and practical estimation."[91]

In Coleridge's terms, Iago wills to silence conscience, living as an
intellectually superior animal; but since humanity *is* conscience, that is
strictly impossible. Shakespeare portrays the character of Iago as inconsistent because, denying his own higher nature, he restlessly seeks substitutes for it. Thus Iago's final soliloquy, noted Coleridge for a lecture,
displays "the motive-hunting of motiveless Malignity."[92] "Yet," continues Coleridge in the *Opus Maximum*, "how many among our modern

[89] *Op Max*, 33.
[90] For a detailed discussion, see Jeffrey Hipolito, "'Conscience the Ground of Consciousness': The Moral Epistemology of Coleridge's *Aids to Reflection*," *Journal of the
History of Ideas* 65 (2004): 454–74.
[91] *Op Max*, 33–34. Elinor Shaffer discusses this passage extensively ("Iago's Malignity Motivated: Coleridge's Unpublished 'Opus Magnum,'" *Shakespeare Quarterly* 19
[1968]: 195–203), arguing helpfully for "the very close connection between Coleridge's
metaphysical preoccupations and his practical criticism" (195).
[92] *Lects 1808–1819*, II, 315.

critics have attributed to the profound author this, the appropriate incon-sistency of the character itself."[93] Critics, in other words, accuse Shake-speare of endowing Iago with insufficient motive for his crimes, of char-acterizing him inconsistently. But in Coleridge's view "motives" are precisely the red-herrings Iago grasps at in order to disguise from him-self the diseased state of his own will — his bad conscience. Inconsis-tency of character is the inevitable result of such a desperate moral state. A priori reasoning can establish this truth, but for Coleridge it was Shake-speare "who alone could feel & yet know how to embody these concep-tions, with as curious a felicity as the thoughts are subtle."[94] As the invo-cation of Shakespeare as quasi-scriptural suggests, Coleridge saw examples of the primacy of conscience in several of his characters: like Iago, Macbeth seeks to evade the whispers of conscience, but "[e]ver & ever mistaking the anguish of Conscience for Fears of Selfishness, and thus as a punishment of that Selfishness, plunging deeper in guilt & ruin."[95] The exemplarity of Iago in the *Opus Maximum* is significantly double. Iago is immoral and hence inconsistent. Behind Iago, though, is the perfectly consistent and moral author, Shakespeare himself.

The inconsistency of Iago is evidently the condition opposite to that wholeness, connectedness, or sincerity which Coleridge exhorts and attempts to exemplify in his writing. Because of his elevation of the intel-lectual over the moral, Iago could not be farther removed from the ideal of method articulated in *The Friend* and achieved in the *Opus Maximum*. For the man of method, according to *The Friend*, embodies the proper synthesis of conscience and consciousness: "If the idle are described as killing time, he may be justly said to call it into life and moral being, while he makes it the distinct object not only of the consciousness, but of the conscience."[96] The methodical consciousness imparts a moral imperative to each chain of thoughts. In *The Friend*, too, Coleridge turns to a Shakespearean character to exemplify the ideal. Hamlet, the literary character in whom Coleridge most saw his own reflection, always refers particular observations to "general truth," and displays maximum "exu-berance of mind."[97] Thus in the midst of his narrative of his eventful

---

[93] *Op Max*, 34. To my knowledge this sentence is not to be found in Coleridge's ear-lier comments on Iago and so is unique to the *Opus Maximum*.

[94] *CN*, II, 3215.

[95] *Lects 1808–1819*, II, 309–10.

[96] *Friend*, I, 450.

[97] *Friend*, I, 454. For a clear, critical account, see J. R. de J. Jackson, *Method and Imag-ination in Coleridge's Criticism* (London: Routledge & K. Paul, 1969), esp. 36–47, 149–56.

voyage to England, he remarks as an apparently irrelevant, but in fact connected aside, *"There's a divinity that shapes our ends ..."* Yet once again the exemplarity is double: the example of the character Hamlet is partly negative, the example of Shakespeare himself perfectly positive. The intensely unworldly Hamlet is "meditative to excess," so should in fact be followed as an illustration of method only with "due abatement and reduction."[98] It is "our 'myriad-minded Bard'" who by his own methodical consciousness animates his characters to epitomize certain states of mind.

Conclusion

To compare the *Opus Maximum* with *The Friend* and *Biographia Literaria* might appear odd, unless to note that Coleridge's literary interests were in the later work firmly subordinated to the theological and philosophical. This is partly true: liberated from anxiety about his readership, Coleridge came closer than ever before to an "unliterary" work written in an austere, connected prose. Yet Coleridge is not a straightforward Kantian: he at no stage regards *a priori* reasoning as the exclusive tool for the communication of truth. That which demonstrative language cannot express, the ground or initiative Idea from which demonstration or method proceeds, must be evoked by other means. At several pivotal moments, Coleridge summons the sublime through warning about its opposite, the trap of the despotism of the eye. He achieves this through quotation or citation, of Wordsworth as a negative exemplar, of Milton and Shakespeare as positive. Milton especially functions as an authority within the text, a role Scripture cannot play. It would be possible to accuse Coleridge of inconsistency in introducing such moments into a work of logic. The apologies with which he prefaces some of the "literary" citations suggest that he feared this. Yet just as Coleridge's Shakespeare is exonerated from inconsistency because he methodically animates his inconsistent characters, so Coleridge himself manifests a level of connectedness which should prevent us from consigning his works to different disciplines. "Blind is that man," wrote De Quincey combatively in 1845, "who can persuade himself that the interest in Coleridge, *taken as a total object*, is becoming an obsolete

---

[98] *Friend*, I, 452.

interest."[99] 160 years later, with the benefit of a complete *Collected Coleridge*, the opportunity for taking Coleridge as a total object is greater than ever.

---

[99] De Quincey, *Works*, 15:105.

DUTY AND POWER: CONFLICTS OF THE WILL IN COLERIDGE'S CREATION OF THE SELF

By GRAHAM DAVIDSON

The Duty of Reason

Forms of the Will

The existence of the Will as the foundation of human individuality is an idea that permeates Coleridge's thinking. In 1803, for instance, he asserted that "My will and I seem perfect Synonimes,"[1] contradicting Kant's association of Will and Reason. Twenty-seven years later, in 1830, pretty much the same thought recurs to him: "The deep confirmation of the I with the Will —."[2] By this conjunction he opposed the discrete conceptions of the self proposed by the materialists,[3] and eventually sought to ground and unify all experience in the absolute. So it is no surprise to find that the Will takes center stage as the postulate and premise of the *Opus Maximum*.[4]

But manifestations of the Will are complex, and I think we can distinguish something like three orders in Coleridge's thinking in the *Opus*: the first is materialist, serving our appetites and desires, the will of self-love which Coleridge associated with what he calls the animal part of our double nature and which if given primacy creates a phantom self; the second is rational, of Reason, the law of conscience, the moral moving towards the spiritual in us, and which identifies self as other; the third is what Coleridge calls "the Absolute will" that transcends finite existence, and to borrow Emily Bronte's words, would not cease to be, though earth and man were gone.

---

[1] *CN*, I, 1717.

[2] *CN*, V, 6274.

[3] Cf. Anya Taylor, *Coleridge's Defense of the Human* (Columbus: Ohio State University Press, 1986), *passim*.

[4] For a résumé of Coleridge's concept of the will, see Thomas McFarland's "Prolegomena," part XVII (*Op Max*, cxix–cxxv). McFarland regards Boehme as the source of Romantic interest in the will for all but Kant. Yet, despite his early disagreement with Kant, Coleridge's thinking is closer to Kant than to Boehme, whose "eternal unfathomable will of life" (*Op Max*, cxxi) seems to have inspired later thinkers such as Nietzsche, whose views are antithetical to Coleridge's concept of the spiritual, and closer to his concept of a *"blind Will"* (*CN*, V, 6143).

I want to consider the ways in which Coleridge has worked out the relations between these modes or types of the will; and I am going to pay particular attention to the *rational* and the *animal*,[5] which he often opposed to each other, and which become the prime sources of Duty and Power. What I hope to show is that the theoretical opposition he posited in the realization of the adult self is not consistent with what he says about the development of the self through the relations between mother and child. His insistence on this polarization, maintained in the *Opus* fragments, is less assertive in some notebook entries, and we will see that the theoretical conflict is partially unmasked by his own, almost tragic, experience later in life.

Sciential Reason and the Moral Will

The moral will is an idea or truth of Reason, and, Coleridge believed, is not a proper subject of the discursive Understanding unless the Understanding is itself informed by the ideas of Reason. To deny this, as materialist schools of philosophy certainly do, is to remove the prime distinction between humanity and the animals, to remove the possibility of the soul, and therefore the hope of immortality. However, although Coleridge believes that the truths of Reason are the truths of our distinct humanity, he also thinks that they are of the same order as the intellectual and logical truths to which we are bound to give our assent, and "the act itself of reasoning and imagining" is "the only practical ingredient" in the developing "superstructures of the pure intellect."[6] That is, these orders of truth may be arrived at by acts of reasoning and imagining which are independent of our assent to them; they have a logical necessity, assent to which is not in the gift of the will, but in the power of the intellect. The kind of truths that Coleridge is likely to have used for illustration are the theorems of geometry,[7] failure to understand which does not put the status of our humanity in question.

Rather than treating moral ideas and insights as an order of truth distinct from the sciential or logical, Coleridge seeks to substantiate moral thought with the same system of logic as that which substantiates the truths of the pure intellect. From his point of view one can see the dangers of doing it any other way. If truths of the pure intellect, and subsequently of the practical intellect, are permitted to exist on a different basis

---

[5] *Op Max*, 14.
[6] *Op Max*, 5.
[7] *Op Max*, 6.

than that of the moral or human, then at some stage there will inevitably be a severance of the two. Moreover, our experience will tell us that nothing "out there," which is how we think of sciential truths, bears any relationship to what is "in here," which is how we think of moral truths. The truths of our humanity will therefore have no belonging in this world, and the subjective and the objective will have no correlation, no interdependence. In the terms of his essay "On the Prometheus of Aeschylus," our *nous* will have no *nomos*, our being will have no home.[8]

But if assent to sciential truths is unconditionally necessary just to the extent that the intellect is capable of comprehending them, then these truths remain independent of personal volition. Further, if that unconditional necessity also applied to moral truths, then of course we would become automata, not persons, not human beings. In other words, the moral "must in some sense... be necessary, or it could have no point of connexion with the sciences; and yet it must not be unconditionally so, or it would be one and the same with science."[9] So Coleridge declares that "the power of withholding and, indirectly at least, of refusing our assent to the necessary foundation of an intellectual superstructure forms the essential difference between the moral and sciential systems."[10] I think it is worth noting here his use of the word "necessary." The difference between sciential truths and moral truths is not the universality of the first and the diversity or relativeness of the second: both are "necessary" since they both exist under the same conditions of logical necessity as truths of Reason. The difference is only in our ability to deny moral ideas without intellectual absurdity. Both sciential and moral truths belong to the order of Reason and are universal; but that raises the question whether Coleridge has not conflated two terms that ought to be distinct even if not divided: reason, intellectual and logical, and Reason, spiritual and moral.

However, Coleridge's determination to maintain the co-ordination of sciential and moral truths has consequences that move us towards the polarization of the will, and thus of the self, into its two opposing forms of the animal and the rational. Since moral ideas are the mark of our humanity, their rejection is a rejection of our humanity, the rejection of the difference between our self and the animal. To all those who justify

---

[8] This is perhaps the origin of the division between Faith and Reason that so troubled subsequent generations, and which Coleridge had the wisdom to foresee and attempted to forestall.

[9] *Op Max*, 8.

[10] *Op Max*, 6.

their appetites and desires by comparing them with those of animals or beasts, Coleridge declares, "[b]ut you are not a beast, for beasts are not capable of reasoning; and you are not a man, for you disown the principles of reason."[11] So the very close association Coleridge has made here between reasoning, the logical and intellectual process, and the principles of Reason, the generic term for moral and spiritual truths, is the foundation of his system. To reject unconditionally necessary intellectual truths is simply an absurdity; to reject moral truths, though these are conditional, constitutes a dereliction of one's humanity.

Moral Responsibility and the Existence of the Will

This system of sciential reasoning appears to be an attempt to place the moral Will upon a firm foundation. But though the existence of the Will is the general premise of the *Opus*, it is not postulated just at the outset, but repeatedly throughout "Fragment 1," and each appeal carries with it some variation. For instance, Coleridge writes that if the assumption of "the Existence of the *Will*" is granted, then "a moment's reflexion will convince us [that it is] the same as *Moral Responsibility*, and that again with the reality and essential difference of moral *Good* and *Evil*."[12] Coleridge refers back to this concatenation of terms as "the one great and inclusive postulate and moral axiom — the actual being of a *responsible Will*. À fortiori, therefore, the actual being of WILL in genere."[13] What I sense, though this may be more a matter of grammar than logic, is that these successive appeals involve a reversal of terms. In the first the postulated existence of the will leads to moral responsibility, and in the second "the inclusive postulate" of a "*responsible Will*" leads to the conception of will in general. Later, he speaks of having proved that "a responsible Will is not only the postulate of all religion but the necessary datum incapable from its very nature of any direct proof."[14] Further still, Coleridge affirms the assumption that one cannot reject moral ideas without forfeiting one's distinction from "bestial nature" as "comprized in one position: *man is a responsible agent*, and in consequence *hath a Will*." Immediately Coleridge goes on to question his own

---

[11] *Op Max*, 9.
[12] *Op Max*, 11.
[13] *Op Max*, 17.
[14] *Op Max*, 32; though isn't this the first we have heard of a lack of direct proof?

assertion, "'Have I a responsible Will? Concerning this each individual must be himself exclusively both querist and respondent."[15]

What is evident here, beneath any superficial inconsistency, is the unlikeness of moral truths to "the structures of the pure intellect." The admission of the impossibility of direct proof, of the necessity of each individual making one's own inquiries as to the existence of the will, puts the whole argument on a footing quite different to that with which it originated, and it now begins to move under the shadow of "duty." Thus, after discussing the injunction, "Do to others as ye would that others should do unto you," he looks to Kant for support: "... I am conscious of a somewhat within me which peremptorily commands the above, that it is a primary and unconditional injunction (hence termed the *categorical imperative*) which neither derives its authority nor permits it to be derived from any reason or source extrinsic to itself, nor anterior except where it is implied in itself..."[16] This is a looking in of the individual upon oneself, not a looking outward to external, logical, and verifiable proofs.[17] If Coleridge appears to have abandoned his original hope of demonstrating the co-ordination of sciential and moral truths, some anticipation of this difficulty is present much earlier in his argument. Chapter IV of "Fragment 1" begins with his making the distinction "between the two possible assertions, 'such a truth may be known as truth by the light of reason' and 'the same truth was discovered, or might have been discovered, by men by means of their reason exclusively.'"[18] It is the exclusive use of reason to discover the truths of Reason which

---

[15] *Op Max*, 54.

[16] *Op Max*, 58–59. The moral precept is, of course, derived from the biblical accounts of Matt. 7:12 and Luke 6:31.

[17] The proposition that the will is at the heart of the matter, and is not susceptible of rational proof, points us towards existentialism. Should we therefore think of Coleridge as some sort of proto-existentialist, as did Herbert Read (*Friend*, I, 514n.2)? Probably not, principally because he did not abandon the idea of God, and so some ultimate authority to which the human will must refer. Coleridge is conscious of "the twofold will, of Grace & of the Flesh" (*CN*, V, 6274) and associates the former with the absolute Will of God to realize that which in ourselves is the object of our duty. Secondly, he offers both a description and condemnation of the existential will in a note in *The Friend*: "When I call duelling, and similar aberrations of honor, a moral heresy, I refer to the force of the Greek αιρεσιξ, as signifying a principle or opinion taken up by THE WILL for *the will's sake*, as a proof and pledge to itself of its own power of self-determination, independent of all other motives" (*Friend*, I, 426–27*). The note goes on to use the word "existentialism" in respect of this function of the will. Coleridge would clearly not have accepted the moral independence that current existentialists are happy to associate with the will.

[18] *Op Max*, 12.

Coleridge rejects, and he develops the metaphor of priming a pump to illustrate his point.[19] He is open therefore to reflection on what the senses can bring as aids to Reason, and affirms this position clearly towards the end of the chapter: "… when we affirm of any moral or religious truth [that] it is susceptible of rational or philosophic demonstration, we are so far from implying that the knowledge of its truth had its primary origin in the unaided efforts of human reason that we regard the present existence and actual exercise of such a power as the result of a revelation which had, by enlightening the mind, roused, disciplined, and invigorated all its faculties and appealed to experience and history for the confirmation of the fact."[20] This would legitimize any use of sense and appearance which reveals or promises to reveal a truth of Reason. And such an opportunity does seem to arise early in his argument. For example, there is a particularly attractive definition of the will: he describes it as "the *power* of *originating* a *state*."[21] We can see its general applicability: I close a door. Have I originated a state? Certainly I have changed one, yet if a closed door is a state, then I have originated it. Of course, from Coleridge's point of view, this application is fraught with difficulty: what if a dog pushes the door open again? We have to say that the dog has originated another state; but it is a beast, and has no morally responsible will, and therefore, presumably, it is incapable of originating a state. Previously, Coleridge provided the basis of a solution to these potential difficulties by describing such non-human acts as "Tendencies, Propensities," denying that we need "the term 'Will' to express them."[22] Nonetheless, because he granted a measure of Understanding to animals, it may be more difficult to create a clear distinction between the Will and Tendencies than he admits, and this is why he would not readily associate the Understanding with his definitions of the Will.

And yet his metaphor of sense priming the pump of Reason, his belief that "[t]hroughout all Nature there is seen an evolution from within"[23] seems a principle perfectly applicable to the natural impulse of men for women, avoiding what I feel is a damaging division between the animal and the rational — of the natural impulse of women for men he says nothing. He might have looked upon the actual

---

[19] *Op Max*, 14–15.
[20] *Op Max*, 15.
[21] *Op Max*, 18; cf. *CN*, IV, 5256.
[22] *Op Max*, 17.
[23] *Op Max*, 120.

behavior of men and women, rather than looking at the rakes of his time or the rakish feelings most have and few act on. The habits of the English working classes may not seem to offer a propitious beginning to the proponents of idealism, but I remember some years ago seeing a Ford Escort with a green sunvisor stuck to the inside of the windscreen, and "Tracy and Trevor 2gether 4 ever" inscribed into it. Well, where did that idea of permanence, even of eternity, come from? Not out of Trevor's lust for Tracy, or Tracy's feeling that Trevor was "fit." That hint of the ideal embedded in a world of sense might have served as a very good beginning for Coleridge, which late in his life and in another context he took. In the album of a young lady about to be married, he wrote that "it is the blest prerogative of conjugal Faith & Love to turn the common water of our animal life to the wine of *Human Gladness!*"[24]

Or to consider an internal rather than an external act: I wish a man success. The condition of my mind has moved from either not wanting or indifference to another's success to wishing it, and the act has originated in my will. So we can see how this attractive definition of the will could be applied to the many levels of human action, and we could imagine, say, that in the proposed fashion of the *Biographia*, Coleridge might have begun in the Cis-Alpine regions of the Understanding, and worked his way up the rivers and streams of consciousness to the Trans-Alpine territories of Reason. However, he steers us clear of attempting any immediate application by calling this "but a verbal definition of the Will," which neither tells us what it really is nor whether the power really exists. We are immediately prevented from sinking into the comfort of a reliable definition, of a definition that can be discerned or discussed by the Understanding, and told that because of its power to "absolutely begin a state or mode of being... It must be ens simplicissimum, and therefore incapable of explication or explanation."[25] This is moving us towards an idea of the absolute will, and it is one of the curiosities of Coleridge's system that not only does the moral will not have its origins in the Understanding, but that it very rarely seems to call upon the Understanding for its functioning; if one can speak of a will of the Understanding at all, then Coleridge tends to think of it as the will of the flesh, the will of self-love and of what is fallen or evil.

[24] *SW&F*, II, 1507; Coleridge's comment is founded on Luther's *Colloquia mensalia*.
[25] *Op Max*, 18.

The Phantom Self

Though he is not an out-and-out soul and bodyist, Coleridge's system is
an *either/or* rather than a *both/and*, requiring the fully independent existence of the soul to exist at all, as McFarland points out.[26] The consequence of this severe distinction, if not absolute division, is that the will
of the individual may orientate itself in one way or the other, but not in
a way that permits the full co-ordination of the animal and the rational,
or the progression from one to the other. Sense is not allowed its priming function. The demands of the natural life are at best servants in the
kingdom of Reason; at worst, and more often in Coleridge's terms, they
are little more than muzzled beasts. Indeed, Coleridge speaks of the pleasure derived from sense as no more than a "harnessed buffalo," an image
which bespeaks considerable power, if nothing human.[27] His habitually
pejorative language in respect of ordinary human hopes and desires
ensures that there is no path from sense to spirit, nothing that might "body
up to spirit work."[28] In turn, we move towards the creation of a self that
is either evil or good. In one's original choice lies one's final destiny, and
thus those who begin in sense create "a false and phantom self"[29] as he
describes in a notebook entry of 1829: "The Voluptuary *begins* with a
desperate error — he seeks his *Self* in that which is only the common root
of his animal Life, i.e. in his *Nature*... And then having given this false
meaning to *the Self*, he offends by *seeking* it, when he should be seeking
and finding a nobler Self in the love and Service of his Neighbor — first,
his Neighbors *in place* — secondly, *in time* — i.e. his own FUTURE
Self, his *Soul*."[30] And so, paradoxically, anyone who does not seek the
self in this second or third person sense, as Thou, or as a neighbor, is at
risk of finding one's "conscience... suspended, or, as it were, drowned
in the inundations of the appetites, passions, and imaginations to which
the man had, and in the beginning willingly, resigned himself, making use
of his Will in order to abandon his Free-will."[31]

---

[26] *Op Max*, 14n.22.

[27] *Op Max*, 48.

[28] A phrase from *Paradise Lost* V, prefacing Chapter XIII, on the Imagination, in the
Biographia (*BL*, I, 295).

[29] *Op Max*, 31.

[30] *CN*, V, 6144.

[31] *Op Max*, 71–72; cf. Coleridge's earlier suggestion that "... we have it in our power
to contemplate our objective self and our neighbour as morally equidistant..." (69).
Coleridge's co-ordination of a sense of duty with the idea of self as a third party can be
traced back some years; cf. an earlier notebook in which he speaks of "the unindividual

Coleridge has steadily boxed himself in. Reticulating the ideas of Reason, Conscience and Duty he notes that if "nothing diverse from the position ("it is my duty") can be true, and nothing different can be placed
before it, it follows that the moral imperative or obligation of duty is...
underived, self-grounded, therefore unconditional..."[32] It is an act, in his
system, preceding all others; he often states, the act of conscience precedes consciousness and so it is "the indispensable pre-condition of all
experience."[33] This act, of conscience or duty, is one "in which and by
which we take upon ourselves an allegiance, and consequently the obligations of fealty. And this fealty, or fidelity, implying the power of being
unfaithful, is the *primary* and *fundamental meaning* of FAITH."[34]
Towards the end of the first chapter of "Fragment 2," one in which he
has been describing paragraph by paragraph "those constituents of the
total man, which are either contrary to or disparate from the reason,"[35]
Coleridge summarizes his findings in this remarkable peroration: "This
brings us to the last and fullest sense of 'Faith': namely, Faith is the obedience of the individual Will to reason — in the lusts of the flesh, opposed
to the supersensual (§1); in the lusts of eye, as opposed to the supersen-
suous (§2); in the pride of the understanding, or faculty of the finite, as
opposed to the super-finite, the mind of the flesh... in contrariety to spiritual truth (§3); in the lusts of the Will, as opposed to the absolute and
universal (§4); and in the love of the creature, as far as it is in opposition to the love which is one with reason, namely the love of God (§5)."[36]
This is a reality which few of us can contemplate with much equanim-
ity, and which Coleridge only began to realize towards the end of his life.

Sense, Understanding, and the Sources of Power

Coleridge's conception of the harmfulness of any realization of the self
that begins with the will looking to the finite is of course not shared by
those whom he calls "the Doctors of Self-love,"[37] whom he barely distinguishes from "voluptuaries." Though he clearly equates atheism with

---

nature of the idea, Self or Soul... conceived apart from our present living Body and the
world of the senses" (*CN*, III, 4007; November 1810).

[32] *Op Max*, 64–65.
[33] *Op Max*, 72.
[34] *Op Max*, 72.
[35] *Op Max*, 85.
[36] *Op Max*, 93–94. This chapter comprises the *Essay on Faith*.
[37] *Op Max*, 29.

this method of creating the self, not all are as materialistic and atheistic as he likes to paint them. He believed, for instance, that Vico, a thinker he much admired after he began to read him in 1825, asserted that self-love is the origin of society. Coleridge described what he took as Vico's idea of the individual's progress to a social being having its beginning in Self-love, or *amour propre*: "Hence the single Savage is influenced solely by the principle of Self-preservation. He takes a woman, begets children, who remain with him. Habit, Appetite, the Services of the Woman, gradually form a part of the confused reflection, or mental Object, which he calls himself, and he then seeks the safety of his Family." From families develop a rising hierarchy of tribes, towns, and cities that are incorporated into the state. It is not this fact, but the limitation of this process to the rules of the Understanding with which Coleridge takes issue: "All this is true as far as Conduct depends on the Understanding: The mistake consists in taking it, either as the adequate description of *Human Nature*, of the entire Man, on the one hand, or as the ground and rule of Morality on the other."[38] As a description of human nature, Coleridge calls this flattery, there are passions and prejudices in us *below* the Understanding that will undermine this simplistic progress; as a basis of moral action he calls it "detraction"; there is something in us *above* the Understanding, a greatness, a spiritual hope not accounted for by this scheme. Still, earlier in his life Coleridge was himself open to very similar schemes. In a lecture on *Romeo and Juliet*, given in 1811 or 1812, Coleridge discusses marriage, without which "the world and its business may be carried on"; but, "[f]rom this union arose the filial[,] maternal[,] brotherly and sisterly relations of life[;] and every State is but a family magnified: all the operations of the mind — all that distinguished us from mere brute animals arises from the more perfect state of domestic life."[39]

It is a powerful thought that in the idea of marriage are present "all the operations of mind" that distinguish us from brutes: whatever marriage

---

[38] *CN*, IV, 5209; May 1825.

[39] *Lects 1808–19*, I, 315. Coleridge rehearses variants of this idea in the next lecture: "… for without marriage, without exclusive attachment there could be no human society: herds there might be but society there could not be: there could be none of that delightful intercourse between Father & child: none of the sacred affections none of the charities of humanity" (330); "[b]y dividing the sisterly & fraternal from the conjugal affections we have in truth two loves; each of them as strong as any affection can be or ought to be consistently with the performance of our duty and the love we bear to our neighbour... To all this is to be added the beautiful gradations of attachment which distinguishes human nature: from sister to wife[,] from wife to child, to Uncle, cousin, one of our kin, one of our blood, our mere neighbour, our county-man or our countryman" (332).

is, it is certainly something that belongs to the body as well as to the soul, to the Understanding as much as to Reason. Interestingly, in his Shakespeare lectures Coleridge recognizes the method by which "the body may up to spirit work," and that it is of a kind with the method by which the Imagination produces poetry: Collier's notes state that, "[i]n poetry Coleridge had shewn that it was the blending of passion with order & still more in morals & more than all was it (which woe be to us if we did not at some time contemplate in a moral view solely) the exclusive attachment of the Sexes to each other."[40]

Later, the nature of this progress is made explicit. Referring to the power of reverence, Coleridge records that Plato "had said that by this we rose from sensuality to affection, from affection to love, & from love to pure intellectual delight… by which we became worthy to conceive that infinite in ourselves without which it were impossible for man to have believed in a God. In short to sum up all, the most delightful of all promises was expressed to us by this practical state, namely our marriage with the Redeemer of Mankind."[41] In this instance, "reverence" may be taken as that power which stands behind or beneath the Understanding, substantiating it. But this does not prevent the process having its initiation in the demands of sense and proceeding under at least the partial control of sense and Understanding.

The real difference, then, between Coleridge's position and Vico's is not the method, but the potential destination. Though both assert that it begins with an "exclusive attachment" that may take its lead from the senses, Coleridge believes that the same journey will take one further, indeed to the ultimate destination. However, in the *Opus*, Coleridge both seems to deny the efficacy of a process that begins in sense and has changed his focus from the relations of husband and wife to the relations of mother and child. I suspect that by this time he had put the success or failure of marriage into the category of a "hap," or the "fortunate chance" of the individual, and that he rejected any notion that the self can rest securely in the "haps" of time and place.[42] Certainly, there is very little indication in the *Opus Maximum* that he finds in marriage the idea of a secure resting place for the self.[43]

---

[40] *Lects 1808–19*, I, 314.
[41] *Lects 1808–19*, I, 315.
[42] *Op Max*, 27; cf. *CN*, V, 6143.
[43] Notably, there is no entry for "marriage" in the index to the *Opus Maximum*.

Sense and Reason — Child and Adult

To find a foundation for the self in the principles of Reason, Coleridge proposed that personal identity is discovered through love of another, that second or third party in which the self can find itself as an object. However, because nothing "can become the object of consciousness but by reflection" so the self can be made known to the mind "only by a representative."[44] This representative must also substantiate the ideas and principles of Reason, which implies that the self cannot have rest except in an absolute — the absolute will, or the absolute good, or, in other words, in the idea of God. To demonstrate this, he draws not upon our experience of loving our neighbor as ourselves, which he had used in describing the proper function of conscience, but of mother and child, an image woven into the fabric of the *Opus Maximum*. In "Fragment 1," discussing how personal identity need not be confined to consciousness of our body, he suggests that "the mother or the nurse is the self of the child" and that in dreams we attach our identity "to forms the most remote from our own." Whereas in the adult this act of finding our self in another is going to be a moral and volitional act — an act of duty, done because it *should* be done[45] — in the young child it is clearly a tendency or a propensity. He attempts to establish the connection between parents, children, and the idea of God in what is perhaps the most remarkable and readable chapter of the *Opus Maximum*, entitled "Of the Origin of the Idea of God in the Mind of Man."[46] He summarizes his findings quite early in the chapter: "Why have men a Faith in God? There is but one answer: the Man, and the Man alone, has a Father and a Mother."[47]

My purpose, though, is not to decide whether Coleridge makes his case, but to point out that the method he uses is the very method he has abandoned in his discussion of instinct and duty in respect of adults. Here he notes that the "young Bull butts ere yet its horns are formed," and makes the generalization that "[t]hrough all Nature there is a manifestation of power pre-existent to the product."[48] He substantiates this idea in respect of mother and child in a delightful, rhapsodic paragraph:

> Even in its very first Week of Being, the holy quiet of its first days must be sustain'd by the warmth of the maternal bosom. The first dawnings of its humanity will break forth in the Eye that connects the Mother's face with

[44] *Op Max*, 30.
[45] *Op Max*, 31.
[46] *Op Max*, 119–27.
[47] *Op Max*, 122.
[48] *Op Max*, 119.

the warmth of the mother's bosom, the support of the mother's arms. A thousand tender kisses excite a finer life in its lips, and there first language is imitated from the mother's smiles. Ere yet a conscious self exists, the love begins; and the first love is love of... another. The Babe acknowledges a self in the mother's form years before it can recognize a self in its own... Faith, implicit Faith, the offspring of unreflecting love, is the antecedent and indispensable condition of all its knowledge: the life is the light thereof... When the little Being newly nourished, or awakening from its heaving pillow, begins its murmuring song for pleasure, and for pleasure leaps on the arm, begins to smile and laugh to the moving head of the Mother, who is to it its all the World. It knows not what the Mother is, but still less does it know what itself is.[49]

In the bosoms and heaving pillows it is possible to see a subliminal eroticism, something written from the father's point of view, rather than that of either mother or child.[50] But Coleridge is asking us to take this as sense priming the pump of Reason, something made explicit ten pages later: "The infant follows its mother's face as, glowing with love and beaming protection, it is raised heavenward, and with the word 'GOD' it combines in feeling whatever there is of reality in the warm touch, in the supporting grasp, in the glorious countenance. The whole problem of existence is present as a sum total in the mother..."[51] Again, the question is not so much whether Coleridge is right, whether he has managed a Rhodean leap in seven-league boots, but to ask why he permits a process in the child that he will not permit in the adult — a process that for the adult may even be seen as a rehearsal of his relationship with his mother. If we turn back to his earlier, anti-Epicurean, descriptions of self development, he asserts that "[a]ll actions... which proceed directly from the individual without reflection, as those of a hungry beast rushing to its food" create a demeaning identity of self and object; perception becomes a substitute for reflection so that "the food in the trough is the temporary *self* of the hog."[52]

But Coleridge makes no attempt to decide whether there is any real difference between the baby crying for the breast and the hog grunting at the trough. Indeed, the only difference might be the language used, and the potential development of deferred gratification in the child. Interestingly, a note in 1817 indicates a closer identification of self with appetite

---

[49] *Op Max*, 120–21.
[50] Cf. "The Pang More Sharp than All," stanza II (*PW*, I.2, 826), for a similar connection between father, mother, and child at the breast; see also stanza 3 of "The Day Dream" (*PW*, I.2, 703) for another take on the complex relations between mother, father, and child.
[51] *Op Max*, 131.
[52] *Op Max*, 30–31.

than Coleridge here admits as he speaks of the baby waking from its feed:
"When the little creature has slept out its sleep and stilled its hunger at
the mother's bosom/ that very hunger a mode of Love, all made up of
Kisses — and coos and wantons with pleasure, and laughs and plays bob
cherry with the Mother, that is all, all to it..."[53] The positive spin
Coleridge puts upon his identification of hunger with love is derived from
his belief that this is how the child learns to love; it is the beginning of
the process by which one eventually comes to have a faith in God. It is
a delightful observation, but there is, I think, something more here. Consider the language: not only the conjunction of "hunger" and "love,"
but "Kisses," "coos," "wantons," "pleasure," "laughs," and "plays."
What is this but the language of dalliance, of happy lovers who are all in
all to each other — and it has begun with appetite. The child has identified the mother as its whole being, and of this experience Coleridge says
"it clings to her, and has a right, an undescribable Right to cling to her."[54]
Here lie the origins of power. And we shall see that the child is the father
of the poet.

Whereas I do not want to undermine Coleridge's belief that here we
may see something of the origins of our faith in God, I do want to suggest that another kind of ability is also being developed. Sense is priming the pump of Reason in a way that Coleridge is, perhaps, reluctant to
admit: a power is being fostered that in the adult will enable close relationships with other people and, in fact, upon which some of the future
adult's happiness will depend. In his ten page discussion in the
Biographia of the character of Don John from Shadwell's play *The Lib-
ertine*, Coleridge distinguishes the means at the hero's disposal from the
ends to which he puts them. He concludes, "[i]n fine the character of
Don John consists in the union of every thing desirable to human
nature."[55] The implication is clear, but not delineated by Coleridge, that
while such a power might be termed "an undescribable Right," it does
not have to be put to evil ends. Still, it is a power Coleridge has trouble
in permitting in himself. On the one hand, "... to possess such a power
of captivating and enchanting the affections of the other sex! to be capable of inspiring... a love so deep, and so entirely personal to *me*! that
even my worst vices... could not eradicate the passion! To be so loved
for my *own self*, that even with a distinct knowledge of my character,

[53] *CN*, III, 4348; cf. *Op Max*, 121n.156.
[54] *CN*, III, 4348.
[55] *BL*, II, 219.

she yet died to save me!..." and, on the other, "... it is among the mysteries, and abides in the dark ground-work of our nature, to crave an outward confirmation of that *something* within us, which is our *very self*, that something, not *made up* of our qualities and relations, but itself the supporter and substantial basis of all these. Love *me*, and not my qualities, may be a vicious and an insane wish, but it is not a wish wholly without a meaning."[56] Indeed not, and not quite as vicious and insane as Coleridge declares. This is the phantom self, of course, but which nonetheless he qualifies, in a notebook, by indicating that loving someone for their qualities alone is a cold and mechanical business: "... as if a human Soul were made like a watch, or loved for this or that tangible & verbally expressible quality!"[57] We admire the fidelity of a spouse to a person who has failed in or has betrayed the "outside" world. "Love me, not my qualities" may not only be a perfectly *sensible* beginning to a relationship, it is almost a *sine qua non* of marriage.

Life and Power: Unmasking the Conflict

Having said that "Through all Nature there is a manifestation of power pre-existent to the product,"[58] Coleridge has assigned such manifestations in *adult* life to a disorientated will, the will to self-love, materialist, epicurean and dark to the love of God. None of the energies he so admired in Don John's character are seen as potentially symbolic of a higher good. Therefore Coleridge chooses to construct a self from the law of conscience and the idea of duty. Instead of making a self that begins in appetite, "... he should be seeking and finding a nobler Self in the love and Service of his Neighbor."[59] Note the "should": it is imperative, a command from the outside, and so perhaps separated from the source of internal power. But the power typified in Don John is a singular quality, and belongs to us as human beings. After the paragraph ending, "Love *me*, and not my qualities... is not a wish wholly without a meaning," the very next paragraph begins, "[w]ithout power, virtue would be insufficient and incapable of revealing its being. It would resemble the magic transformation of Tasso's heroine into a tree, in which she

---

[56] *BL*, II, 216–17.
[57] *CN*, III, 3991.
[58] *Op Max*, 119.
[59] *CN*, V, 6144. Coleridge always constructs the self, especially the "phantom self," as masculine.

could only groan and bleed. (Hence power is necessarily an object of our desire and of our admiration.)"[60] Does this mean that, in Coleridge's system, virtue can only reveal its being in *opposition* to power? Probably, because Coleridge goes on to discuss the nature of power, and his examples are all drawn from the evil characters of literature: Satan, Richard, Iago, Edmund. But this of course prevents power having any symbolic function at all, in contrast to the rest of nature. I think Coleridge has gotten himself into something of a pickle, and the very unhappy image of the confined spirit, without power, only able to groan and bleed, is one that he uses to describe his own condition in 1826: "For nearly three months I have not known a single genial Sensation; but have felt, even in the intervals of Freedom from Pain and distressful Feelings, just as the imprisoned Spirit in the enchanted Wood of Tasso, or in Virgil's Tree — like a naked Intelligence, a Mind detached from Life. — Mrs Gillman desires her kind regards to You and Your's —."[61] Although we should note the primacy Coleridge gives to Mind and Intelligence, here again we see Prometheus chained to the mountain, virtue without power, a naked Intelligence — a powerful phrase in itself — and though Life might be a difficult entity to define, he clearly feels that his mind is imprisoned as a consequence of detachment from it.

Life, Love, and Hope

In 1823, three years before this letter, and when just fifty, he had written, or finished writing "Youth and Age," in which Life, in the form of Nature, Hope, and Poesy, are all emanations of Youth. The poems ends by defying the external appearances of age: "Life is but thought: so think I will/ That YOUTH and I are House-mates still." However, though making only a single appearance in the poem, Hope sustains this complex, as can be seen from four lines that may have been part of the original poem, but which Coleridge cut because he felt they made the conclusion too cheerless, or "a religious one too elevated for the character of the Ode."

---

[60] *BL*, II, 217.
[61] *CL*, VI, 605; another image of imprisonment written a few months earlier, to Mrs. Charles Aders, is equally powerful in conveying a trapped spirit: "For in this bleak World of Mutabilities, & where what is not changed, is chilled, and in this winter-time of my own Being, I resemble a Bottle of Brandy in Spitzbergen — a Dram of alcoholic Fire in the center of a Cake of Ice" (*CL*, VI, 532).

Dewdrops are the Gems of Morning,
But the Tears of mournful Eve:
Where no Hope is, Life's a Warning
That only serves to make us grieve.[62]

Hope for what? Love is the answer, and here, as often but not only in Coleridge's later poetry, love of the person and presence of Ann Gillman. On January 3, 1825, he looks back to these lines, when he jots down, "… Jacob and Rachel… Youth and Age. Third Stanza — Estrangement. Indifference of…" and an indecipherable name follows that Kathleen Coburn associates with Ann Gillman.[63] If Ann Gillman is indifferent to Coleridge, then he feels all hope withdrawn, and Life only a cause for grief.

The middle 1820s seem to have been difficult years for Coleridge. He had been in the Gillman household since 1816 and was fully established as a member of the family, even to the extent of going on holiday with Ann Gillman without her husband and so enduring rumors of their living openly in sin. Though there is almost certainly no truth in this, Coleridge and Mrs. Gillman did look to each other for emotional support. But the intimacy they shared had no external or public form and was thus dependent almost wholly on their sense of each other's sympathy, probably excluding even modest kinds of physical contact.

Early in 1825, Coleridge felt nagged by Mrs. Gillman, and treated "as if I were Henry at his Lesson."[64] He seems to have felt that the sympathy he looked for was being replaced by her insistence that he work methodically, and this perhaps invoked uncomfortable memories of his time in the Wordsworth household. This withdrawing caused him intense anxiety, expressed in a notebook letter prefacing "Work without Hope," and in some additional lines. The published poem concludes with the couplet "WORK without Hope draws nectar in a sieve;/ And HOPE without an Object cannot live."[65] The nature of this hope is made clear in the prefatory letter: "Strain in the manner of G. HERBERT —: which might be entitled, THE ALONE MOST DEAR: a Complaint of Jacob to Rachel as in the tenth year of his Service he saw in her or *fancied* that he saw Symptoms of Alienation."[66] Mrs. Gillman has written on this page of the notebook, "It *was* fancy," though of course we do not know when she

[62] *PW*, I.2, 1013.

[63] *CN*, IV, 5184; via the allusion to Jacob and Rachel, this association is made explicit in *CN*, IV, 5192 and *CL*, V, 414–16; see *PW*, I.2, 1030–31.

[64] *CL*, V, 411.

[65] *PW*, I.2, 1033.

[66] *CN*, IV, 5192.

set down those words. But she thus accepts her Rachel to Coleridge's Jacob. Fourteen years was the final term of Jacob's service to Laban for Rachel,[67] and it is remarkable that Coleridge and Ann Gillman are willing to see their relationship as rehearsing this great biblical romance. The additional lines suppose the loss of Ann Gillman's love, and describe the world drawing its web tighter and tighter round the poet; but mirrors on opposite walls hide the narrowness of the room, and these mirrors are a symbol of the faith that Ann Gillman and Coleridge had in each other:

> My FAITH — (say, I: I and my Faith are one!)
> Hung, as a Mirror there! and face to face
>   For nothing else there was, between or near
> (For not a thing between us did appear)
> One Sister Mirror hid the dreary Wall.
> But *that* is broke — and with that bright Compeer
> I lost my Object and my inmost All —
> Faith *in* the Faith of THE ALONE MOST DEAR![68]

He signs off, "JACOB HODIERNUS," or "Modern Jacob." This is quite consistent with Coleridge's belief that the self can only be known to the mind by a representative,[69] but does not tackle the question as to whether "The Alone Most Dear" should be another man's wife. What is duty in principle, to find one's self through love of a neighbor, is in fact an impetuous need in Coleridge, surmounting moral obstacles.

How deep that need is can be seen by his apparently turning from Mrs. Gillman, for a short period of time, to search for sympathy from another beautiful and accomplished woman. Even if this turning and returning (Sara Hutchinson is also in his consciousness in the mid 1820s) does not make him the Don Juan manqué of Highgate, we can see that he had not given up hope of discovering or expressing a sense of power. On June 3, 1826, Mrs. Charles Aders received from Coleridge the following astonishing tribute, as well as a very flattering poem, "The Two Founts." First de-clichéing the phrase "My dear Friend," he begins again with "My dear Friend and Sister": "I have during the last fortnight or more been so haunted by day-thoughts and night-fancies of and concerning *you*, that *if* I had been some 25 or 30 [years] younger; and *if*... I had not been possessed and lorded over in the very same way & with the same exclusiveness and monopoly of my Thoughts, Solicitudes and

---

[67] Fourteen years total service, but she was given to him as a wife seven days after his marriage to Leah.

[68] *CN*, IV, 5192.

[69] *Op Max*, 30.

Imaginations by Mr. Aders's Image; I should verily have been half afraid that I was in love…"[70] Curiously enough this awkward letter, in which confession and denial follow hard upon each other's heels and in which Mrs. Gillman is evoked as a competing muse, or as Coleridge puts it, "another Object," was written just three months before he described himself as an "imprisoned Spirit in the enchanted Wood."[71] Perhaps his letter had so worried his correspondent that relations were interrupted, and Coleridge thus lost a focus for the expression of his sense of power or love, and felt himself trapped.[72] There are no further letters extant to Mrs. Aders until December 1826, which begins almost as awkwardly as the earlier and with a spirit of self-justification that might be referring to the June letter: "My dear Friend, and (by the privilege of silvery Locks and a heart pure as burnished Silver, in defiance of Beauty and Genius I dare add) beloved Sister!"[73] Is there a bit too much self-conscious protestation here? Too much assertion of the purity of his heart? And why "in defiance" of the Beauty hers and the Genius perhaps his? Is the hint that this combination, under other conditions, would have produced something more powerful than filial affection?[74]

Duty Surviving Self-love

The letter describing himself as "a naked Intelligence, a Mind detached from Life"[75] was written a few weeks before "Duty, Surviving Self-love"[76] and so that poem should, I think, be set in the context of Coleridge's likely sense of alienation from both Mrs. Aders and Ann Gillman. There is a prose preface in the manuscript, which is a debate between "Alia" — who appears to be a personification of Mrs. Gillman

---

[70] *CL*, VI, 581–82.

[71] *CL*, VI, 605.

[72] The impression that Coleridge allows us to form is that such conditions originate in physical causes; but it seems just as likely that they were psychosomatic.

[73] *CL*, VI, 651.

[74] In celebrating Derwent's engagement to Mary Pridham, Coleridge first declares that he has "left behind/ Life's gayer views and all that stir the Mind," but then feels his hope revived "Since I have heard…/ That all, my glad eyes would grow bright to see,/ My Derwent hath found realiz'd in Thee!" He sounds slightly fired up by the reports of her beauty, and perhaps there is a hint of proper paternal jealousy in his compliment. He goes on to praise her as the "Crown of [Derwent's] Cup, and Garnish of his Dish;/ The fair Fulfilment of his Poesy" (*PW*, I.2, 1077), thus reminding us of the connection he had made between poetry and marriage in his lectures on *Romeo and Juliet*.

[75] *CL*, VI, 605.

[76] *PW*, I.2, 1067–68, and *PW*, II.2, 1266–68.

— and "Constantius," the philosopher-poet, and thus a debate between constancy or mind, and something "other" which constitutes ordinary life. This choice of name, Alia, also points to the sense of alienation Coleridge is conscious of. Alia asks Constantius, "Are *you* the happier for your Philosophy?" and Constantius, though skeptical as to what Alia means by happiness, answers in just the manner which we would expect from the author of the *Opus Maximum*: "The calmer at least, and less *un*happy... for it has enabled me to find that selfless Reason is the best Comforter and only sure Friend, of declining Life." This is pointed, suggesting that Reason, not Alia, is his only reliable friend. At that point a carriage arrives, "followed by the usual bravura executed on the brazen Knocker...," a phrase hinting at both a modest excitement in the party arriving and skepticism in the poet. Alia responds by hastening, again Coleridge's ironic word, to receive them. These phrases reflect the distaste with which the poet views Alia welcoming Life. The poet is left by himself — he is not going to join the party — and, a little unsettled by Alia's question, he mutters the words that, punctuated by rhymes, become the poem.

The title of the poem epitomizes the contrast Coleridge has made throughout the *Opus Maximum*: between the material impulses of the self and the law of conscience, between nature and Reason. The poem opens with the hard business of coming to terms with one's outward decline, despite feeling very little changed inwardly. This, the theme of "Youth and Age," is also touched on here in the preface: "And the smile of Constantius was as the Light from a purple Cluster of grapes of the Vine gleaming thro' snow-flakes..."[77] So why, if one is in decline oneself, the poet asks, should one fret at the "wanings" of others? A subtle modulation of meaning is present here: the poet thinks of his waning in terms of his body not matching his inward youth — the purple light of fresh grapes still glows from the eyes in a head capped with white hair — whereas the waning he ascribes to others, notably expressed in the plural, is more a waning of their love for him; so there may be a buried reference to Mrs. Gillman and Mrs. Aders:

> Yet why at others' Wanings should'st thou fret?
> Then only might'st thou feel a just regret,
> Hadst thou withheld thy love or hid thy light
> In selfish fore-thought of Neglect or Slight.

---

[77] These lines of the Preface are crossed out in the ms. (*PW*, II.2, 1267).

Even if his body has the marks of old age upon it, his waning is not going
to take the form of a reduction of "love" and "light" that the fear of
being neglected might initiate. Indeed, he then asserts a heroic indifference to the outcome of his continued pouring forth, and takes this indifference as a mark of wisdom:

> O wiselier from feeble Yearnings free'd,
> *While*, and *on whom*, thou may'st — shine on! nor heed,
> Whether the Object by reflected light
> Return thy radiance, or absorb it quite.

To expect the radiance to be returned is, the poet implies, the mark of self-
love. And, to use the metaphor central to the additional lines in "Work
without Hope," he is not going to be the mirror that breaks; he is going
to keep faith. But the crucial point is that Coleridge recognizes the process
of receiving reflected light from the mirror opposite as that of self-love,
and, as he was to put it in a note of 1830, "*anti-redemptive*," having the
mark of Hades about it.[78]

The objects we create in our consciousness by reflection become the
representations of the self.[79] The distinction between self-love and a self
that loves depends upon the individual: the former arises out of the
senses, while the latter emerges from "a higher law," the law of conscience.[80] The friends he is thinking of in this poem appear as objects
given to him through the senses; there is a curious conjunction of the
personal and the impersonal in the two lines, "*While*, and *on whom*, thou
may'st — shine on! nor heed/ Whether the Object by reflected light…"
The person, "whom," becomes an "Object"; in a draft the "Object" was
"Body." The energy that Coleridge still feels called upon to expend is
nonetheless the energy of self-love, and if the objects upon which it falls
fail to return it, no matter, because it does not represent either the poet's
or his friends *true* selves. This is constructed according to the law of conscience, the imperative of duty, and lies deep to the immediate presence
of the dim-burning friends; but in that phrase "dim-burning" also lies the
rub — there is no power associated with this duty.[81] Though Coleridge
in the final line of the poem issues himself with an injunction not to love

[78] *CN*, V, 6444.
[79] *Op Max*, 30.
[80] *Op Max*, 31; cf. *CN*, III, 3559.
[81] In discussing this passage in the *Opus* conference held at Clare College (see "Preface"), John Beer suggested that Coleridge's fullest realization of the essential person is the
historically but ineptly titled "Phantom" (*PW*, I.2, 763).

them less because they are not what they were to him, we sense that all the power lies in the *"were,"* all the spirit of delight that pervades "Youth and Age" and which is so notably absent in the versification of this poem. Self-love, we might think, is not so much a kind of cold self-interest but rather consists of the energies that bind people together into a society; and that duty, only conceived as loving one's neighbor as oneself in the most absolute or ideal sense, is the colder quality, the "naked Intelligence," or the "Mind detached from life." The exercise of duty corresponds to no exercise of power, and so this kind of dutiful love is disengaged, and has become a love which does not involve one with another, which is not sociable, allowing the poet to contemplate his friends in isolation, from his "safe recess"; thus the time when Youth "went a maying" as a "Masker bold," that spirit of revelry with which Coleridge invested his earlier days, is left behind.

Or almost. Though his relationship with Mrs. Gillman may have faltered, it did not fail. Her sympathy restored, some two years later in 1828, he finished his last great poem, "The Garden of Boccaccio,"[82] comparable in kind and excellence to Keats' odes. His spirits of poetic and amatory power were freed for the last time. It is a consummate poem, and if we are tempted to suggest that it is at best a vicarious experience, disconnected from the realities of the poet's life, we should remember whose hand placed the engraving on his desk. It is a celebration of Jacob and Rachel's long fidelity.

But it is not the end of the debate between the powers of sense and the duties of Reason. Coleridge's journey was "from love to pure intellectual delight... by which we became worthy to conceive that infinite in ourselves,"[83] from life to the absolute, a journey which can be traced in the development of the cancelled lines of "Youth and Age."[84] The four lines are:

> Dewdrops are the Gems of Morning,
> But the Tears of mournful Eve;
> Where no Hope is, Life's a Warning
> That only serves to make us grieve.

In versions of 1829 and 1832, these lines are retained, and are given different additions. In 1829 he removed the stop after "grieve," adding "When we go tottering down Life's Slope!" and then

---

[82] *PW*, I.2, 1089–95.
[83] *Lects 1808–1819*, I, 315.
[84] *PW*, I.2, 1013–15.

> And yet, fair Maid! accept this truth,
> Hope leaves not us but we leave Hope,
>   And quench the light of inward Youth.

The poem is addressed to a person, and so we see the vestiges of a hadistic search for sympathy. But is the leaving of hope voluntary or involuntary? Certainly hope, as a thing in itself, is not lost, but perhaps because we cannot avoid tottering down life's slope, neither can we avoid leaving hope standing on the hill behind us, and so quenching the light of inward Youth. That combined act, of leaving hope and quenching youth seems to be a thing regretted, but ineluctable. Not so in the last version, which after "Life's a Warning" runs

> That only serves to make us grieve,
>   In our Old Age!
> That only serves to make us grieve
> With oft and tedious *taking-leave* —
> Like a poor related Guest,
> Who may not rudely be dimiss'd;
> Yet hath outstay'd his welcome while,
> And tells the jest without the smile!

The whole focus has turned round. Here Life is compared to a guest no longer welcome, but to whom the rules of hospitality still apply, and rather like the dim-burning friends of "Duty" this guest reflects no radiance, no warmth, no smile. But quite how deeply Coleridge feels this condition is made ruthlessly explicit in the final couplet:

> O! might Life *cease*, and selfless *Mind*,
> Whose Being is *Act*, alone remain behind![85]

Age has entirely supplanted Youth, and with it, Life. So what of the gifts reserved for age? In the last six years of his life, as his body and soul began to fall asunder, Coleridge seems to have embraced "the cold friction of expiring sense." His refining fire is the conception of the absolute. John Beer's final entry in his selection of Coleridge's reflections on religion and psychology is the wish expressed to J. H. Green the night before he died "to remember that, first of all is the Absolute Good..."[86] The very last entry in his notebooks, except for Mrs. Dashwood's address, and probably written in the month he died, runs, in part: "O grace of God! if only a believing Mind... could indeed be possessed by, and

---

[85] *PW*, I.2, 1014–15.
[86] John Beer, ed., *Coleridge's Writings. Volume 4, On Religion and Psychology* (New York: Palgrave, 2002), 257.

possess, the full Idea of the Reality of the Absolute Will, the Good! — tho yet — higher shall I see or deeper than *reality*, the Will as the Ground essentially causative of all *real* Being, and therefore essentially of it's own Being…" then, he says "o with what deep devotion of Delight, Awe & Thanksgiving would he read every sentence" of chapters 13 to 17 of St. John's Gospel.[87]

Conclusion

That last note is certainly striking in its intensity, but after a lifetime's striving it speaks of a condition still to be achieved. Duty, as he conceived it, required him to possess or be possessed by the idea of the absolute or the infinite, and in that idea he grounded his conception of the human self Divine. Such a conception asked him, he believed, to reject any other method of realizing the self in the adult, which proved in practice to be a rejection of the kind of power that the child first found in its mother, and upon which the poet's creativity depended. However, if there is one thing we take away from a reading of the *Opus Maximum* and the last volume of the Notebooks, it is his utter conviction of the truth he was seeking. Coleridge was not afraid to take the journey out of life into eternity.

[87] *CN*, V, 6918.

REPEATING THE ACT OF THE INFINITE IN THE FINITE: THEOLOGICAL ANTHROPOLOGY IN COLERIDGE'S *OPUS MAXIMUM*

By SCOTT MASSON

Coleridge's *Opus Maximum* is certainly not the most accessible of the author's numerous challenging works, and this judgement lies not merely in the fact that it only recently came into print within the edition of his *Collected Works* after 170 years of near oblivion. While not constituting the "immethodical miscellany" of some of his works — in fact, it provides an extended, albeit fragmentary, and at times directionless examination of matters closely related to theological anthropology — it requires greater than usual patience and persistence to follow what its editor, Thomas McFarland, judiciously describes to be at times "a swamp of near-unintelligibility."[1] In fact, were it not for his sterling work in adding a lengthy "Prolegomena," it would be difficult to detect what he describes as its "intellectual coordinates."[2] The very need for it unfortunately suggests that these documents gathered under the title of *Opus Maximum* will always lack the authority a completed work would have possessed.[3]

Be that as it may, there are so many fertile areas in this swamp that it should not be abandoned precipitously, or at least not without some attempt to cultivate them and reap their benefits. A closer engagement with the *Opus Maximum* is particularly compelling insofar as it seems to anticipate and proleptically refute the "atheistic humanism" of mid-twentieth century communism and fascism, rooted as it was in "the positivism of Comte, the subjectivism of Feuerbach, the materialism of Marx, and the radical wilfulness of Nietzsche."[4] Coleridge's attack on forms of intellectual positivism, his framing of the dynamics of what came to be called

---

[1] *Op Max*, cxliii.

[2] *Op Max*, xiii.

[3] Without wishing to be too critical of the editor, while his "Prolegomena" is much to be praised, its stated purpose to function in the stead of "a larger and more ambitious work that does not exist, the fabled *magnum opus*" (*Op Max*, xiii) is problematic. Not only does he thereby tacitly undermine his attempt to establish the four fragments *as* Coleridge's *opus*, he almost appears to present his own "Prolegomena" as such.

[4] This is a case that George Weigel makes, citing the work of Henri de Lubac, S.J., in his recent assessment of the intellectual disparity that has emerged between the intellectuals

human "subjectivism" in terms of a personal relationship of I and Thou, his grounding of consciousness in conscience, and his discussion of the role of the human will, all argue the prescience and importance of these fragments collected as his *Opus Maximum*.

The contradiction in the materialist's position that Coleridge continually exposes in the *Opus Maximum* is this: whenever he wishes to advance an argument for his position, he is required to draw rational inferences, that is, to employ the voluntary powers that reveal him to be a rational agent. For "nature itself, as soon as we apply reason to its contemplation, forces us back to a something higher than nature as that on which it depends."[5] The materialist, however, would deny that he uses such powers as he is not actually an agent, i.e. one to whom we could attribute definite judgments or cause-and-effect statements. He would attribute those powers to *involuntary* processes of the brain, much as we attribute the circulation of the blood to the heart or the secretion of bile to the liver; and in the process would subordinate thinking to the laws of chemistry, physics, and biology. Coleridge argues that it is only a sign of *wilful* perversity that he would deny the very capacity that he *necessarily* employs in making the denial. Nonetheless, he commits an obvious intellectual error as well. For if the materialist's contentions were true, what we call thinking would become nothing but a symptom of non-rational processes from which nothing *could* be concluded. And this uncertainty would necessarily extend to include the materialist's own conclusions, rendering even his own argument absurd. In either case, the position is untenable.

It is this fact that explains Coleridge's attraction to transcendental philosophy; the fact that it recognizes the inherent contradiction of a materialist system of thought, and offers an escape from it. Its future implications far transcended anthropology alone. The growing materialism and scientism in Coleridge's time[6] combined with the radical scepticism

of contemporary Western Europe and many of their counterparts in the United States; cf. "Europe's Problem — and Ours," *First Things* 140 (February 2004), 22.

[5] *Op Max*, 140.

[6] There are countless examples of this, but that of Joseph Priestley, whom Coleridge admired early on in his Unitarian/Socinian days, is one of the clearest: "Lastly, the doctrine of *necessity* ... is the immediate result of the doctrine of the materiality of man; for mechanism is the undoubted consequence of materialism. But whether man be wholly material or not, I apprehend that proof enough is advanced that every human volition is subject to certain fixed laws, and that the potential *self-determining power* is altogether imaginary and impossible. In short, it is my firm persuasion, that the three doctrines of *materialism*, of that which is commonly called *Socinianism*, and of philosophical *necessity*, are equally parts of *one system*..." (Joseph Priestley, *Disquisitions Relating to Matter and Spirit* [London, 1777], 356).

bequeathed by Descartes' "ghost-in-the-machine" anthropology to form the nineteenth century's two-tiered hierarchy of truth in which matters that employed the will — such as those that entailed beliefs, aesthetic judgments, or moral judgments — came to be regarded as wholly arbitrary and "relative"; whereas those that were cognitive came to be regarded as the stuff of real knowledge. As Nancy Pearcey argues in a recent book, this separation has had devastating social consequences, for its inevitable effect has been to make it intellectually unacceptable to make a case for the public good according to beliefs or moral judgments, or for social institutions to serve it according to them.[7] Thus while the restriction of the term "science" to material phenomena has cloaked itself with the mantle of scientific detachment and objectivity, it has in fact imposed an intellectually disingenuous framework for thought that appealed to the conventions of "rationality" or even "common sense" — but only insofar as these were consistent with a materialist view of the world. This became a sort of Procrustean bed on which the facts were stretched, to the extent that genes can now be attributed "mind" and agency, yet individuals cannot.[8]

The fragments that constitute the *Opus Maximum* also justify further exploration on purely scholarly grounds, for they do provide an extended discussion of so many of the matters that Coleridge deemed of such paramount importance that he deferred them to a grand, but as it happened, never quite forthcoming project. Were it for that reason alone they would be worth exploring. The most fertile area of his discussion may well lie in the demonstration of how the relationship of I and Thou (a relationship with theological import for Coleridge) arises "naturally" in an individual's consciousness,[9] accounting for both his conscience and consciousness (in that order), and the pattern of relationships for all human community. There can be little dispute about the novelty of this angle of approach, though McFarland catalogues an impressive array of precedents in writers with similarly apologetic intent throughout the seventeenth and eighteenth centuries.[10] For almost unique to Coleridge's *Opus*

---

[7] Cf. Nancy Pearcey, *Total Truth: Liberating Christianity from its Cultural Captivity* (Wheaton: Crossway, 2004), 295–324.

[8] Cf. Richard Dawkins' popular scientific books such as *The Selfish Gene*.

[9] Nature is of course one of the many terms that Coleridge is at pains to desynonimize precisely because of its unreflective appropriation by his positivistic contemporaries to the science of nature, including the human nature that Coleridge is at pains to distinguish from it.

[10] Cf. his discussion of "The Genre of the *Magnum Opus*," ch. XXIII, clix–clxiv.

Maximum, though as we shall see it is certainly anticipated in his *Biographia Literaria*, is his attempt to develop his anthropological understanding dyadically, quintessentially in *relation* to another (God), rather than in a self-referential fashion as would modern psychology (and the human sciences in general). In this sense he also anticipates Martin Buber's magnificent work *I and Thou* by a century.[11] It is a tack that sets him at odds not only with the philosophy of his German contemporaries, but with the post-Heideggerian school that has so dominated contemporary scholarship.

Precedents for Theological Anthropology: *Biographia Literaria*

In trying to establish intellectual coherence for Coleridge's thought in the absence of a *magnum opus*, a great deal of the scholarship on Coleridge over the years has rightly been devoted to the numerous debts his work owes to the German philosophers of his age, many of whom presented their ideas more systematically. The cumulative effect of the impressive scholarship that has been done in excavating Coleridge's sources however has been to create a general portrait of Coleridge as a grand accumulator and assimilator, a mediator of the grand thoughts of his contemporaries, and at times even a plagiarist. There are many studies of course that have not followed this path, but when it comes to the matter of how to understand Coleridge, he has generally been moulded into the die cast by others.

However, there is a problem with this model. Understanding the coherence of Coleridge's thought to lie within the confines of the German philosophical tradition makes his subsequent repudiation of many of these same philosophers, not just on minor points but on the general direction of their work, all the more puzzling, indeed inexplicable.[12] Moreover, while Coleridge's role in introducing German thought to the English speaking world is incontestable, understanding him largely as a mediator does insufficient credit to the ways in which his thought deviates from what he mediates, even where he uses its terminology. This is particularly evident in his later work and this is perhaps the prime reason why the

---

[11] Martin Buber, *I and Thou*, trans. Walter Kaufmann (New York: Simon & Schuster, 1970).

[12] Even McFarland's magisterial work *Coleridge and the Pantheist Tradition* (1969) is of little help here, for observing Coleridge's opposition to various forms of Spinozism is in and of itself no form of unity.

Opus Maximum is so significant. In it, Coleridge's distinctiveness as a thinker becomes far clearer, in part because it is only there that he has extricated himself from what he mediated. Above all, it sets into bold relief the difficulties with reading Coleridge as if the *Biographia Literaria* had been his *magnum opus*, which was never the author's intention but which has happened almost by default in the absence of such a work.

But if the angle of approach of Coleridge's apologetics in the *Opus Maximum* is virtually unprecedented among his predecessors and contemporaries, it is certainly not without precedent in his own work. It might be useful to take a look at how it appears in the *Biographia*, that most famous of his critical works, where we can find shafts of the light that we see more fully in the *Opus Maximum*. Chiefly we see this in the heart of that work, in his idea of asserting human identity — that is constructing an anthropology — to be a finite corollary to God and his self-revelation in his Son (a personal relationality to be found throughout the Trinity). This is evident in his famous definition of the activity/personeity of the primary Imagination in Book XIII: "The primary IMAGINATION I hold to be the living Power and prime Agent of all human Perception, and as a repetition in the finite mind of the eternal act of creation in the infinite I AM."[13]

The great difficulty with this particular formulation, at least with respect to the position he later advances in the *Opus Maximum*, is the fact that the agency it mentions threatens to be defined as a mental function or process because of the overarching term "Imagination." This has in fact been the conventional reading of Coleridge's definition: it is, it is said, the quintessential "Romantic" definition of the Imagination. Since Kant's *Critique of Judgment* (1790), the Romantic poets and Idealist philosophers concurred in regarding the Imagination as a Divine faculty, and associated it with the production of sublime poetry. For Keats, the Imagination and "its empyreal reflection is the same as human Life and its spiritual repetition"; for Shelley, the Imagination was the portal into the "invisible nature of man"; for Wordsworth, it was like the "workings of one mind, the features/ Of the same face," which suggested "the great Apocalypse,/ The types and symbols of Eternity,/ Of first, and last, and midst, and without end."[14] Despite some of the overt similarities of these statements to Coleridge's, it was clearly possible to deny the need to understand who Christ was in order to understand human nature, or to

---

[13] *BL*, I, 304.
[14] 1850 *Prelude*, VI, 636–40.

"imagine" as a function of our sharing the Divine image. To understand how, we perhaps need to look to Kant's discussion of the sublime.

Throughout the eighteenth century, the sublime had been an aesthetic category associated with powers that produced overwhelming sensations, whether they were wrought by the poet's hand — Shakespeare and Milton were by many accounts the most sublime poets — or through the sheer grandeur of nature. *Mont Blanc* was perhaps the most common *topos* of the sublime in nature. Unlike preceding philosophers, however, Kant was not interested in art as such; indeed, he made the unprecedented move of dissociating his notion of sublimity from objects of art. Kant was only interested in discussing the sublime in the context of its association with the objects of nature, and it formed the key point in his argument for the "purposiveness without purpose" in aesthetic objects. This focus displayed his opposition to the Deists who tended to regard nature as a book that revealed its Divine author's intentions. But the more obvious purpose, at least in the light of its place in the *Critique*, is that by doing so, it made it far easier for him to avoid the subject of intentionality, and thus to illustrate the *power* of judgment.[15] One could easily discuss the sublime in nature without discussing what its Author thereby intended; but it is virtually impossible to discuss the sublimity of a passage in Shakespeare or Milton without doing so.

The importance of avoiding any connection between the experience of the sublime and the idea of purpose or intent only became clear in what he thereby concluded. Since the sublime in nature was, according to his definition, evoked in instances when our senses *failed to comprehend* their object, such as they did in the presence of a huge mountain whose summit we could not see, it stood to reason that it was the very *absence* that we enjoyed. Kant argued that the reason why is that it brought the previously hidden role of the judgment as a *form-giving faculty* to our awareness. In other words, we received a sort of self-conscious pleasure when we became aware of the *formative* power of our Imagination; and this awareness was prompted by an "object" of thought that lacked any form of its own. From this, it is perfectly possible to regard the Imagination as self-authorizing, and thus like Shelley to speak to the sublime landscape: "And what were thou/ And earth, and stars, and sea/ If to the human mind's imaginings/ Silence and solitude were but vacancy?"[16]

---

[15] Kant's third Critique is entitled the *Kritik der Urteilskraft* in German, and the final word is conventionally translated as "Judgment." This is understandable in terms of dynamic equivalence, yet it does tend to somewhat confuse the purpose of Kant's critique.

[16] "Mont Blanc," 142–44.

Yet for Coleridge, such a view of the Imagination has missed the point.[17] He would concur that we cannot know God from nature, not even in those sublime instances in which it suggests the Infinite. To conclude otherwise is to mistakenly place God in the category of things and, in this particular instance, only more deceivingly so by suggesting that the sublime is more like "the invisible God" because it represents *no thing*; and he would also accept that the instances of the sublime in nature in which we encounter nothing are a means of discovering the hidden power of the Imagination. But he would not thereby conclude that our relationship to the world and to others is somehow internally constituted as a *result* of our self-consciousness. The consequence of that would be that personal distinctiveness would lose its integrity. I shall explore that further when I look at what Coleridge says about "I and Thou" in the *Opus Maximum* below.

Here we should observe that there is a similarly *personal* dimension to Coleridge's use of the term Imagination in the *Biographia* that goes beyond that of his contemporaries' divinization of the mind's *powers*, although it is less distinctive than one would like.[18] It comes through his analogy of the finite mind to the eternal. This analogy of man to the biblical God in the sense of *person* as well as in power is clearer when we consider the remarks Coleridge makes immediately prior to his famous definition in the *Biographia*.[19] Having just announced at the end of his twelfth chapter his disagreement with Wordsworth over his remarks on the Imagination in his 1815 *Preface to Poems* (a theological disagreement that extends into the second half of the *Biographia*),[20] the thirteenth chapter of the *Biographia* commences with what we must presume to be an elaboration. At any rate, he offers an extended quote from *Paradise Lost* v. 469–88 and its description of the great chain of being.[21]

This is but a prelude to a series of references *relating* the lesser to the greater and the finite to the infinite. As in the subsequent definition of the Imagination, he immediately modifies what he says, in this instance by

---

[17] Coleridge attacks the idea of the self as the first principle in *Op Max*, 62.

[18] For an excellent discussion of the similarities in diction that lie between Coleridge and his German contemporaries, see Engell's introduction to the *Biographia*, xcvii–xciv.

[19] I believe a case can be made that these concerns appear throughout the *Biographia*, and may well constitute its underlying thread, but since the purpose here is to discuss the *Opus Maximum*, I shall postpone a more extended discussion of that for another occasion.

[20] Thereby demonstrating the unity of the two halves of the work around a theological anthropology, as I argue at greater length in the third chapter of my *Romanticism, Hermeneutics and the Crisis of the Human Sciences* (Hampshire: Ashgate, 2004).

[21] *BL*, I, 295.

approving of a statement from Leibniz that rejects the materialist hypothesis that corporeal beings are merely material and contends that they must be referred to the idea of *powers* if they are to be explained (or understood) at all.[22] The relevance of *both* quotes to his definition of the primary Imagination is clear: the one emphasizes the personal agency, the other the activity (or power). A further dimension is added by the Greek lines from Synesius he cites, translated to say "I venerate the hidden ordering of intellectual things, but there is some medial element that may not be distributed." Such sentiments will sound familiar to readers of the *Opus Maximum*, as we shall see in a moment, but the question is, what might this "medial element" be?

He elaborates somewhat on what he means in what follows, referring once again to Kant and the significance of "his introduction of negative quantities in philosophy," particularly his discussion of opposites. Here we need to keep in mind what he will say about the relationship of the human to God, for he notes how Kant had rightly observed that opposition could be conceived not only in a logical sense, i.e. absolutely incompatibly, but also in a sense that was "real without being contradictory."[23] He concludes the discussion like this: "The counteraction then of the two assumed forces does not depend on their meeting from opposite directions; the power which acts in them is indestructible; it is therefore inexhaustibly re-ebullient; and as something must be the result of these two forces, both alike infinite, and both alike indestructible; and as rest or neutralization cannot be this result; no other conception is possible, but that the product must be a tertium aliquid, or finite generation. Consequently this conception is necessary. Now the tertium aliquid can be no other than an inter-penetration of the counteracting powers, partaking of both."[24] Are we to understand an idea of concurrence here? That is, does Coleridge mean to suggest that the attributes that humanity receives *in imago Dei*, such as the freedom of the will to act, in no way impedes its apparent contrary, Divine foreknowledge, but rather that God grants the free choices of his creatures — to deny them would deny their status as image-bearers — while yet avoiding the opportunity for His providence to be ultimately thwarted?

Whatever he does mean, it is not yet clear, and the reader is thankful for the letter that intervenes at this point in the *Biographia*. It seems to

---

[22] *BL*, I, 296.
[23] *BL*, I, 297, 298.
[24] *BL*, I, 300.

indicate that Coleridge is still struggling, and is not entirely sure how to make the connection between the idea of personhood and activity. Later in life, Coleridge was to regard his "metaphysical disquisition at the end of the first volume" of the *Biographia* as "unformed and immature," with at best "fragments of the truth."[25] Yet there is more to it than that. The chapter preceding this drew deeply from Schelling's *Naturphiloso-phie*, in fact, as numerous scholars have observed, it was a verbatim translation. And while it promised to overcome the problem of reconciling the dualistic relationship of "I am" with "it is," the discussion of which had commenced in the fifth chapter, it had only done so at the terrible cost of identifying God with the mysterious forces of nature. The idea of process had eradicated identity. In other words, Coleridge himself had been like those he warned against latterly in his *Opus Maximum*, one who had ignored that "every reality must have its own form," and had thus fallen into "one of the great errors of the mystics at the close of the fifteenth century and in the recent writings of Schelling and his followers, as often as they attempt to clothe the skeleton of the Spinozistic pantheism and breathe a life thereinto."[26]

The Discussion in the *Opus Maximum*

The theological correlation often only implicit in Coleridge's anthropology becomes clearer in his subsequent writing, such as his 1820 *Essay on Faith* and of course his 1825 *Aids to Reflection*, but it is perhaps most extensively explored in his *Opus Maximum*. Without these subsequent works, it could be argued (though I think still mistakenly) that his discussion of the human Imagination, Reason, and Understanding were self-referential epistemological notions *alone* — as Kant argues, creative insofar as we understand the world to conform to our capacities for thought. Yet Coleridge was always of the conviction that theological truths underlay philosophical arguments, even where they were unacknowledged. In fact, he observed that it was often the case that the most important truths were unacknowledged: "Truths of all others the most awful and mysterious, yet being at the same time of universal interest, are too often considered as *so* true, that they lose all the life and efficiency of truth, and lie bed-ridden in the dormitory of the soul, side by side, with the most

---

[25] *TT*, II, 293; June 28, 1834.
[26] *Op Max*, 204–5.

despised and exploded errors."[27] Having observed the abiding theological correlation in Coleridge's anthropology though, we are required to consider its orthodoxy, particularly since many of his opponents would call themselves co-religionists, and few would openly avow to being atheists.

In a sense, we are not helped by the genre of the *Opus Maximum*. Apologetics not only tends to be rationalistic in nature (rarely referring to the biblical texts that would ground its own orthodoxy) it becomes dated the more immediately pointed it is. Particularly confusing for us is the fact that Coleridge tends to use terms he has borrowed from Kant and the German idealists, even though he occasionally rails against pure rationalism. How do we explain this? It seems to me that his context is as important as anything else in this respect. In the Britain of Coleridge's day, the field had not yet been won by the subjective turn of transcendental philosophy that is now almost taken for granted; it was occupied by various forms of mechanistic and materialist philosophies, the like of which Kant's vocabulary had allowed him to escape. They were his chief opponents, and he used the armament provided by Kant and his successors. Nevertheless, he never subordinated what he wrote to their framework. He appropriated their terminology and attempted to re-orient it so that "philosophy would pass into religion, and religion become inclusive of philosophy,"[28] not vice versa. It must be acknowledged that this proves a significant difficulty for contemporary readers not only because we are almost certainly less biblically literate than Coleridge's contemporaries and less attuned to the logic of the Reformation, but also operate almost two centuries after religion has in fact largely been subsumed in the academy under a form of philosophy (or history, or literature).

Nonetheless, acquaintance with the manner in which he uses these terms in the *Opus Maximum* makes it clear that although he would agree with Heidegger's formulation that "language is the house of being," i.e. that language actually forms the reality we understand, he differs from him insofar as he insists that this can only be understood as a function of man's being *in imago Dei*. This is a point that Coleridge is at pains to explain in the *Opus Maximum* in distinguishing humans from the other animals. Unlike the other animals, humankind alone is addressed by God (Gen. 1:28–30), and is required to respond in kind (Gen. 2:15–20). The very fact that we are thus respons*able* to God entails that we are also

---

[27] *Friend*, II, 74.
[28] *BL*, I, 283.

responsible, and it is clear that what that entails is that we are account-able to him. This conviction that an ineradicable state of being underlies a necessity of conduct underlies Coleridge's attempt to argue the *logical necessity* of the responsible will, an issue over which he spills much ink.[29]

The underlying ontological basis of Coleridge's anthropology should prompt a revision in how we understand the *Biographia*, and such sem-inal concepts to posterity as the symbol and Imagination, but it is impor-tant here to explore some of the ways in which Coleridge expands upon it. Perhaps the best way to do so is to subdivide his treatment into cer-tain key areas.

On Revelation

Coleridge's view of revelation is in many ways the most crucial aspect of his thought, again not so much because he discusses it with any regu-larity in the *Opus Maximum* as that it provides the light and evidence for what he asserts on other matters. It is the subtext that lends comprehen-sibility to his subsequent claims. Although its role is perhaps unsurpris-ing given his professed allegiance to Protestant theology, announced in the *Opus Maximum* by his praise of Luther and the Thirty-Nine Articles, it is somewhat ignored in studies of Coleridge for the simple reason that it does not *appear* to be a matter over which he expends a great deal of thought. Indeed he does not seem to be much exercised, despite his acquaintance with the Higher Criticism, to defend the veracity of the bib-lical witness. He assumes it, though he also defends it, in his eyes, in the very manner in which he defends the logic of the faith.

Furthermore, it underlies not only the emphasis but the scope of what he says on the Word. It informs his remarks on the Trinity, which in turn underlies his discussion of the human person, perhaps the primary sub-ject matter in the *Opus Maximum*. His views on the subject of revelation

---

[29] Cf. *Op Max*, 53–54: "Now as in all reasoning, even in the simplest physical sciences, the argument must commence with some assumption which is supposed and may be demanded but cannot be proved, so in the present subject. But as it belongs to the moral world, its postulates are of necessity different from those of geometry in this one respect: that though both may with equal right be demanded, the latter can not be extorted. In geom-etry, a negative answer to the postulate would prove only either the conscious falsehood or jest of the denier, or the suspension of his humanity by madness or idiotcy [*sic*]. But the assumptions of morality [are that] it is in a man's power to reject believingly without the absolute forfeiture of his human understanding, though not without forfeiting that which, even more than the understanding, forms the contradistinction of the human from the bestial nature... *man is a responsible agent* ..."

are perhaps most cogently expressed in an 1816 fragment of the same name: "Striking fact. That the great Truths of Revelation all transcend the Understanding, are inconceivable; but being granted, they are not only consonant with our conceptions of all we are capable of understanding, and of all we know by inner or outward experience, but improve those conceptions, solve the enigma of the World, the phænomena of Sense and the facts of Self-Consciousness; and inconceivable themselves give conceivability to all else."[30] Here already we can see the ground of what will become a standby in Coleridgean thought, the fundamental divergence between the function and material of the Reason and that of the Understanding. Just as Revelation transcends all Understanding, so too does what Coleridge defines, in Kantian language, as the Reason.

Of course, there is a difference: Coleridge's view of revelation always underlies what he asserts about the Reason, and it is the primary reason why Kant's definition is so attractive to him. Not only does it allow him to escape the shackles of associationism, it permits him to articulate the hidden character of the human person, and, in particular, its analogy to the Godhead. It was Coleridge's opinion that Kant intended much the same as he, though he never articulated it as such, he speculated, out of fear of religious persecution: "In spite therefore of his own declarations, I could never believe, it was possible for him to have meant no more by his *Noumenon*, or THING IN ITSELF, than his mere words express; or that in his own conception he confined the whole *plastic* power to the forms of the intellect, leaving for the external cause, for the *materiale* of our sensations, a matter without form, which is doubtless inconceivable. I entertained doubts likewise, whether in his own mind, he even laid *all* the stress, which he appears to do on the moral postulates.[31]

Coleridge's maintained his rather singular reading of Kant fairly consistently in his work. I believe it is what he has in mind in a key section of "Fragment 1" at the outset of the *Opus Maximum*. In it, we see that he forefends any possible misunderstanding that by referring to Reason, one of the key planks to his subsequent argument (and his thought as a whole), he might mean what Kant and the Enlightenment appear to have had in mind by their formless use of the term: "There is one point on which we are particularly anxious to prevent any misunderstanding. This respects the difference between the two (possible) assertions, 'such a truth may be known as truth by the light of reason' and 'the same truth was

---

[30] "On Revelation," in *SW&F*, I, 417.
[31] *BL*, I, 155.

discovered, or might have been discovered, by men by means of their reason exclusively.' We may assert the former, and in the course of this work shall find occasion to assert it without involving, nay, we altogether disbelieve and deny, the latter."[32] Nonetheless, if what Coleridge means here by Reason is the character of the Divine in the human, we must acknowledge that his argument does not take the expected tack of referring to Scripture to support it. Once again, this is one of the main reasons that his emphasis upon revelation has been too little acknowledged.

Yet there is a more significant reason. It is because in his appeal to Reason, as numerous scholars have observed, Coleridge has placed a great deal of weight on the significance of the line in John's Gospel "the light that lighteth every man that cometh into the world."[33] For Coleridge, this line not only refers to the universal human significance of the coming of Christ, but to the place of the word in forming the human capacity to understand the truth, as it were, "naturally." This is not a contradiction, or a denial of the primacy of revelation to subsequent human understanding. It is the point that lies behind his unusual emphasis on the anteriority of conscience to consciousness: "… when we affirm of any moral or religious truth [that] it is susceptible of rational or philosophical demonstration, we are so far from implying that the knowledge of its truth had its primary origin in the unaided efforts of human reason that we regard the present existence and actual exercise of such a power as the result of a revelation which had, by enlightening the mind, roused, disciplined, and invigorated all its faculties and appealed to experience and history for the confirmation of the fact."[34] What is more surprising here is that Coleridge's use of the term "revelation" is so general, referring here to the role prophecy played in developing the mind of Egypt, India and even the thought of the pre-Socratic philosophers of Greece.

It could then beg the question of whether Coleridge does actually attribute any *particular* status to the Bible as revelation. It is true that elsewhere he asserts that "in the Bible there is more, *that finds me* than… in all other books put together,"[35] but this in itself is hardly an affirmation of the Scriptures as the divinely appointed means by which God has revealed himself to humankind. Nonetheless, it is plain from any acquaintance with Coleridge's work that he does hold this, and that although he

---

[32] *Op Max*, 12.
[33] John 1:9.
[34] *Op Max*, 15.
[35] Coleridge, *Confessions of an Inquiring Spirit*, in *SW&F*, II, 1123.

does wish to make the point that *"revealed religion"* is "a pleonasm or definitio per idem" — in other words that there is no such thing as natural religion — it does not justify regarding all revelation indiscriminately: in fact, he maintains that "christianity is the only revelation of universal *validity*."[36] This raises some rather complicated issues, for Coleridge seems to hold that it is not necessary to deny any and all revelation to other religions in order to hold the truth revealed in the Christian faith.

While that may be so, his purpose is not to make a comment on comparative religion, let alone a justification for it. It is to make clear what he describes, by analogy, as the "Lutheran" as opposed to "Grotian" spirit of his own approach: "... the Grotian essays to prove the truth of the christian revelation and our obligation to believe the same by the miracles recorded in the biography of Christ, while the Lutheran would place the credibility of the miracles mainly on their strong previous probability, and this again on the truth and necessity of the revelation."[37] When Coleridge asserts the necessary truth of the Christian faith, therefore, and the primacy of biblical revelation, what he is asserting is what he elsewhere declares, that "the truth is its own light *and* evidence":[38] "Our problem, therefore, must be thus stated. From the necessity of the objects of the christian religion and from its correspondency, adequateness, and divine character, to establish the perfect à priori probability of the miracles attributed to Christ — which being satisfactorily done, the very fact of their having recorded by contemporaries becomes a *sufficient proof* of the facts themselves."[39] This functions in precisely the same way that self-consciousness does: "If I am asked how I know that I am, I can only reply, 'because I am': this is the absolute ground of my knowledge. But if I were asked for the cause not of my knowledge but of the thing known,

---

[36] *Op Max*, 48 (emphasis added).

[37] *Op Max*, 50.

[38] He uses this phrase to describe the way in which the poet, in this case Wordsworth, could know how to write as he had: "For even as truth is its own light and evidence, discovering at once itself and falsehood, so is it the prerogative of poetic genius to distinguish by parental instinct its proper offspring from the changelings, which the gnomes of vanity or the fairies of fashion may have laid in its cradle or called by its names. Could a rule be given from *without*, poetry would cease to be poetry, and sink into a mechanical art" (*BL*, II, 83). Nonetheless, there is an analogy to be made between the poet and the Christian. The Christian too has been apprehended by the Spirit so that he knows Christ. What Coleridge's *Opus Maximum* attempts to do, however, is to show that although it is in God's will to choose his people, that choice does not deny the order of nature, in fact it fulfills it.

[39] *Op Max*, 50–51.

and in this sense the question were put, 'How came you to be?,' the answer must be, 'Because God is.' And vice versâ. The knowledge is derived from the former knowledge as the cause is known in and through its effect: 'quod prius est in ordine essendi, posterius in ordine sciendi.'"[40] Coleridge's emphasis on the anteriority of conscience to consciousness clearly sets him at odds with his contemporaries and their variations on Spinozism, but we will need to conclude by turning to his discussion of how the "I" is discovered in relation to the Divine "Thou," and set it against his contemporaries' formulations to understand it.

I and Thou

The aim of Coleridge's thinking was "to make the senses out of the mind — not the mind out of the senses, as Locke did."[41] Yet the subjective mind cannot regard itself in any scientific way without treating itself as an object. To do so autonomously however would be to be trapped in the sort of solipsistic circular process that Coleridge was at pains to avoid ever since he became aware of Schelling's error. It can only ever be in activity, but never take form. We can see this problem illustrated in the ruminations of his contemporary, Shelley, in his essay "On Life": "Nothing exists but as it is perceived. The difference is merely nominal between those two classes of thought, which are vulgarly distinguished by the names of ideas and of external objects... The words *I* and *you*, and *they* are grammatical devices invented simply for arrangement, and totally devoid of the intense and exclusive sense we usually attach to them." Coleridge's view on these matters, seen in a comparable passage in the *Opus Maximum*, is noticeably different: "Henceforward, I shall presume my reader's recognition of the 'conscire' as equal with 'scire aliquid cum me,' i.e. to know something in its relation to myself in and with the act of knowing myself as acted on by that something... If, then, there can be no '*He*' nor '*It*' without an '*I*,' and no '*I*' without a '*Thou*,' the solution of the problem must be sought for in the genesis or origin of the '*Thou*.'"[42] This is where we see the significance he places upon the relationship of *I* and *Thou* in the *Opus Maximum*, which McFarland even goes so far as to designate as his "philosophical fulcrum."[43] In that sense,

---

[40] *Op Max*, 66–67 ("what is first in the order of being is last in the order of knowing").
[41] *TT*, II, 179; July 25, 1832.
[42] *Op Max*, 74–75.
[43] *Op Max*, cxxxv.

the relationship of *I* to *Thou* has an analogous role to the relation of the
finite mind to the Infinite in his definition of the Imagination in the heart
of his *Biographia*.

At its heart, it is not just an issue of relationship, but of human identity, though implicit in this identity is not only the revelation of our moral
nature, our conscience, but our subsequent capacity to know, our consciousness. Behind all his thoughts on the subject is doubtless the passage
in Genesis 1:26–27 in which human nature is presented *in imagine Dei*:
"Then God said, 'Let us make man in our image, in our likeness, and let
them rule over the fish of the sea and the birds of the air, over the live-
stock, over all the earth, and over all the creatures that move along the
ground.' So God created man in his own image, in the image of God created he him: male and female he created them."[44] In this formulation, not
only do we see something revealed about human nature that is not altogether self-evident and wholly opposed to the Enlightenment's characteristic anthropology based on the postulate of autonomy, namely the fact
that the fundamental human condition is that of *plurality*, and only subsequently of individuality.[45] Yet it also follows that if the two together
are in God's image, this also says something about God.

To illustrate the point we can compare what Coleridge writes in the
Opus Maximum about the process of becoming conscious of the analogy
of Divine love to us in reflection upon another's selfless act, "[a]s sure
as ever the heart of man is made tender by the presence of a love that has
no self, by a joy in the protection of the helpless which is at once impulse,
motive, and reward, so surely is it elevated to the universal Parent,"[46] to
Shelley's remarks on love, which he defines self-reflexively as a process
of outward *self-aggrandizement*: "Love is that powerful attraction...
beyond ourselves, when we find within ourselves the chasm of an insufficient void, and seek to awaken in all things that are, a community with

---

[44] Cf. Colossians 1:15–17 in this respect as well: "(Jesus) is the image of the invisible God, the firstborn over all creation. For by him all things were created: things in
heaven and on earth, visible and invisible, whether thrones or powers or rulers or authorities; all things were created by him and for him. He is before all things, and in him all
things hold together."

[45] Cf. *CL*, II, 1197: "A male & female Tyger is neither more or less whether you suppose them only existing in their appropriate wilderness, or whether you suppose a thousand Pairs. But Man is truly altered by the co-existence of other men; his faculties cannot
be developed in himself alone, & only by himself... Hence with a certain degree of satisfaction to my own mind I can define the human Soul to be that class of Being, as far as
we are permitted to know... which is endued with a reflex consciousness of it's own consciousness..."

[46] *Op Max*, 126.

what we experience within ourselves."[47] This is, however, but an analogy of lesser to greater, and only part of the manner in which Coleridge relates the relationship of I to Thou. Nor is it the most significant to him, though it is perhaps the most persuasive.

The most significant "proof" of Christianity actually sounds very similar to Shelley's formulation, and it may be because he is reflecting more upon human logic than on the logic of Scripture, though it could also lie in his project's whole attempt to access the evidence of Scripture by the back door. It is "the mind, exerting its powers unaided on such factors alone as are found within its own consciousness…"[48] As McFarland rightly notes in his "Prolegomena," Coleridge's conception of God as "Thou" thus lacks the immediacy of the only two comparable authors, Jacobi and Martin Buber, the latter of whom has written a most profound book on the subject.[49] Their formulation would seem to be far more in tune with the logic of Scripture, which presents God as the reality against which everything else, including man, is but a vanity, a puff of wind.

Given the fact that we do deny that reality however, and Coleridge discusses this at considerable length in "Fragment 1," it is questionable whether it can be more readily obtained by a process of introspection. That is Coleridge's project though. For Coleridge, the awareness of God is something that begins with self-consciousness, and moves outward from thence: the "equation of *Thou* with *I*, by means of a free act by which we negative the sameness in order to establish the equality — this, I say, is the true definition of Conscience."[50] Far from being immediate, it is hard won, and only emerges after a process that he likens to watching the intellectual growth of an infant as a parent, whereby "he, and he only, will detect the formation of a language, while to all others the tones of the child are still inarticulate." Without such careful attention "the consciousness itself has the appearance of another,"[51] and an other whom we do not know.

Yet the awareness actually begins not with an intellectual observation as such, but with a favourable assent of the will. It cannot be otherwise. To make God, in the first order, an object of intellectual assent is, once again, to make him out to be a thing, an "It." God does not suffer us to know him in that way any more than a cause suffers an effect to become *its* effect. Thus he writes "quod prius est in ordine essendi, posterius in

---

[47] Percy Bysshe Shelley, "On Love."
[48] *Op Max*, 80–81.
[49] Cf. Buber, *I and Thou*.
[50] *Op Max*, 76.
[51] *Op Max*, 127.

ordine sciendi," that God, though first in the order of being, is last in our order of knowing. Yet although we know ourselves first, our being is always contingent upon His, and relates to it even if we deny it: "Man, with all finite self-conscious beings, knows himself to be because he is a man, but he is a man because God is and hath so willed it. It is the great 'I AM' only, who is because he affirmeth himself to be, because, or rather in that, He is. Thus in like manner, because we have a conscience, we know that there is a God, i.e. that God is the reality of the Conscience, on the principle that the necessary condition of a certain truth must itself be true. Thus in the order of dignity and objective dependency, the principle of religion is before the moral principle, but in the order of knowledge; the moral principle is the antecedent of *our* Faith in the principle of religion."[52] It follows that because knowing God involves an assent of the will, just as the human can suspend consciousness of conscience, overcome it by wicked indulgence, or even through the use of "his Will in order to abandon his Free-Will," we can deny any knowledge of Him.

Ultimately to know God is always an act of faith, though in Coleridge's view, so too is all knowledge: "becoming conscious of a conscience... is an act, namely, in which and by which we take upon ourselves an allegiance, and consequently the obligations of fealty. And this fealty, or fidelity, implying the power of being unfaithful, is the *primary* and *fundamental meaning* of FAITH. But it is likewise, paradoxical as it may appear, the commencement of experience and the indispensable precondition of all experience."[53]

Conclusion

Coleridge's *Opus Maximum* makes a number of fascinating elaborations, clarifying what he had intended in the mysterious transcendental deduction of the Imagination at the center of his most famous critical work, the *Biographia Literaria* (1817). It is apparent from what he later wrote that this definition cannot serve, as it long has, as an articulation of Romantic poetics. Not only does this force us to reassess Coleridge's relationship to Romanticism, his emphasis on the problematic anthropology of his contemporaries should also make an important contribution to the debate over the problem of selfhood bequeathed by the Enlightenment, and perhaps even the current debate surrounding "the body."

[52] *Op Max*, 67.
[53] *Op Max*, 72.

SCIENCE AND THE DEPERSONALIZATION OF THE DIVINE: PANTHEISM, UNITARIANISM, AND THE LIMITS OF NATURAL THEOLOGY

By Jeffrey W. Barbeau

Coleridge's seminal influence on the development of English Romanticism, with its reflective interest in nature, would appear to confirm the judgment that Coleridge was "Nature's Priest." One recent historian has suggested that "[t]he Sage of Highgate was uniquely qualified, appointed by heaven and earth, to fulfill the office of natural theologian."[1] In fact, in the manuscripts that form the published *Opus Maximum*, nature, the idea of God, and the philosophical demonstration of the existence of God apart from biblical revelation are topics of chief interest. Perhaps surprisingly, however, Coleridge's posture towards nature is far less amenable than might be suspected. In the wake of English Deism, the critique of natural religion advocated by David Hume and the prominent response by evidentiary theologians such as William Paley led Coleridge to seek a distinct solution to the question of God that has often gone unnoticed in the history of ideas. Through a careful study of Coleridge's comments on natural theology in the *Opus Maximum*, especially in "Fragment 2" of the text, a vital dimension of Coleridge's long-planned *magnum opus* emerges. In fact, in an argument that both parallels and advances a similar claim made in *Aids to Reflection*, Coleridge's critique in the *Opus Maximum* demonstrates that natural theology employed as a philosophical apologetic for the existence of God terminates in atheism. Coleridge instead advocates reliance on conscience and moral sense predicated on his concomitant belief in the human need for redemption. In this way, Coleridge's *Opus Maximum* presents a trenchant critique of the limits of natural theology based upon an affirmation of the Triune God against both pantheism (explicitly) and Unitarianism (implicitly).

---

[1] Tod E. Jones, *The Broad Church: A Biography of a Movement* (Lanham: Lexington, 2003), 42.

The Intelligibility of God

The evidences for the existence of God occupied a prominent place in eighteenth- and nineteenth-century philosophical theology. The rise of English Deism and correspondent riposte by a throng of the defenders of the Christian faith in England, chief among them (in popularity) William Paley, thrust forward not only a demonstration of God's existence but, more particularly, raised to prominence the vitality of an investigation of the natural world as a source or means of attaining a knowledge of God's existence. The theological reliance on nature, a mode of investigation reliant on the human mind and the world, was hardly a new solution to the question of God's existence, but its prominence in modern controversies is partly the result of a scientific rationalism that infiltrated theological and ecclesial debates.

Natural theology, or physico-theology, as it was often denominated, found biblical support in a series of key Scriptures. Theologians unearthed ample evidence in the Psalms, which suggested that "[t]he works of the Lord are great, sought out of all them that have pleasure therein" (111:2). Throughout the Old Testament, a consistent portrait of the world as a reflection of the Divine emerged. Creation spoke in the landscape and through the starry heavens; the world proclaimed the God who tamed the beasts and brought the sea under his command. Likewise, Paul's injunction to the Romans served as the basis of a veritable proof of the existence of God: "that which may be known of God is manifest in them; for God hath shewed it unto them. For the invisible things of him from the creation of the world are clearly seen, being understood by the things that are made, even his eternal power and Godhead; so that they are without excuse." More than a sufficient source of reflection for the discerning eye, creation through the Pauline lens brought all humanity under the judgment of God ("so that they are without excuse"). Paul's words on creation provided a means not only for the knowledge of right action, or morality, but for the knowledge of God's existence and attributes ("even his eternal power and Godhead").

Rooted in the biblical injunction to survey the creation to gain knowledge of the Creator, many Christian thinkers renewed classic theistic claims, probing the depths of nature in response to what they perceived to be an emerging skepticism. Armed with the latest scientific research on the created order, theologians explored the vast reaches of the globe down to the intricacy of the human eye in an epistemological and unfailingly apologetic quest for their Creator. William Derham (1657–1735) produced one of the most substantial statements of natural theology in his formidable *Physico-Theology* (1713). The subtitle of the volume is a telling indicator of the philosophical end of anatomical and physiological investigation: "A Demonstration of the Being and Attributes of God, from His Works of Creation." Psalm 111:2 serves as the basis for Derham's "Introduction"; for Derham, the verse points to the necessity that all the world be "heedfully and deeply pried into, solicitously observed, and enquired out, especially when clearly discovered to us."[2] Derham vigorously proceeds through the study of the laws of the earth and various animals and rests on a series of six practical inferences of the excellence of God's works. Most important of all, however, is the third inference on infidelity: "the Works of GOD are so visible to all the World... that they plainly argue the vileness and perverseness of the Atheist, and leave him inexcusable. For it is a sign a Man is a willful and perverse Atheist, that will impute so glorious a Work, as the Creation is, to any thing, yea, a mere *Nothing* (as Chance is) rather than GOD."[3] Of course, Derham's research and argument from design applied equally to the theist as the overtly Christian, since it had little to say of Christ.

David Hume, however, sent shockwaves throughout Christianity in his shrewd critique of the claims of natural religion. In his *Dialogues Concerning Natural Religion* (1779), Hume questioned the capacity of reason to access knowledge of the Divine nature and, by implication, to know the very existence of God. What must be recognized here of the conversation between Cleanthes, Demea and Philo is a central problem, identified by Philo, with the rational claim that the cause of the universe can be known through an analysis of effects. Cleanthes rejects Philo's skepticism through an appeal to design reminiscent of the argumentation of Derham's natural theology: "The order and arrangement of nature, the curious adjustment of final causes, the plain use and intention of every part and organ — all these bespeak in the clearest language an intelligent cause or author. The heavens and the earth join in the same testimony: The whole chorus of nature raises one hymn to the praises of its Creator."[4] Philo remains less convinced that the assumption of a cause provides substantial knowledge of a wise Creator. Neither infinity nor perfection need be assigned to Cleanthes' Creator on the basis of an

---

[2] William Derham, *Physico-theology*, reprint of the fourth ed. (1716), History of Ecology (New York: Arno, 1977), 1.

[3] Derham, *Physico-theology*, 428.

[4] David Hume, *Dialogues Concerning Natural Religion*, The Hafner Library of Classics, 5 (New York: Hafner, 1957), 35.

observation of the creation. The case is demonstrated with appeal to a vessel prepared for sea: "If we survey a ship, what an exalted idea must we form of the ingenuity of the carpenter who framed so complicated, useful, and beautiful a machine? And what surprise must we feel when we find him a stupid mechanic who imitated others, and copied an art which, through a long succession of ages, after multiplied trials, mistakes, corrections, deliberations, and controversies, had been gradually improving?"[5] In the same way, many worlds may have been created before our own of less perfect design. Likewise, the unity of the deity, a near universal assumption in the eighteenth century, could hardly be presupposed, since any collection of gods might have equally served as the cause of all. Though something like design might be conjectured, "beyond that position he cannot ascertain one single circumstance, and is left afterwards to fix every point of his theology by the utmost license of fancy and hypothesis."[6] Indeed, on this trajectory of thought, one wonders how the material order might be distinguished from the Divine at all: "There can be no doubt that if we try to draw a positive view out of the discussion in the *Dialogues*, it must either be plain atheism, or atheism in the thin disguise of pantheism."[7] For Philo, if an analogy between the Divine and human be allowed, as the rationalist wishes, the conclusion must be that the universe was formed by a being indifferent to evil. The end result of Hume's *Dialogues*, through the entire conversation and especially through Philo's skepticism, is an undermining of the power of reason to make truth claims about matters of belief, since our experience is so limited and imperfect that it "can afford us no probable conjecture concerning the whole of things."[8]

---

[5] Hume, *Dialogues*, 39.

[6] Hume, *Dialogues*, 40.

[7] Peter Addinall, *Philosophy and Biblical Interpretation: A Study in Nineteenth-Century Conflict* (Cambridge: Cambridge University Press, 1991), 32. Addinall highlights Hume's use of Spinoza for skepticism against theologians, but maintains that "[o]nce we step outside the charmed circle of scepticism and try to give a positive account of experience along the lines laid down by Hume in the *Dialogues*, our ultimate destination is Spinozistic monism, and this is as good as admitted in the words of Philo in which he refers to the world as an organism containing the principle of its order within itself and thereby really asserts it to be God" (32).

[8] Hume, *Dialogues*, 48. Cragg effectively summarizes Hume's contribution to the history of ideas in the *Dialogues*: "Theologically Hume's importance lies less in what he himself taught than in what he henceforth made it impossible for others to say. He destroyed the basis for the glib rationalism of the early part of the century. The complacent assurance that man's mind can dissipate all mysteries and resolve all difficulties could not survive the astringent effect of Hume's cool and searching analysis" (Gerald R. Cragg,

Though Hume's critique of natural religion proved a powerfully devastating blow to Christian apologetics, evidentiary theology in England continued. William Paley, among the foremost natural theologians of the early-nineteenth century, wrote a series of apologetic works demonstrating the veracity of Christianity in the face of criticisms founded on biblical and natural grounds. Paley's biological treatment of the world in *Natural Theology* (1802) shows the impact of Hume's critique of classic approaches to Christian arguments for the existence of God.[9] As LeMahieu explains, natural religion relied on a basic syllogism:

> Major Premise: Nature everywhere exhibits elements of purpose and design.
> Minor Premise: Design must always be the product of a designer.
> Conclusion: Nature is the product of a designer [who is God].[10]

The distinction Paley recognized, after Hume, was the fundamental necessity of substantiating the teleological argument that had been shattered. Thus, Paley brought the minor premise of the syllogism more prominently into play and, quite famously, founded his argument on the necessity of recognizing that all design was the product of a Designer. It is for this reason that Paley commences his argument for the existence of God not on the vast beauty of creation, as Derham and others had so thoroughly emphasized in prior generations, but through the careful explication of why nature's complexity serves as irrefutable evidence of the existence of God: "In crossing a heath, suppose I pitched my foot against a *stone*, and were asked how the stone came to be there; I might possibly answer, that, for any thing I knew to the contrary, it had lain there for ever: nor would it perhaps be very easy to show the absurdity of this answer. But suppose I had found a *watch* upon the ground, and it should be inquired how the watch happened to be in that place... the inference, we think, is inevitable, that the watch must have had a maker: that there must have existed, at some time, and at some place or other, an artificer or artificers who formed it for the purpose which we find it actually to answer; who comprehended its construction, and designed its use."[11]

The Church and the Age of Reason, 1648–1789, The Penguin History of the Church, 4 [London: Penguin, 1990], 168–69).

[9] Addinall maintains that while some believe that Paley simply failed to address Hume's challenge, in fact he wrote *Natural Theology* as "a deliberate reply to Hume's *Dialogues*" (*Philosophy and Biblical Interpretation*, 37).

[10] D. L. LeMahieu, *The Mind of William Paley: A Philosopher and His Age* (Lincoln: University of Nebraska Press, 1976), 58.

[11] William Paley, *Natural Theology; or Evidences of the Existence and Attributes of the Deity. Collected from the Appearances of Nature*, twelfth ed. (Reprint: Lincoln-Rembrandt, n.d.), 1, 3. LeMahieu notes that Paley's watch analogy was derived from the

Unlike a watch, however, the natural order differs in one major respect for Paley: although both the complexity of a ticking watch and that of creation may both imply the existence of a Designer, creation actually generates new structures through the purposeful organization of its parts. This "new discovery" ought to bring greater "admiration of the skill" required to form such a machine, the denial of which amounts to atheism.[12] Under Paley's careful analysis of the organization of bodily structures, even the seemingly defective facets of animal life are elevated. The sloth, for example, appears to have imperfectly formed limbs and "has often been reproached for the slowness of its motions," but this, "tardiness of his pace seems to have reference to the capacity of his organs," while the apparent enjoyment of cattle that "chew the cud" suggests that it is they, perhaps, that "best relish their food."[13] Thus, what may initially appear to be a sign of awkwardness or structural disarray becomes, under the inspection of the natural theologian, a mark of intricacy and purposefulness that identify the Cause of the universe. Indeed, the persistent appearance of pleasure as a dimension of the natural order (in both humans and animals) serves as a sign of the benevolence of a Divine Artificer, despite Hume's supposal of apparent Divine indifference.[14] For Paley, the singular conclusion cannot be avoided: "The marks of *design* are too strong to be gotten over. Design must have had a designer. That designer must have been a person. That person is GOD."[15] Yet, Paley, though his argument is complete, does not conclude his work here. For Paley, merely proving the existence of a Designer is not satisfactory, since he also wishes to suggest that a particular God exists that may be differentiated from a deistic conception of the Divine. Though the mind

Dutch theologian Bernard Nieuwentyt; however, in one respect the two differ: "For Nieuwentyt, the watch analogy did not occupy center stage in his overall production; it played only a minor role and was included, almost casually, as a useful illustration of a larger, more dramatic principle. For Paley, the watch became the controlling motif of his entire book" (LeMahieu, *The Mind of William Paley*, 61).

[12] Paley, *Natural Theology*, 17.

[13] Paley, *Natural Theology*, 285, 287.

[14] LeMahieu notes that "nature for Paley was a vibrant and live carnival of pleasurable activity where even swarms of shrimp on an ocean shore huddle 'in a state of positive enjoyment'" (*The Mind of William Paley*, 83).

[15] Paley, *Natural Theology*, 441. Addinall notes that while Paley's argument that the world may be described according to an analogy of machines, we nevertheless "have no right to assume or deduce that what is convenient or even almost unavoidable in human ways of thinking about the natural world is a characteristic of that world in itself" and, thus, "[t]he fatal flaw in Paley's classic statement of a classic argument is that he assumes just that which he is attempting to demonstrate" (*Philosophy and Biblical Interpretation*, 46).

"feels its powers sink under the subject," still reflection on nature through the lens of the teleological argument yields clear knowledge of the Divine attributes of a unified, benevolent Creator.[16] Built on the theoretical foundation of Butler's analogical argument as well as the empirically-derived scientific and physiological evidence of Derham, Paley's *Natural Theology* formed a penetrating and immensely popular volume demonstrating the existence of the Divine on the basis of evidences from nature.[17]

It was in reaction to Paley, especially, that Coleridge famously disclaimed the value of evidences in *Aids to Reflection*. In *Aids*, Coleridge proposed that the work of physico-theologists had disrupted the work of Christianity in contemporary society by effectively enslaving the Christian to empirical knowledge derived from the senses: "I more than fear, the prevailing taste for Books of Natural Theology, Physico-theology, Demonstrations of God from Nature, Evidences of Christianity, &c. &c. *Evidences* of Christianity! I am weary of the Word! Make a man feel the *want* of it; rouse him, if you can, to the self-knowledge of his *need* of it; and you may safely trust it to its own Evidence."[18] Coleridge's claim contains an implicit appeal to the moral conscience worth noting. Yet, in an earlier day, the "Mechanico-corpuscular Philosophy" had some appeal for even Coleridge. As a man in his thirties, Coleridge studied Derham and seems to have admired his ability to vividly describe nature.[19] Moreover, Coleridge appeared willing, at an earlier stage, to overlook the

---

[16] Paley, *Natural Theology*, 442, 443. Though LeMahieu suggests that "Paley never claimed that his cautious and generally sober lucubrations on the argument from design were intended to persuade the nonbeliever or convert the atheist" (*The Mind of William Paley*, 89), Addinall counters that an ambiguity exists that requires further scrutiny: "There can be no doubt that Paley and many of the thinkers who agreed with him believed that they were putting forward a conclusive argument which if not sufficient of itself to make someone a Christian would lead any honest thinker to revelation and ultimate commitment to the Christian faith. From beginning to end the *Natural Theology* is dominated by the feeling that those who fail to draw the proper conclusion are being willfully blind" (*Philosophy and Biblical Interpretation*, 40–41); for a rhetorical approach to Paley's argument against atheism, see also, M. D. Eddy, "The Rhetoric and Science of William Paley's *Natural Theology*," *Literature & Theology* 18 (2004): 1–22.

[17] The empirical nature of the project is vital, as LeMahieu explains: "To prove that the structure of various creatures in nature was, like a watch, designed for a specific purpose could be neither intuited nor deduced without concrete evidence. The proboscis attached to the head of a butterfly could not be explained by sitting alone with a pencil in an oak-paneled room; you needed the butterfly. For the teleological argument to succeed, it was first necessary to compile a significant number of observations which showed that the individual parts of nature worked together for specific ends; that, like the mainspring of a watch, the proboscis was *telic*" (*The Mind of William Paley*, 63).

[18] *AR*, 405–6.

[19] Consider Coburn's comments in *CN*, II, 3074n.

"pedantry" of Durham and Paley, even if they had "carried the observation of the aptitudes of Things too far, too habitually — into Pedantry…
O how many worse Pedantries! how few so harmless with so much efficient Good!"[20] Coleridge's thinking on these matters changed significantly in later years as a persistent interest in the Logos and moral conscience emerged as the centerpiece of his philosophical theology.
Coleridge develops the concern in the *Opus Maximum* through an examination of the viability of arguments for the existence of God based on
classic Christian propositions deduced from nature. Indeed, in the next
section, I suggest that Coleridge subtly associates an anti-Unitarian
polemic with a philosophical critique of the limits of natural theology in
a prominent chapter of "Fragment 2" of the *Opus Maximum*.

Natural Theology and Atheism

Coleridge's mature critique of natural theology appears in a powerful chapter of "Fragment 2" of the *Opus Maximum*: "On the existential reality of
the Idea of the Supreme Being, i.e. of God."[21] It is here that Coleridge's distinct concern for the philosophical and theological impairment of natural theology comes to the fore. Notably, Coleridge's concern for pantheism and
atheism in this chapter raises to prominence a related notion less recogniz-
ably present in the text: the inadequacy of Unitarianism.

   "Fragment 2" is the longest of the four major manuscripts in the *Collected Coleridge* edition of the *Opus Maximum*. It flows quite naturally
out of the closing section of "Fragment 1" in its immediate recognition
of the relationship between the "I" and "Thou" as factors denominated
"A" and "Z."[22] One of the distinctive features of the fragment is the
wholesale appropriation of the manuscript known as Coleridge's *Essay on
Faith*.[23] The *Essay* is taken up quite early in the text, continuing the discussion of conscience in the first fragment, and serves as the basis for a
connection between Reason and will. Coleridge explains that the "Will
of God is the last and final claim of all our duties" and, thereby, faith as
a form of knowing or beholding, "must be a total, not a partial."[24]

---

[20] *CN*, I, 1616.
[21] *Op Max*, 96–119.
[22] *Op Max*, 80–81.
[23] The *Essay on Faith* can be found in *SW&F*, II, 833–44.
[24] *Op Max*, 93–94. For more on the role of Will in the *Essay on Faith*, see Jeffrey W.
Barbeau, "The Development of Coleridge's Notion of Human Freedom: The Translation

The following chapter, not numbered, is the discussion entitled, "On the existential reality of the Idea of the Supreme Being, i.e. of God." Here, Coleridge turns to the idea of God and poignantly explains the limits of the speculative intellect. Coleridge offers assent to Luther, that "mighty minister of truth," that "without that inward revelation by which we know ourselves responsible… [i]n vain should we endeavour to make up the notion of a divinity out of any materials which the senses can convey, or the world afford."[25] Coleridge's anti-empirical argument is grounded in moral sense and the practical Reason as he proclaims the "logic of human nature by which the soul announces its superiority over the senses and notices of the senses" through the "negation of the senses."[26] Of course, as the work of Derham and Paley suggest, natural theology in the eighteenth and early-nineteenth centuries relies heavily on empirical, sensory-based knowledge as evidence of a Designer. Looking to the world around them, natural theologians examined the world through the eyes of the scientist and discovered a Divine Artificer.

The heart of the chapter turns specifically to the limitations of natural theology in reference to its popular use in the Christian tradition. Coleridge suggests that the belief that the existence of God may be demonstrated from nature is so widespread that "it becomes more than merely expedient not to rest in an assertion if we cannot demonstrate by reason the existence of God, yet by reason itself to demonstrate its indemonstrability." Why? Coleridge is unbending: "For the most dangerous of all weakness is a false presumption of strength."[27] While nature, one of the "two books of God" (along with the Bible), may appear to provide precisely the type of evidence needed to prove the existence of God, in fact it is decidedly limited and, as we shall see, may be extraordinarily pernicious.

The very notion that God cannot be demonstrated is, by Coleridge's own estimation, disquieting. He suggests that his readers will no doubt be "startled at the position that the existence of the Supreme Being in any religious sense is indemonstrable," but the demolition of a false argument will open up "a new world of harmonies" and reestablish "the transcendent dignity of the doctrine itself."[28] By opening the section with a

and Re-formation of German Idealism in England," *The Journal of Religion* 80 (2000): 576–94.

[25] *Op Max*, 102.
[26] *Op Max*, 98.
[27] *Op Max*, 102.
[28] *Op Max*, 103.

clear statement of his conclusion, Coleridge sets the reader along a trajectory of thought that challenges the foundation of modern Christian
apologetics. Although reflection on nature may appear to prove the existence of God, Coleridge maintains that, pressed to its logical conclusions,
Christians will be hard pressed to show the existence of any god other
than the world when reliant on "consequent reasoning."

Coleridge's mastery of language throughout this section plays a vital
role in the rhetoric of a philosophical assertion of religion. Although he
briefly describes the relationship between forms of "consequent reasoning" and pantheism, Coleridge rather briskly takes his reader to the heart
of the popular concern for his proposal; it is a characteristically
Coleridgean defense of the legitimacy and necessity of his project: "I am
only too well aware that an attempt to detect error and weakness in the
ordinary proofs of truths dear to us beyond all others, and the very dear-
ness of which is itself a presumptive proof of their verity... cannot but
seem invidious and be met with the chill, and the shock, which it had
itself occasioned." There is something quite commonsensical and apparently rational about the proofs for God derived from nature. Coleridge
asks, what "can be more delightful, more suited to our nature, than the
argument from the order and harmony of the visible World, from the general adaptation of means to ends, and of an infinity and intrication of
means and proximate ends, to the one ultimate end of beauty in all and
enjoyment in all, that live?"[29]

It is surely a hallmark of Christian theology — even outside the ranks
of the English rationalist debates found in Paley and Hume — to reflect
on the beauty of nature and perceive the glory of God. The North American theologian Jonathan Edwards, whose writings on the human will
were especially irksome to Coleridge, described the beauty of nature as
a "voice or language of God to instruct intelligent beings in things per-
taining to Himself."[30] Edwards reflects a Reformed tradition familiar to
Coleridge. Although Coleridge subjects Sir Thomas Browne's *Religio
Medici* to criticism in *Aids to Reflection* for its "ultra-fidianism," he could
no doubt appreciate the logic and attractiveness of an assertion that nature
acts as an instrument of God. For Browne, the warted toad or seemingly
misshapen elephant are creatures whose outward forms express the visi-
tation of the Creator: "There is no deformity but in Monstrosity; wherein,

---

[29] *Op Max*, 108.
[30] Jonathan Edwards, *The Images of Divine Things*, ed. Perry Miller (New Haven: Yale
University Press, 1948), 61.

notwithstanding, there is a kind of Beauty... there was never any thing ugly or mis-shapen, but the Chaos."[31] Coleridge echoes Browne's appreciation of the natural world in *The Statesman's Manual* when he calls Nature "the music of gentle and pious minds in all ages... the poetry of all human nature." The soothing power of the flowering meadow and the sleeping infant at its mother's breast are alike chapters of "the great book of his servant Nature."[32]

Yet, in the *Opus Maximum*, Coleridge's expression of this deeply Christian tradition serves as a blunt contrast to the apparent absurdity of his own effort to posit any argument to the contrary: "The self-evidence of the great Truth that there is a divine Author of an order so excellent seems to us to supersede all detail of proof... the Heavens declare the Glory of God and the Firmament sheweth his handiwork."[33] For the Christian, the evidence for an intelligent author of nature is weighty. Above all, the proof is sensible and clear in its lack of abstraction. The evidence of nature seems to speak in a voice perceptible to even the least discerning.[34] Moreover, the demonstration of God seems, in many ways, as if it has been "dictated to us by Nature herself, or rather by God in our human Nature."[35] Finally, the evidence is directly connected with "a sense of the high Wisdom, Providence, and adorable Powers of that Being, the existence of which it sets forth." In this way, it would seem that the demonstration of God in nature is not only reflective of the characteristic wisdom and power associated with God, but further provides a deeply practical and persistently fresh impression on the observer that may be more forceful than the insights of a philosopher. In sum, Coleridge stirs the imagination of his audience by envisioning the delight of a reader who follows the "physico-theologist, volume after volume, through the Heavens, through the Waters, into the depths of Earth. Each realm of Nature has had its own religious display, and these works are in every language among the most popular."[36]

---

[31] Thomas Browne, *Religio Medici*, I.II.xvi; for Coleridge's critique of Browne, *AR*, 207–8.

[32] *LS*, 70–71. Coleridge's mention of the infant presages the wonderful analysis of self in "Fragment 2" of the *Op Max*, 120ff.

[33] *Op Max*, 108–9; cf. Ps. 19:1.

[34] Coleridge's use of the imagery of sight and sound reinforces his anti-empiricism: "the whole train of reasoning such as might be conveyed in a series of pictures even to the deaf... it is at once lively, affecting, and comprehensible by the meanest capacity" (*Op Max*, 109).

[35] *Op Max*, 109.

[36] *Op Max*, 110.

In the midst of such weighty evidence, Coleridge rather suddenly offers a statement of powerful subtlety that contradicts the prevalent claims of a Christian devotion to the natural world: "Can it then be the purpose of a wise man to evacuate the force, to throw doubt on the sufficiency of such an evidence?" The voice of popular wisdom underscores the irony of Coleridge's seemingly skeptical question: "As well might he seek to cast a shade on the Sun in Heaven. The Cloud that conceals this, our better Sun, must exhale from the evil heart of unbelief, and rises no higher than to the unbeliever's own Head."[37] Here Coleridge requires careful scrutiny. He does not wish to suggest that nature fails to offer insight into God, but rather that the argument itself ought not be made to carry a weight it cannot bear. On this basis, he can question and even "deny the validity of an argument" while willingly examining its true nature in order "to prevent it from being passed off for a proof of a different kind, for a something which it neither can be nor ought to be, as an argument which addresses itself to the whole man collectively, as an inducement with which each and every distinct faculty of our nature coincides and co-operates."

It may be helpful to remember that this is the same line of argumentation that one finds in *Aids to Reflection* when Coleridge examines the rational basis for Trinitarian doctrine. In *Aids* Coleridge acknowledges that the Trinity may, in fact, be "the hardest to demonstrate," but he also believes that it remains "the one [doctrine] which of all others least needs to be demonstrated," since the lack of conclusive proof does not indicate its irrationality: "though there may be no conclusive demonstrations of a good, wise, living, and personal God, there are so many convincing reasons for it, within and without... the Truth which it is the least possible to prove, it is little less than impossible not to believe!"[38] For Coleridge, it remains possible to disbelieve in the Trinity only so as "to leave some room for the will and the moral election, and thereby to keep it a truth of Religion." The real question for those who disbelieve is not why the Trinity is illogical or should not be believed, but rather why it should. For Coleridge, the answer is plain because it is rooted in the moral conscience of individuals: "because the doctrine of Redemption from Sin supplies the Christian with motives and reasons for the divinity of the Redeemer far more *concerning* and coercive *subjectively*, i.e. in the economy of his own Soul, than are all the inducements that can influence

---

[37] *Op Max*, 110.
[38] *AR*, 186.

the Deist *objectively*, i.e. in the interpretation of Nature."[39] What Deism looks to through the objective inducements of nature, the Christian considers through the moral lens of conscience.

The argument for the Trinity founded on conscience in *Aids to Reflection* serves as a parallel impulse for Coleridge's description of the limits of natural theology and the demonstration of the Divine in the *Opus Maximum*. Coleridge does not wish to deny the value of some aspects of nature in developing a language for the doctrine of God, but he will not accept such argumentation as the basis of proof or a demonstration of Christianity. Natural theology is "an efficient ally" above all by "demonstrating the impossibility of any rational objection" and, further, by "evincing that its indemonstrableness by mere reason results wholly from its transcendent excellency."[40] But the argument presupposes, according to Coleridge, that the idea of God already exists within the mind of the reader of the Book of Nature. In this way, to observe the Book of Nature is not to examine a series of facts and inductively propose the existence of God; it is, rather, to "remember," for learning is "a process of reminiscence."[41]

More importantly, Coleridge questions the allegedly boundless intellect of the rational mind. The human intellect may ultimately be able to establish the existence of God, but cannot proceed to the degree of knowledge frequently presumed: "the dialectic of intellect, by the exertion of its own powers exclusively, is sufficient to establish the general affirmation of a supreme reality, of an absolute being, but this is all — [for] here the power of the scientific reason stops; it is utterly incapable of communicating insight, or conviction, concerning the existence of a world different from Deity. The very possibility is hidden from the reason."[42] The affirmation of a "supreme reality" and "absolute being" fails to communicate the difference between the world and the Creator. Pantheism stems from the identification of deity through the created order and inevitably, "cutting the knot which it cannot untwist," results in the denial of all finite existence. Moreover, Coleridge maintains that the effort to demonstrate God on such a basis is to establish its antecedent, "and thus to construct the thing anew."[43] Under such a system, Coleridge believes that both the philosopher and the theologian are alike left without alternatives: "the inevitable result of all *consequent* Reasoning, in which the

---

[39] *AR*, 188.
[40] *Op Max*, 110.
[41] *Op Max*, 111. McFarland links this to Plato's *Phaedo* and *Meno* (111n.121).
[42] *Op Max*, 104.
[43] *Op Max*, 103.

Speculative intellect refuses to acknowledge a higher or deeper ground than it can itself supply, is... Pantheism."[44]

Consequent reasoning, then, leads to pantheism and, for Coleridge, atheism. Polytheism, similarly, results from the identification of an effect in nature with its cause. Modern science explored through the intricate studies of the physico-theologian finds a parallel in the observations of the natural order by humans in prior eras. Coleridge suggests that the personification of conceptions abstracted from nature has led, in a popular form, to the belief of ancients in "Naiads from the rivulets, their Driads from the Mountain, their Aurae and Aephyri from the Gales and Breeze, and an Hemadryad from every Oak."[45] This popular polytheism is really a mere pantheism that stems from the "habitual referring" of the "Divine Idea to Nature" and ends in the "identification of the one with the other." In later times, the plurality of polytheism was rejected and replaced by similar models such as the Stoic *anima mundi* (spirit of the universe) and, in Spinoza, the whole of creation was reduced "to a nothing."[46] Thus, for Coleridge, the pantheism that natural theology continuously risks slipping into amounts to practical atheism.

Apart from this distinctly philosophical concern, yet closely associated with it, Coleridge's *Opus Maximum* suggests that the deleterious effect of the displacement of the Divine by nature is a shrinking away from the use of the personal in reference to the Deity: "how often have I not observed men of ardent Minds, in the early glow of self-thinking and in the first efforts of supposed emancipation from the prejudices of the popular faith, shrink from the use of the personal as spoken of the Deity, and disposed... to substitute for the living Jehovah the Creator of the Heaven and the Earth, 'a sense sublime / Of something far more deeply interfused... A motion and a spirit, that impels / All thinking things, all objects of all thoughts / And rolls through all things.'"[47] Coleridge is overtly distancing his early poetry (and Wordsworth's) from pantheism and, implicitly, the underlying atheism he now perceives. He strains to justify an earlier stage of his life by interpreting it as a time of incipient development: "Be it,

---

[44] *Op Max*, 106–7. Relevant clarity on the multifarious definitions of the term "pantheism" may be found in Douglas Hedley, "Pantheism, Trinitarian Theism and the Idea of Unity: Reflections on the Christian Concept of God," *Religious Studies* 32 (1996): 61–77.

[45] *Op Max*, 111.

[46] *Op Max*, 112.

[47] *Op Max*, 113; quoting from "Tintern Abbey," 93–102.

however, that the number of such men is comparatively small, and be it, as in truth it often is, a brief stage, a transitional period in the process of intellectual growth, yet among a number great and daily increasing there may be observed an almost entire withdrawing from the life and personal Being of God... a Fate, in short, not a moral Creator and Governor."

What is the consequence of the kind of thinking in which God is identified as more a "Fate" than a "moral Creator and Governor"? In the *Opus Maximum*, as in *Aids to Reflection*, the habitual identification of the laws of nature with the Deity has led most significantly to a complete loss of the idea of sin. The language of "sin" and "holiness" had been lost or ignored as language synonymous with "defect" or "calamity"; sin and the biblical conception of "the hatred of Sin" "are words without meaning, or metaphorical accommodation to the prejudices of a rude and barbarous age."[48] If it is natural phenomena that guides the demonstration of God, as Paley seems to suggest, one wonders how it could be otherwise. Coleridge insists that a religion founded on insights drawn from nature will unavoidably lose sight of the reality of sin. It is for precisely this reason that Coleridge's *Aids to Reflection* points to this passage of the *Opus Maximum*, it seems to me, when he highlights the "hollowness" and "tricksy sophistry" of natural theology: "both Reason and Experience have convinced me, that in the greater number of our ALOGI, who feed on the husks of Christianity, the disbelief of the Trinity, the Divinity of Christ included, has its origin and support in the assumed self-evidence of this Natural Theology, and in their ignorance of the insurmountable difficulties which (on the same mode of reasoning) press upon the fundamental articles of their own Remnant of a creed."[49] In *Aids*, Coleridge suggests that his readers can find a further discussion of the injurious effects of natural theology for Christianity in his *opus* ("[t]he Reader desirous of more is again referred to the Work already announced"), but he uses his attack on natural theology as the basis for a subsequent discussion of the doctrines of original sin and redemption.

Here is where Coleridge's argument takes what many will deem a rather peculiar turn. In the *Opus Maximum*, Coleridge's attack on forms of natural theology in "Fragment 2" is almost wholly focused on the impact of evidential theologies such as Paley and the pantheistic atheism

---

[48] *Op Max*, 115.
[49] *AR*, 255; "ALOGI" suggests the "wordless," "without the Logos," or the "unreasonable" (see 254n.15).

he perceives in Spinoza. Yet, by drawing the doctrine of sin into his discussion, Coleridge rather surreptitiously incorporates a distinctly anti-
Unitarian dimension to his argument. Coleridge poses a seemingly-
innocent question to the reader as a means of drawing together the several
strands of his argument: "And yet how is it possible this should not be
so, if the idea wholly originates in the experience of Nature? For what
can we infer from natural phenomena but the laws that at once constitute
and regulate them. Dr. Priestley, therefore, spoke with perfect consistency when, having affirmed that God did every thing, he added, and is
every thing; for such is the true and adequate idea of the laws of
Nature."[50] The mention of Joseph Priestley here is not accidental, especially when linked to the parallel critique of natural theology and sin in
Aids to Reflection. In the *Opus Maximum*, Coleridge suggests that the
error of natural theology — and those, like Priestley, who risk identifying God with nature — is the loss of personality. God is distanced, in this
way, from the personal attributes that distinguish an active Being from a
mere law or force of nature. Although nature may provide a basis for
curiosity or the advancement of intellectual stimulation, nature fails to
recognize a personal God to be associated with the attributes of faith,
hope, and love. What is intimated in the language of "Divine personality" in the *Opus Maximum*, however, is made explicit in the more overtly
theological concerns of *Aids to Reflection*. Immediately after referring
his readers to the work completed towards his planned *magnum opus*,
Coleridge describes his conviction that all inquirers must come to the
recognition of the necessity of a redeemer: "Remove for him the difficulties and objections, that oppose or perplex his belief of a crucified
Saviour; convince him of the reality of Sin, which is impossible without
a knowledge of its true nature and inevitable Consequences; and then
satisfy him as to the *fact* historically; and as to the truth spiritually, of a
redemption therefrom by Christ."[51]

Coleridge's attempt to develop a line of philosophical argumentation
on the grounds that reflection on the laws of nature fails to bring to attention the nature of a personal God accentuates a latent anti-Unitarian argument in the *Opus Maximum*. The loss of personality collapses the distinction between Deity and nature that Coleridge regarded as fundamental
to rightly describing the difference, for example, between God and grav-
itation. For Coleridge, Priestleyan Unitarianism, like pantheism, amounted

---

[50] *Op Max*, 115–16.
[51] *AR*, 255–56.

to practical atheism because it failed to recognize the need for a personal God who actively engaged humanity's sinful condition: Christ the Mediator. Coleridge believed that the reality of sin (understood as more than a "calamity" or "defect") and the universal need for a redeemer both point to the distinct role of the conscience as the proper ground for the demonstration of God. It is this trajectory of thought that led Coleridge to what might otherwise remain rather baffling comments on the connection between Unitarianism and atheism. Coleridge, for example, cantankerously jokes in one 1824 notebook on the relationship between the two: "I was once asked by a Unitarian, What God made Atheists for? Answer. To cure Deists and Unitarians; or [to] counteract the contagion at least by showing their shallowness and inconsistency."[52] Coleridge's seemingly-paradoxical association between pantheism, Unitarianism, and atheism is similarly expressed in a notebook entry in 1833. There, Coleridge lists the salient points of his argument: "1. That Pantheism is Atheism: 2. that there is no other form of *speculative* Atheism but the pantheistic... 3. That Pantheism, i.e. Atheism disguised under the self-annulling term Pantheism... is essentially immoral... 4. That Socinianism, fairly pursued into it's legitimate Consequences leads to & ends in Pantheism, i.e. Atheism."[53] The language is stark and unexpected for those more familiar with the young poet-preacher of Unitarianism around Bristol during the 1790s. Yet, Coleridge is careful to distinguish between the individuals and the system itself, condemning Unitarian*ism* while remaining silent about the faith of Unitarians. The system undermines the need for Christ as Redeemer and inevitably elevates the divinity of all nature: "In it's zeal to ungod the Redeemer it goddifies Cats, and Mice, Toads, Frogs, and Fleas." The connection between Unitarianism and Nature is prominent; so, too, is Coleridge's antidote: "Pater, Filius, Spiritus sunt Deus, the one only God!"[54] If Coleridge's many attempts to delineate the contents of the *magnum opus* may be trusted and, I believe, if we are to adequately comprehend the content of the *Opus Maximum*, an anti-Unitarian dimension undoubtedly remains among his foremost concerns.

As a matter of fact, it is not always remembered that Coleridge was raised in a vicar's home.[55] Coleridge's father, John Coleridge, was not

---

[52] *CN*, IV, 5120.

[53] *CN*, V, 6753.

[54] *CN*, V, 6753.

[55] A number of useful biographies may be consulted, including Walter Jackson Bate, *Coleridge*, Masters of World Literature Series (London: Weidenfeld and Nicolson, 1968)

only the vicar at Ottery St. Mary, but an author of textbooks in Latin and Hebrew, including a *Dissertation on the Book of Judges* in 1768. Coleridge humorously refers to his father in one letter as "not a first-rate Genius — he was however a first-rate Christian."[56] Although his father died when Coleridge was only nine years old, there can be little doubt that the precocious youth gained an early acquaintance with Christian doctrine — including a framework for interpreting the faith in relation to doctrines of sin and redemption — that maintained some hold on him throughout his more radical years in the Unitarian circles of Cambridge University and the Bristol region.

One could argue that Coleridge's Unitarian impulses, nurtured in the 1790s at Jesus College through the influence of William Frend (1757–1841), are far more the consequence of political dissent than a spiritual conversion from the orthodox Anglicanism of his youth. Although political dissent carried a specifically religious impulse, it was parliamentary reform and the abolition of the slave trade that dominated the radical wings of the period.[57] Still, as a Unitarian lecturer in Bristol, Coleridge's anti-Trinitarian stance, informed by the writings of Joseph Priestley, is resolute. In the fifth of Coleridge's *Lectures on Revealed Religion*, devoted to the "Corruptions of Christianity," Coleridge opens his discourse by affirming a Unitarian vision of Christian theology: "That there is one God infinitely wise, powerful and good, and that a future state of Retribution is made certain by the Resurrection of Jesus who is the Messiah — are all the *doctrines* of the Gospel. That Christians must behave towards the majority with loving kindness and submission preserving among themselves a perfect Equality is a Synopsis of its Precepts."[58] For the young Coleridge, the doctrine of the Trinity must be rejected, as it was by Priestley, because it is a truth above reason itself: "A mysterious Doctrine is never more keenly ridiculed, than when a man of sense, who professes it from interested motives, endeavors to make it appear consistent with Reason."[59] The language of

---

and Rosemary Ashton, *The Life of Samuel Taylor Coleridge: A Critical Biography*, Blackwell Critical Biographies: 7 (Oxford: Blackwell, 1996).

[56] *CL*, I, 310.

[57] One helpful account of Coleridge's connection to the Unitarian climate in England around this time is H. W. Piper's "Coleridge and the Unitarian Consensus," in *The Coleridge Connection: Essays for Thomas McFarland*, ed. Richard Gravil and Molly Lefebure (New York: St. Martin's Press, 1990), 273–90.

[58] *Lects 1795*, 195.

[59] *Lects 1795*, 206–7.

"mystery" had garbled the pristine message of Jesus, volatizing "absurdity into nothingness," and, shackled by the Neoplatonism of the early Christian Fathers, obscured truth under the "dazzle of fantastic allegory."[60] Nonetheless, even in these early years of Unitarian allegiance, the germ of a Trinitarian theology lies latent in Coleridge's lectures. Despite his objections, Coleridge supposes that the Trinity is but "a mysterious way of telling a plain Truth, namely that God is a living Spirit, infinitely powerful, wise and benevolent."[61]

In time, the philosophical legitimacy of Unitarianism became a matter of private concern as Coleridge hoped to locate a *via media* between religious enthusiasm and rationalism. Late in 1799, Coleridge privately composed a profound meditation suggestive of his private doubts: "Socinianism Moonlight — Methodism &c A Stove! O for some Sun that shall unite Light & Warmth."[62] This surging pursuit of a faith uniting head and heart was shortly thereafter coupled with personal crisis. Indeed, by 1804, Coleridge's marriage had largely failed, he was addicted to opium, and he had suffered the loss of several loved ones (most notably his own son Berkeley Coleridge in 1799). All the while, the Socinian conception of God cultivated during prior years at Cambridge was now facing direct scrutiny through private study. Most notable among Coleridge's study of a doctrine of God are the controversial writings between Priestley and Bishop Samuel Horsley (1733–1806). After reading Horsley's 1784 *Letters in Rep. to Dr. P.*, Coleridge wrote with a consuming terseness: "No Trinity, no God."[63] His explanation encapsulates the biography to follow in subsequent decades as he passed from Unitarianism to resolute Trinitarianism: his was "the Religion of a man, whose Reason would make him an Atheist but whose Heart and Common sense will not permit him to be so," as one which came "thro' Spinosism into Plato and St. John."[64] Coleridge's penetrating statement of faith infused by Reason provides us with an acute image of a man in pursuit of a middle way and a determination to integrate the historical and spiritual aspects of the Christian faith. Unitarianism, by Coleridge's account, could not stand in the

---

[60] *Lects 1795*, 207.

[61] *Lects 1795*, 208.

[62] *CN*, I, 467; September–October 1799.

[63] *CN*, II, 2448; February 12, 1805.

[64] *CN*, II, 2448; notably, Coleridge's shift in thinking was deeply informed by his reading of Immanuel Kant — who had himself been "awakened" by Hume's critique of rationalism.

face of a Trinitarian Christian teaching and ought to be cast off as an idolatrous form of worship. Trinitarianism, for Coleridge, provided a distinct means of casting off false notions of God — precisely the concerns reflected in his account of the demonstration of God in the *Opus Maximum*, viz. the atheism implicit in Spinozistic pantheism and, allegedly, Unitarianism.

Coleridge's Trinitarian development sets the stage for a better understanding of the distinctive impulse and nomenclature of later accounts of the *magnum opus* such as the "Logosophia." Coleridge's proposed treatise on Unitarianism, for example, denominated in 1814 as "Logos alogos" or "logos illogicus," suggests the centrality of the Incarnation, but rather shyly fails to explicate Coleridge's full intention. It is notable, too, that the modern proclivity for natural theology enters this same plan, as Coleridge mentions his intention to apply his constructive philosophy to "Metaphysics & Natural Theology" under the heading of "Logos architectonicus." The whole could be encapsulated under a single title: "Christianity the one true Philosophy — or 5 Treatises on the Logos, or communicative Intelligence, Natural, Human, and Divine."[65]

It is due to this shift in thinking that the Trinity lies at the heart of Coleridge's aphoristic treatment of the Christian faith in *Aids to Reflection*. As Douglas Hedley has ably explained, the proper context of *Aids* is "the English Unitarian-Trinitarian controversy of the eighteenth and nineteenth centuries."[66] Although reluctant to write expansively on the Trinity (elsewhere Coleridge suggests that the Trinity is only dealt with in *Aids* "in a *negative* way"),[67] Coleridge willingly deviates from his "first intention" so as to "at least indicate the point on which I stand." Parallel to the argument that I have identified in "Fragment 2" of the *Opus Maximum*, Coleridge maintains that the idea of the Trinity is a matter of "legitimate Contemplation for a speculative philosopher" even while also affirming the importance of Divine revelation for its full disclosure.[68] For Coleridge, the crux of the Trinitarian-Unitarian controversy as developed in *Aids* lies not in the mere possibility of an intellectual assent to the idea of God, but rather in the more probing

---

[65] *CL*, III, 533; September 12, 1814.
[66] Douglas Hedley, *Coleridge, Philosophy and Religion: Aids to Reflection and the Mirror of the Spirit* (Cambridge: Cambridge University Press), 16. As I have suggested at a number of points in this essay, Hedley's thesis could profitably be applied to the *Opus Maximum*.
[67] *CL*, V, 444.
[68] *AR*, 177.

consideration of belief, redemption and, ultimately, the priority of human conscience. It is to prevent this kind of thinking, the kind of thinking that does more damage "to the moral character than it can ever promise as serviceable to the intellect," that Coleridge writes against false demonstrations of God in the *Opus Maximum*.[69] Evidences or demonstrations from the natural order are not wholly without merit. Rather, Coleridge posits the centrality of Reason, that "*immediate recognition of the Necessary and the Universal in negative and positive positions*,"[70] as the true origin of the idea of God. The idea of God finds its "ground of reality" in the moral order of the conscience. This is the basis for Coleridge's claim that one cannot look to nature for a true demonstration of God: "To deduce a Deity wholly from Nature is in the result to substitute an Apotheosis of Nature for Deity."[71] Rather, Coleridge places the reliance on sensory observation and empirical evidence in opposition to the role of the conscience and the claims of morality. Within the individual may be found a basis for the demonstration of God that "the light of the Sun can never reveal": "we must... either despair of finding, or must seek and find within ourselves."[72]

In more overtly theological language, Coleridge relates this same conception to Divine revelation. Coleridge suggests that it is not by discursive reasoning but by the "knowledge being given" that God is known.[73] One cannot properly read the "Book of Nature" so firmly recommended by the physico-theologian until revelation has "assured it" and the conscience has "required it."[74] Though many look to nature as the source of a knowledge of God, for Coleridge, natural theology, by reflecting on the "order and harmony of the visible world," provides an "efficient ally" or the means by which the dictates of Reason and the conscience may find "confirmation, reproduction, and progressive development."[75] Still, one cannot discern true divinity through the lens of nature until the Divine light has revealed it and, thereby, "taught him to read and construe it."[76]

---

[69] *Op Max*, 116.
[70] *LS*, 60n.1.
[71] *Op Max*, 118.
[72] *Op Max*, 118–19.
[73] *Op Max*, 117.
[74] *AR*, 183–84.
[75] *Op Max*, 117.
[76] *AR*, 183.

Conclusion: A Personal God

Although delivered nearly ten years after the death of Coleridge, a passage from the closing of John Henry Newman's 1843 Oxford University sermon, "The Theory of Developments in Religious Doctrine," may provide a fitting interlocutor for Coleridge's insights on the demonstration of God in the *Opus Maximum*: "If we know any thing of Him, — if we may emerge from Atheism or Pantheism into religious faith, — if we would have any saving hope, any life of truth and holiness within us, — this only do we know, with this only confession, we must begin and end our worship — that the Father is the One God, the Son the One God, and the Holy Ghost the One God; and that the Father is not the Son, the Son not the Holy Ghost, and the Holy Ghost not the Father."[77] For Coleridge, as for Newman, the doctrine of the Trinity identifies the heart of the Christian notion of God because it demands reflection on personality.[78] Coleridge's words to Green on the night before his death, though articulated in his distinctive philosophical language, express a similar devotion to attend to a more adequate demonstration of God: "first of all is the Absolute Good whose self-affirmation is the 'I am,' as the eternal reality in itself... And next... as manifested in the person of the Logos by whom that reality is communicated to all other beings."[79] Reliance on empirical knowledge fails to adequately ground a discussion of Divinity because it cannot distinguish between the world and God, nor can it reveal the fundamental importance of Divine redemption in Christ.

Coleridge's seemingly reckless disavowal of the widely popular, scientifically-grounded claims of natural theology in "Fragment 2" of the *Opus Maximum* is, thus, directly tied to his fervent rejection of both pantheism *and* Unitarianism. The recognition of this aspect of Coleridge's argument may provide some perspective on the seeming disappearance of

[77] John Henry Newman, "The Theory of Developments in Religious Doctrine," in *Fifteen Sermons Preached Before the University of Oxford Between A.D. 1826 and 1843* (Notre Dame: University of Notre Dame Press, 1997), 350–51. The centrality of conscience in the *Opus Maximum* has recently been brought into a helpful dialogue with the theology of John Henry Newman's 1859 manuscript, "Proof for Theism" (Philip C. Rule, *Coleridge and Newman: The Centrality of Conscience* [New York: Fordham University Press, 2004], 41–64).

[78] For more on Coleridge and the Trinity, see Alan P. R. Gregory, "'That I may be here'" (ch. 9); cf. Daniel W. Hardy, "Coleridge on the Trinity," *Anglican Theological Review* 69 (1987): 145–55.

[79] In John Beer, ed., *Coleridge's Writings. Vol. 4, On Religion and Psychology* (New York: Palgrave, 2002), 257.

the anti-Unitarian dimension when one compares the *Opus Maximum* to Coleridge's proposed *magnum opus*. Rather than imagining that *Aids to Reflection* alone develops a stance against Unitarianism, it is clear that the *Opus Maximum* not only parallels but even extends the argument of *Aids to Reflection*. Moreover, when we attend carefully to Coleridge's chapter "On the existential reality of the Idea of the Supreme Being" in "Fragment 2" of the *Opus Maximum*, it comes as no surprise to find that Coleridge begins the manuscript with a discussion of moral conscience and Reason through the appropriation of the manuscript *Essay on Faith*. Nor is it a surprise that "Fragment 2" ends with a discussion of Trinitarian theology and redemption.[80] Coleridge insists that a right understanding of God depends on both the capability and possibility of redemption by a personal God; without such a stance, Coleridge believed that theology risked "reducing the idea of God into a formless and hollow unity, or rather sameness, like the unity of space... Such would be the unity of the universe considered as God." In the words of *Aids to Reflection*, "the Demonstrators presuppose the Idea or Conception of a God without being able to authenticate it."[81] The act and duty of beholding in faith remains, and "these are Derivatives from the practical, moral, and spiritual Nature and Being of Man."[82]

---

[80] *Op Max*, 212.
[81] *AR*, 185.
[82] *AR*, 188.

"THAT I MAY BE HERE": HUMAN PERSONS AND DIVINE PERSONEITY IN THE *OPUS MAXIMUM*

By Alan P. R. Gregory

Joe Simpson shattered his knee near the top of a hitherto unclimbed peak in the Andes. For several days, he crawled in agony over snow and rock back to his colleagues at base camp. Within yards of their tent, he screamed uselessly for help. Recalling the moment he believed himself abandoned, he said, "it was then I lost me."[1] Coleridge reminds us that in childhood we are closer to such psychic extremes and do not have to fall off mountains to suffer them. A three-year old, he writes, "I myself heard using these very words in answer to the mother's enquiries, half hushing and half chiding, 'I am not here, touch me, Mother, that I may be here!' The witness of its own being had been suspended in the loss of the mother's presence by sight or sound or feeling."[2] This essay introduces Coleridge's account of personality and, especially, of personality as grounded in relations: there is "no '*I*' without a '*Thou*.'"[3] My guiding purpose is to examine the extent to which Coleridge, in developing his Trinitarianism, provides an ontology able to support the moral and religious weight he places upon the distinction between "persons" and "things."

Persons and Relations

Coleridge worried over a public conscience dozing in the satisfactions of mechanistic thinking and utilitarian ethics. Among varied attempts to slap it awake, he attacked the laissez-faire arguments of "political economy." The critique in *A Lay Sermon* finds its rhetorical climax in anecdotes drawn from a trip to the Scottish Highlands. A widow ejected from her farm laments the social destruction that followed upon the clearing of the

---

[1] Joe Simpson, "Touching the Void," directed by Kevin Macdonald (IFC Films, 2004), videocassette.
[2] *Op Max*, 132.
[3] *Op Max*, 75.

Highlands in the interests of profitable sheep farming: "Within this space
— how short a time back! there lived a hundred and seventy-three persons: and now there is only a shepherd, and an underling or two. Yes, Sir!
One hundred and seventy-three Christian souls, man, woman, boy, girl,
and babe; and in almost every home an old man by the fire-side... Instead
of us all, there is one shepherd man, and it may be a pair of small lads
— and a many, many sheep!"[4]

Coleridge makes a point of stressing the woman's animation, she
begins "with a deep sigh and a suppressed and slow voice which she suddenly raised and quickened after a first drop or cadence" and as she
spoke, "she made a movement with her hand in a circle, directing my eye
meanwhile to various objects as marking its outline." Her moral energy
makes her an icon of "personality," a proof upon the feelings of what distinguishes persons from things. In the social history she describes, moral
community is trumped by economic interest. The logic of political economy strides past the irreducible particularity of persons as it counts units
rather than weighing value: surely, "[i]f three were fed at Manchester
instead of two at Glencoe or the Trossacs, the balance of human enjoyment was in favor of the former."[5]

This passage and the Trinitarian arguments of the *Opus Maximum* are
closely related, despite the contrasting discourse. The distinction between
persons and things, between the "I" and the "non-I," is an ontological
one and — as Kant's successors, Coleridge amongst them, recognized
— needs securing philosophically within a fundamental ontology. Is the
"personal" really an ultimate category? Does the political argument that
limits the application of political economy in the name of this category
have its grounds in the ultimate conditions of being? Do we live in a universe fitted for the making of persons and promising their fulfillment,
their eternity?[6] These questions undoubtedly haunted Coleridge and to a
considerable extent took the more existentially pointed form of desire for
salvation. Is a life crossed by broken relationships, moral failure, and

---

[4] *LS*, 209–10.

[5] *LS*, 211.

[6] In various writings, Colin Gunton has drawn attention to the importance of ontological questions within theological discussion in general and Trinitarian theology, in particular; see especially, Colin Gunton, *The Promise of Trinitarian Theology*, second ed. (London: T & T Clarke, 1977); *The One, the Three, and the Many: God, Creation, and the
Culture of Modernity*. The 1992 Bampton Lectures (Cambridge: Cambridge University
Press, 1993); "Trinity, Ontology and Anthropology: Towards a Renewal of the Doctrine
of the *Imago Dei*," in *Persons, Divine and Human: King's College Essays in Theological Anthropology*, eds. C. Schwobel and Colin E. Gunton (Edinburgh: T & T Clark, 1991).

unsubstantiated commitments, just a life lost? Are years lived as an unkept promise redeemable?

The most familiar targets of Coleridge's cultural and philosophical polemic were chosen largely because they failed to provide an ontology that preserves the personal from extinction. In the Necessitarianism of Hartley and Priestley, that "hybrid of Death and Sin," personal freedom disappears into the determining laws of association; virtue vanishes as those with a prudent eye on the afterlife follow William Paley in his cost/benefit analysis of moral action; while Spinozistic pantheism, in all its guises, absorbs personal significance without remainder in "that mysterious nothing which alone is."[7] Only, Coleridge argues, in the acknowledgement of a personal God to whom love and gratitude are due, do we find a ground that guarantees the eternal significance of persons. Coleridge arrives at this acknowledgement in two distinct intellectual movements, the internal relations of which he never fully clarified. Theologically, he proceeds from biblical narrative and creedal authority to confession of the God who — as Father, Son, and Spirit — reveals himself as love. Philosophically, however, the starting-point is moral responsibility and the landing-place, the necessary distinctions of the God who is "Idem," "Alter," and "Copula." This latter movement is the one developed in the *Opus Maximum* and its relationship with the former; that between the doctrinal and the philosophical remains largely the subject of Coleridgean promise.

Clearly, though, if the philosophical tradition he so strongly opposed sought to interpret revelation through reason, as in Locke's paradigmatic defense of revelation, *The Reasonableness of Christianity*, Coleridge interpreted reason through revelation. There is, therefore, no "natural religion" or "religion of reason." A religion not revealed is "no religion at all" and the "Ideas" of Reason, and preeminently the doctrine of the Trinity, are the *revelation* of "Supreme Reason."[8] From an analysis of moral responsibility and "conscience," the arguments of the *Opus Maximum* plot how they require the development of a Trinitarian account of God. The point of departure itself, the reality of the conscience, cannot be demonstrated, it can only be accepted in an act of self-recognition: "consciousness of a conscience is itself conscience."[9] Arguments from

---

[7] *Op Max*, 112. For one history of Coleridge's critique of pantheism, see Thomas McFarland, *Coleridge and the Pantheistic Tradition* (Oxford: Clarendon Press, 1969).

[8] *AR*, 184; *Op Max*, 160.

[9] *Op Max*, 21.

social function, for instance, or human behavior, can never get beyond the empirical sphere of cause and effect to arrive at the knowledge of freedom. Freedom is manifest in the act of "faith" in which we trust the witness of conscience.[10] An argument that begins from this starting-point remains, therefore, hypothetical: we learn "not indeed whether a true religion exists, but what it must be, and what it cannot be, if it have or at any future time should have, a real existence."[11] Furthermore, though Coleridge's philosophical procedure uses "no arguments" or "authorities borrowed from or grounded upon any particular supposed revelation," he is careful to insist that the actual existence and practice of such a procedure does depend upon historical revelation: "we may be abundantly convinced that but for a particular revelation this sufficiency of the reason for itself would not have existed. The Boy walks unaided, though without aid he never might have learnt to walk."[12] Thus, theological argument, even when it prescinds from any "supposed revelation" and proceeds "unaided," never leaves the sphere of revelation either in terms of its historical possibility or, transcendentally, in the revelation that is Reason, in which all human beings participate even as their sinful wills resist its light.

Contemporary Trinitarian theologies frequently argue the dangers, indeed, hopelessness, of any account of the Trinity that does not remain close to the shape and detail of biblical narrative.[13] In some respects, Coleridge provides evidence for such argument. However, what is remarkable is the degree to which his guiding urgency concerning the ultimacy of personality opens the prospect of a Trinitarianism formative of Christian faith and practice. Biblical exegesis may be at the margins of the *Opus Maximum*, but its fragments map a suggestive conceptual strategy for thinking the Triunity of God and unfold the logic of the connections between "persons," a "personal" God, and the God who is "Trinity."

Coleridge learned the distinction between "persons" and "things" from Kant and, up to a point, his account of "personality" is, again, Kantian. The "predisposition to personality," Kant tells us, lies in our "capacity for respect for the moral law as in itself a sufficient incentive of the will."

---

[10] *Op Max*, 72.
[11] *Op Max*, 83.
[12] *Op Max*, 57–58.
[13] David Brown, *The Divine Trinity* (London: Duckworth, 1985), 52–101; Walter Kasper, *The God of Jesus Christ* (London: SCM, 1984), 233–63.

On the ground of practical reason, reason as it governs our willing, a person is "a rational and at the same time an accountable being."[14] Persons, therefore, are "ends in themselves" and distinguished from "things" in that they demand respect "in every case as an end withal, never as means only."[15] Moral agency is also decisive for Coleridge, however, his treatment is distinctive in that the moral will and, therefore, personality, is conceived in terms of relations — human relationships being constitutive of persons. In addition, Coleridge's is a more thoroughly theological enterprise than Kant's, and, from the outset, he has his eye on the theological deployment of concepts such as "will," "reason," and "person." Again, though Christian doctrine may be strategically eclipsed, the argument always moves in its attraction.

Animals, of course, know and, what is more, they are aware of themselves in relation to the objects of their knowledge. This self-awareness, however, must, Coleridge argues, be carefully distinguished from the "self-consciousness" that is the privilege of humanity. Human knowing, the knowing that is proper to persons, is "*con*-sciousness," the knowing of self that accompanies, goes along with, all empirical knowledge: "In the subjective sense, the 'I' is able to know this or that as one with its own self."[16] This is the general form of human knowing but it is dependent upon a specific form of "con-scire," that which we familiarly call "conscience." Conscience, the inward measure of the conformity of the will to the moral law, is "the root and precondition of all other consciousness."[17] Coleridge admits that this appears paradoxical, and we shall return to his specific argument below, but the claim has an important place in developing the theological case. It provides for a radical break between the animal and the human creation and ensures a thoroughly theological anthropology in that the orientation to God, via the conscience, is the origin of human consciousness and, therefore, of *human* experience. All reductionist accounts of human experience in terms of psychological, economic, or sociological causation, whatever their specific and relative usefulness, are, by the dependence of consciousness on conscience, judged and found wanting.

---

[14] Immanuel Kant, *Religion Within the Limits of Reason Alone*, trans. T. M. Greene and H. H. Hudson (New York: Harper & Brothers, 1960), 23.
[15] Immanuel Kant, *Groundwork of the Metaphysic of Morals*, trans. H. J. Paton (New York: Harper & Row, 1956), 95.
[16] *Op Max*, 74 (translation). Coleridge has "ego sensu subjectivo scire posse hoc vel illud un cum se ipsis."
[17] *Op Max*, 84.

Conscience is the inward mediator of Reason as it governs, or should
govern and guide our willing. Conscience, therefore, is the knowledge of
Reason as representing the will of God.[18] By virtue of conscience, human
beings are summoned into moral agency and know themselves free and
responsible. "Will" thus moves into the center of Coleridge's anthropology, as it does in his doctrine of the Triune God. Humanity is constituted
in acts of will, even as "becoming conscious of a conscience, partakes of
the nature of an act."[19] The conscience demands a synthesis between our
individual will and the Divine Reason it represents. Righteousness, therefore, is a likeness to the God in whom will and Reason are not synthe-
sized but in the identity of "co-inherence." While conscience has a bearing on all acts of will, of course, not all acts of will unite with conscience.
Our finite wills make play with other partners, ambition, appetite, power,
and so on. This returns us to "personality." Persons are particular, inex-
changeable, a point Coleridge exemplified in the figure of the Highland
widow. As Reason is necessarily universal, whereas will is particular
(there being many wills but one "Reason"), Coleridge concludes that
"we become persons exclusively in consequence of the Will."[20] However,
since wills are free and only become so in relation to conscience, we correctly term "will" unrelated to Reason, "instinct" or "impulse." Personality, therefore, involves the co-presence of Reason and Will.[21] Since
Coleridge has correlated "personality" with will in its varying relation to
Reason, personality is not a psychological given, an individual confluence
of characteristics, but a vocation. We become persons and, through our
aggravated self-alienation from God, we diminish ourselves as persons,
though Coleridge acknowledges that personality cannot be entirely lost as
long as Reason continues at all.[22] Conceiving personality in dynamic
terms, as a matter of degrees in relation to the unity of will and Reason,
secures Coleridge two great advantages. He has an anthropology oriented
towards sanctification, our vocation being what makes us human, and a
concept of personality open to the idea of "absolute personality," the
identity of will and Reason. "Person" is understood so as to make it possible to apply that term to God.

[18] *Op Max*, 84.
[19] *Op Max*, 72.
[20] *Op Max*, 165, cf. "Reason is incompatible with individuality, or *peculiar* possession"
(167).
[21] *Op Max*, 175.
[22] "For as long as the reason continues, so long must the conscience exist in some
form, as a good conscience or as a bad" (*Op Max*, 72).

Thus far, Coleridge's account of personality may appear as firmly in an individualistic tradition as Boethius' classic definition, "an individual substance of rational nature."[23] Certainly, persons are related to one another through the universal, the voice of conscience, as it were, constituting the common life of reason. Coleridge, however, departs radically from an individualistic understanding of personality by deriving the particularity of each person, self-consciousness as person, from relations with others. Identification in terms of "he," "she," or "it" presupposes, Coleridge argues, the recognition of "Thou." The third person is thus a displaced or denied "Thou." "Thou," though, remains at the center of the system of pronouns as "Thou" involves the recognition of the "other as same" and self-consciousness, the "I," is the reflex of this recognition. Thus, "no He without a previous Thou — and of course, no *I* without a *Thou*."[24] What, however, has all this to do with the claim that "*Conscience* is not a Result or Modification of Self-Consciousness; but its Ground and Antecedent Condition"?[25]

The answer is dense even by Coleridge's standards and he admits that he "must require from the reader an energy of attention… far beyond what I shall have occasion to require in any following part of the work."[26] Coleridgean apologies are generally markers that something is "going on," either very important or somewhat shifty. Here the apology indicates the importance the argument has within the *Opus Maximum* and the author's sense of going out on a philosophical limb. What takes place when we recognize that which confronts us as "Thou"? A simultaneous identification and distinction: "an equation in which '*I*' is taken as equal to but yet not the same as '*Thou*.'" '*I*' and '*Thou*' are established as "correspondent opposites, as harmonies or correlatives."[27] There is, then, a double action or, perhaps better, a single action with two reciprocating poles: an identifying and a distinguishing, the former affirming sameness, the latter "negativing the sameness in order to establish the equality."[28] What, though, is the difference between the two poles of this action? The difference lies in the role of Coleridge's key term, "will." Will is not involved in the movement by which I acknowledge sameness,

---

[23] "Naturae rationabilis individual substantia," Boethius, *Contra Eutychem*, III.4f.
[24] *Essay on Faith,* in *SW&F*, II, 837; cf. *Op Max*, 75.
[25] *CN*, IV, 5167; cited in *Op Max*, 73n.202.
[26] *Op Max*, 75.
[27] *Op Max*, 75.
[28] *Essay on Faith*, in *SW&F*, II, 837; cf. *Op Max*, 76. As regards the two "poles," Coleridge, of course, uses the language of "thesis" and "antithesis."

the pole of *self*-consciousness: "I do not will to consider myself equal to myself." Put more technically, that is, "the affirmation of the *I* primary as equal to the reflex *I* — in other words, that in the identification of the subject and object in which self-consciousness consists, there is no application or intervention of the Will"[29] The case of the other, simultaneous, action of distinguishing is different. Here, there is an act of will, an act whereby I differentiate to establish an equality: the acknowledgement of the "*Thou.*" Self-consciousness is thus a reflex pole of the act by which I recognize the same as other, the "Thou." This action, however, by which the "Thou" is known and is the condition of self-consciousness is "a free act by which we negative the sameness in order to establish the equality," and this is "the true definition of Conscience."[30] More concretely, I see myself in another person but recognize that that one is not a part of me or an extension of me, but different and equal, and because equal, a neighbor and demanding of love: "thou shalt love thy neighbor as thyself."

The free act, the will that acknowledges the "Thou," establishes a measure by which all my willing is judged. The distinction between "persons and things" follows from the original movement in which "Thou" and "I" are established as "correlatives." This is the act of conscience without which there would be no self-consciousness, no recognition of "he," "she," "it," "we," or "they," and no *human* experience. The triumphant conclusion — provided in a rather breathless statement with a relieved "Q.E.D" to finish — is that therefore "the conscience in its first revelation cannot have been deduced from experience" and, we may add, applying the point, it cannot be *re*duced to experience, either, psychological, sociological, or otherwise. Coleridge has gotten to his first "landing-place" in securing the personal as an ultimate and irreducible category. In this relational account of the person he also has a potential point of correspondence between his anthropology and a doctrine of the Triune God. The argument we have reviewed, of course, is a transcendental one, an analysis of the conditions of experience. It may find its experiential analogue, though, in those Copernican moments when our recognition of another person has a peculiar intensity and jerks us out of our presumptive place at the center of the universe. A loved one or, sometimes, an arresting stranger, awes us into the depths of their equality as another "I," and thereby we also find ourselves and are "put in our place."

---

[29] *Op Max*, 76.
[30] *Op Max*, 76.

Cultural assessment and critique are never far away from Coleridge's philosophical or theological arguments. His basic epistemological distinction between "Reason" and "Understanding" is elaborated in polemic against an age that had "fallen captive to the understanding and the senses." It is, then, not surprising that when "personality" is elaborated as a central concept, we also find Coleridge bemoaning de-personalizing tendencies in his society and that "among a number great and daily increasing there may be observed an almost entire withdrawing from the life and personal Being of God."[31] When theological argument loses itself in the explanation of "Nature," then God becomes a "hypothetical Watch-maker," if not identified with the system of laws itself, a solution that Coleridge regards as at least having the merit of greater consistency.[32] Personal language and the piety it supports atrophy in a culture for which God has become a "Fate... not a moral Creator and Governor."[33] The ideological changes gift their authority to the undermining of personal relationships in, for instance, economics, education, and child-rearing. Coleridge's next approach to finding the origins of personality in relations, here the relationship of infant and mother in particular, is an exercise in both psychological reflection and cultural critique.

Once again, the stakes are high since the formation of personality, Coleridge argues, takes place by means of relationships: first with the mother, then with the father and others. This formation, however, is theologically significant as the formation of personality, from its earliest moments, is a stage in the relationship with God. From this perspective, ideologies and practices that objectify human beings or that represent human satisfaction in sub-personal ways are blind to the dynamics of human development because they fail to distinguish between the level of personal relations and material goods. Personal relationships are irreducible. They are not just one form of good alongside others but the good that determines personality and humanity. Such an argument begs the ontological question with a renewed intensity: is there ultimate grounding for this personal reality?

The cuddled child intuits the mother in the warm security of embrace. She is a complete environment, the various sensory stimuli of sight, touch, sound, smell, and taste, not discrete but combining within this "World" in which the infant's own self will be formed: "The Babe acknowledges

---

[31] *Op Max*, 114.
[32] For "hypothetical Watch-maker," see *CL*, IV, 768; September 1817.
[33] *Op Max*, 114.

a self in the mother's form years before it can recognize a self in its own."[34] What is sensed is connected as an environing whole that emerges as "Thou": "The Eye... connects the Mother's face with the warmth of the mother's bosom, the support of the mother's arms."[35] The child is "Eye," not yet "I," but still this is no construction of the animal instinct, but the "first dawnings of humanity" or "Reason itself mutely prophesying of its own future advent."[36] The child is humanity throughout, animal instinct subsumed into the pre-conscious intuitions of Reason, the revelatory power that discloses those "truths above sense" which provide the context and order for the objects of sense and, eventually, of reflection.[37] The Mother intuited — through and beyond the sensory experience, as a "whole," a loving environment in person — is the gift of Reason. Coleridge pushes the dynamics of Reason back into a time before the conscious exercise of "Understanding," the activity in which we negotiate the world of objects, analyze, abstract and generalize, plot cause and effect, discover means for ends.[38] Where Reason reveals itself, though, there must also be the form of its reception, which for Coleridge is "faith."[39] In this way, the "will," too, makes its way into Coleridge's depiction of our earliest experience: "Faith, implicit Faith, the offspring of unreflecting love, is the antecedent and indispensable condition of all [the child's] knowledge."[40] Coleridge, here, shifts the meaning of faith away from the stress he has placed on "fidelity," as "keeping faith," towards "trust."

[34] *Op Max*, 121. According to a slightly later passage in "Fragment 2" of the *Opus Maximum*, between the mother/child relationship and the development of full self-consciousness, there is the experience of the father and the mother's relationship with both the child's visible father and the heavenly father, both of whom are "other" to the maternal "Thou." This experience of "distinction and alterity," visible and invisible, is the catalyst of the child's own sense of being an "I," visible and invisible, empirical and transcendent: "The child now learns its own alterity, and sooner or later... it forgets henceforward to speak of itself by imitation, that is, by the name which it had caught from without. It becomes a person; it is and speaks of itself as "I," and from that moment it has acquired... a sense of alterity in itself, which no eye can see, neither his own nor others" (*Op Max*, 132).

[35] *Op Max*, 121.

[36] *Op Max*, 122.

[37] "Reason is the Power of universal and necessary Convictions, the Source and Substance of Truths above Sense, and having their evidence in themselves" (*AR*, 216).

[38] The "Understanding" is also, and first, "the faculty by which we generalize and arrange the phenomena of perception." As such, the activity of the Understanding is a priori and thus the condition of all human experience.

[39] For one of the clearer statements of the Reason/Understanding distinction, see *AR*, 216–18.

[40] *Op Max*, 121.

"Why have men a Faith in God?," Coleridge asks. "There is but one answer: the Man, and the Man alone, has a Father and a Mother."[41] Coleridge is not interested in establishing the nurturing relationship of parents to children as an analogy for the relationship of God and human beings. This is not to say such an analogy is worthless but unless carefully controlled it crops up in crude anthropomorphisms and embarrassing homiletic exhortations to "childlikeness." Rather, the relationship of mother and child, as Coleridge interprets it, is a stage in the formation of persons and thus the psychological preparation and initiating context for our relationship with God, since that relationship is personal in form and the fulfillment of our personality. As we have seen, persons are constituted by relations. Indeed, so much so that a hiatus in relationship may be experienced as the loss of self: "I am not here, touch me, Mother, that I may be here!" The terms of the relations, however, are from the beginning essentially mysterious. Beyond the elements felt, heard, seen, the child intuits the mother as a loving "whole," a sum that always remains greater than the parts. Intuition thereafter comes to exceed the form of the mother towards the horizon of an encompassing whole that bears up the loving environment of the mother/child relationship itself.

"Personality" is an "Idea" in the Coleridgean sense, that is, not fully objectifiable in discursive terms. Whether grasped implicitly or explicitly, it is formative, ordering, and supplies a context that transcends the sensible world. Coleridge elevates "personality" as the ordering power upon which psychological, social, and cultural good depends, not to say religious truth and faithfulness.[42] In healthy development, Coleridge suggests, happiness is so thoroughly involved with persons that "the pleasures of its senses... have become their representative, their denominator" and "[o]ften have I see a child of two or three years old seated at the homely table with healthful hunger, and yet incapable of gratifying it, because the father had not yet come in, or the accustomed faces of brother, sister, or playmate, were wanting."[43]

The intuitions of Reason provide the divinely significant environment of "ideas" that are prior to and should order the conscious reflections, analyses, and investigations of the "Understanding." Coleridge, though, identifies a psychological and cultural tragedy in which we close off our

---

[41] *Op Max*, 122.

[42] "An Idea is not simply knowledge or perception as distinguished from the thing perceived: it is a realizing knowledge, a knowledge causative of its own reality" (*Op Max*, 223).

[43] *Op Max*, 125.

experience from the horizon opened in our earliest intuitions. The false
clarities of the Understanding occlude the sense of the whole and leave
the world a heap of "little things."[44] Since personality is formed within
these intuitions of an encompassing and loving environment, an environment of human and Divine persons, then the more fully the diversities of human knowledge and experience are integrated with these, the
more culture will approach its Divine vocation as an order for the formation of persons. The alternative, according to Coleridge, is a fragmented world in which persons suffer violence, reification, and the loss
of freedom.

In order to sustain this vision, Coleridge must develop an ontology that
does justice to the crucial role of personality in his thought. If personality is the form of humanity's eternal relationship with God, then this
ontology will take form as a doctrine of "the living Jehovah whose name
is I AM!, whose first and Eternal Name is in the declaration of that personality, which nature hath not and cannot declare."[45]

Maintaining the "personal Being of God," however, commits
Coleridge to facing a critique that proceeds aggressively from his own
philosophical sources. In 1798, an accusation of atheism derailed
J. G. Fichte's philosophical career in Jena. The immediate provocation
was the brief essay, "On the Foundation of Our Belief in a Divine Government of the Universe," though, in substance, the theological argument
was anticipated as early as the *Attempt at a Critique of all Revelation* of
1792. Fichte started, as did Coleridge, with the Kantian moral subject
and, theologically, with God as the ground of human freedom. Coleridge
credited Fichte with "the first mortal blow to Spinozism" and he also
acknowledged the philosopher's precedence in preparing for the placing,
so important in the *Opus Maximum*, of "will" as an originating act in priority over "being."[46] In the 1798 essay, though, Fichte concluded that theism was incompatible with moral freedom. What we know, Fichte argued,
is our freedom and our moral vocation to conform the world of appearances to the purposes of reason. That vocation, and the "moral world-
order" it implies, is self-dependent and self-authenticating. Theistic arguments attempt to explain and find security for this moral vocation and thus
they falsify the freedom and faith that make it a *moral* vocation. They

---

[44] Letter to Thomas Poole (*CL*, I, 354; October 16, 1797).

[45] *Op Max*, 119.

[46] *BL*, I, 158; elsewhere Coleridge suggests that "[Fichte] has the merit of having prepared the ground for, and laid the first stone of, the *Dynamic* Philosophy by the substitution of Act for Thing" (*CL*, IV, 792).

seek a reason for that which is and must be its own reason. There is no ground, therefore, "outside" the moral order: that order is the Divine and to do the deeds of duty is to know the Divine: "This living and effective moral order is identical with God."[47] Furthermore, the theistic concept of God, as a creator distinct from the moral world order is, in itself, "impossible and full of contradictions."[48] Above all, to ascribe "personality" or consciousness to God is useless anthropomorphism. "Personality" is necessarily finite; persons, particular.

Coleridge frequently accused the post-Kantian Idealists of collapsing back into the pantheism their point of departure should have enabled them to avoid. Fichte's essay serves as one example of the tendency Coleridge deplored. He most frequently attacks Schelling in this respect, but "On the Foundation of Our Belief in a Divine Government of the Universe" is particularly appropriate here for Fichte's uncompromising attack on Divine personality.[49] From Coleridge's perspective, Fichte is trying to ground the value of persons upon an impersonal context. One might object to this that the "moral world order" is itself an order of rational persons and, as Fichte argues, it is, and must be, its own sole justification. This response, however, does not deal with Coleridge's central concern as we find it in the *Opus Maximum*. Persons are irreducibly particular. Within Fichte's scheme, the general activity of persons in moral world-making may be upheld but the particular persons are only of instrumental value in the evolving order. There is utilization of their dutiful acts, but no redemption of persons who are, as Coleridge knew rather painfully, more than their good deeds. Coleridge counters the opposition Fichte finds between the inherent rationality of the moral order and a God distinct from that order and believed to explain it with an account of Reason as both transcendent and immanent. Reason is "act," revelation: it is the manifestation of the Logos whose plenitude is the formative system of "Ideas." Rationality, both subjective and objective, is the "living

---

[47] Fichte, "On the Foundation of Our Belief in a Divine Government of the Universe," trans. Patrick L. Gardiner, in *Nineteenth Century Philosophy*, ed. Gardiner (New York: The Free Press, 1969), 25.

[48] Fichte, "On the Foundation," 26.

[49] One comment in the *Biographia Literaria* strongly suggests that Coleridge knew this essay, "[Fichte's] *religion* consisted in the assumption of a mere ORDO ORDINANS, which we were permitted *exoteric* to call GOD" (*BL*, I, 159–60); see also, Gian N. G. Orsini, *Coleridge and German Idealism: A Study in the History of Philosophy with Unpublished Materials from Coleridge's Manuscripts* (Carbondale: Southern Illinois University Press, 1969), 190.

Light" of the God whose being is act, the self-affirmation of the
"I AM."[50] Against Fichte, too, "personality" is not necessarily finite. By
conceiving it in terms of the unity of universal Reason and particular will,
Coleridge locates human personality within the context of absolute personality. Finally, Coleridge moves beyond "a personal God" to the "persons" of the Trinity united in an eternal and eternally complete circulation of love. If persons are constituted by relations and "personal" is not
to be equivocal and, therefore, uninformative, then God cannot be personal without relations. We might, of course, nominate the world as God's
eternal "correspondent opposite," but then we return to a variation on
pantheism. The doctrine of the Trinity, on the other hand, offers Coleridge
a way to affirm the personality of God and, through the eternal com-
pleteness of the Divine communion, maintain that creation is not neces-
sitated but God's free act, the making of a world distinct from God and
bearing its own forms of freedom.

Human Personality and Divine Persons

To what extent does Coleridge succeed in conceiving the Triune God as
the ultimate context for the formation and fulfillment of persons? In the
fragments of the *Opus Maximum*, Coleridge sets about showing the logic
of Trinitarianism. First, he elaborates a doctrine of God as Absolute Will.
From that doctrine he proceeds to a derivation of the persons, moving in
the classically familiar order of the Son's generation by the Father, followed by the procession of the Spirit from the Father and the Son. I will
describe this strategy in broad outline before returning to pursue my question through some of the details.

   Personality, as we have seen, is an "essential attribute" of the "will."
To the degree that our willing is not limited by our self-concern, constrained by a narrowness of purpose or deformed by the pursuit of irra-
tional goals destructive of other wills, our personality is enriched and liberated. The "Absolute Will," therefore, is the absolute instance of
personality, in which Reason and will are one. Coleridge recommends
the term "personeity" with respect to God, though he does not use it
quite consistently. He introduces it simply as a device to avoid the common associations of limitation that "personality" carries. Later, though,

---

[50] *Op Max*, 223.

he distinguishes "personeity" as "the source of personality," and attributes "personality," again, to God.[51] The decisive point, though, is that God is the "absolute person and the ground of all personality" and is so by virtue of being "Absolute Will," "having the... ground and principle of its own being, in its own inexhaustible causative might."[52] Coleridge draws both a key theological term and a defining biblical moment into this doctrine of God as Absolute Will. As "Spirit," he argues, the reality of God is the act of self-causation, a truth witnessed to in the Divine name given to Moses, "I Am that I Am," or as Coleridge prefers to translate it, "[t]hat which I will to be I shall be."[53] This translation provides biblical focus for Coleridge's ontological bulwark against pantheism. As *causa sui*, Absolute Will is the eternal condition of the Divine Being. Insisting on the priority of will over being, though not, of course, in a temporal sense, is necessary as soon as we understand "will" for what it is. There is no contradiction in thinking of being as a "product," however, the very idea of will is abandoned as soon as being is regarded as the condition of will: "no other definition of Will is possible but, *verbally*, 'that which originates,' and *really* 'that which is essentially causative of reality.'"[54] The causative priority of Divine Will over Divine Being distinguishes the personal God from an impersonal Spinozistic substance.

From Absolute Will as "essential causativeness... abiding undiminished and indiminishable," Coleridge begins his mapping of Trinitarian logic. If the Absolute Will is eternally and essentially causative, then it requires an eternal object of causation, an object that is the full realization of its own self: "The causativeness hath not ceased, and what shall the product be? — All power, and all reality, are already present... what, then, remains to be communicated? It must in some high sense be other, and yet it must be a Self. For there is no other than Self."[55] Eternal causativeness must, therefore, be *self*-communication and this leads us to the idea of a second co-eternal reality or "a self wholly and adequately repeated, yet so that the very repetition contains the distinction from the primary act, a Self which in both is self-subsistent but which yet is not the same, because the one only is self-originated."[56] As the *Deus alter*, the perfect "Idea" of the "Supreme Mind," it must be no less than the

---

[51] *Op Max*, 195.
[52] *Op Max*, 176, 195.
[53] *Op Max*, 189.
[54] *Op Max*, 194.
[55] *Op Max*, 195–96.
[56] *Op Max*, 199.

Father, the *Deus Idem*; it must be "substantial" and "consubstantial...
with the Father."[57] The Son, therefore, is "from all eternity personal" as
is the Father, a truth that Coleridge, in conclusion, renders in biblical
form, "as the Father knoweth the Son, even so the Son knoweth the
Father."[58]

There is a danger that we will understand "knowledge," here, in terms
of human knowing. The concept of Absolute Will as "essential causativeness" should guard against this. The Father knows the Son in the act of
communicating his own self to the Son, the act in which the Son eternally
"becomes." Divine knowing is "causative," a term by which Coleridge
preserves the possibility of distinguishing begetting, proceeding, and creating as different forms of such "causativeness." In like fashion, as *Deus
alter*, eternally causative, the Son wills the completion of the Divine communication by returning his own fullness to the Father. This "perichoresis" is the reciprocal *act* of the Father and the Son, and as a Divine act
it is causative of reality. The Spirit is thus the being of the reciprocal
willing of Father and Son: the substance of mutual love. As the "eternal
unity in the eternal alterity and distinction," the *act* of uniting, the Spirit
completes "the venerable Tetractys of the most ancient philosophy, the
absolute or the prothesis, the Idem, the Alter, and the Copula by which
both are one, and the copula one with them."[59] The Absolute Willing that
is the Mosaic "I AM," Coleridge thus unfolds as the communion of Trinitarian love.

Augustine is the decisive figure for the development of Western Trinitarianism. His work, and especially the *De Trinitate*, "laid the foundation
for most all subsequent trinitarian theology."[60] To some degree, Coleridge
clearly stands within the Augustinian tradition. The Kantian account of
consciousness as self-reflective provides the guiding analogy. The *Deus
alter* is God's co-eternal "Idea" of himself; the *Deus idem et alter* is
thus "Supreme Mind" and its "adequate Idea." Whilst the philosophical
psychology is different, Coleridge follows the direction of Augustine's
search. The mind's operations are privileged as the analogical basis for
an exposition of the Trinity. Augustine exhorts his readers that "as far as
relates to the discerning in some way by the understanding that highest,
ineffable, incorporeal, and unchangeable nature, the sight of the human

[57] *Op Max*, 203–4.
[58] *Op Max*, 199–200.
[59] *Op Max*, 209–10.
[60] Edmund J. Fortman, *The Triune God: A Historical Study of the Doctrine of the Trinity* (London: Hutchinson, 1972), 150.

mind can nowhere better exercise itself, so only that the rule of faith govern it, than in that which man himself has in his own nature better than
the other animals, better also than the other parts of his own soul, which
is the mind itself."[61] The Spirit, Coleridge proposes, is the "act substantial," uniting the Father and the Son. This is traditionally Augustinian
insofar as the Spirit is made the bond of union.[62] Also traditional is the
anxiety Coleridge expresses about its biblical basis.[63]

One of Augustine's most theologically freighted innovations involved
the relationship between the deity of God and the Triunity. Eastern Trinitarianism and earlier Western writers, identified the Father with God's
deity. The Son and the Spirit receive their deity, therefore, as well as
their subsistence as persons, from the Father. Augustine, however, distinguished Divine "essence" as common to all three persons and wholly
in each from the structure of Trinitarian relations. Whilst the Father is the
origin of the relations, it is "through the sole godhood [*sic*] [that] the
same Trinity is said to be God."[64] Coleridge, too, appears to follow this
when he refers to the "Supreme" or "absolute" mind, the "identity," or
the "prothesis" as prior to the distinctions of the persons.

"Personality," we have argued, that of God and of human beings, is
the focal point of Coleridge's theological task in the *Opus Maximum*
and elsewhere. "Persons," routinely sacrificed to various human interests, are also vulnerable to philosophers. Coleridge, therefore, seeks the
source by which persons are holy. Put philosophically, he pursues an
ontology that secures eternity for the particular. As Coleridge assesses
the philosophical and theological possibilities, only Trinitarianism maintains both the freedom of God and the relative freedom of a creation that
is not Divine, thus avoiding any collapse into pantheism. Absolute Will
is fully expressed within the mutual giving and receiving of Father, Son,
and Spirit, and thus absolute freedom is preserved. The Divine Will
does not "need" creation for its self-expression. The history of creation
and redemption follows, then, as a history that begins in Divine and
human freedom. Created as persons before God, will has priority over
being in the human creation, too. This priority is lost, though not completely, in the Fall and redeemed through Christ. Human personality
and freedom are thus God's gift, both a finite correspondence to God

---

[61] *De Trinitate*, 15.27.49.
[62] *De Trinitate*, 15.17.27, for example.
[63] *Op Max*, 201.
[64] H. A. Wolfson, *The Philosophy of the Church Fathers: Faith, Trinity, Incarnation*,
third edition (Cambridge: Harvard University Press, 1970), 354.

and the form of human relationship to God. Human vocation, destiny, and fulfillment are thus irreducibly personal. Finally, Coleridge understands "person" as a relational term. Persons are constituted in and by relationships. Without a "Thou," there is no "I" and the child bereft loses consciousness of self, "Touch me... that I may be here!" Coleridge appears to need a doctrine of the Trinity in which Divine freedom is realized and unfolded in the relations that constitute God as Father, Son, and Spirit, and in which Divine unity is the love that is their *act* of unity.

Coleridge, however, inherits some stumbling blocks from his Augustinian heritage. There are two problems in particular. Augustine chooses the inner activity of mind as the most adequate finite analogue to God. Certainly, he stresses that likeness is bounded by infinitely greater difference. The fittest analogue, too, is the mind in its sanctifying contemplation and love of God; the one "who is day by day renewed by making progress in the knowledge of God, and in righteousness and true holiness, transfers his love from things temporal to things eternal, from things visible to things intelligible, from things carnal to things spiritual."[65]

The lens, though, that focuses contemplation of the Trinity is still that of the individual mind. Precisely because of that, the distinction of the persons is weakened and may approach, in practice if not always admission, a Unitarianism in which persons become "aspects" of the one God, unknowable in himself.[66] In Coleridge's case, the stakes are very high. Unless the distinction-in-relation of the persons is strongly represented, the ontological status of human relations is undermined and, therefore, Coleridge's account of the personal itself.

A corresponding danger attaches to Augustine's suggestion that the Divine nature is a "common substratum" to all three persons.[67] Augustine denies, of course, that the "Godhead" is *distinct* from the persons, a "fourth" within the Divine life. Nevertheless, "it is divine substance and

---

[65] *De Trinitate*, 14.17.23.

[66] Traditionally known as the heresy of "modalism." The modalistic tendencies of Augustine's Trinitarianism and of the Western tradition as a whole have been widely noted, see Fortman, *Triune God*, 152; Gunton, *Promise of Trinitarian Theology*, 42; Wolfhart Pannenberg, *Systematic Theology*, vol. 1 (Grand Rapids: Eerdmans, 1991), 294–95, 298. Moltmann notes that "[i]f the subjectivity of acting and receiving is transferred from the three divine Persons to the one divine subject, then the three Persons are bound to be degraded to modes of being, or modes of subsistence, of the one identical subject" (Jürgen Moltmann, *The Trinity and the Kingdom of God: The Doctrine of God* [London: SCM Press, 1981], 139).

[67] Wolfson, *Philosophy of the Fathers*, 352–54.

not the Father that is the basis of the being of God, and, therefore, *a fortiori*, of everything else."[68] The Trinitarian relations, in other words, are eternal but not *essential* to what makes God, "God." As Christians presented their beliefs as formal theology, Augustine's innovation encouraged discussion of the Divine nature, what we mean by "God," prior to treating of the Trinity. By the time theologians got around to the latter, it looked "as if everything that matters for us in God ha[d] already been said."[69] The Trinitarian relations are not decisive for our understanding of deity. We can discuss "God" very well, it seems, in abstraction from the Trinity, a position that leaves the latter doctrine vulnerable to marginalization.[70] Coleridge has argued, on the one hand, that only if God is Absolute Will is he personal and, on the other, that because God is Absolute Will, he is necessarily triune. If God's Triunity is not determinative of his being as God, then his personality becomes questionable and the slide towards pantheism begins. Coleridge's success in developing a doctrine of God as the source and promise of personality, depends, therefore, on his breaking through the constraining liabilities of his own Augustinianism.

The exposition of the Spirit concludes with a summary statement: "this, indeed, completes the venerable Tetractys of the most ancient philosophy, the absolute or the prothesis, the Idem, the Alter, and the Copula by which both are one."[71] The "most ancient" and "venerable Tetractys," was the supreme symbol of the Pythagoreans, based upon the fundamental elements of order, 1 (point), 2 (line) 3 (surface), and 4 (solid), together adding up to the sacred number ten. The tetractys, "the Fountain of the Eternal order of things" was represented as lines of dots in the form of a triangle, rising from four at the base, through three, and two, to one at the apex.[72] The "Producer and Cause of the Universe," the Tetractys or Tetrad, "is the Intelligible God, the Author of the heavenly

---

[68] Gunton, *The Promise of Trinitarian Theology*, 54.

[69] Karl Rahner, *The Trinity* (London: Burns & Oates, 1970), 17.

[70] Some have seen this as the primary reason for the relative marginalization of the doctrine of the Trinity in Western theology. Certainly, the separation of "general" discussion of the being of God from Trinitarian reflection favored the developments described by Michael Buckley in his *At the Origins of Modern Atheism* (New Haven: Yale University Press, 1990). Buckley makes the case that early modern apologetics directed against atheism abandoned argument from the distinctive doctrines of Christianity for a defense based on the necessity of God as demonstrated by the sciences of nature. This cure, he argues, only promoted the disease.

[71] *Op Max*, 209–10.

[72] Hierocles of Alexandria, *Hierocles upon the Golden Verses* (printed for Thomas Fickus, bookseller in Oxford, for M. Flesher, 1682), 115.

and sensible Gods."[73] Coleridge's appeal to the fourfold structure of the Tetractys in a Trinitarian context has occasioned some alarm. Is he suggesting that the "prothesis" is an original Divine unity, prior to the Trinity itself? Were that so, we would now have a "Monad which originally *is* not a Triad, but *becomes* one — whereby four factors are introduced into the problem."[74] If the prothesis is indeed a "fourth," then Coleridge has gone beyond Augustine in finding an undifferentiated and ultimate unity "behind" the persons. The "prothesis," then, is "not in its own nature either Triune or personal, but is merely the impersonal base from which the Trinity proper is evolved."[75] This, however, is so wildly at variance with Coleridge's interests that we should be cautious about the interpretation.

As the first thinker to seek the essence of things in ideas rather than in material realities, Pythagoras was one of Coleridge's philosophical heroes.[76] The Greek philosopher appeared as a proto-Trinitarian in Ralph Cudworth's *True Intellectual System of the Universe*, a work Coleridge used and admired.[77] Cudworth finds no tension between his claim that Pythagoras affirmed a "Trinity of Divine Hypostases" and the Tetractys, deriving the latter from the four consonants of the Tetragrammaton.[78] Though he does not follow the derivation itself, Coleridge also links the Tetrad to the Divine "I Am." His rendering of the Tetragrammaton as "[t]hat which I will to be I shall be," points towards a genuinely Trinitarian interpretation of the Tetractys.[79] We must not understand the "prothesis" in terms of "substance" but of "will."

Taking issue with the language of another admired writer, Jacob Boehme, Coleridge steers the unwary from the "depth" that is said to "[beget] the paternal Deity."[80] This is the stuff of theogony and to be

---

[73] Hierocles of Alexandria, 116.

[74] J. Robert Barth, *Coleridge and Christian Doctrine* (Cambridge: Harvard University Press, 1969), 93. Barth is citing, with agreement, Coleridge's American editor, W. G. T. Shedd. Compare these positions, and my own, with Daniel W. Hardy, "Coleridge on the Trinity," *Anglican Theological Review* 69 (1987): 147–55.

[75] Barth, *Coleridge and Christian Doctrine*, 94.

[76] *Lectures 1818–1819*, 78–80.

[77] Mary Anne Perkins, *Coleridge's Philosophy: The Logos as Unifying Principle* (Oxford: Clarendon Press, 1994), 64–65.

[78] Ralph Cudworth, *The True Intellectual System of the Universe* (printed for Richard Royston, 1678), 373–75.

[79] *Op Max*, 189.

[80] *Op Max*, 232. Boehme is not mentioned in the *Opus Maximum* passage but the text is virtually identical to a marginal comment on Boehme's *Of the Election of Grace* (*CM*, I, 694).

strenuously avoided. Yet, the "ground" and even the "depth" of deity are still terms we need. They keep our attention on the priority of will over being. The ground or "abysmal depth," therefore, is "not to be called God, much less God the Father." It is rather, "the abysmal depth... of the eternal act by which God... affirmeth himself eternally." This act is "in and together with" but to be distinguished from the threefold becoming of Father, Son, and Spirit. The act of "self-realization" is not prior to the Trinitarian relations but "in and together with" the begetting and pro- ceeding, their "effusion and refundence."[81] In a series of notes, written almost at the end of his life, Coleridge again gave his Trinitarianism a four-fold structure. "Absolute Will" is the "Identity," the *causa sui* that is realized in "Ipseity," "Alterity," and "Community," Father, Son, and Spirit. Coleridge stays with Augustine in that "Absolute Will" is not identified with the Father. "Absolute Will," however, is the single Divine willing that wills *God* as, not apart from, the unfolding of Trinitarian life. The Father, Son, and Spirit do not emerge from a prior and undifferenti- ated unity but rather share in the single act of self-realization that accom- panies and affirms the differentiated dynamics of Trinitarian order. "Prothesis," then, in its Trinitarian application, refers to the Absolute Will, the power of Self-causation that is expressed in and as the recipro- cal willing of Father, Son, and Spirit. Coleridge, of course, also developed the Tetractys in the form of his widely applied logical grid: prothesis, the- sis, antithesis, synthesis. This opens up another possibility. If the "proth- esis" is not a "something," prior to the Trinity, but the act of self-affir- mation as God, then the completion of the Trinitarian relations in the Spirit, the act of unity, is the "synthesis." The unity of God, then, is not prior to the "persons" but realized in their relations. Far from relativiz- ing the Trinity through a prior, undifferentiated unity, the Tetrad opens the possibility of seeing the unity of God as the uniting of the persons.

The Augustinian individual mind or the Kantian self-consciousness might still, however, be the focal analogy for these Trinitarian dynamics. Certainly, Coleridge invites this reading. The Trinity is "the supreme Being, his reflex act of self-consciousness and his love, all forming one supreme mind."[82] This formulation will not, however, do all that Coleridge wants to do. As Pannenberg sums up the entire history of the "psychological analogy": "for all the differentiation in the self- consciousness, the God of this understanding is a single subject. The

---

[81] *Op Max*, 232–33.
[82] Coleridge, quoted in *Op Max*, cxlii.

moments in the self-consciousness have no subjectivity of their own."[83] In practice, Coleridge strains the analogy beyond its breaking-point — and he has to. There can be no persons without relations and without relations between the Divine persons, such that there is mutual knowing and loving, we are back with that uni-personal God needing an eternal world as counterpart. In Augustine's famous triad of memory, understanding, and will, the Spirit is specially appropriated to the will. Will, however, is Coleridge's determining concept for his doctrine of personality and for his exposition of the Trinity. The Father's will is fully expressed in the Son, his *alter*, only if the Son is also "personal" and "becomes" in his *own* act of will: will, after all, must precede being in the Son, also. By the same logic, personality and, therefore, will must be affirmed of the Spirit, as well.[84] When we conceive the Divine persons as "substantial acts," as wills in perichoresis, we have left the psychological analogy behind. Coleridge also acknowledges that "[Theos] *becomes* [ho pater] by the Act of realizing in the Son," and that the "primal Self... becometh God the Father" through the Son.[85] This is undeveloped but it brings the making of human persons into finite correspondence with the mutually constituting Divine relations.

Surely, "if three were fed at Manchester instead of two at Glencoe or the Trossacs, the balance of human enjoyment was in favor of the former."[86] In conjunction with the multiplicity of decisions, more or less good and necessary or more or less bad and willful, that dispose of human lives, Coleridge sets the final distinction between persons and things. The person is an irreducible particular, one that cannot be calculated away and so remains to qualify any assessment of advantage and loss. That particularity is the inevitable bad conscience of all policy, whatever its wisdom, that determines the fortune of persons. No anthropological reductionism and no appeals, even to the best of common goods, will or should salve it. Coleridge understood that all forms of pantheism leave the category of person vulnerable. Particularity and distinction are not ultimate, the One is above the many. Trinitarianism, however, does ground the particularity of persons and also the multiplicity of all creation in the being of a God for whom relation is equiprimordial with unity. The unity of God is thus the unity of eternal distinctions, the eternal generation and

[83] Pannenberg, *Systematic Theology*, I:295.
[84] *Op Max*, 201, 206–8.
[85] *CL*, VI, 537; *Op Max*, 232.
[86] *LS*, 211.

communion of difference. Coleridge develops this point explicitly in connection with the Son. The distinction of the Son from the Father, the particularity by which he is "Thou" for the Father, is the basis of all created
distinction and particularity: "in this other all others are included, that in
this first substantial intelligible distinction... all other distinctions that
can subsist in the indivisible unity... are included."[87] The Son, as the
Idea Idearum, contains and refers to the Father, the Ideas, the creative
powers, of all non-Divine reality: "the same reason which has compelled
us to the conclusion that whatever is distinct in the Deity must be real,
substantially distinct, and distinctly substantial — that the same reason,
which has led us to admit the self-subsistence of the adequate idea of the
supreme mind, must hold equally good of whatever ideas are distinctly
contained in that adequate idea, and that these distinctities are both real
and actual, as in whom and through whom the eternal act of the Father
and the Son, the uniting, receiving, and communicating Spirit lives and
moves."[88] Distinction and plurality are ontologically fundamental. In the
eternal act by which the Son "becomes," is distinguished from the Father,
all God's creative possibilities are established as finite expressions of the
eternal distinction and self-referral of the Son from and to the Father.

A good few readers have considered Coleridge a would-be German
Idealist, too nervous to remove his theistic stabilizers.[89] The place of "persons" and "personality" within Coleridge's thought, however, shows that
his appropriation of Kantianism is a critical one in the interests of a distinct project. Post-Kantian developments run aground for Coleridge on
their failure to avoid pantheism and, therefore, the demise of the personal
as an irreducible category. Not only is Trinitarianism important here but
also the interpretation of personality that accompanies it. How we think
of "persons" affects how we can conceive of reciprocity within the
Divine Being without becoming tri-theistic.[90] To the extent that "person"
is, as generally during the modern period, defined in terms of individuality and free independent action or, to put it differently, to the extent

[87] *Op Max*, 207.
[88] *Op Max*, 220.
[89] A classic example is provided by James Mackinnon Robertson in his 1910 article
for the eleventh edition of the *Encyclopedia Britannica* (see Alan Gregory, "Putting Him
in His Place: Coleridge in the Encyclopaedia Britannica," *The Coleridge Bulletin* n.s. 20
[2002]: 137–40). More recently, Orsini in *Coleridge and German Idealism*, a careful and
sympathetic treatment of Coleridge's debts to the Idealists, still treats his "theism" rather
as a sign of cold feet.
[90] Kasper, *The God of Jesus Christ*, 285–90, 299–308; Gunton, *Promise of Trinitarian Theology*, chs. 3 & 5.

that freedom and independence are correlated within the idea of "person," then talk of persons within the Divine life is going to sound hopelessly like three gods. Coleridge's significance is that he does develop an account of persons that, bursting the confines of his own Kantianism, points towards an understanding of the persons of the Trinity as constituted in their mutual acts of giving, receiving, and returning.

A further consequence of Coleridge's insistence on Divine personality and the Triunity that follows from it is a reworking of the long-conflicted relationship between reason and revelation. With a God conceived so resolutely in terms of "act," the nature of reason is reconfigured, becoming itself manifestation, revelatory, an active illumination.[91] The affirmation of Divine personality again places revelation as the central epistemological category through which "Reason" is understood. Revelation is, after all, what *persons* do — not by virtue of their limitations or their individual isolation, but by virtue of their being persons. The revelation of persons takes place in a communion of giving and receiving. As Coleridge explored quite brilliantly in connection with the relationship of mother and infant, persons find themselves as such through the revealing presence of others. Revelation, therefore, is given with the notion of a personal God, as the only way in which God can be known as personal. If God is not known as personal, we do not know God but only "a Fate."[92] Hence the phrase "revealed religion" is a "pleonasm."[93]

Colin Gunton has credited Coleridge with being "the first to have developed both a trinitarian understanding of God and a relational view of the human person."[94] He is, however, rather more wary about the particular way in which Coleridge set about developing his Trinitarianism, suggesting, in particular, that his emphasis on the will threatens to end in the very "monism" he abhorred.[95] I have suggested here that Coleridge's understanding of "Absolute Will" and its relation to "Being" not only turns his thought decisively away from monism but also that his conception is fruitful in breaking through the "uni-personal" psychological analogy on which he is still, as he might say, "belimned." Would Coleridge, though, not have done better to have abandoned his tetractys, within which, as I have argued, will plays such an important role, and returned to another venerable tradition: the Eastern identification of the Father as

[91] In this connection, Boehme was an important influence on Coleridge.
[92] *Op Max*, 118.
[93] *Op Max*, 48.
[94] Gunton, *The Promise of Trinitarian Theology*, 97.
[95] Gunton, "Trinity, Ontology and Anthropology," 54.

the source of deity? The answer, I think, lies in the possibilities opened up for us by Coleridge's account of the Divine willing. Distinguishing the act of "self-causation" from the role of the Father in the origin of Trinitarian relations enables us to affirm that the will to be is a single act shared by all the persons, though expressed in the Trinitarian ordering of Father, Son, and Spirit. This avoids the monarchical implications of the Father as "source of deity" and allows for an account of the Trinitarian relations as more fully reciprocal. Coleridge's exploration of the relational origin of persons allows, against all pantheism but also against monotheism, a doctrine of God in which the movement of reciprocity, of communion, is as ontologically fundamental as unity.

PHILOSOPHIA TRINITATIS: COLERIDGE, PANTHEISM, AND A CHRISTIAN CABBALA

By Douglas Hedley

Coleridge compares his "system" with that of the so-called Neoplatonists and Indic Thought. I shall leave aside Coleridge's discussion of Indian theology. It is largely polemic and Coleridge was not an adept. However, his knowledge of the Neoplatonists was considerable. Hence the negative tone of much of his reflection upon Neoplatonism as the "Degenerate Platonists" is *prima facie* rather puzzling. This is the man whom Charles Lamb, recalling the young Coleridge at Christ's Hospital, described as the captivating young "Mirandula" who unfolded "deep and sweet intonations, the mysteries of Jamblichus, or Plotinus."[1] McFarland's edition of the *Opus Maximum* relates closely to his massively influential, landmark study, *Coleridge and the Pantheist Tradition*, and may provide a decisive moment in the continued evaluation of Coleridge's complex relationship to Neoplatonism. This pivotal study was the first to consider Coleridge's work in the context of the *Pantheismusstreit* as the context of Coleridge's philosophical theology. This was the debate between Jacobi and Mendelssohn concerning Lessing's alleged pantheism. It took place while Schelling and Hegel were students of theology in the Tübingen Stift. Jacobi published (rather scandalously) a conversation he had enjoyed with Lessing in which Lessing openly avowed his "Spinozism." Jacobi was intent upon contrasting Lessing's Spinozism with Christian theism: the former as deterministic nihilism, the latter presupposing inexplicable freedom.

One of the great achievements of Thomas McFarland has been to emphasize the importance of the so-called "Pantheism controversy" between Jacobi and Mendelssohn, which was such a momentous influence upon the post-Kantian philosophers. The line "give me a firm spot to stand on," quoted by Coleridge in "Fragment 3" of the *Opus Maximum*, is, in fact, the motto of F. H. Jacobi's *Über die Lehre des Spinoza*.[2]

---

[1] Charles Lamb, "Christ's Hospital Five and Twenty Years Ago" (1820), in *Essays of Elia: First Series* (Moxon, 1840), 13.

[2] *Op Max*, 219; Friedrich Heinrich Jacobi, *Über die Lehre des Spinoza* (Hamburg: Felix Meiner, 2000), 3.

Spinoza was, indeed, a vital part of the development of German Idealism. Yet we have to be careful in considering the context of this reception. Spinoza's "pantheism" upon which McFarland concentrates needs very careful handling. Jacobi's interpretation of Spinoza is coloured by a particular "cabbalistic" context. As McFarland notes, Coleridge himself in the *Philosophical Lectures* speaks of Spinoza as holding "the opinions of the most learned Jews, particularly the Cabbalistic philosophers."[3]

In this essay I wish to suggest that the editor has misunderstood Coleridge's position. McFarland's mistake is to construe Coleridge in a manner too akin to F. H. Jacobi, as primarily a warrior in the cause against "pantheism." This clouds the fact that Coleridge's invective against Plotinus (or indeed Schelling) is not so much the rejection of an attractive external enemy as an *internal* battle within the same camp. Crabb Robinson was quite correct when he observed that Coleridge "metaphysicized à la Schelling while he abused him."[4] McFarland has often emphasized that the dogma of the Trinity is quite essential for a proper understanding of Coleridge's thought. Yet he seems to think that this means that Coleridge "moved out of the sphere of philosophy into the sphere of religion."[5] However, I suggest that Coleridge's Trinitarian speculations are a key to his *philosophical* concerns. Jacobi does not engage in any speculative exposition of the Trinity. Indeed, the renewal of Trinitarian thought was to be found in Lessing and Schelling.[6] Moreover, the roots of this can be found in the Enlightenment, especially in the Cambridge Platonists.

Of course, in the case of Coleridge we are considering a specific tradition of Christian Platonism.[7] In this tradition of specifically *Christian* Platonism the doctrine of the Logos is seen as the key to any apology for the doctrine of the Trinity and I have discussed the relevance of Cudworth for Coleridge on this elsewhere.[8] In this essay I wish to pursue in

[3] *Op Max*, cxcv.

[4] Henry Crabb Robinson, *Diary*, ed. T. Sadler (London, 1869), II, 273.

[5] Thomas McFarland, *Coleridge and the Pantheist Tradition* (Oxford: Clarendon, 1969), 202.

[6] See H. B. Nisbet, "The Rationalisation of the Holy Trinity from Lessing to Hegel," *Lessing Yearbook* 31 (1999): 65–89; see also my book, *Coleridge, Philosophy and Religion: Aids to Reflection and the Mirror of the Spirit* (Cambridge: Cambridge University Press, 2000), 40ff. For Lessing's theological works, see Lessing, *Philosophical and Theological Writings*, ed. H. B. Nisbet (Cambridge: Cambridge University Press, 2005).

[7] See Douglas Hedley, "Cudworth, Coleridge and Schelling," *The Coleridge Bulletin* n.s. 16 (2000): 63–70.

[8] See Douglas Hedley, "The Platonick Trinity: Philology and Divinity in Cudworth's Philosophy of Religion," in *Philologie und Erkenntnis Beiträge zu Begriff und Problem früneuzeitlicher 'Philologie'*, ed. R. Häfner (Tübingen: Niemeyer, 2001), 247–63.

part the influence of the Christian cabbala of Henry More (1614–87) upon Coleridge, whom Coleridge quotes explicitly in the *Opus Maximum*.[9] My point is that the German philosophical tradition employs the term *causa sui* because of the *Pantheismusstreit* and ultimately Spinoza. Hence we might think that Coleridge's usage of the term reflects his fascination with Spinozistic pantheism. Spinoza, however, uses the idea of Divine self-generation in a completely different manner from Plotinus. In Spinoza's Divine substance as *causa sui*, there is no trace of will. For Plotinus the point of the concept rests in his assertion of the radical transcendence and freedom of the supreme principle: the Good. Spinoza's pantheism precludes any such meaning: employment of the ideas of the freedom and the will of supreme reality appears as absurd anthropomorphism. However, the "Spinozism" of the Christian Cabbala was inclined to re-invest Spinoza's Divine substance with the dynamic qualities of the Neoplatonism of Plotinus. Schelling's seminal *On Human Freedom* of 1809, with its claim that "will is primordial being" is a striking index of the transformation of Spinoza beyond recognition — and in a manner redolent of the audacious theology of Plotinus. Reflections upon Coleridge's usage of the notion of *causa sui* reveal his deep debt to Neoplatonism, not his rejection of it.

The Ambiguities of Coleridge's Christian Platonism

We should consider at least two distinct meanings of "Neoplatonism." The first sense is that of an anti-Christian late Antique philosophy, and declared as such under the Emperor Julian the Apostate (Emp. 361–63). This anti-Christian, pagan philosophical school was closed down by Justinian in 529 AD. As such Neoplatonism was a rival theory of *salvation* as much as a philosophy in the modern sense. In this sense Coleridge is vehemently and polemically anti-Platonic, and, in the *Opus Maximum*, he refers to "Platonism" in this sense scathingly as a "rival of Christianity."[10]

There is another most pertinent sense of "Platonic," however. This is the sense in which Augustine explains how the books of the Platonists led him to the threshold of the Church.[11] Coleridge explicitly appeals to

---

[9] *Op Max*, 244.
[10] *Op Max*, 252.
[11] Augustine, *Confessions* (7.9–21), trans R. S. Pine Coffin (Harmondsworth: Penguin, 1961), 144ff.

Augustine's *Confessions* in his *Biographia Literaria*, where he notes that the "books of certain Platonic philosophers... commenced the rescue of St. Augustine's faith."[12] Coleridge and Augustine knew these books well enough to realize that they were not pantheistic.

Pace McFarland, it is clear that Coleridge's objection to Plotinian Neoplatonism is not *pantheism* in any clear sense. If this were the case he would have examined and criticized Stoic theology, which he refers to in passing as the "Jupiter est quodcunque vides of the Philosophic Roman."[13] Coleridge criticizes Neoplatonism precisely because, like St. Augustine, he knows the proximity of his own thought to the "books of the Platonists" and this is why he wants to distance his own position.[14] Coleridge is completely aware that the Platonists posit a transcendent spiritual source of the material cosmos. This is why in the center of "Fragment 3" Coleridge quotes from Plotinus' magnificent vision of the intelligible cosmos, which Coleridge uses as a justification for his own definition of a "divine Idea."[15] The ideas are not abstract theorems or universals but living powers in vibrant harmony of translucent unity: "every thing is more eminently some one thing, and yet all things fairly shine in every thing."[16] This is not some realm of "ghostly Platonic forms" but the creative energy of the Divine Mind.

Coleridge's critique of Plotinus is aimed at the incoherence of the idea of a hierarchy of three Divine hypostases and the superiority of Christian theology, which affirms the consubstantiality of the three persons of the Godhead: "'God' or 'Deity' in its philosophic sense is wholly incompatible with comparative debility, obscurity, and progressive deterioration; or where these qualities can be predicated of a subject, to call it God is to affirm of the same thing that it is and that it is not."[17]

But Coleridge is also aware that the stronger divide between Divine and created in Christian theology raises its own problems. In particular the question of evil becomes much sharper. And the origin of evil is a central question of "Fragment 3" of the *Opus*. However, Spinoza regards this whole question of "evil" as ridiculous on the basis that he cannot allow for any difference between actuality and possibility. Complaint about evils in the world is, for Spinoza, the product of the unchastened

---

[12] *BL*, I, 205.
[13] *Op Max*, 264 ("Jupiter is whatever you see").
[14] Cf. *BL*, I, 205.
[15] *Op Max*, 236.
[16] *Op Max*, 236; Coleridge cites Plotinus, *Enn.* V.8.31.4.
[17] *Op Max*, 259.

imagination rather than reason.[18] The Platonic tradition was committed to Divine providence from Plato's *Laws* up to the *De providentia et fato* of Proclus: theodicy was a central part of Platonic and Neoplatonic theism.

Coleridge's repeated use of the word *"apostasy"* where he speaks of the "apostate self will" shows how close he is to Plotinus.[19] Speaking of the "audacity" of finite being separating itself from its source, Plotinus describes finite beings "running the opposite course" and "getting as far away as possible."[20] Spinoza cannot envisage the modes of the Divine substance considered as *natura naturata* as an "apostasy" from the *natura naturans* of God as a free cause (in Spinoza's somewhat Pickwickian sense of Divine freedom), any more than Spinoza could follow Plotinus in seeing salvation as fleeing from the world to the intelligible homeland of the soul.

The Christian Cabbalistic Interpretation of Spinoza

The cabbalistic Spinoza points to F. H. Jacobi: he uses the Cabbalistic term "Das Immanente Ensoph" or the cabbalistic concept of immanent Ensoph in order to expound Spinoza.[21] Jacobi's intention is manifestly polemical, but it reveals a very interesting aspect of the interpretation of Spinoza that became a cardinal element in the Romantic-idealistic reception of Spinoza.[22] The "substance" of Spinoza's *Ethics* is interpreted through the Ensoph: Spinoza is drawn into an orbit of Neoplatonic Protestant Mysticism. Hence, Spinoza can be seen as much closer to the *philosophus teutonicus* Jacob Boehme. Spinoza's substance is transformed into a dynamic source of cosmic processions.

In *Über die Lehre des Spinoza* Jacobi describes how, before he realized the nature of Lessing's pantheism, he was puzzled by a passage in Lessing's *Education of the Human Race* (¶73), which identifies the Father of the Christian Trinity with *natura naturans* and the Son of the Christian Trinity with *natura naturata*.[23] Lessing in *Die Erziehung des*

---

[18] See Spinoza's *Ethics*, Book 1, Appendix.
[19] See, for example, *Op Max*, 390; cf. 263, 324, 363, 377.
[20] Plotinus, *Enn.* V.1.1.1ff.
[21] Jacobi, *Über die Lehre des Spinoza*, 182.
[22] See Eveline Goodman-Thau, Gert Mattenklott, Christoph Schulte, eds., *Kabbala und die Literatur der Romantik: zwischen Magie und Trope* (Tübingen: M. Niemeyer, 1999).
[23] "Ehe mir Lessings Meinungen auf die bisher erzählte Weise bekannt geworden, und in der festen Überzeugung, die sich auf Zeugnisse stützte; Lessing sei ein rechtgläubiger Deist, war mir in seiner Erziehung des Menschengeschlechtes einiges ganz unverstandlich, besonders der 73 ¶. Ich möchte wissen, ob jemand diese Stelle anders, als nach Spinozistischen Ideen deutlich machen kann. Nach diesen aber wird der Kommentar sehr leicht.

Menschengeschlechts (¶ 73) actually writes: "On the doctrine of the Trinity — if we try to sort out intellectually this doctrine after infinite confusions left and right, that God cannot be one object — that his unity is a transcendent unity that does not exclude plurality. Does not God require a representation of himself? That is to say a representation in which all that constitutes him is contained... how better and more concrete than by calling this representation the son, Divine begotten from eternity?"[24]

This "Christological" passage is linked by Jacobi to Spinoza's metaphysics. Such a Christological reading of Spinoza via Lessing is quite incredible apart from the view of Spinoza as a Cabbalist propagated by Johann Georg Wachter at the beginning of the eighteenth century. On this the relationship between Substance and modes is linked to a Christian Neoplatonic logos speculation. Thus the Spinozistic (and pantheistic) idea of modifications of the one Substance is mysteriously interpreted as procession or emanation from the First Cause. Of primary importance is the role of the Cabbalistic figure of Adam Kadmon who stands for the Christ-Logos figure.[25] The immediate source of Wachter's Christian Cabbalism was the remarkable friend and pupil of Henry More: Anne Conway and her *Principia philosophiae Antiquissimae & Recentissimae* (1690).[26] Wachter tells us that the Cabbalists speak of two principles

Der Gott des Spinoza, ist das lautere Principium der Würklichkeit in allem Würklichen, das Seins in allem Dasein, durchaus ohne Individualität, und schlechterdings unendlich. Die Einheit dieses Gottes beruhet auf der Identität des nicht zu unterscheidenden, und schließet folglich eine Art der Mehrheit nicht aus. Bloß in dieser transcendentalen Einheit angesehen, muß die Gottheit aber schlechterdings der Würklichkeit entbehren, die nur im bestimmten Einzelnen sich ausgedrückt befinden kann. Diese, die Würklichkeit mit ihrem Begriffe, beruhet also auf der natura naturata (dem Sohn von Ewigkeit); so wie jene, die Möglichkeit, das Wesen, das Substantielle des Unendlichen, mit seinem Begriffe, auf der Natura naturanti (dem Vater)" (Jacobi, *Über die Lehre des Spinoza*, 45).

[24] Z.E. die Lehre von der Dreieinigkeit. — Wie, wenn diese Lehre den menschlichen Verstand, nach unendlichen Verirrungen rechts und links, nur endlich auf den Weg bringen sollte, zu erkennen, daß Gott in dem Verstande, in welchem endliche Dinge *eins* sind, unmöglich *eins* sein könne; daß auch seine Einheit eine transcendentale Einheit sein müsse, welche eine Art von Mehrheit nicht ausschließt? Muß Gott wenigstens nicht die Vollständigste Vorstellung von sich selbst haben? d.i. eine Vorstellung, in der alles befindet, was in ihm selbst ist... so viel bleibt doch immer unwidersprechlich, daß diejenigen, welche die Idee davon populär machen wollen, sich schwerlich faßlicher und schicklicher hätten ausdrücken können, als durch die Benennung eines *Sohnes*, den Gott von Ewigkeit zeugt (Gotthold Ephraim Lessing, *Werke in drei Bänden* [Muenchen: Carl Hanser, 1982], III, 653).

[25] Wilhelm Schmidt-Biggemann, *Philosophia perennis. Historische Umrisse abendländischer Spiritualität in Antike, Mittelalter und Früher Neuzeit* (Frankfurt: Suhrkamp, 1998), 304ff.

[26] Anne Conway, *The Principles of the Most Ancient and Modern Philosophy*, eds. Allison P Coudert and Taylor Corse (Cambridge: Cambridge University Press, 1996).

within the Deity, the second of which is called variously Adam Kadmon, the Logos, or the Word and mentions in this connection expressly Spinoza.[27] Wachter sees Spinoza as presenting an intellectually rigorous exposition of a Christian metaphysics of a fundamentally Neoplatonic kind in which the Logos stands for the Divine intellect.[28] Hence Wachter was convinced that in this manner he could acquit Spinozism of the twin accusations: pantheism and materialism. Wachter's speculative Spinozistic Christology is not completely absurd: in Spinoza's *Short Treatise*, *natura naturata* is described as the "son." However, Wachter did not know this text.[29] Furthermore, in a letter to Heinrich Oldenburg Spinoza says that his theory of God as the immanent rather than transcendent cause of the world is akin to ideas of St. Paul in Acts 17:28, various antique philosophers, and "the ancient Hebrews" in as far as one can infer their views from the corrupted traditions.[30] Wachter did not, however, think that Spinozism was compatible with the personality of the Divine or the immortality of the soul. Winfried Schröder observes that Wachter had no illusions about Spinoza as "Spinoza Christianus" or even "christianissimus" (Goethe).[31] Brucker in his celebrated *Historia critica philosophiae* knew that "the difference between modifications and emanations is far greater than the famous Wachter admits; modifications are within in the Substance, emanations proceed without."[32]

Jacobi's pantheism polemic depends upon his bizarre interpretation of Spinoza. Jacobi insists: "The Cabbalistic philosophy as far as research reveals, and according to the best commentators like the younger van

---

[27] The Cabbalists "loquuntur de principiato quodam primo, quod Deus immediate ex se effluere fecerit, & quo mediante caetera in serie & ordine sint producta, idque variis nominibus salutare solent, qualia sunt, Adam Kadmon, Messias, Christus, Logos, verbum, Filius, Primogenitus, Homo Primus, Homo Coelestis, Dux, Pastor, Mediator, & reliqua... rem ipsam agnovit SPINOZA, ut praeter nomen nihil desiderare possis" (Johann Georg Wachter, *Elucidarius cabalisticus*, ed. W. Schröder, *Dokumente: Johann Georg Wachter: De primordiis Christianae religionis, Elucidarius cabalisticus, Origines juris naturalis* [Stuttgart-Bad Cannstatt: frommann-holzboog, 1995], 167).

[28] "Et de intellectu quidem divino (cujus modo mentio facta) plane ad mentem Cabalistarum philosophatur, qui duplicem lógon DEI, statuunt, unum DEO internum, alternum, externum" (Schröder, *Dokumente*, 171).

[29] Winfried Schröder, *Spinoza in der deutschen Frühaufklärung* (Würzburg: Königshausen und Neumann, 1987), 99.

[30] Baruch de Spinoza, *Briefwechsel*, trans. into German by C. Gebhardt (Hamburg: Felix Meiner, 1986), 276.

[31] Schröder, *Spinoza in der deutschen Frühaufklärung*, 101–2.

[32] "Longius inter se distant modificationes et emanationes, quam vult cl. Wachterus; modificationes enim substantiae immanent, emanationes progrediuntur" (Leipzig, 1742-67; quoted in Schröder, *Spinoza in der deutschen Frühaufklärung*, 103).

Helmont and Wachter, is nothing but an underdeveloped or newly confused Spinozism."[33] These works that Jacobi refers to as Cabbalistic are,
in fact, Christian. Henry More, Anne Conway, van Helmont and Wachter
were all Christian thinkers, and Jacobi's polemical identification of Cabbala and Spinozism as forms pantheism was not based on any direct
knowledge of Jewish sources. M. Freystadt clearly demonstrated the error
of such a depiction of Cabbalistic theology as pantheistic in his
Philosophia cabbalistica et Pantheismus in 1832. However, the identification of Cabbala and pantheism is an index of Jacobi's influence.

The "Cabbalistic" Legacy in German Idealism

In "Fragment 2" of the *Opus Maximum* Coleridge is dismissive of "the
recent writings of Schelling and his followers, as often as they attempt to
clothe the skeleton of the Spinozistic pantheism and breathe a life thereinto."[34] Yet this is sheer polemic. An investigation of the topics of the
Opus Maximum shows a profound proximity to these "recent writings of
Schelling" in his Munich phase: Divine Will, evil, freedom, system, etc.

The topic of the Divine Will and potentiality is *the* problem that
Schelling after 1809 is attempting to answer. This is not a question that
a *genuine* pantheist like Spinoza (unlike perhaps his Cabbalistic alter ego)
would regard as worth contemplating. Indeed, Spinoza is quite adamant
that the religious imagination is the source of such an absurd anthropomorphism as the belief in a *personal* Deity.[35]

One reason why Coleridge was so close to Schelling can be explained
in terms of a *shared* Christian Cabbala. When Coleridge refers to "the
Hebrew sages" or "the Rabbinical writings," McFarland refers to the
possible influence of Hyman Hurwitz.[36] But we should not ignore the
role of Henry More, whose deeply Neoplatonic *Psychozoia* is quoted in
"Fragment 3" of the *Opus Maximum*.[37] Moreover, Coleridge's speculation in "Fragment 2" about the "tetractys of the most ancient philosophy"

---

[33] "Die Kabbalistische Philosophie, so viel davon der Untersuchung offen liegt, und
nach ihren besten Kommentatoren, von Helmont dem Jüngeren, und Wachter, ist als
Philosophie, nichts anders, als unterentwickelter, oder neu verworrener Spinozismus"
(Jacobi, *Über die Lehre des Spinoza*, 120).

[34] *Op Max*, 205.

[35] See the scarcely veiled contempt for the idea of the personality of the Deity in the
Appendix to Book 1 of Spinoza's *Ethics*.

[36] *Op Max*, 275 and n.183.

[37] *Op Max*, 244.

draws on a tradition of Pythagorean-Cabbalistic numerology.[38] Schmidt-Biggemann writes of Reuchlin's Cabbalistic use of the four: "The Four is the order, which neighbours upon the Trinity — it is the last, before the divine number three: it is the number of wisdom."[39] I do not wish to suggest that Coleridge is merely repeating Cabbalistic lore. However, we clearly have clues about the provenance of his thought. This provenance is far closer to what McFarland summarily describes as the "pantheistic tradition" than Jacobi's own Pascalian philosophy of faith.

Schelling's Christian Neoplatonism is deeply rooted in this Christian cabbalism that can be traced to Henry More and Anne Conway. This son of a Professor of oriental languages, who knew Persian and Arabic as well as Hebrew, Schelling never studied the Jewish Cabbala. But he was influenced by *Christian* Cabbalistic ideas mediated by figures such as More and Conway — a system of Christian Neoplatonism revolving around the Logos concept. The decisive shift in Schelling's thought was in 1809 and onwards. At this point Schelling was, for the first time, in the physical proximity of Jacobi himself and Franz von Baader, an exponent of Christian Cabbala and a great admirer of Boehme.[40] Schelling's *On Human Freedom* reflects this influence, as does *Über die Gottheiten von Samothrace* (1815).

One of the most eminent figures in the Christian Cabbalistic tradition was the Cambridge Platonist Henry More. More is referred to by both Wachter in his *Elucidarius Cabalisticus*[41] and by Jacobi in *Über die Lehre des Spinoza*. The passage in which Jacobi describes how Lessing reminded him of a doctrine in Henry More deserves special note: "Once Lessing said — with half a laugh — that he was perhaps the highest being and present in the state of its most extreme contraction. I pleaded for my existence. He replied that it was not meant thus, and explained himself in a manner reminiscent of Henry More and van Helmont. He further explained himself still more clearly, and so that I was driven once again to suspect him of Cabbalism."[42] The concept to which Jacobi refers in this passage is the

---

[38] *Op Max*, 209; cf. 259.

[39] "Die Vier ist die Ordnung, die der Trinität benachbart ist, es ist die letzte — vor — der göttlichen Zahl Drei, es ist auch die Zahl der Weisheit" (Willhelm Schmidt-Biggemann, *Philosophia Perennis*, 181). In the Pythagorean tradition Tetrad and the Decad are closely related: $10 = 1 + 2 + 3 + 4$ (see K. S. Guthrie, *The Pythagorean Sourcebook and the Library* [Grand Rapids: Eerdmans, 1987], 27ff.).

[40] Ernst Benz, *Die Christliche Cabbala. Ein Stiefkind der Theologie* (Zürich: Rhein-Verlag, 1958).

[41] Schröder, *Dokumente*, 150.

[42] "Einmal sagte Lessing, mit halbem Lächeln: Er selbst wäre vielleicht das höchste Wesen, und gegenwärtig in dem Zustand der äußersten Kontraktion. Ich bat um meine

Cabbalistic idea of the contraction of the Deity or the "Zimzum." This
concept played a role in German mystical pietism: Friedrich Christoph
Oetinger (1702–82) says explicitly: "For without attraction, what the
Hebrews call 'Zimzum,' there can be neither creation nor manifestation."[43]
Schelling was demonstrably familiar with the work of his Schwabian pre-
decessor. Schelling first uses the concept of Zimzum in his *Stuttgarter
Privatvorlesungen* of 1810. However, he employs this concept to express
the ideas expounded in *On Human Freedom*. In this period of his thought,
Schelling moves from the static conception of the Absolute in his Philosophy of Identity and *Naturphilosophie* of his earlier period to the emphat-
ically dynamic philosophy of a living, personal God in *On Human Freedom* and his subsequent thought. "Wollen ist Ursein": Will is primordial
Being and in this period of his thought God produces the world by a willed
self division (*Entscheidung*), and this self division belongs to Trinitarian
self-unfolding of the Absolute. Spurred by Hegel's pun about the "night
in which all cows are black," "the one Knowledge that in the Absolute
all is alike" ("*Dies Eine Wissen, daß im Absoluten Alles gleich ist*"),
Schelling develops a theology of distinction or division within the
Absolute, a theology that is expressly intended to avoid the abstract perfection of the *actus purus* of the inherited scholastic tradition whose relation to the cosmos seems deeply mysterious and also the other extreme of
a pantheism in the sense of a mere reduction of God to world. Schelling
never completed this project, but its themes were clear from the published
fragments and it clearly exerted a fascination for Coleridge.

Coleridge on *Causa Sui*

The editor of the *Opus Maximum* seems to have been oblivious to a striking paradox. Coleridge says quite explicitly that the tenet of God as self
caused is his starting point: "The Will, the absolute Will, is that which is
essentially causative of reality, essentially, and absolutely, that is, boundless

---

Existenz. — Er antwortete, es wäre nicht allerdings so gemeint, und erklärte sich auf eine
Weise, die mich an Heinrich Morus and von Helmont errinerte. Lessing erklärte sich noch
deutlicher; doch so, daß ich ihn abermals, zur Not, der Kabblisterie verdächtig machen kon-
nte" (Jacobi, *Über die Lehre des Spinoza*, 36–37).
    [43] "Nulla enim neque manifestatio fieri potest sine attractione, quod Hebraeis est
Zimzum" (F. C. Oetinger, *Theologia ex idea vitae deducta*, ed. Konrad Ohly, Texte zur
Geschichte des Pietismus [Herrenberg, 1765; Berlin: W. de Gruyter, 1979], part I, 151
[216]).

from without and from within. This is our first principle."[44] And he explicit refers to the tenet of God as *causa sui* throughout his mature writings, that "which admits of no question out of itself, acknowledges no predicate but the I AM IN THAT I AM."[45] Coleridge also talks of the linking of "self-existence" with "Spirit" by the "Fathers and the School Divines," yet the editor does not reflect on the oddity of such a claim.[46] Certainly he cannot mean Augustine or Aquinas. The most important of the Fathers, St. Augustine, in *De Trinitate*, says explicitly, "... those who suppose that God is of such power that he actually begets himself, are... wrong, since not only is God not like that, but neither is anything in the world of body or spirit. There is absolutely no thing whatsoever that brings itself into existence.[47] The most influential Schoolman, St. Thomas Aquinas, in his *Summa contra Gentiles* is equally adamant: "The existence of the cause is prior to that of the effect. If, then something were its own cause of being, it would be understood to be before it had being — which is impossible...[48] Aquinas is making the commonsense point that causation presupposes a distinction between cause and that which is caused, and hence the idea of self causation is a contradiction in terms. Needless to say, the concept of *causa sui* is utterly meaningless to Kant, though for more complex reasons, namely, his Transcendental Idealism wherein causality is a concept that cannot be legitimately employed beyond the limits of possible experience. *Causa prima* may be vacuous for Kant, but *causa sui* unintelligible.

Of course, the immediate source of the language of *causa sui* is that of Spinoza, and his enormous influence upon the eighteenth century. Yet self generation or auto-constitution of the Divine is not problematic for a pantheist. If the world is identical with the Divine and vice versa, then the Creator creates himself in the generation of the cosmos. Hence a Stoic like Seneca can happily say: *deus ipse se fecit* ("God made himself"), but this is merely expressing conceptual truth within pantheistic parameters. Such a position would be untenable for Coleridge, or any pagan Platonist who holds to a self-generating transcendent god, and a radical distinction between God and world.[49]

[44] *Op Max*, 220.

[45] *Friend*, I, 519.

[46] *Op Max*, 189.

[47] Augustine, *The Trinity* (1.1) (Hyde Park, NY: New City Press, 1991), 66.

[48] Thomas Aquinas, *Summa Contra Gentiles* (I, 22), trans. A. C. Pegis (Notre Dame: University of Notre Dame Press, 1975), 119.

[49] Jean-Marc Narbonne, "La notion de puissance dans son rapport à la *causa sui* chez les stoïciens et dans la philosophie de Spinoza," *Archives de Philosophie* 58 (1995): 35–53.

Hence our puzzle. Coleridge is claiming as a tenet, his central tenet, furthermore, a principle that is clearly *rejected* by the great theological authorities and Coleridge's own much admired Kant. It is also a tenet *accepted* by pantheists such as the ancient Stoics or Spinoza. Is this an instance of Coleridge vacillating between pantheism and theism? McFarland's cavalier association of Plotinus with Spinoza and Schelling has muddied the waters since the publication of his massive and provocative book *Coleridge and the Pantheist Tradition* and, unfortunately, this error pervades the new edition of the *Opus Maximum*. Hilary Armstrong, the great translator of Plotinus, makes the pertinent point about Divine "personality": "The Christian Fathers never allow us to forget that they are speaking of an infinite and incomprehensible person, however much his infinite personality may transcend the limited personalities of experience; for they are always speaking of God as he is revealed in the Scriptures. Plotinus too thinks of the One or Good as a personal God in the sense that he attributes to him something analogous to what we know as intellect and will in a manner proper to his transcendent unity."[50] And Coleridge employs Plotinus when he attempts to explain the contemplation of the Divine ideas by quoting the great passage "On the Intelligible Beauty," in which Plotinus describes the dynamic reality of the transcendent realm.[51] This is the transcendent domain in which the ideas are "distinct beings in the plenitude of the Supreme Mind, whose essence is Will."[52] Coleridge was perfectly well aware that Plotinus was not a pantheist in any ordinary signification of the word.

When we come to consider the concept of the One as *causa sui*, we can see how the transcendence of the One is an essential part of Plotinus' metaphysics. In *Ennead* VI.8, Plotinus argues that the One is "the father of reason and cause and causative substance, which are certainly all far from chance, he would be the principle and in a way the exemplar of all things which have no part in chance, truly and primarily, uncontaminated by chances and coincidence and happening, cause of himself and himself from himself and through himself; for he is primarily self and self beyond being."[53] Plotinus was the first Greek philosopher to identify the Good as "will": "If then the Good is established in existence, and choice and will join in establishing it — for without these it will not be — but this

[50] A. H. Armstrong, *Christian Faith and Greek Philosophy* (London: Darton, Longman and Todd, 1960), 13–14.
[51] Plotinus, *Enn.* V.8.31.
[52] *Op Max*, 236.
[53] Plotinus, *Enn.* VI.8.14.40ff.

Good must not be many, its will and substance must be brought into one; but if its willing comes from itself, it is necessary that it also gets its being from itself, so that our discourse has discovered that he has made himself. For if his will comes from himself and is something like his own work, and this will is the same thing as his existence, then in this way he will have brought himself into existence; so that he is not what he happened to be but what he himself willed."[54] The concept of *causa sui* for Plotinus is inextricably related to the "will" of the One.

We cannot, however, attribute the concept of the One as *causa sui* to Neoplatonic lore. The Athenian Neoplatonist, Proclus (410–85), for one, rejects the idea. Proclus, who exerted an enormous influence upon Christian theologians such as Denys the Areopagite, Thomas Aquinas or Nicholas of Cusa, explicitly rejects the idea of the self-generation of the One. He writes: "For some want to say that the first principle is self-constituted, arguing that even as the first principle of moving things is the first moved, even so the first principle of all those things which have any sort of existence is self constituted; for all things subsequent to the first principle also derive from the first principle.[55] Proclus' own typically measured opinion is that the One is "superior to all such causality."[56] Dillon suggests that Plotinus is probably the target of Proclus's rejection of the doctrine of *causa sui* for the First Principle.[57] In his *Commentary on the Republic*, Proclus argues that the One is above self generation since he transcends any kind of multiplicity.[58] Perhaps this is one of the reasons why Coleridge greatly preferred Plotinus to Proclus; the former being "beyond all comparison the profoundest philosopher" of the "Aegypto-Graecian school, or the Alexandrine philosophy."[59]

One of the problems of intellectual history is discovering the significance of certain issues within a constellation of ideas. Plotinus in third-century Rome is clearly very concerned about Gnosticism; Proclus in fifth-century Athens is not. Plotinus can ignore Christianity; Proclus cannot. The theology of both writers is deeply affected by these concerns, which may not be explicitly mentioned. This being said, Plotinus seems a far more radical and innovative thinker than Proclus, and Coleridge is

---

[54] Plotinus, *Enn.* VI 8.13.50ff.

[55] Proclus, *Commentary on Plato's Parmenides*, trans. G. R. Morrow and J. M. Dillon (Princeton: Princeton University Press, 1987), 505.

[56] Proclus, *Commentary*, 506.

[57] Proclus, *Commentary*, 505.

[58] Proclus, *Commentaire sur la Timée*, trans. and notes by A. J. Festugiére (Paris: Vrin, 1967), II.2.59.

[59] *Op Max*, 251.

quite aware of the special genius of Plotinus. Within the legacy of Plato's reflections on the Good and Aristotle's idea of God as "Thought thinking itself" and the teleological unmoved mover,[60] the first Greek philosopher who identifies the transcendent principle of thought and being (*arche*) with will (*boulesis*) is Plotinus. There are Gnostic and pre-Neoplatonic sources that refer to Divine self generation, and Plotinus may well have been influenced by such sources. But whatever the main inspiration for the highly speculative and abstruse doctrine of the self generation of the First Principle, Plotinus' own reasoning is clear: the origin of the One is neither happenstance (chance) nor blind necessity (fate) but result of the free will of the One. Plotinus seems to be steering a middle way between an arbitrary deity (of possibly Gnostic provenance) and some principle of inexorable higher destiny.[61]

Causa Sui and the Absolute Subjectivity of the Christian Trinity

Coleridge employs the concept of *causa sui* throughout "Fragment 3" of the *Opus Maximum*. The Index refers to pages 222–25 only, but 220–247 is more accurate, and the discussion is closely linked to references to Neoplatonism. His usage makes it clear that he is not using the concept in the Spinozistic-pantheistic manner. Coleridge, moreover, seems perfectly aware of the Neoplatonic (or rather Plotinian) provenance of the idea.[62]

Throughout the *Opus Maximum*, Coleridge emphasizes the inadequacy of human language for the expression of the noetic domain. He even makes the paradoxical point of Denys Areopagite that "the more sensuous, the less abstract these words are; the more appropriate, the less deceptive."[63] Yet generally the Fathers (and the Schoolmen) did not take up the question of the origin of the Father and thus gave some account

---

[60] *Metaphysics*, XII, 7; 1072 b 7.

[61] John Whittaker, "The Historical Background of Proclus' Doctrine of Authypostata," in *De Jamblique à Proclus: neuf exposés suivis de discussions*, Entretiens sur l'antiquité classique, 21 (Vandœuvres-Genève: Fondation Hardt, 1974), 193–237.

[62] See W. Beierwaltes, "Causa Sui: Plotins Begriff des Einen als Ursprung des Gedankens der Selbstursächlichkeit," in *Traditions of Platonism: Essays in Honour of John Dillon*, ed. John Cleary (Aldershot: Ashgate, 1999), 191–226.

[63] *Op Max*, 226; cf. Dionysius, "I doubt that anyone would refuse to acknowledge that incongruities are more suitable for lifting our minds up into the domain of the spiritual than similarities are" (Celestial Hierarchy 141B, *Pseudo-Dionysius: The Complete Works*, trans. Colm Luibheid [New York: Paulist, 1987], 150).

of the Divine aseity without compromising the consubstantial relation between the persons.

Previously, in the *Biographia Literaria*, Coleridge takes up the ancient tenet that an ultimate principle must be postulated in order to avoid an infinite regress: "we must be whirl'd down the gulph of an infinite series. But this would make our reason baffle the end and purpose of all reason, namely, unity and system. Or we must break off the series arbitrarily, and affirm an absolute something that is in and of itself at once cause and effect (*causa sui*), subject and object, or rather the absolute identity of both."[64] The link between Trinitarian self realization and the concept of *causa sui* is strikingly evident in the hymns of Synesius of Cyrene, which Coleridge quotes in the *Biographia Literaria*: "Thus the true system of natural philosophy places the sole reality of things in an ABSOLUTE, which is at once causa sui et effectus... in the absolute identity of subject and object, which it calls nature, and which in its highest power is nothing else but self-conscious will or intelligence."[65] In Coleridge's pythagorean terminology, the "abysmal Ground of the Trinity" is the One that is the prothesis, which logically, though not temporally, proceeds the Trinity of Father, Son, and Spirit. The model is that of a Neoplatonic-Neopythagorean series of numbers being generated from a primordial one. The hymns of Synesius are a good instance of this in the Patristic tradition.[66] "God *is* one, but exists or manifests himself to himself, at once in a three-fold Act, total in each and one in all."[67] Coleridge wishes to avoid Sabellianism, Tritheism, and Subordinationism. The three persons are one, but their unity is not grounded in the Father (hence avoiding subordinationism).[68] The One or Monad (prothesis) of the primordial Godhead expresses itself eternally as the triad of thesis qua Father (Ipseity), antithesis qua Son (Alterity) and synthesis qua Spirit (copula) which is "the identity of object and subject... fit alter et idem."[69]

---

[64] *BL*, I, 285.

[65] *BL*, I, 284. On Synesius, see John Whittaker, "Proclus' Doctrine of the Authypostata," 204ff.

[66] Samuel Vollenweider, *Neuplatonischer und christliche Theologie bei Synesios von Kyrene* (Göttingen: Vandenhoeck and Ruprecht, 1985).

[67] *CN*, III, 4427; *c*. Aug–Sept. 1818.

[68] See the remarks of Whittaker in "Proclus' Doctrine of the Authypostata," 204ff: "By failing to take up seriously the problem of the source of the Father's being Christians neglected an important department of theology, and by abandoning the concept of self generation deprived their theology of a suggestive means of expressing the aseity of the supreme deity." This was precisely Coleridge's quarry.

[69] *BL*, I, 279.

Coleridge is attempting to express the central Christian idea of the absolute Divine subjectivity (the great I AM) as constituted by the substantial *relation* between the hypostases of the Father, Son, and Spirit. Whereas Neoplatonism, whether of Plotinian or the post-Iamblichean (e.g. Proclus) form, sees a hierarchy of descending levels of unity in the Divine, Christian Trinitarian theology sees the unity of the Godhead as defined by the relation of the three: "It is an eternal and infinite self-rejoicing, self loving, with a joy unfathomable, with a love all comprehensive. It is absolute; and the absolute is neither singly that which affirms, nor that which is affirmed; but the identity and living copula of both."[70]

Coleridge's daring speculations about the Trinity contain the proviso that all attempts to express the Godhead are deeply inadequate: "in the philosophy of ideas our words can have no meaning for him that uses and for him that hears them, except as far as the mind's eye in both is kept fixed on the idea."[71] Coleridge discusses the "ground or the nature of Deity," but "we nevertheless abjure the rash and dangerous expressions that the depth begetteth the paternal Deity, or that a Not-Good, which yet is not Evil, a Not-Intelligent..."[72] Coleridge is clearly not advocating some irrationalistic voluntarism, for he explicitly claims: "Will is higher and deeper than Power, for it is that which God eternally *is*."[73] This is a criticism of Boehme and possibly Schelling. But here we must, Coleridge insists, proceed with caution: "The ground is not to be called God, much less God the Father; it is the abysmal depth... of the eternal act by which God as the alone causa sûi affirmeth himself eternally. The depth begetteth not, but in and together with the act of self realization the supreme mind begetteth his substantial idea, the primal Self, the adorable *I am*."[74] The use of the terminology of *causa sui* is not a retreat into a comfortable Christian orthodoxy, but shows Coleridge in all his speculative daring.

The Eternal Act of Creation in the Infinite I AM

The relevance of Coleridge's Trinitarian speculations may seem hard to fathom. Yet if one considers his famous definition of Imagination as a

[70] *Friend*, I, 521.
[71] *Op Max*, 225–26.
[72] *Op Max*, 232.
[73] *Op Max*, 240.
[74] *Op Max*, 232.

"repetition in the finite mind of the eternal act of creation in the infinite I AM,"[75] it becomes apparent that the creative act which is the paradigm of artistic activity is not the creation of the cosmos but the self
generation of the Godhead. Creation of the cosmos for Christians is not,
as it is for pagan Platonists, eternal. The self generation of the "adorable
tetractys" is the theory of the "infinite yet self-conscious Creator."[76]
The *Biographia* recounts how Coleridge could not "reconcile personality with infinity,"[77] since a "person" characteristically involves distinction from other persons. Thus an infinite person could have no
"other." The Trinity solves the problem insofar as the Godhead is constituted precisely by the interactions of the persons or hypostases. But
Coleridge is keen to avoid the charge of tritheism. The three persons
are three in one. Coleridge's Trinitarian resolution to the conflict
between personality and infinity is to see personeity (as the root of personality) as essentially relational. The idea of God as *causa sui* is that
of the *abysmal* (without bottom or ground) relationality of the First Principle. The fusing power of the Imagination is a vital and original agency
— it cannot be reduced to mechanical aggregation and association of
images (Fancy).

The finite I Am, for Coleridge, is the manifestation of the Infinite I AM
and as such is an inferior reflection of the absolute subjectivity of the
Triune Godhead.[78] When Coleridge says in the *Biographia* that Spirit is
the mediation of subject and object and that this self representation
implies "an act, and it follows therefore from that intelligence or self-consciousness is impossible, except by and in a will. The self-conscious spirit
therefore is a will; and freedom must be assumed as a *ground* of philosophy, and can never be deduced from it,"[79] he is fusing his Trinitarian
speculations with his metaphysics of mind. Coleridge reflects upon the
aporetic nature of self-consciousness — to what does the personal pro-
noun "I" refer? This aporia drives Coleridge to the self generating,
abysmal or groundless, transcendent I AM of Christian theology. The primary Imagination as the aboriginal and unconscious power of perception
is a faint imitation of the groundless creativity of the Godhead. Like "Bottom's Dream" in *A Midsummer Night's Dream*, "it hath no bottom" (4.1).

---

[75] *BL*, I, 304.

[76] *BL*, I, 203.

[77] *BL*, I, 201.

[78] See Friedrich Uehlein's magnificent *Die Manifestation des Selbstbewußtseins im konkreten 'Ich bin'* (Hamburg: Felix Meiner, 1982).

[79] *BL*, I, 279–80.

The appeal to the God of Abraham and Isaac is also to the God of Exodus 3:14, "I AM who I AM" as grounded in the absymal *causa sui*. This appeal is not, for Coleridge, a *sacrificium intellectus* since "true metaphysics are nothing else but true divinity."[80] It is entirely of a piece with Coleridge's metaphysical and empirical reflections upon the unfathomable mystery of the finite imagination as the image of its transcendent Divine source.

What is Coleridge's project? He wants an Encyclopedia — a *system* of knowledge. This is fundamentally an *Idealistic* project. Coleridge says that it is part of the "logic of human nature" that the soul "announces its superiority over the senses... itself deriving its noblest and most precious possession from the negation of the senses."[81] In the *Table Talk* Coleridge says: "THE pith of my system is to make the senses out of the mind — not the mind out of the senses."[82]

Here is what Coleridge means when he discusses the conflict between the "I am" and the "It is."[83] He thinks that a philosopher can try to understand the higher (mind, rationality, freedom, etc) in terms of the lower (chemistry, biology, instincts, etc) or vice versa: the lower in terms of the higher. This is the path of Idealism or Platonism. He also notes that such Idealism is to be found in Neoplatonism. It should not surprise us that Coleridge is most vehement in his critique of those to whom, intellectually, he is so close. Neoplatonism, Coleridge says, is the "closest approximation" to his own system.[84] Coleridge takes the great Athenian Neoplatonist Proclus as a paradigm of this idealist procedure: "The most beautiful and orderly development of the philosophy which endeavours to explain all things by an analysis of consciousness, and builds up a world in the mind out of materials furnished by the mind itself, is to be found in the Platonic Theology of Proclus."[85] This does not cohere well with McFarland's view of the Neoplatonists as key figures in the "Pantheist tradition" to which — on McFarland's account — Coleridge is both repelled and attracted.[86] Coleridge is also aware that Schelling or the Neoplatonists are also philosophers of the "I am," even though he disagrees with them over points of detail. McFarland tends to lump together

---

[80] *BL*, I, 291.

[81] *Op Max*, 98.

[82] *TT*, II, 179.

[83] See McFarland, *Coleridge and the Pantheist Tradition*, 53ff.

[84] *Op Max*, 205.

[85] Quoted by E. R. Dodds, *Proclus: Elements of Theology* (Oxford: Clarendon, 1963), xxxiii.

[86] McFarland, *Coleridge and the Pantheist Tradition*, *passim*.

the Neoplatonists, Spinoza, and the German Idealists. Yet, in fact, the relations between these philosophical positions are far more complex than McFarland admits. Jacobi's conflation of Spinoza's rigidly mechanistic and deterministic philosophy with a dynamic Neoplatonism is also linked to the rehabilitation of the doctrine of the Trinity via a Christian Neoplatonic Logos speculation. Within this particular reception, the Spinozistic (and pantheistic) idea of modifications of the one Substance is interpreted as procession or emanation from the First Cause. Certainly, Jacobi, ever the provoker of surprising results, helped produce a revival of the doctrine of the Trinity through his polemics. The fascination that the Christian doctrine of the Trinity exerted for Schelling, Hegel, and Coleridge was in part due to the indirect knowledge of the Christian Cabbala inspired by Jacobi's polemical (and inaccurate) yoking of Cabbala with Spinozism and pantheism. The concept of *causa sui* is a good index of this perplexing genealogy. If McFarland were correct, this should take us into the heart of Spinoza's pantheism. But rather the concept takes us via the Christian Cabbala back to Plotinus and Synesius. And yet Coleridge is using the concept of the self constitution of the Godhead for his own distinctively Christian and Platonic interests. His employment of this controversial concept shows Coleridge to be a rather more audacious thinker than is sometimes imagined.

INDIVIDUALITY, UNITY, AND DISTINCTION: PLOTINIAN CONCEPTS IN THE *OPUS MAXIMUM*

By Karen McLean

Introduction

It can be difficult to know where to start when listing the many fundamental ways in which Platonism and Neoplatonism influence the philosophical thought of Samuel Taylor Coleridge. When it came to the *Opus Maximum*, however, I knew I had much of my work cut out for me — Coleridge names Plotinus and Plato outright in a few places; the former he criticizes for coming so close to the truth of reality by way of pantheism,[1] the latter he admires for coming so close to the truth of reality but not telling anyone how to get there.[2] Quite apart from these explicit mentions and some praising, passing references to other Neoplatonists, the *Opus Maximum* borrows and adapts many conventional Neoplatonic concepts.

The *Opus Maximum* sits as a nexus between the aspects of Coleridge's philosophy I find most intriguing, and the characteristics of Neoplatonism that I wish were more discussed. Out of all of Coleridge's philosophical texts, the *Opus Maximum* is the most consistent indication of what Coleridge thought concerning the human personality. The "imperfection and privation"[3] involved in the limitation of personality pointed towards a problematic differentiation between the individual and God — an issue Plotinus places at the heart of his own philosophy.[4] Therefore, I will examine Coleridge's views regarding individuality, personality and, in a broader sense, distinction, which I will compare with parallel concepts developed by Plotinus. I shall show that both philosophers are interested in the same problem, and that Coleridge adopts and modifies aspects of Plotinian theory in order to solve the ramifications involved in an individuality distinct and potentially separate from our origin in God.

---

[1] *Op Max*, 254–61, esp. 232.

[2] *Op Max*, 97, 117, 184; esp. 250, 256.

[3] *Op Max*, 169.

[4] A typical Plotinian view of the necessary distance between humanity and the Divine can be found in "On Providence [I]," *Enneads*, trans. A. H. Armstrong, 7 vols, Loeb Classical Library 440–445 (Cambridge: Harvard University Press, 1966–88), III.2.14.19–20.

Coleridge seeks to reconcile the concept of distinction from our origin in God with the idea of free will, evil and potentiality, and in the *Opus Maximum* he achieves this through the concepts of unity and relationship — two terms central to Plotinus' own investigations into distinction and differentiation from the origin of the One.

Coleridge's Context

The philosophical materials amongst which Coleridge spent much of his time often presented these concepts in a negative light. F. W. J. von Schelling, for instance, describes the distinctive and differentiated parts of nature — inorganic and organic, including humanity — as lapsed versions, failed attempts to represent of the unity of their origin. Heinrich Steffens (1773–1845), a subsequent exponent of *Naturphilosophie*, is referred to throughout "Fragment 4" of the *Opus Maximum*. But both German thinkers were using and adapting concepts such as the many and the One, the "seer and the seen,"[5] being/actuality and non-being/potentiality first hinted at by Plato, developed by Neoplatonists such as Plotinus and Proclus, and adopted by early Christian philosophers, Augustine in particular.[6] Generally speaking, these theological concepts were used within the context of Western philosophy to balance and reconcile, through the notions of God's love and God's ultimate plan, the two otherwise mutually exclusive ideas of original sin and humanity as God's greatest creation. Coleridge desperately wanted to believe in the second concept, but was unable to apply this to himself at all times, finding his "individual Self," "the most unpleasant if not the most worthless Object of direct Thought."[7] Of course, as some scholars have pointed out, the self-worthlessness Coleridge felt was a great motivation to investigate the idea of God's love and plan for humanity, and where we might all stand in relation to the creative act. Jeffrey Barbeau charts the course of

---

[5] Plotinus, *Enn.* V.3.10.5–20. Plotinus believes the relationship between agent and product, particularly in the initial act of Divine creation, is integral to the self-constitution of the One (see below).

[6] Cf. Douglas Hedley, *Coleridge, Philosophy and Religion: Aids to Reflection and the Mirror of the Spirit* (Cambridge: Cambridge University Press, 2000), where Hedley describes Coleridge's philosophical and theological heritage in greater detail (see pp. 7–11 for some differences and parallels between Neoplatonism and early Christian thought; 21 and 38 for a mention of the Augustinian legacy, and its specific connection to Neoplatonism).

[7] *CL*, VI, 984; June 7, 1834.

Coleridge's ideas concerning the relationship between the individual and the Divine Will, revealing how this view of individual will developed and changed over five key works, from the *Biographia Literaria* (written in 1815) to *Aids to Reflection* (1825), influenced in part by the struggle Coleridge had in fighting and finally accepting his opium addiction.[8] James Boulger writes that Coleridge was interested in explaining why the individual human soul had existence seemingly separate from that of the Absolute, and that Coleridge's work on both the creative dynamic of the Trinity and the potentiality of the Will to "actualize into individuality" aimed to give an answer to this question of our distinction from the Absolute.[9]

An Overview of Plotinus

Plotinus was one of many who found within the Platonic Dialogues the idea of a single, perfect, all-powerful and unified origin as the basis for all reality. Many Neoplatonists saw perfection as a synonym for the ability to create, and Plotinus' idea of the One certainly fulfils this tenet — the only thing we can truly say about the One is that it creates, endlessly. The One has no desire and no lack, but its infinity overflows, creating a first product, and thus the first relationship ever that establishes unity. These products gain their existence by turning back to the One and comprehending their origin.[10] But as products emerge from the One, they diminish, and this occurs for two reasons.[11] Initially, diminishment and

---

[8] Jeffrey W. Barbeau, "The Development of Coleridge's Notion of Human Freedom: The Translation and Re-formation of German Idealism in England," *The Journal of Religion* 80 (2000): 576–94.

[9] James D. Boulger, *Coleridge as Religious Thinker* (New Haven: Yale University Press, 1961), 162–63.

[10] Plotinus, *Enn.* V.2.1.8–10.

[11] Coleridge was unsure why things diminished in a Plotinian world, and mentions this uncertainty in the *Opus Maximum* (202, 254–60). Plotinus is able to explain why the influence of the One appears to diminish: through no fault of the One, the rest of creation is simply unable to absorb all that the One emanates. If creation were able to absorb all, creation would no longer merely mimic the One, it would rival the One. As its name suggests, there can only be one ultimate principle of creation and power. Plotinus believes that creation must be subsequent and diminished compared to the One. What is particularly interesting about Coleridge's problems with Plotinian notions of diminishment is that Coleridge himself uses the same argument to propose characteristics of Evil — that it seeks actuality by supplanting the only thing that can give it grounds for actuality: "It must be possible to will a Self that is not God. But in God all Good is, and to will the contrary of Good is to will Evil" (*Op Max*, 237–38; cf. also 225 and 233).

distinction occur because there cannot be two Ones — it is impossible that there be two absolute and infinite sources of origin. Therefore a hierarchy emerges from the creative activity of the One, and while diminishment and distinction occur, those products closest to the One are the things that most resemble it — the first product of the One is Intellect, named thus by Plotinus because of its specific activity of attempting to be like its origin through thinking of itself as a unity. Intellect cannot completely imitate the One, for the One is infinite, and a product cannot supersede the source from which it comes: "[Intellect] was unable to hold the power which it received and broke it up and made the one power many, that it might be able so to bear it part by part."[12]

Intellect successfully echoes the Divine unity of the One by being both thought and the object of its own thought. This Plotinus equates to "sight," inferring a self-consciousness in which Intellect controls its multiplicity and understands its relationship to its origin. This seeing/self-consciousness results in substance, or existence for Intellect.[13] While Intellect cannot attain the absolute simplicity of the One, it can pull its own Many-ness — the multitude of reified/enumerated Forms that distinguish it from the One — into a unity that approaches both the unity and infinity of the One.[14] Intellect "constitutes [its own] being [through] its gaze upon the One… Resembling the One thus, Intellect produces in the same way, pouring forth a multiple power — this is a likeness of it — just as that which was before it poured it forth."[15] The rest of reality is a product of the One, and One is the principle of perfection, and, therefore, of creation within this reality. Subsequent levels of reality, *hypostases*, unfold as a result of this creative activity, and we can see that Intellect is a true child of its source when it creates from itself the next *hypostases*, Soul. From itself and the creative principle, Soul produces again, forming Nature. Nature is the result of Soul recognizing within itself the One as origin, and attempting to pull its Many-ness together into a perfect unity — making itself both unified and quantifiable through the now-perceivable corporeal objects in our material world. Corporeality, without the unifying influence of the One, and the choice of Soul to recognize its source through being creative and unifying, would not even attain a sense of corporeality — it would be an incomprehensible chaos.[16]

---

[12] Plotinus, *Enn.* VI.7.15.21–23.

[13] Plotinus, *Enn.* V.3.10.5–20.

[14] See my "Plotinian Sources for Coleridge's Theories of Evil," *The Coleridge Bulletin* n.s. 20 (2002): 97; see also Hedley, *Coleridge, Philosophy and Religion*, 38.

[15] Plotinus, *Enn.* V.2.1.12–16.

[16] Plotinus distinguishes between "corporeality" and matter (evil) at II.4.14.34–38.

The Alternative to Creative Activity

The flip-side of Soul's choice tells us something about the status of evil. Nature is the last product of the One's creative activity — being inert it lacks the creative agency to produce from itself. But the idea that Nature could have been incomprehensible if Soul had not chosen to recognize the unity of the One within itself is the concept that underlies the production of individual things. When he considers the choice that faced Intellect, Plotinus asks "why did it not on the contrary remain by itself[?]... we think it right to refer back to the One."[17] In this way, the One is transcendent, underlying the reality of everything that exists, and standing as the ultimate example of unity and identity; all things wish to return or be like the One: "things which are not one strive as far as they can to become one... wishing to be united in identity with themselves; for all individual things do not strive to get away from each other, but towards each other and towards themselves; and all souls would like to come to unity, following their own nature."[18]

While on the one hand, each individual chooses to recognize, within itself, both the principles of unity and creation exemplified by the One, there is a third principle at work here, which Plotinus refers to as "otherness," *heterotès*. This principle underlies the breaking away from the One that products must do, to be "other" than the One. As A. H. Armstrong explains, everything other than the One must enact an "illegitimate self-assertion."[19] In addition, each agent that possesses the creative ability from the One is allowed to choose "what is worse," and as this is a tendency not given by the exemplary example of the One, Plotinus blames such a choice on the "self-caused turning."[20] There is no need for the One to be "other" than itself, for it encapsulates infinity and perfection, along with everything else in creation; perhaps even the principle of *heterotès* itself lies unused within the One, a concept that may anticipate Schelling's thoughts on the subject, as we can see from Coleridge's evaluation of both his and Schelling's philosophies: "In short, Schelling's System and mine stand thus: — In the Latter there are God and Chaos: in the former an Absolute Somewhat, which is *alternately* both, the rapid leger de main shifting of which constitutes the delusive appearance of *Poles* —."[21] While for Coleridge there is a fundamental difference between God and

---

[17] Plotinus, *Enn.* V.1.6.6–8.
[18] Plotinus, *Enn.* VI.2.11.21–25.
[19] Armstrong, Preface to *Enneads*, xiii.
[20] Plotinus, III.2.4.37–40.
[21] *CN*, IV, 4662 (*f.*30); 1820.

evil, Schelling locates the origin of evil within a ground that encompasses both God and evil together.[22] Plotinus would say that I am taking things too far to ally his views with Schelling on this point. He argued that while we could say the One is All, we ourselves cannot comprehend the All. We know only of our own intellectual and corporeal experiences of unity, these being compromised and fleeting shadows. Therefore we can say nothing accurate when describing the One.[23] Armstrong suggests that it is a matter of "supreme existence": "the unity of the Good is so absolute that no predicates at all can be applied to Him, not even that of existence; and that as the Source of being to all things He is not a thing Himself."[24] As soon as we attempt to describe any aspect or characteristic, we limit what the One represents.[25] But for those interested in taking things too far, I suggest that all individual aspects of the One lie dormant within it — perhaps all are in perfect balance with each other and do not require representation as together, in infinity, they make up the perfect, supercomplete whole.[26] Against his own warnings never to attempt to describe the One, Plotinus concedes some ground concerning the relation between the One and the products that emanate from it, using terms that evoke Coleridge's description of the pleroma or Divine Ideas. He suggests that "all things" have their origin in the One, and that the One is their "principle" in that it underpins their existence. The One achieves this by "possessing them beforehand" but rather than this making the One a multiplicity, it possesses them in their indistinct form. Multiplicity occurs when "all things" are "distinguished on the second level [Intellect], in the rational form."[27]

While it is problematic that we might posit that *heterotès* is somehow in the One, like "all things," it is not manifested until the One overflows

[22] For a deeper investigation of the contrasts between Coleridge's and Schelling's respective theories of creation, see Nicholas Reid, "The Satanic Principle in the Later Coleridge's Theory of Imagination," *Studies in Romanticism* 37 (1998): 259–77.

[23] Plotinus says this throughout the *Enneads*, but his most famous protestation is at III.8.11.

[24] Armstrong, Preface to *Enneads*, xvi; cf. also John M. Rist, *Eros and Psyche: Studies in Plato, Plotinus, and Origen* (Toronto: University of Toronto Press, 1964), 69–71.

[25] Coleridge complains of Plotinus not taking things too far in *Aids to Reflection*: "the superessential ONE of Plotinus, to whom neither Intelligence, nor Self-consciousness, nor Life, nor even *Being* can be attributed" (*AR*, 169).

[26] Cf. Wallis explains that "the contents of the Intelligible world must already be present in the One in 'unfragmented' or perfectly unified form." Wallis notes that at various points Plotinus suggests that "the One is all things in transcendent mode" (R. T. Wallis, *Neoplatonism* [London: Duckworth, 1995], 60).

[27] Plotinus, *Enn.* V.3.15.25–32.

and the rest of creation exhibits otherness. Everything else that forms from the creative agency of the One must utilize *heterotès* when they distinguish and differentiate themselves from their source. If we can look at the process of how an individual comes about, we can locate the activity of *heterotès* after the event where the One's creative principle goes forth from itself. As the One is the only All/unity there is at that point, this creative principle must find some other place for its existence, and this necessarily and contradictorily has to be "other" than the One, existing as "deficient" Many, which through its aspiration to reunite with the One attains existence as a "one-many."[28]

While I have written elsewhere on the similarity between the concept of *heterotès* and Coleridge's theories regarding the potential and illogical "path not taken" that the Divine Will may choose,[29] I have quickly outlined these Plotinian theories here to focus on the predicament of humanity for both philosophers.

Humanity Spans the *Hypostases*

In Plotinus' system, the choices that face the *hypostases* are the choices humanity must face as well: whether to be other than the One or to contemplate the One as the true basis for a true existence. In a Plotinian world, we too are children of the One in that we possess both creativity and the ability to generalize many things into a unified and thus comprehensible concept. Despite the goodness that the Intellect within us gives,[30] humanity itself is in an interesting position, for it spans the hypostatic levels of Soul and Nature. Our bodies are corporeal and at times lose their hold on unity; we fall apart or render down into other objects. Of course, the upper unities face this problem to a lesser degree. But individual souls span the material world (which threatens to spin out of control into chaos and evil) and the *hypostases* of Intellect and Soul (the latter of which attempts to form matter into a unified many our intellects can comprehend). This is more important to Plotinus than the simple duality of matter and spirit, and it points to a more sophisticated struggle between

---

[28] Plotinus, *Enn.* V.3.15.5–12.

[29] McLean, "Plotinian Sources"; cf. also Reid, "The Satanic Principle," 259–77; and Anthony John Harding, "Imagination, Patriarchy, and Evil in Coleridge and Heidegger," *Studies in Romanticism* 35 (1996): 3–26.

[30] Plotinus, *Enn.* V.3.3.8–15.

the higher and lower self of each individual.[31] As Armstrong explains, an individual's soul can "devote itself selfishly to the interests of the particular body... [becoming] entrapped in the atomistic particularity of the material world... isolated from the whole. The root sin of the soul is self-isolation, by which it is imprisoned in the body and cut off from its high destiny." This "imprisonment" is a state of mind, dependent on whether the soul "surrenders to the body,"[32] or the person rises beyond the particularity and fragmented truths of this world to contemplate the transcendent archetypal truths found in the higher *hypostases*.

Crucially, it is when the individual soul is distracted by and mired in evil that a unique "Intellect" comes into activity. The faculty with which we see matter/evil is "another intellect which is not intellect, since it presumes to see what is not its own": "intellect, leaving its own light in itself and as it were going outside of itself and coming to what is not its own, by not bringing its own light with it experiences something contrary to itself, that it may see its own contrary."[33]

As I will discuss later, this in-between position has huge ramifications for both Plotinus and Coleridge in terms of Reason, its relation to our legitimate existence (for Plotinus) and the finite will (for Coleridge). But my immediate point for now is that the failure of the individual unities to aspire to their respective origins recalls Schelling's view of nature, a level of existence that fails to represent the unity of its origin. What Plotinus considers important in this mired state is that humanity not only shares the same choice as the upper unities, but that the choice to follow the path of *heterotès* is an overwhelming part of our own identities. Quite apart from the fact that our corporeal bodies fall apart[34] is the sensation that we are all individuals that differ from each other — we often value different "truths." As Boulger describes it, when talking of humanity's predicament as Coleridge may have seen it, "man is a spiritual being conscious of evil in himself and around him, of his darkened intellect, and above all of his position as an alien in the world of matter and sense, longing for his God whom he may know only partially, and this through the resources of the internal, the spiritual, alone."[35] Coleridge, like Plotinus, also sees humanity separated from God by a "passage from the

---

[31] Armstrong calls attention to this point in a footnote to *Enn.* III.3.4.36.
[32] Armstrong, Preface to *Enneads*, xxiii–xxiv.
[33] Plotinus, *Enn.* I.8.9.18–27.
[34] Cf. Plotinus on this point, *Enn.* III.6.6.
[35] Boulger, *Coleridge as Religious Thinker*, 202.

absolute to the separated finite… the chasm which ages have tried in vain to overbridge."[36] Plotinus' advice regarding this predicament is an extension of the Platonic suggestion that we give up our earthly pursuits and wait for death — at which point we exit the corporeal prison of the body, and our true spiritual/intellectual selves will re-ascend to some sort of super-communion with each other, possibly to reunify with the One. Plotinus believes that corporality is not the issue — it is merely the end of the line of creation, but it should not be the start of the journey back. He suggests that if we look within ourselves, we will hopefully see a trace of the Intellect that made us.[37] True knowledge of the true self will lead to knowledge of others, and therefore knowledge of archetypal truths. And as like knows like, we must use our own intellects in order to identify the Intellect that constitutes our true selves: "A man has certainly become Intellect when he lets all the rest which belongs to him go and looks at this with this and himself: that is, it is as Intellect he sees himself."[38] As Armstrong points out, this intellectual discovery of the true self is not a matter of "destruction or absorption of the particular personality, but its return to its perfect archetypal reality, distinguished in unity from all other archetypal realities, individual and universal."[39] We have to "cut away [the] excess and straighten the crooked and clear the dark and make it bright… [leaving] no inward mixture of anything else."[40] In this way, when we use the portion of Intellect that we have, we are not merely discovering our true selves, but making our true selves in an action of unity. Plotinus believes that our problem is not in the fact that we are individuals, but that being an individualized self may mean that we are tempted to become even more individual, and seek to follow a course that may end up alienating ourselves from the basis of our existence. What this action of "intellection" shows us is that in a Plotinian world we are children of Intellect in that we find ourselves compelled to mimic what Intellect does when it contemplates the One — to let go of our *heterotès* and contemplate what it possesses from our creator. Intellect, by knowing its true self, becomes intelligible to itself — many-ness no longer chaos because the many is unified. Intellect comprehends itself by finding its true nature and considering the One within its true self. Intellect finally makes itself

---

[36] *Op Max*, 218.
[37] Plotinus, *Enn*. V.3.9.1–10.
[38] Plotinus, *Enn*. V.3.4.29–32.
[39] Armstrong, Preface to *Enneads*, xxii.
[40] Plotinus, *Enn*. I.6.9.12–19.

comprehensible and achieves existence.[41] By founding the self upon unity
and the relationship it thus has with the One, "the Good is said to be the
cause not only of substance but of its being seen."[42]

What if we are mistaken in our attempts to find our true selves? Armstrong notes that there is a danger that our contemplation may not recognize our true self, but cause our identity to dissipate further outwards.[43]
This does not happen with the upper unities — Intellect makes itself Intellect by looking within, grasping what it can of the One. Therefore it is
inconceivable to propose that Intellect ends up being what it is by thinking of something else, or something *other*: "if it thinks from itself and
derives the content of its thought from itself, it is itself what it thinks. For
if its substance was other [here Armstrong inserts "than its thinking"]
and the things which it thought were other than itself, its substance would
itself be unintellectual: and again, potential, not actual."[44] As Intellect has
the choice to favor *heterotès* (but does not), we have the choice also to
lose ourselves in our "other" self; the self that gives us individuality
away from Intellect and Universal Soul.

I believe this Plotinian concept is comparable to Coleridge's stance on
individuality and distinction. While on the one hand *true* personality is
grounded in God (God being the absolute archetype of an agent engaging with an *idem et alter* [same and other] self), there is a rift between
Divine Personeity and human personality. This rift is diversity, a many-
ness, the chaos of which may not be countered by the unity and true existence of God, our basis for true personality: "the essence of Personality
is to be found in none of those qualities, negations, or privations by which
the finite is diverse from the absolute, the human Will from the divine,
man from God — nay, as we have found these diversities proportionally
subtracting from personal perfection, it inevitably follows that by the subtraction of these diversities, the personality must become more perfect,
and that God, therefore, must be at once the absolute person and the
ground of all personality... we have proved that the perfection of person
is in God, and that personeity, differing from personality only as rejecting all commixture of imperfection associated with the latter, is an essential constituent in the Idea of God."[45]

---

[41] Cf. *Enn.* V.3.8.
[42] Plotinus, *Enn.* VI.7.16.23–24.
[43] Armstrong, Preface to *Enneads*, xxvi.
[44] Plotinus, *Enn.* V.9.5.7–9.
[45] *Op Max*, 176–77.

To further investigate Coleridge's views on personality, individuality and distinction, it will be necessary to examine his ideas regarding the relationship between God and the Son, which underlies all of reality, and the actions of the Will that establish this relationship. A sense of otherness is involved in this relationship, as otherness is required by God to have a relationship with his other self, the Son: "while in the mutual act of self-attribution the effusion and refundence, the inspiration and respiration of divine Love, the Son is (or may I innocently say of the eternal that He becometh?) Deus alter et idem."[46] Unlike the Intellect, which must separate from the One and mimic it, the Coleridgean concept of the Son is "alter et idem" — other and same. As I have suggested elsewhere, God the Father contemplates himself, creating a Divine idea, a formal representation of his infinity, in God the Son. The dynamic between the two is one of a relationship through an act, rather than a hierarchical, subsequent simplification. God is contemplator and contemplated; the Son is God as he has acted; God is his own act.[47] But due to the freedom of the Will, there is a possibility that the Will might choose to go against its own nature and actualize chaos instead of order, comprehensibility, and relationship. This is reminiscent of the choice that each individual must make. To follow the path of *heterotès*, to refuse to mimic and make comprehensible the unity and creativity of the One, is to instead attempt (impossibly) to bring chaos into comprehensibility.

This is true of every Plotinian individual, apart from Intellect, which appears to share a superficial similarity with the relationship between God and the Son/Logos. The Intellect employs otherness to survive as something *of* the One. There is no reason why this otherness has to filter down through the hypostatic levels of reality; there could reasonably be a fraternal infinity of Intellects which represent the Many, all of the same level. But unlike the Son, who is the "same and other" to God, the action that the Intellect takes — to separate, be other, and to unify itself by contemplating the One as source — is all the knowledge that Intellect possesses, and this is passed on down through its own product and the subsequent *hypostases*. Intellect's "experience" is limited, it acts for a specific reason, and thus diminishment occurs.

This concerns the "things that are" in Plotinus' system. When we begin to look at evil in Coleridge's system, we begin to see a few more parallels between the two thinkers, and these are concepts that have obvious

---

[46] *Op Max*, 233.
[47] McLean, "Plotinian Sources," 104.

ramifications for human selfhood: "But the power (potentia) here asserted
is the power of losing ['a subsistence in and as one with the eternal
mind'], of substituting a self that is not God, a center in that which cannot be other than peripheric... The potential, still a form of reality, though
its negative role, and therefore a form of Will, willed itself to be actual
under impossible conditions. For to be actual was to will its subsistence
to be in God, and the power of willing otherwise existed potentially, by
necessity part of a Will, and part because it was a particular Will. It could
not but be, because the real was, and the actual was... The result can be
no otherwise expressed, as far as it can be at all expressed, than that a self
became, which was not God, nor One with God."[48] There is a similarity
here between the actions the *hypostases* take after separating from the
One — they contemplate their true source, and unify their own many-ness
into something comprehensible. The same is true for Coleridge's concept
of Will — its true nature is to seek unity — "the *Will* to be one is the
refusing to be divided."[49] This is further illustrated by the following, Plo-
tinian-sounding notebook entry: "The Will, whose other name is the
Good, is the Absolute One pure of the Many, out of whom the Many era-
diates as so many iterations of the One. The Will, which is *Evil*, would
be the Many utterly without the One; therefore *not* the Many but a striving to originate the Many by the destruction of the *One/*. But the One is
essentially indestructible: even to destroy the appearances of the One, it
must be of the One in the Many, and therefore by the destruction of the
Many in the One. It therefore contradicts itself, in one and the same Act
(or rather strife) willing to originate & to destroy. Self-contradiction is its
essence — it is a Lie & the Father of Lies from the beginning. Evil is
antipathy to the One; but the One is the Being of the Many. It destroys
therefore the possibility of its own Being — and Self-destruction *is* its
essential Tendency."[50] So while it is the Will's true nature to unify and
make real, it is evil's true nature to not only make real the Many, but to
do so by necessarily attempting to replace the One — in attempting such
an impossible thing it also must supplant the Many, which indicates that
the evil Will is self-destructive. It would become a Many without any
sense of unity.[51] Coleridge describes this self-contradiction as a type of

[48] *Op Max*, 246–47.
[49] *CN*, V, 5523; June 1827.
[50] *CN*, IV, 5076; December 1823.
[51] Cf. *Op Max*, 354: "in the plenitude we had Number above multeity so in the contrary state we have a multeity alien from number."

"Self-love [that] becomes Hate... in the striving to be one (instead of striving after and toward the One) it becomes the infinite Many."[52]

Strictly speaking, the main difference between humanity and evil is the fact that evil is "baseless." It seeks to be like God, to "have the ground of its existence in its existence." But not only does evil seek to supplant the Many made real by God, it is also, as Boulger suggests, "unintelligible, because an outcast from intelligence even as God [is] incomprehensible as containing all intelligence."[53] On the other hand, humanity at least has a self that is grounded, if we recognize it properly, in God. But as I outlined above, for Coleridge there are elements of imperfections and "diversities" that appear to point towards the Many and chaos, and not the Unity and comprehension that God's gift of actuality gives to us. Coleridge believes that we will fall (from existence) if we fail to recognize the basis of our true being. Writing from God's point-of-view, he explains: "so far as my Will gave you being, I gave you actual being, and begot you in the only begotten, begotten before all creation, and while your Will was one with my Will, ye were my offspring, the children of the most High. But there is a possibility of a Will that is not a Holy Will, and that ye will to be by your own Will; and hence there is a futurity, a fearful futurity, a change which cannot be without destruction of that actuality which ye would but have transferred to another source, without a fall proportioned to its height."[54] As Boulger has pointed out, "[a] will is free if it avoids contradiction with the Absolute Will."[55] It has to recognize what it is, where it comes from, its true nature, and not the "satanic" aspect that limits it or leads it to contradict the Absolute Will and therefore its own essence. Like the Intellect of Plotinus, we must turn to contemplate our origin and not go down the path of further separation. Though it may seem that we can base our existence within ourselves, this is a satanic fallacy: there is only God/the One, and to seek to supplant or separate ourselves from this origin is to forget our true selves. Plotinus describes this when he uses the allegory of souls running away from "their father, God": "[They are] ignorant of themselves and him, even though they are parts which come from his higher

---

[52] CN, IV, 5076; December, 1823. Cf. Plotinus Enn. III.6.14.7–10; "its self-assertion and a kind of begging and its poverty makes a sort of violent attempt to grasp, and is cheated by not grasping, so that its poverty may remain and it may be always begging."
[53] Boulger, Coleridge as Religious Thinker, 155.
[54] Op Max, 233.
[55] Boulger, Coleridge as Religious Thinker, 152.

world and altogether belong it[.] The beginning of evil for them was
audacity and coming to birth and the first otherness [*heterotès*] and the
wishing to belong to themselves. Since they were clearly delighted with
their own independence, and made great use of self-improvement, running the opposite course and getting as far away as possible, they were
ignorant even that they themselves came from that world... they despise
themselves through ignorance of their birth and honour other things."[56]
Recalling the Plotinian situation of spanning two *hypsostases*, one
dynamic, creative and unified, the other sometimes incomprehensible,
fragmented and inert, "its being is actual as far as it is in the being of God
and potential in relation to itself as particular existence."[57] We need to
recognize the basis of the reality we live in and affirm God as the basis
of our own Wills, as "it is in the Will itself and not in its limitations,
whether deficiency or defect, that the personality consists, as far as the
element of the Will is concerned."[58]

Should a Will actualize its particularity instead of its true relationship
with God, it does not simply disappear as its connection with God is sev-
ered. The potentiality itself remains, "by virtue of the Will, which as Will
is indestructible and eternal." This potentiality forever "annihilates the
actual, and in the potential swallowing up all actuality, so that the potential as merely potential remains the only form of its reality, it is an act
that may be said to realize the potential in the moment of potentializing
the alone truly real."[59] Plotinus discusses particularity in a similar way,
proposing that it be in some way the counterpoint to not only unity, but
subsistence. Consider Plotinus' view of the potentiality of Intellect to be
something other than the wonderfully varied representation of the One it
tries to be: "If the potential, without the prior existence of what is actual
and of Intellect, were to come into existence it could not attain to actuality. For what will be the principle which will bring it there if there is
not one different from and prior to itself? But if it is going to bring itself
to actuality, which is absurd, all the same it will bring itself by looking
to something, which will exist not potentially, but actually..."[60] In terms
of individual soul and human selfhood, we may mistakenly start "looking towards becoming, not being," and this of course is because evil has

[56] Plotinus, *Enn.* V.1.1.2–14.
[57] *Op Max*, 230.
[58] *Op Max*, 175.
[59] *Op Max*, 225.
[60] Plotinus, *Enn.* IV.7.8^3.14–19.

no being, or actuality, at all.[61] Individual soul, therefore, starts to contradict its own existence, no longer recognizing that it has a valid basis to exist, due to the influence of the One within it. Distracted by the evil which underlies corporeality, it mistakenly believes it should forever "become," instead of celebrating the fact that it already *is*. Coleridge believes "a world of contradictions" would follow this "first self-constituting act [which is in] essence a contradiction": "The Will, to make a centre which is not a centre, a Will not the same with the absolute Will, and yet not contained in the absolute, that is, an absolute that is not absolute... A world of contradictions, I have said, commences. The father of self, alien from God, was a liar from beginning and the father of lies."[62] As finite wills, our existence is only "actual as far as it is in the being of God and potential in relation to itself as particular existence."[63] Yet there is something deeply personal about the Divine Will that appears to underlie all of the seemingly limitless and varied personalities that we can think of: "we become persons exclusively in consequence of the Will... a source of personality must therefore be conceived in the Will, and lastly... a Will not personal is no idea at all but an impossible conception."[64] The major difference between our own personalities and the Divine, is again, a matter of unity, as J. H. Green suggests: "the Will must will, what it cannot otherwise than will, its own Being as one undivided Will; — it must will itself continuously, permanently, invariably, self-consistently; — and this is what we mean by an *individual Will* or a *Person*... eternal act of self-affirmation... the Absolute Will causative of reality, is in this relation, the essential act of Personeity... Ipseity, the Absolute Subject, 'I am.'"[65]

Other than the Pleroma

Coleridge spends a significant part of the *Opus Maximum* describing distinction in terms of the pleroma, or Divine Ideas. Having done this, he begins to discuss "the very attempt to pass beyond [the pleroma][66] is to plunge instantly from light into mere unsubstantial darkness."[67]

[61] Plotinus, *Enn.* I.8.4.20–21.
[62] *Op Max*, 225–26.
[63] *Op Max*, 230.
[64] *Op Max*, 165.
[65] Quoted in *Op Max*, ccxxxix–ccxl.
[66] Or, in this specific context, the "indivisible unity (*logoi theioi*) [Divine Ideas]."
[67] *Op Max*, 207.

The attempt he is explaining here covers the doomed effort to use a will
other to God's when trying to bring into existence the apostatic will. In
this way, human selfhood seems as precarious as it does when spanning
the *hypostases* — but what particularly interests me about the pleroma is
the fact that it encapsulates multeity in the comprehensible manner in which
Plotinian Intellect encapsulates the Forms. Again, this is due to unity; but
there is also a different type of distinction which is no longer about mul-
teity-in-unity, but a multeity which is distinctive to the point of chaos.[68]

Coleridge examines the idea of chaos in "Fragment 4" of the *Opus
Maximum*, when he describes the unity that "Indistinction" reaches,
through the process of actualization: it never reaches true unity as it
retains "its former nature, i.e. indistinction... without distinction of
parts," but a type of Multeity arises, now comprehensible as it possesses
a "semblance of distinction."[69] This semblance of distinction means that
there is meaning sprinkled throughout the world; objects approach a unity
which is comprehensible to us; this applies to self identity also.[70] Reminiscent of Plotinus' advice above, Coleridge believes that we must seek
unity by finding within ourselves some trace of the action that made us,[71]
"the realizing unity by which multeity is raised into figure and relation":
"we must gather strength... and with cleansed eye refuse to behold any
true unity but in the Deity, any true and essential distinction except in that
divine Unity. Out of this, the Alpha and Omega, we can find no attributes but those of Allness and Multeity — and as long, therefore, as we
speak of that which is not God, we can comprehend no other Allness
which is the reflex and Symbol of unity but that which is derived from
the multeity — become conceivable as component parts. An Allness that
in its Unity is the causative principle of its comprehended distinctions

---

[68] *Op Max*, 298–99.
[69] *Op Max*, 320.
[70] Cf. Reid in "'That Eternal Language,' or Why Coleridge was Right about Imaging
and Meaning," *Romanticism on the Net* 28 (2002). Reid describes in greater detail the
relation of form, meaning, and language to the gift of actuality and its effects on Nature.
Hedley also touches upon the philosophical heritage of the concept of Nature, language,
and intelligibility in *Coleridge, Philosophy and Religion* (see in particular p. 119, which
relates to Augustine but is equally attributable to Plotinus).
[71] A sentiment echoed by Plotinus at *Enn.* V.3.3.32–46 ("On the Knowing
Hypostases"): "we ourselves are not Intellect. We are... in accord with it by our rational
power which first receives it... The activities of Intellect are from above in the same way
that those of sense-perception are from below; we are this, the principal part of the soul,
in the middle between two powers, a worse and a better, the worse that of sense-perception, the better that of Intellect... Sense-perception is our messenger, but Intellect is our
king."

would be = God."[72] What this comes down to is a struggle between an individual's Reason, which sees things as they are, and an individual's will, which may either fall into despair (seen often as the greatest sin, in Christianity, as it leads to an inability to recognizes the self's basis in God)[73] or use its freedom to choose itself as a basis, instead of God. An individual's will has to recognize what it truly is, and attempting to understand where it comes from leads directly to it establishing, or at least comprehending, its true nature and avoiding the limitation of self basis that contradicts the Absolute Will and therefore the finite will's own essence. The freedom that God has in bringing itself into a comprehensible unity and true existence is the same choice we have.[74] As Harding has explained, humanity has the same basis as God does in his will; the same choice between selfishness or a creative principle that is based upon Reason.[75] Should we will ourselves apart from God, where would we go? Coleridge provides a description that recalls Plotinus' concept of *heterotès*: "Hence we have in the first place three forms of agency contained in the act of light (lucific act) as realized in a diverse materia: 1st, the evocation, which can only be represented by its contrariety to the former creaturely or self-seeking direction. If that former be a fleeing back in upon the self and relative to that self be the actual, then the power of moving, or being influenced to move away from, Self and to a center out of Self (which we know is realizable only as a return to God, but which in the present stage of our enquiry must, relatively to the creature, be confined to the notion of a center out of itself, i.e. ad extra, as in opposition to ad intra) — then, we repeat, this power must be opposed to the former as the potential, but this power is called into act by an influence of the Divine Will, which is essentially realizing."[76] If the will brings itself through the freedom that it has in accordance with Reason, it communes, as Hedley suggests, with the Divine.[77] This sense of communion

---

[72] *Op Max*, 313.

[73] Cf. Boulger, *Coleridge as Religious Thinker*, 210.

[74] Although it is impossible "for God not to be God," such freedom "is not precluded in the Will, or in a realization of the Will through and in the Divine Will: it is precluded only by the absolute self-realization of the absolute Will." For humanity, however, "the potential necessarily co-exists as alternable with the actual. And this by virtue of the Will, which is the common essence of all; for all are as realization of the Will, and yet not exempted from potentiality by being in their own forms or necessarily absolute" (*Op Max*, 222, 232).

[75] Harding, "Imagination, Patriarchy, and Evil," 12.

[76] *Op Max*, 381 ["Appendix A"].

[77] Hedley, *Coleridge, Philosophy and Religion*, 185.

is at the very core of Coleridge's idea of true personality, as it relates to the sense of reciprocation that the Son has towards the Father at the (on-going) act of Divine actualization, as well as the temptation to divide without "that distinction which necessarily implies a community, or the existence of another in the self, as another and yet equal to self."[78] It is no longer a matter of an individual falling into apostasy like the recalci-trant gods who run away from their Creator in Plotinus' *Ennead* V.1, but that our personality must include a sense of community with something other than ourselves; otherwise, we risk isolating ourselves, half-actual-ized, half potential, and free to choose either, approaching the state of things logically prior to the Divine actualization. An individual who seeks to base oneself in one's own will is in danger of falling into indistinction, for this is no community. The relationship must be with a true other, as the Logos is in its filial relationship with the Father.

Dyad as the Essential Form of Unity

From the fallen point of view of humans, we need to recognize the ulti-mate polarity of comprehensible things when we exercise our Reason and our Will. For Coleridge, everything that has achieved actuality in some way must be in a relationship with something else. Hence "[t]he Dyad is the essential form of Unity";[79] it is not that unity has fallen apart or split, but that unity is manifested through the willing communication/commu-nion of two agents, who through the self-realization of their mutual inter-connectedness, establish a relationship with each other (and within their own selves). Therefore a comprehensible distinctity can exist without falling into self-isolation and indistinction. I propose, for Coleridge, this is where our true personalities find their grounding: we can be distinctive from each other, reflecting the relationship and overall unity of the *logoi theioi* or Divine Ideas, as long as we are connected through community and avoid self-isolation. Boulger cuts to the very heart of this concept when he states that "Alterity in the Trinity provides the ontological grounds for 'distinctity' of beings, and creation is merely the transmission of this distinction into the cosmological order."[80] Creation underlies this community, because Creation establishes God's communion with his self

---

[78] *Op Max*, 324.
[79] *CN*, IV, 4829; c. 1821.
[80] Boulger, *Coleridge as Religious Thinker*, 149.

and other. And, as Boulger remarks, "unity is the source of true functional diversity," and our Reason helps us realize and perceive this.[81]

Plotinus would wholeheartedly agree with this concept, for it underlies not only the manner in which the One brings itself into existence, but also the way in which the *hypostases* and ourselves recognize our true selves and our ultimate unity with the whole of creation. For Plotinus, Reason is sinless, as it is the formula, the *logos*, by which the whole of creation unfolds.[82] Reason differs from opinion in that opinion can lead us to think that we are chasing the true self and contemplating truth within ourselves: "wishing itself to be directed towards itself[, the individual soul may make] an image of itself, the non-existent, as if walking on emptiness and becoming more indefinite... it is altogether without reason and unintelligent and stands far removed from reality."[83] When we use Reason, we transform — the seer becomes the seen, we suddenly unify within ourselves, becoming Intellect, much in the same way the One creates from itself, eternally: "[The One's] activities are what we might call his substance, his will and his substance will be the same thing... then as he willed, so also he is... [H]e is not what he happened to be but what he himself willed."[84]

So it seems there is one thing we can say about the One. We may ascribe to him a sort of activity-in-being through an act of will: "his will is in his substance... there is nothing different from his substance... he was all will... he himself is primarily his will [and] it generated nothing further in himself, for he was this already."[85] When the perceiver "comes into unity with what is known," she is truly contemplating the course that leads to the One. Reason, as the influence of Intellect (the true basis of which is its own thinking of itself as a unity that approaches the absolute unity of the One), is at the heart of the One's self-creation, as it is at the heart of unity: "For if they are two, the knower will be one thing and the known another, so that there is a sort of juxtaposition, and contemplation has not yet made this pair akin to each other, as when the rational principles present in the soul do nothing. For this reason the rational principle must not be outside but must be united with the soul of the learner, until it finds that it is its own."[86] In a Coleridgean world, God's

---

[81] Boulger, *Coleridge as Religious Thinker*, 135.
[82] Plotinus, *Enn.* I.1.9, 4–16.
[83] Plotinus, *Enn.* III.9.3.10–14; cf. I.8.4.9–13.
[84] Plotinus, *Enn.* VI.8.13.7–59; cf. VI.8.16.15–21.
[85] Plotinus, *Enn.* VI.8.21.12–19.
[86] Plotinus, *Enn.* III.8.6.17–22.

alterity manifests both community and being for the first time, for both
God and the Logos. As Boulger attests, the distinctity between God and
the Son/Logos is made valid through a "greater unity of the Identity...
a philosophical dualism of Creator and created, Absolute and individual
will, God and created finite substance."[87] In an orthodox Christian sense,
the Son is the perfect archetype of humanity we all should aspire to, for
in the Divine unity he reciprocates, introducing communication to the
concept of unity: "It has been stated as the act of the Father in the generation and contemplation of the Son, and directed towards the Son. But
it is likewise, and simultaneously, as it were, the act of the Son in referring himself, and in him the plenitude of divine forms to the Father, and
thus directed towards the Father... such procession being in its nature
circular, at once ever refluent and ever profluent, the Greek Fathers have
entitled the [*perichōresis*], or the primary, absolute, co-eternal intercir-
culation of Deity."[88] Therefore, Reason has a proper object of thought,
which is itself, or simply the self.[89]

Conclusion

The concept of contemplation through the Reason is of great importance
to both Plotinus and Coleridge in terms of anchoring an individual's personality in reality, allowing it to be manifested through the distinction
and unity that echoes the initial Divine self-creation. Like Plotinus' idea
of return contemplation, we find our true selves (in the Coleridgean
world) by contemplating and loving that which our Creator founded our
own being upon: "Himself being all, he communicated himself to another
as to a Self. But such communication is Love, and in what is the re-
attribution of that Self to the Communicator but Love? This, too, is Love,
filial Love — Love is the Spirit of God, and God is love."[90] A sense of
atonement is applicable to both Plotinus and Coleridge. For the latter, an

---

[87] Boulger, *Coleridge as Religious Thinker*, 138.

[88] *Op Max*, 205–6.

[89] Boulger, *Coleridge as Religious Thinker*, 76; cf. Plotinus, *Enn.* V.3.10: "The thinking principle, then, when it thinks, must be in two parts, and either one must be external
to the other or both must be in the same, and the thinking must be in otherness and necessarily also in sameness; and the proper objects of thought must be the same and other
in relation to the intellect." See also the *Essay on Faith*, where Coleridge states that Reason should be the object of its own thought — use of the Understanding can lead to a pride
that places the finite will above that of the Divine (*SW&F*, II, 839–44); cf. *Op Max*, 104–6.

[90] *Op Max*, 210.

individual must place the will in "harmony with, and in subordination to, the reason."[91] For Plotinus, an individual must recognize the true basis of being and align self-contemplation with the logic that underlay the One's self-creation and the subsequent creation of the hypostatic levels of reality, not the *heterotès* that is also part of identity as something other than the One. As Armstrong suggests, what this means in terms of personality is not "the destruction or absorption of the particular personality but its return to its perfect archetypal reality, distinguished in unity from all other archetypal realities, individual and universal."[92] The *heterotès* in our personality may mean that we are tempted to become even more individual, and seek to follow a course that may end up alienating ourselves from the origin and basis of our existence, whether that be God (for Coleridge) or the One (for Plotinus). As Armstrong explains, the focus for Plotinus is on "a return [via] Intellect," where our individual personalities unite and rediscover our true selves in the unity we establish in the Intellectual realm, mirroring the Divine unity and selfhood of the One. Through true self-knowledge, "we rise above Intellect to a state in which there is no consciousness of difference from the One, in which there is no longer seer and seen, but only unity."[93] Coleridge believes relationship is linked to unity and the concept of our true selves as well, and it is in the *Opus Maximum* that we see him succeeding to reconcile the necessity of distinction and differentiation from our origin in God with the concept of relationship and unity, particularly in terms of the Will and its freedom of choice, and how we might use our Reason to notice relationships between disparate things, to notice polarities, and comprehend how these and our selves are reflections of the relationships within the Trinity.

---

[91] *AR*, 42; cf. Barbeau, "The Development of Coleridge's Notion of Human Freedom," 592.

[92] Armstrong, Preface to *Enneads*, xxii.

[93] Armstrong, Preface to *Enneads*, xxvi–xxviii.

THE LOGOSOPHIA: HOW THE LOGOS ACTS AS UNIFYING PRINCIPLE IN COLERIDGE'S THOUGHT

By Nicholas Reid

In this chapter I shall examine the broader context in which Coleridge wrote his *Opus Maximum*, the context provided by his "Logosophia." I shall rely heavily, indeed, somewhat audaciously, on what is much the best book on Coleridge's systematic thought, Mary Anne Perkins's *Coleridge's Philosophy*, for Perkins has dealt with the subject more comprehensively than any other commentator, and allowed us for the first time to see how the various parts of the Coleridgean project related to one another. But I shall also bring to the table some of my own arguments about Schelling and about the role of form in the Coleridgean Logos.[1] And where Perkins's book is long and demanding, I hope, and this can be my only claim on the reader's indulgence, to present a short synthesis of what can be said about the role of the Logos in Coleridge's thought.

For I think that there are few things in Coleridge's thought that are as hard to grasp as his Logosophia. McFarland has, of course, done much to put Coleridge's aspiration in its historical context, pointing to the development in the eighteenth century of the genre of the universal history in writers like Bossuet, Pascal, Ficino, Bacon, Burnet, Cudworth, Ramsay and Berkeley.[2] But many of us will have read Coleridge's descriptions of the proposed "Logosophia," even in the very detailed version reproduced by McFarland in the *Opus Maximum*, with a certain incomprehension.[3] Its desire to bring together all branches of knowledge is evident, a desire, as Fletcher put it, to transform "some vast labyrinthine body of inchoate materials into an equally vast, but now

---

[1] Mary Anne Perkins, *Coleridge's Philosophy: The Logos as Unifying Principle* (Oxford: Clarendon Press, 1994). The best introduction to Coleridge's philosophy remains John H. Muirhead's *Coleridge as Philosopher* (London: George Allen & Unwin, 1930/1954).

[2] See *Op Max*, clx–clxiii. McFarland's argument has, of course, a subtext, aimed at those who wish to deny the systematic dimension to Coleridge's thought.

[3] *Op Max*, c–civ; the full notebook entry, as discussed in chapter 1, is found in *CN*, V, 5868.

perfectly lucid..., temple of ideal order."[4] But how was this inchoate
mass to be made lucid? And how was the Logos to function within the
system?

These are the questions that this essay seeks to answer. I shall begin
with the deep logic of alterity that is founded in the Logos, before moving to the quasi-sensuous nature of form, the necessity of personality
for the instantiation of the infinite, and the role of the Logos in language, history, and Reason. From there I shall move to the finite creation, and to the Logos as both archetype and vital influence within the
fallen world of Schelling's understanding. In each of these fields, which
broaden out to include literary and biblical criticism and politics, the
Logos turns out to be central — and I shall conclude with a brief examination of just how much of the long-fabled "Logosophia" is in fact
extant.

Triune Logic and Alterity

We should begin at the most fundamental level, with the Trinity and the
role of the Logos within the act of instantiation through which the Father
brings Himself and all reality into being. Coleridge's triune logic is well
known and, if his own account is to be believed, dated from at least 1796,
for he claims that "I was at that time and long after, though a Trinitarian
(i.e. ad norman Platonis) in philosophy, yet a zealous Unitarian in Religion."[5] The evidence of the notebooks suggests that the triune logic dates
from early in 1801; and his formal conversion to Trinitarianism dates
from about February 1805.[6] Coleridge discusses the triune logic in the
Opus Maximum, but more substantive discussions appear in the *Logic*
and in the hundreds of notebook entries and marginal annotations where
the implications of the *Logic* are drawn out.[7]

In any case, as his own comments in the *Opus Maximum* show,
Coleridge's triune logic derives from a set of arguments that are first
found in Plato's *Parmenides*, where Plato presents without endorsement
arguments showing that the many must be one — because, as Spinoza

---

[4] Angus Fletcher, "Positive Negation: Threshold, Sequence and Personification in
Coleridge" in *New Perspectives on Coleridge and Wordsworth,* ed. Geoffrey Hartman
(New York: Columbia University Press, 1972), 149; *Op Max,* cv.

[5] *BL,* I, 179–80.

[6] *CN,* I, 922; II, 2444, 2445, 2448.

[7] *Op Max,* 104–5; *Logic,* 241.

was later to argue, if two different entities occur in the same universe, they must have something in common.[8] Added to this was the converse argument, that no two objects can ever be exactly the same, an argument for an ultimate manyness, and the result was the problem of the One and the Many — or an example of Kant's antinomies, arguments that appear to license directly contradictory conclusions.

But the Christian Neoplatonists posited a God who is simultaneously one and many, or rather one and three, and Coleridge sharpened this apparently paradoxical state by arguing that selfhood is an implicitly communal concept — that the oneness of self implicitly demands the manyness implied by the necessity of an other. For the Father instantiates himself in a moment of self-recognition, but self-recognition depends upon the recognition of the other, in this case, of the Son. To put it another way, consciousness is dependent, as Coleridge says in the *Opus Maximum*, on conscience — again, a recognition of the other.[9] Ipseity (sameness) depends upon Alterity (otherness), though for Parmenidean reasons that Alterity must ultimately be one with the Ipseity. And so, if we include the Spirit as the community of the Ipseity and the Alterity, we are left with a God who is both one and three. Instantiation requires the principle of alterity; and the real presence of the Logos is thus necessary for Coleridge's system. That the Logos is fully substantial is clear in Coleridge's claim that "Philo names the Logos the only-begotten Son of God to distinguish the Word from a Thought," for a mere thought would not embody the alterity needed for the Father's self-instantiation.[10] The Logos is the energy which lies behind a thought, and the principle that gives form to a thought. But it is fundamentally a principle of alterity, a principle that proves to be central to many of the functions of the Logos in Coleridge's system, as we shall see below.

In the *Opus Maximum* and in other later writings, Coleridge refined his triune views into a fourfold schema, the tetractys, and indeed lamented the "failure of the 'Fathers… from Justin Martyr to Augustine' to hold on to the truth of the *tetractys*, substituting for it the less adequate *trias*.'"[11] But the tetractys still incorporated the triad described above, along with the principle of alterity. It added a ground to the triad, and has

[8] *Op Max*, 184.
[9] *Op Max*, 21.
[10] *CM*, II, 458; Perkins, *Coleridge's Philosophy*, 70.
[11] Perkins, *Coleridge's Philosophy*, 64; *CN*, V, 6761 (*f*.16v).

been the cause of some controversy, but since the ground is not existential, it does not radically change the picture just given and need not further detain us here.[12]

Alterity, Sensousness, and Form

In a move thoroughly presupposed by the discussion in the *Opus Maximum*, Coleridge argues that the Father does not merely recognize the alterity of the Son: he also recognizes himself in the Son, for Father and Son are one. The Son's alterity comes not from a difference of substance but of form — for the Son turns out to be the formal embodiment of the Father. We might think of this as being like the way in which the formal qualities of a work of art embody artistic intentions. Indeed, Coleridge suggests that the forms of nature, or "that eternal language which thy God/Utters," are reflections of the archetypal forms that constitute the Logos. As the well known notebook entry from 1805 puts it: "In looking at objects of Nature while I am thinking, as at yonder moon dim-glimmering thro' the dewy window-pane, I seem rather to be seeking, as it were *asking*, a symbolical language for something within me that already and forever exists, than observing any thing new. Even when that latter is the case, yet still I have always an obscure feeling as if that new phænomenon were the dim Awaking of a forgotten or hidden Truth of my inner Nature/It is still interesting as a Word, a Symbol! It is <u>Logos</u>, the Creator! and the Evolver!"[13] The question now arises as to how the Logos can be a formal entity, for clearly the Logos differs from an artistic work in being immaterial. The answer is to be found, I think, in something analogous to vision (or any of the senses), for the images (or acts of imaging) that form in our heads when we look at a tree are not material things or objects, lacking for instance spatial extension, though they are undoubtedly the products of material brains, and are material in that sense.[14] Images,

[12] *Op Max*, 209, 254. See my "Coleridge and Schelling: The Missing Transcendental Deduction," *Studies in Romanticism* 33.3 (Fall 1994): 472; and a more detailed discussion of the Ground in an endnote to chapter 6 of my *Coleridge, Form and Symbol*; see also Perkins, *Coleridge's Philosophy*, 192. Others who have written on the subject include Harding, McLean, Barth, Modiano, Hardy, and Shedd.

[13] *CN*, II, 2546. I have transliterated "Logos" from Coleridge's Greek. The poetry is quoted from "Frost at Midnight," lines 60–61.

[14] Berkeley argued correctly that the distinction between primary and secondary qualities is misleading, since there is no question of the "images" within our heads having

then, are in this sense not material *objects*, but they do, like the Logos, embody meaning. Our most basic understandings about the external world come to us through the senses and in sensory form; and the Father's recognition of himself in the Son is similarly basic, and quasi-sensory.

Indeed, the analogy is more straightforward for Coleridge than it is for us, for Coleridge was an idealist, and sensory images thus involved no reference to a physical world but were purely mental. Of course, some qualification of this is necessary. Sensory intuition for Coleridge derives from the fallen Understanding, which contributes amongst other things the forms of time and space, and Coleridge's early rejection of empiricism was followed by a deep distrust of the attractions (and lusts) of the senses. But these are objections to an inappropriate reification, and not to the archetypal forms that underlie that kind of sensation (or, better, intuition) which Coleridge calls Imagination. It follows that the Father's perception of the Son might be called quasi-sensuous — an act of Imagination shorn of course of all the limitations of the Understanding, but in some sense at least akin to the qualitative experience of sensation.[15]

So, form means something quasi-sensory. It is important to note, with Coleridge, that form is not reducible to *forma formata*, the "outward forms," which Coleridge rejected in "Dejection: An Ode" (l.45), or what the Notebooks term "mould" or "shape."[16] Rather, as Susanne Langer has argued, form is a generative principle of order, or a concept which is fundamentally relational.[17] And relationality turns out to be central to Coleridge's conception of the Logos. The alterity of the Son

---

actual length or breadth. This way of thinking of images goes back to Plato's *Phaedo*, where Socrates argues that minds do not have physical locations — though one does not have to accept Socrates' argument to agree with Berkeley about images. L. A. Reid further argued that it is better to avoid talk of images, since the thought that our brains might contain something analogous to Polaroid snaps is absurd. He therefore preferred to speak of acts in which we image the world — for he did not want to go as far as the ultra-materialist position of denying that qualitative experience occurs; see Nicholas Reid, "Form in Coleridge; and in Perception and Art more generally," *Romanticism on the Net* 26 (2002): http://www.erudit.org/revue/ron/2002/v/n26/005699ar.html.

[15] Perhaps one might suggest facetiously that the Logos, like nature, is mostly green. Or perhaps like the model demiurge in Plato's *Timeaus* it is spherical, but with the addition of lots of blue bits. But that would be to push the analogy too far, for while images in themselves may lack spatial dimension, they do refer to a world that is spatially extended, and that the Logos is not.

[16] *CN*, I, 1433 (August 1803); *CN*, IV, 5377 (f.44v) (May 1826).

[17] Susanne K. Langer, *An Introduction to Symbolic Logic*, second ed. (1937; New York: Dover Publications, 1953), 23–24.

means that the Son is not "like" the Father in the way, for instance, that a picture of a cat is "like" a cat. Nor for that matter is the green in which I image grass "like," in any direct or representational sense, any quality of the grass itself, for "green" is a secondary quality, a kind of mental or qualitative stuff, while grass is merely a physical substance with certain surface properties.[18] In both cases, there is a relation between the "image" and the thing imaged, but it is not a relation of immediate likeness.[19]

I have argued elsewhere that *relations* are formal when they present (not *re*present) an entity within a new medium, where immediate likeness is precluded.[20] Coleridge adopts exactly this language of relation in a marginal note on Schelling, when he insists on the *difference* or "otherness" of the Son *vis-à-vis* the Father: "It [i.e. the Father] has all reality in itself; but it must likewise have all reality in another."[21] He goes on to say that "all eternal Relations are included in all reality — and there can be difference but of *relation*" (Coleridge's emphasis). But he further insists that "this must be a *real* relation," that is, one in which there is genuine difference or Alterity (a difference in *medium*). This is the basis of Perkins's claim that Coleridge views "the Logos as the mediation between transcendent principle and finite form."[22] It is also the basis of Perkins's broader claim that "[f]rom the time of his adoption of orthodox Christianity, he maintained that reality was most adequately expressed and communicated in terms of relationality, whether in the form of triunity or polarity, or... the *tetractys* [etc]."[23]

---

[18] On "presentation" see Susanne Langer, *Philosophy in a New Key* (London: Oxford University Press, 1951), 92 and ch. IV more generally; and Coleridge, *LS*, 113. Given that "images" are not the "representations" spoken of in empiricist theory, Coleridge and Langer prefer to speak of them as "presentations." In Langer's case, the use of the term "presentation" grew out of L. A. Reid's rejection of "representational" views, in his *Knowledge and Truth* (London: MacMillan, 1923), 8 and *passim*.

[19] The relation is between the surface qualities of the grass (how much energy is required to jump the outermost electron to its next highest orbit, and therefore which wavelengths of light it will absorb) and the spectral qualities of the light — for again these two things are not "like" in kind, and so their likeness can only be one of relation. There is also a relation between the spectral quality of the light and the stimulation of the cones within the eye, and thus a relation between the light and the qualitative experience of green.

[20] Reid, "Form in Coleridge."

[21] *CM*, IV, 400 (my emphasis).

[22] Perkins, *Coleridge's Philosophy*, xi.

[23] Perkins, *Coleridge's Philosophy*, 43; see also 252.

Personality and Infinity

In moving away from his Unitarian phase, Perkins claims, the Logos became "the means by which he was finally able 'to reconcile personality with infinity.'"[24] The problem is that personhood, even in its Divine form, seemed for Coleridge to be an implicitly social concept, implying distinction (I am not you: I recognize you as other; conscience, or recognition of the other, is the basis of consciousness) though not, after 1818, Schellingian limitation. How then could the infinite be personal, when the personal appears to be distinct and non-inclusive? The answer is that the infinite only exists when the Father instantiates himself *personally* by recognizing the otherness of the Son. The Father is an infinite fullness, and the Son an infinite capacity.[25] The Logos is thus both the condition of the infinite, and the condition of the personeity of the infinite. And, on the level of logic, the Logos is the driving concept behind triune logic (that the One must be Three). It is also the driving concept behind the converse, that the Three must be One, and that that One must be personal in Nature rather than the "pantheistic" or impersonal One of Plotinus or Schelling.[26] Hence Coleridge's claim, "No Christ, No God," the insight in February of 1805 that converted his triune view of logic into an orthodox Trinitarian view of God.[27]

It is worth noting that such considerations ease the passage from Christ as Logos to Christ as Man, for as Coleridge wrote in 1820, "as the fontal God can only be known in the Logos, so neither can the Logos be sought aright but in the divine Humanity."[28] Christ is both the ideal of humanity and immanent within humanity, being "the Self of every creature."[29] As Perkins notes, this relation became increasingly important to Coleridge in his later life, and underlies his claim: "More & more I see the necessity of devoting my best powers, & prayers as the best means of power, to the enucleation of this latter title, Son of Man."[30] As Perkins points out, this required a balance between the Greek, triune conception of the Logos, and the Hebraic doctrine of the God-Man, conceptions that derive respectively from a Greek emphasis on the "it is," and a Hebrew emphasis on

---

[24] Perkins, *Coleridge's Philosophy*, 16; *BL*, I, 201.
[25] *Op Max*, 199.
[26] Perkins, *Coleridge's Philosophy*, 19; Karen McLean, "Plotinian Sources for Coleridge's Theories of Evil," *The Coleridge Bulletin* n.s. 20 (Winter 2002): 93–104.
[27] Perkins, *Coleridge's Philosophy*, 16; *CN*, II, 2448.
[28] *CN*, IV, 4671; Perkins, *Coleridge's Philosophy*, 207.
[29] *CM*, I, 629; Perkins, *Coleridge's Philosophy*, 207.
[30] *CN*, V, 6521 (*f.*12v); Perkins, *Coleridge's Philosophy*, 207.

the "I AM."[31] She traces these views to Philo, Origen, and Eriugena, though she also points to the difficulties Coleridge experienced in conceptualizing the relation.[32]

Perkins perhaps too easily takes at face value some of Coleridge's later attempts, in the notebooks, to argue that while the Father and the Holy Ghost are possessed of "personeity," only the Logos is possessed of "personhood."[33] For while the distinction is first raised in the *Opus Maximum*, personeity is there distinguished from personality "only as rejecting all commixture of imperfection associated with the latter" and, therefore, without any attempt to distinguish between the three persons of the Trinity.[34] In the later notebooks it is true that the Logos is granted a more exclusive personhood, in part out of a desire to avoid any notion of Tritheism, of the sort which Coleridge feared could be read into the Athanasian creed.[35] But I do not believe that we fully understand the distinction Coleridge thought he was making in the later notebooks, for Coleridge's picture of a Father who instantiates himself in recognizing himself in the Son certainly requires that the Father possess some sense of selfhood; and thus, at the very least, "personeity" will need to retain some of the qualities of personhood. Perhaps the distinction is akin to that between ego and Zenist detachment — a distinction that, if purged of the negative qualities associated with the ego, might recognize the role of the Logos as the one who acts within the Creation, or the one who in Coleridge's terms is the "exegesis" of the Godhead.[36] But I can offer little evidence for such a position.[37]

---

[31] Perkins, *Coleridge's Philosophy*, 208, 209.

[32] Perkins, *Coleridge's Philosophy*, 207, 209, 213, 215, 219, 223.

[33] Perkins, *Coleridge's Philosophy*, 228, 229, 230–35. Perkins depends heavily on the view that the Logos is *"Deitas objectiva,"* but in quoting *The Friend* here, she relies on a text that predates Coleridge's abandonment of subject/object language in descriptions of the Godhead — an abandonment that dates from his rejection of Schelling in the letter to Green of September 1818 (Perkins, *Coleridge's Philosophy*, 229; *CL*, IV, 1145). Coleridge's later uses of the terms "subject" and "object" are qualified by the term "relatively," for instance in the "Formula Fidei" where Coleridge reuses the term *"Deitas objectiva"* (*SW&F*, II, 1510–12 ["On the Trinity"]). Subject and object are polarized terms, and as such belong, as I have argued above, solely within the finite realm; see Excursus note 3 on this subject in Chapter 6 of my book, *Coleridge, Form and Symbol.*

[34] *Op Max*, 177; see also 164 and 166.

[35] Perkins, *Coleridge's Philosophy*, 233.

[36] Perkins, *Coleridge's Philosophy*, 228. Zenist detachment of course has its correlatives in the Bible's demand that we must lose the illusory self of the ego in order to find a deeper or truer self in the immanent Logos.

[37] Perkins makes a similar suggestion in describing "personeity" as "Coleridge's term for the living energy of the distinction-in-unity of reason, will, and love, which is what

Logos and Human Language

The one perhaps regrettable aspect of Perkins's analysis lies in her desire
to assimilate Coleridge's theory of language to late-twentieth-century linguistic theories, though this desire is shared by a number of recent commentators.[38] Such arguments begin with the premise that words "are the
tools through which... reality is constituted," and move from there to the
claim that the Coleridgean Trinity is founded on the role of the Logos,
or Divine Word, conceived as a quasi-linguistic utterance.[39] The Father
speaks and the Son is the linguistic word spoken, a creation constituted
in much the same way as meaning is alleged to be constituted within and
by linguistic utterance.

Fortunately Perkins does not press the analogy to that conclusion,
for when Coleridge speaks of language he does not think of it as only
a system of arbitrary and conventional signifiers (though he is of course
aware that this is one aspect of language, asking in his famous letter
of September 22, 1800, to Godwin, "[i]s *thinking* impossible without
arbitrary signs?").[40] As Perkins herself is aware, Coleridge's position
has the psychologistic foundation (and indeed the basis in faculty psychology) that twentieth-century thought for the most part tried to elide,
and she thus characterizes Coleridge's position by the claim that
"[w]ords which are unconnected to ideas are mere sound."[41] As the
Opus Maximum argues, "our words can have no meaning for him that

might rather be called 'personhood,' suggesting a state of being, [rather] than 'personality,' which might be understood as character or quality" (*Coleridge's Philosophy*, 84n.).
And my talk of Zenist detachment finds an echo in Coleridge's analysis of love. He speaks
of a beloved human partner as a symbol of God, for in love of another the self finds "its
self-oblivion united with *Self-warmth*, & still approximates to God!" (*CN*, II, 2540;
Perkins, *Coleridge's Philosophy*, 54).

[38] Perkins, *Coleridge's Philosophy*, 89–90. Critics who take a "linguistic" approach to
Coleridge's Trinity include Jerome C. Christensen, *Coleridge's Blessed Machine of Language* (Ithaca: Cornell University Press, 1981); Angela Esterhammer, *The Romantic Per-
formative* (Stanford: Stanford University Press, 2001); Tim Fulford, *Coleridge's Figura-
tive Language* (London: Macmillan, 1991); John A. Hodson, "Transcendental Tropes:
Coleridge's Rhetoric of Allegory and Symbol," in *Allegory Myth and Symbol*, ed. Mor-
ton W. Bloomfield (Cambridge Massachusetts: Harvard University Press, 1981), 273–92;
James C. McKusick, *Coleridge's Philosophy of Language* (New Haven: Yale University
Press, 1986); Elinor S. Shaffer, *Kubla Khan and The Fall of Jerusalem: The Mythologi-
cal School in British Criticism and Secular Literature 1770–1880* (Cambridge: Cambridge
University Press, 1975); and K. M. Wheeler, *The Creative Mind in Coleridge's Poetry*
(London: Heineman, 1981).

[39] Perkins, *Coleridge's Philosophy*, 28.

[40] *CL*, I, 625.

[41] Perkins, *Coleridge's Philosophy*, 28.

uses and for him that hears them, except as far as the mind's eye in both is kept fixed on the idea."[42] Once Ideas are admitted as extra-verbal entities, the idea that meaning is solely constituted by language evaporates.[43]

What then does Coleridge think is the essence of language? As I have argued elsewhere, I think he was struck by the mystery of the way in which something as subjective as an idea can be captured and conveyed in the external and relatively objective form of language.[44] For instance, in the *Opus Maximum* Coleridge claims that utterance is "outerance" — and that outering function goes to the heart of language for Coleridge.[45] Coleridge claims that "that which goeth forth yet so as in its essence to remain, is a Word."[46] And this is also the basis of the claim that the Son is the Word, for as we have seen the Son embodies the Father in a relatively external form. But that form is not linguistic if by "linguistic" we mean a structure of conventional and arbitrary symbols. For as we have seen, the Son is a *formal* embodiment, an embodiment in a form that is essential rather than conventional, and that is closer in kind to a sensory image than to a linguistic word.

Coleridge brings together these themes of "word" and "outering" in an analysis of the creation account in Genesis: "you are likewise to keep in mind with regard to the Power, *Light*, that the word in Gen. I. v.3 does not mean visual Light or solar Light, which was not yet in existence; but that which is no less present in Sound, Odor and in whatever else *goes forth to declare*, like a word *spoken*; or remains on the surface (or *out*side) to *distinguish*, like a word *written*; and in both cases, makes the thing *out*ward, and *outers* (now spelt utters) its nature. P.S. Hence the Son of God is called indifferently The Light, that lighteth, and the Word."[47]

[42] *Op Max*, 225–26.
[43] See my "'That Eternal Language,' or Why Coleridge was Right about Imaging and Meaning" (*Romanticism on the Net* 28 [November 2002]: http://www.erudit.org/revue/ron/2002/v/n28/007208ar.html) for a discussion of the way in which the sensory imaging process acts as the ideas or the extra-verbal source to which words are indexed. George Lakoff and Mark Johnson present similar arguments in *Philosophy in the Flesh: The Embodied Mind and its Challenge to Western Thought* (New York: Basic Books, 1999).
[44] See my "Coleridge, Language and Imagination," *Romanticism on the Net* 22 (2001): http://www.erudit.org/revue/ron/2001/v/n22/005977ar.html.
[45] *Op Max*, 312; Perkins, *Coleridge's Philosophy*, 29.
[46] *SW&F*, II, 870; cf. Perkins, *Coleridge's Philosophy*, 72.
[47] Cited in Perkins, *Coleridge's Philosophy*, 89.

The Fall and Redemption of Language

What then is Coleridge's view of human language? His view is complex, for on the one hand he describes human language as an instrument of the Understanding, a fallen and limited human faculty that is to be distinguished from transcendent Reason, and which, as Vallins argues, leaves language prey to the contradictions implicit in Kant's antinomies.[48] And for Coleridge, human words are merely "the faint types or reflexes" of the Logos, rather than its constituent elements.[49] As Perkins argues, Coleridge was influenced by the Stoic distinction, later taken up by Philo, between logos *prophorikos*, uttered speech, and logos *endiathetos*, unuttered speech or thought. Augustine similarly "devalued the external word," saying: "Thou didst speak thy thought; and, that the thought which was hid with thee might come to me, thou didst sound syllables; the sound of the syllables conveyed thy thought to my ear; through my ear thy thought descended into my heart, the intermediate sound flew away; but that word which took to itself sound was with thee before thou didst sound it, and is with me."[50]

But given these caveats, language is nonetheless the necessary tool that finite minds must use to think, for finite minds are caught within the limitations of the Understanding and are not capable of immediate intuition. This is a theme more explored in the *Philosophical Lectures* than in the *Opus Maximum*. Language is the tool in which distinctions (ideas) can be captured and preserved, and which therefore allows the building of complex meanings.[51] The resulting linguistic structure is a communal resource, just like roads and railways, though as we have seen it is a resource that has been constructed by thinking people, and which is indexed to psychological intentions. Further, it is a tool which develops over time, in a process which Coleridge called desynonymization, a process in which words which in earlier periods were synonymous, like property and propriety, came to be distinguished and to have their meanings refined.[52]

---

[48] David Vallins, *Coleridge and the Psychology of Romanticism: Feeling and Thought* (London: Macmillan, 2000), ch. 6.

[49] Perkins, *Coleridge's Philosophy*, 46.

[50] Perkins, *Coleridge's Philosophy*, 79, 71n.96.

[51] In *The Philosophical Lectures of Samuel Taylor Coleridge* (ed. Kathleen Coburn [London: The Pilot Press, 1949], 257), Coleridge describes words as "the great mighty instruments"; and in *Aids to Reflection* he famously compares language to the chariot of Ezekiel, a vehicle for conveying ideas but (for humans) an essential vehicle since immediate intuition is not possible (*AR*, 6–7).

[52] *BL*, I, 82–83.

While I have been stressing the limitations of human language in the last few paragraphs, it is important to add that the Logos nonetheless has a role to play in its history. As Perkins points out, the Logos principle introduces the logic of distinction into Coleridge's system; and "[t]o Coleridge, words were distinctions within an underlying unity of thought."[53] This extends to their syntax, for words, as Perkins puts it, "were not simply accumulated end to end, but each had its own distinct reality and yet was part of a whole (for example, in the sentence)."[54] Coleridge bemoaned the loss in eighteenth-century philosophy of the Scholastic sense of the relationality of words.[55] And the logic of distinction also underlies the process of desynonymization, the reflection within the language of polarity, which is in turn the engine that drives all activity within the fallen realm for Coleridge.

But language has a higher significance than this, for as Perkins puts it, "Coleridge believed that the restoration of the veracity of 'living words' must be an integral part of the regeneration of human nature."[56] Luther had argued that human language reflects the fallenness of humanity, a view that Coleridge to some extent accepted given human language's origin in the Understanding. But Coleridge also accepted Augustine's view of the redemptive power of the Logos upon human language, a power which emerges in an inspirited reading of the Bible, and which will presumably emerge when Christ returns to reign on Earth. Augustine said, "[t]he word which sounds without is a sign of the word that shines within, to which the name of word more properly belongs."[57] And in an unusual passage, Coleridge seems to allow language, and even the Understanding, the possibility of an unfallen form: "Contemplated in its… Absoluteness, Speech (… Logos…) denotes the essence of the filial Deity; but in its finite and derivative existence, it is the act, attribute, and in the most ancient languages the name, of the *human* Understanding — i.e. the Understanding as distinct from Reason but not, as in inferior Natures, *contra*-distinguished therefrom."[58] The passage, which dates from July to September 1823 (and which therefore predates Coleridge's later and darker reflections on the Satanic underpinnings of the Understanding), is certainly unusual in its view of the Understanding, and I am not aware

[53] Perkins, *Coleridge's Philosophy*, 38, 43.
[54] Perkins, *Coleridge's Philosophy*, 43.
[55] Perkins, *Coleridge's Philosophy*, 44.
[56] Perkins, *Coleridge's Philosophy*, 32.
[57] Augustine, *De Trinitate*, 15.11.20, cited in Perkins, *Coleridge's Philosophy*, 35.
[58] Perkins, *Coleridge's Philosophy*, 43; *CN*, IV, 4984.

of that view being repeated elsewhere, but it may derive from an attempt to conceptualize humanity in an unfallen, or in a redeemed, existence.[59] In any case, it points to a redemptive potential in language.

Coleridge also believed that the German Higher Critics, in their sensitivity to the historical contexts in which the language of the Scriptures was written, had nonetheless underestimated the Christian historicity of the specifically linguistic process of desynonymization by which language evolves.[60] For, as the *Philosophical Lectures* suggest, that history is part of the history of redemption.[61] As Perkins puts it, "[j]ust as the Logos is both Creator and the life within the evolving forms of his creation, so words and language are... the evolved products of man's life in community."[62] The point is not merely theoretical: the redemption of language was presumably a precondition for salvation, while an acknowledgement of the changing nature of language over time allows us to see scriptural language not as merely historically situated and therefore to be dismissed (the tendency of the more secular higher critics). It allows scriptural language to be seen as itself a part of history, with all the significance which that concept has within the Christian world view. It also allows the later interpreter a *via media* between ultra-Protestant bibliolatry and eighteenth-century free thinking, for it allows later understandings of scriptural texts without the need to accept in full the presumed understandings of the original writers.

History

In the paragraphs above I have begun to broach the view that the Logos is immanent within history, being indeed the alpha and the omega of time. The *Opus Maximum* provides the metaphysical foundations for this view, but it is more broadly discussed elsewhere.[63] For instance, in his marginal comments, Coleridge reveals the ambition behind his "Logosophia," and its treatment of history, in describing it as an attempt to discover, "if Christ be that Logos or Word that was in the beginning,

[59] See my "The Satanic Principle in the Later Coleridge's Theory of Imagination," *Studies in Romanticism* 37 (1998): 259–77.
[60] Stephen Prickett discusses desynonymization in *Words and The Word: Language, Poetics, and Biblical Interpretation* (Cambridge: Cambridge University Press, 1986).
[61] Coleridge (ed. Coburn), *Philosophical Lectures*, 212.
[62] Perkins, *Coleridge's Philosophy*, 37.
[63] *Op Max*, 368.

by whom all things *became*; if it was the same Christ [NB the Son, not the Father], who said, Let there be *Light*; who in and by the Creation commenced that great redemptive Process, the history of LIFE which begins in its detachment from Nature and is to end in its union with God."[64] And it follows that "Homo est historicus ut esset propheticus" (or, as Perkins translates it, "a man is a historian inasmuch as he might be a prophet") — that is, one who has grasped the driving force behind history — for "[t]o prophecy is to unroll and draw out the involved consequences" of the world.[65] And in the higher-critical domain, the inconsistencies in the New Testament seemed to Coleridge "a work of Providence, in order to preserve the necessity of internal evidence, of individual illumination & inward experience.'"[66] Coleridge's broader faith is that (as Perkins puts it) "progress in human learning... would make possible a progressive revelation of God."[67]

Biblical Language

This salvatory dimension to language (and the role of the Logos within it) finds its most important dimension in the Bible. In part this is because "the teaching of Christ as Word is the universal content of the Old and New Testaments," for, as Coleridge put it, the "Sethian, Noetic, Patriarchal, Mosaic, Prophetic and Messianic" all tend to the same end: the message of the Word is the message of salvation.[68] But for Coleridge, the Bible is also denominated the Word because it is uniquely personal, speaking to our deepest need for redemption.[69] The Bible's power might thus be understood in reader-response terms: it represents the Word not in its reified form (as a book made out of paper), but in the spiritual act of reading which it draws forth. Thus in *Confessions of an Inquiring Spirit*, Coleridge says that in Scripture "I have met every where more or less copious sources of truth, and power, and purifying impulses... I have found words for my inmost thoughts, songs for my joy, utterances for

---

[64] Perkins, *Coleridge's Philosophy*, 12, 255ff.; *CM*, III, 919.
[65] Perkins, *Coleridge's Philosophy*, 83; *CN*, V, 6028. The full quotation reads, "[a man is a historian inasmuch as he might be a prophet]; to exhortation, to edification and to comfort."
[66] Perkins, *Coleridge's Philosophy*, 23; *CN*, V, 5605.
[67] Perkins, *Coleridge's Philosophy*, 81.
[68] Perkins, *Coleridge's Philosophy*, 77.
[69] Perkins, *Coleridge's Philosophy*, 76.

my hidden griefs, and pleadings for my shame and my feebleness... In short whatever finds me, bears witness for itself that it has proceeded from a Holy Spirit."[70] And in his marginal comments, he says, "[i]f even through the words [of] a powerful and perspicuous author... I identify myself with the excellent writer, and his thoughts become my thoughts: what must not the blessing be to be thus identified first with the Filial Word, and then with the Father in and through Him?"[71] But while these quotations speak of the way in which the Logos can be immanent within the Bible, Coleridge also criticized Luther for overemphasizing the infallibility of Scripture — for Luther "every where identifies the Living Word of God with the Written Word."[72] Coleridge called such views of Scripture "bibliolatry," a term which Lessing had used and which owes its English origin to the earlier, eighteenth-century writer, John Byrom.[73] Coleridge contrasted Luther's views to those of Bullinger "who contended that the [written word] is the Word of God only as far as and for whom it is the Vehicle of [God]."[74]

The Name of God

Some years after the writing of the *Opus Maximum*, Coleridge extended the identification between the Logos and the written word — for as Perkins suggests, in the notebook entries from 1827 on, Coleridge strikingly denominates the Logos the *Name* of God.[75] Coleridge argues that where the Bible speaks of Jehovah, it in fact refers to the Logos, the second person of the Trinity, a point he finds evidence for in John 12:20, where "our Lord expressly calls himself the Father's *Name*."[76] This claim presumably relates to the idea that the Word is an exponent, an outward-putting of a divinity that, in the Father, is entirely internal or "hidden" and accordingly has no form, let alone phenomenal appearance.[77] Such was the view of Pseudo-Dionysius, whose *Celestial Hierarchy*, though not admired by Coleridge, was the standard text on the subject in the

---

[70] Perkins, *Coleridge's Philosophy*, 76.

[71] *CM*, III, 522–23; Perkins, *Coleridge's Philosophy*, 88.

[72] *CM*, III, 762; Perkins, *Coleridge's Philosophy*, 78.

[73] Jeffrey W. Barbeau, review of Coleridge, *Marginalia*, Part V, *The Coleridge Bulletin* n.s. 20 (2002): 145.

[74] Perkins, *Coleridge's Philosophy*, 78; *CM*, III, 762–63.

[75] Perkins, *Coleridge's Philosophy*, 83.

[76] *CN*, V, 5746 (*f.62*); Perkins, *Coleridge's Philosophy*, 84–85.

[77] *CN*, V, 5691 (*f.22v*); Perkins, *Coleridge's Philosophy*, 86.

Medieval period.[78] Pseudo-Dionysius, writing sometime before 533 AD, images God as an entirely incorporeal entity, lost in the Divine light which the angels crowd around — a view which *Paradise Lost* repeats in its treatment of the Father.[79] Jehovah, the God who appears in history and who speaks to his followers in the Old Testament, is clearly different from this, for he has the ability to take on an outward form. As such, he is an "exponent," and is thus to be identified with the Logos.

Coleridge takes the argument further, with a technical definition of *Nomen*, or name. *Nomen*, he says, "expresses that which is *understood* in an appearance," or the deeper substance that is understood to underlie the appearance, which is why the term Logos is so appropriate for the second person of the Trinity.[80] For *Nomen*, on this definition, equates with *Numen*, what Perkins calls the "intelligible presence, the spirit, will, and power of a thing," just as the Son equates with, but is distinct from, the Father.[81] The terms of Coleridge's definition are, as Perkins points out, Kantian, though used to assert an identity between phenomenon and noumenon that Kant would have denied.[82] Coleridge's argument thus goes beyond the Mosaic identification of the Logos with the act of creation, arguing both that the God who acts in history is the Logos, and that the Logos is the name of God — not in the sense in which Muslims assert that Allah is the name of God, but in the sense that naming is a form of outering, and that the Logos is the outering, or utterance, of God. One might add that the references in the Bible to the Word of God grew out of the ancient Hebraic view that Adamic language was essential in its relation to the object named, rather than conventional, and that Coleridge's explanation nicely "explains" the references without adopting the absurdity of their origins.

The Logos as Inner Revelation

For Coleridge, the Logos is central to Revelation, in part because of its particular relation to the Bible as the Word of God (see above), in part

---

[78] *Op Max*, 215.

[79] Book III of *Paradise Lost* describes God as "… Author of all being,/ Fountain of Light, thyself invisible/ Amidst the glorious brightness where thou sit'st/ Thron'd inaccessible…" (III, 374–77).

[80] Perkins, *Coleridge's Philosophy*, 84; *AR*, 230.

[81] Perkins, *Coleridge's Philosophy*, 85.

[82] Perkins, *Coleridge's Philosophy*, 84.

because the Logos is the person of the Trinity who "outers" or "utters," and in part because Nature is a form of revelation that reflects the archetypal forms of the Logos. But for Coleridge revelation is not merely external: it extends to internal, spiritual experiences (as one might expect), but also to Reason. The Logos is both the "outer" Light of objective truth and the "inner" Light of Reason, for "Reason is *subjective* Revelation."[83] This identity was foreshadowed in the announcement of the "Logosophia" in the *Biographia*, and is thoroughly implicit in the opening pages of both fragments "1" and "2" of the *Opus Maximum*.[84] It is of course a thoroughly Protestant position, for despite what Coleridge saw (perhaps unfairly) as Luther's emphasis on the reified word of the Bible, Luther himself had argued that the truth of revelation was not to be demonstrated by the miracles recorded in the New Testament, but in "the truth and necessity of the revelation" — a position that puts human Reason on a par with revelation, and points to their essential union.[85]

There is, as Perkins argues, a deeper connection between Reason and revelation. Humanity is made in the image of God, and therefore at least potentially inherits the Divine psychology. More particularly, Coleridge maintained that human Reason reflects the nature of the Divine Logos, communicated to humanity. It is the Logos that Coleridge associates with Reason and intelligence, while the Father is associated with the Will — though this distinction should not be taken too far since all the persons of the Trinity are psychologically complete persons.[86] Since Reason is a direct reflection of the Divine nature, it is also (in humans) a form of revelation. Coleridge reinforces this potential identification between the human and the Divine when he describes Logos as the "Idea of Man," an idea which incorporates the suggestion that Christ, in his human guise, represents humankind in perfection, and which also underlies the typological identification of Adam with Christ.[87]

The suggestion, in Perkins's words, that Reason is "not a divine attribute, but the divine Person," requires a little more explanation.[88] In a sense it is a very literal take on the view of the Church Fathers that the

[83] Perkins, *Coleridge's Philosophy*, 75; *CL*, VI, 895.
[84] *BL*, I, 263, 302; *Op Max*, 90, 122, 5–23, 83–85. The identity is discussed in a note (dated 1827) to *The Statesman's Manual* (*LS*, 73n) and in *On the Constitution of the Church and State* (*C&S*, 182).
[85] *Op Max*, 50.
[86] Perkins, *Coleridge's Philosophy*, 9.
[87] Perkins, *Coleridge's Philosophy*, 61.
[88] Perkins, *Coleridge's Philosophy*, 146.

Godhead is a Trinity of Will, Reason, and Love — an insistence that
these attributes are literally persons. As Coleridge says in Notebook 35,
slightly varying the terms, "I find it the most difficult of all the labors of
Faith to disenthral my spirit from the tendency to think of Truth, Reason,
Wisdom as accidents, properties of this or that Being — to raise it into a
more satisfying contemplation of Truth, as *Being*, as = ['The True' — in
person]."[89]

Coleridge does not so far as I know explain the basis of this striking
claim, but it can be rendered consistent with his views more generally.
For we need to remember that for Coleridge persons are not *things*.
Rather, he identifies personhood with *will*, and, like will, personhood
must be a form of energy or act.[90] Reason is also a form of energy or act,
but more particularly it also is a form (literally a form) of will, and must
therefore be personal in nature.[91] Reason is thus person. The intuitive
immediacy of Reason also allies it with personhood, for the Logos is the
immediate and intuitive form in which the Father knows himself.

Coleridge suggests a fundamental identity with the Logos in the human
possession of "no mean symbol of Tri-unity, in Reason, Religion, and the
Will" — the three truly human (and therefore transcendent) faculties in
Coleridge's psychology.[92] It follows, in Perkins's words, that "[b]oth the
essence and the ideal existence of humanity were to be found in the Logos
as Principle and Person; true philosophy must therefore be both logo-
centric and anthropocentric."[93] The Logos also functions for Coleridge as
a response to one of the pressing issues in mid-eighteenth-century philosophy — Hume's reduction of reason to passion, an alienation that
Coleridge would have derived from the Fall.[94]

---

[89] Perkins, *Coleridge's Philosophy*, 165; *CN*, V, 5664.

[90] *Op Max*, 172.

[91] See for instance a marginal note in which Coleridge speaks of "the will, which is
the reason, — Will in the form of Reason" (*CM*, III, 720; Perkins, *Coleridge's Philosophy*, 190). Another marginal note claims that "a will not intelligent is no Will," thus showing the intimate union of will and Reason (Perkins, *Coleridge's Philosophy*, 197; *CM*, I,
355).

[92] Perkins, *Coleridge's Philosophy*, 62; *LS*, 62.

[93] Perkins, *Coleridge's Philosophy*, 22.

[94] Perkins, *Coleridge's Philosophy*, 22. One might suggest, with Akenside, that the
Fall leads to an inappropriate objectification, and that Love becomes alienated when inap-
propriately objectified — a theme Akenside deals with in Version 1, Book II of *The Plea-
sures of Imagination*; see Mark Akenside, *The Poetical Works of Mark Akenside*, ed. Robin
Dix (London: Associated University Presses, 1996); and my "Coleridge, Akenside and the
Platonic Tradition: Reading in *The Pleasures of Imagination*," *AUMLA* 80 (1993): 31–56.
Coleridge's remarks on the love between the sexes suggests both an appropriate

The Archetypal Symbol

While Reason is a form of revelation, its modes are not primarily those of logical syllogism nor the manipulation of sentences. Those operations belong within the domain of the Understanding, though their grasp *is* a product of Reason.[95] Instead, and as we have seen, human Reason is a form of subjective revelation, a power induced by the influence of the Logos. Just as the Logos was a *formal* or aesthetic embodiment of the Father (a quasi-sensory expression of the Father, rather than an expression of the Father in a conventional language), so Reason's primary mode is that of the *formal* symbol. Thus Perkins says that: "the divine Word is, for Coleridge, the transcendent source of all symbols and, at the same time, immanent within them as their reconciling power. The Logos is the life and power of mind, the ground of relationship, the revelation of prophetic utterance, the completion and presence of love... yet the Word can never be reduced to words, and the mystery of the true Symbol remains."[96] Coleridge believed that certain kinds of mystery are legitimate, for explanation in terms of cause and effect can only operate within the world of phenomena. Symbol is able to convey the truths of Reason at the point where explanation fails. Coleridge thus found in Greek and Egyptian religion "the peculiar force of the Symbol, as omening the presence of the Divine, the sense of the inexplicable, or aboriginal —. That which unexpectedly, from the depths of Nature, started upon the Eye as Prediction or Warning..."[97] And he was interested in the hermetic tradition, and its views on the role of symbol; his naturphilosophie contains much alchemical symbolism based on the view that there are correspondences between inert physical substances and life itself — though it is important to remember that Coleridge's views were based not on mysticism, but on what he took to be a scientific approach: one based on deductions drawn from newly published experimental work by Davy, amongst others.

The link between Reason and symbol is again implicit in the *Opus Maximum*, but can most clearly be seen in Coleridge's famous discussion in *The Statesman's Manual*.[98] There he describes scriptural symbols as the

---

objectification (though with St. Paul we may ask how far it is appropriate), and the mechanism for its derangement.

[95] Perkins, *Coleridge's Philosophy*, 144.
[96] Perkins, *Coleridge's Philosophy*, 68.
[97] Perkins, *Coleridge's Philosophy*, 67; *CN*, IV, 4831 (*f*.57v).
[98] The role of form, which underlies symbol, is discussed in the *Opus Maximum* (296), but the formal symbol itself is not discussed.

products of Imagination, "that reconciling and mediatory power, which incorporating the Reason in Images of the Sense, and organizing (as it were) the flux of the Senses by the permanence and self-circling energies of the Reason, gives birth to a system of symbols... consubstantial with the truths, of which they are the *conductors*."[99] It is worth noting that the symbols here are not reified forms (the picture-language of allegory), but products of acts and energies. Indeed, as Perkins says, it is only through the inner light of the Logos that the symbol can "reveal the full truth of the universal in which it participates."[100]

Thinking back to our discussion of the role of alterity in the Logos, it is also worth noting, as Gregg Biglieri does, Coleridge's emphasis on the role of the medium in the production of the symbol.[101] In the "Essay on Genial Criticism," Coleridge says: "Something there must be to realize the form, something in and by which the forma informans reveals itself: and these, less than any that could be substituted, and in the least possible degree, distract the attention, in the least possible degree obscure the idea, of which they (composed into outline and surface) are the symbol."[102] Biglieri goes on to point to Coleridge's example of the translucent gemstone, as (with peculiar recursiveness) a symbol for the Divine presence within a symbol. It is an example that reminds us of the brilliance of Coleridge's play with image in his criticism: "An illustrative hint may be taken from a pure chrystal, as compared with an opaque, semi-opaque, or clouded mass on the one hand, and with a perfectly transparent body, such as the air is, on the other. The chrystal is lost in the light, which yet it contains, embodies, and gives a shape to; but which passes shapeless through the air, and in the ruder body is either quenched or dissipated."[103] This image of the crystal takes us back to the definition of symbol in *The Statesman's Manual*, with its talk of "the translucence of the Eternal through and in the Temporal."[104] For while in this essay I have focused on form, we must always recall that form is essentially an inner, vital principle, *forma formans*, rather than a reified entity, *forma formata*. Its archetype is found in the recirculating energies of the Trinity — and what better figure could there be for the Logos than as

[99] *LS*, 29.
[100] Perkins, *Coleridge's Philosophy*, 52.
[101] Gregg Biglieri, "Medium Coleridge: Thinking the Relation in-between Poet and Critic," *Schuylkill* 2.2 (1999), http://temple.edu/gradmag/summer99/biglier.htm.
[102] *SW&F*, I, 377.
[103] *SW&F*, I, 377.
[104] *LS*, 30.

something "lost in the light, which yet it contains, embodies, gives shape to." In this giving of shape or form, the Divine self is instantiated, and so the whole of reality emerges from the principle of form.

As Perkins suggests, Coleridge's view of symbol paralleled Goethe's, who claimed that "[t]hat is true symbolism, where the more particular represents the more general, not as a dream or shade, but as a vivid, instantaneous revelation of the Inscrutable."[105]

The Finite Creation

In the pages above, I have described the finite creation as reflecting the formal archetypes that are to be found in the Logos. But while this is true of both human persons and Nature, they are also both fallen and as such lacking entirely in "actuality." It is only through the Logos, and through its gift of actuality in its gift of form, that the finite world comes into being — and in this returns us more squarely within the concerns of the *Opus Maximum*.

The story told in the *Opus Maximum* begins with the Divine Will, which is a will to unity, as an expression of the love which is the communal principle underlying it.[106] Coleridge, however, argues that it is in the nature of will to be free, and that freedom includes the freedom to will itself as something separate from its own unity — a freedom that Coleridge calls apostatic and one that is clearly self-frustrative.[107] It is the Satanic principle, the origin of evil, but while (in the terms that Coleridge uses) it is *real*, it lacks the self-instantiating *actuality* necessary for being, and is in its own terms merely a *potential* and (in a tradition which goes back to the *Timaeus* and Genesis) is thought of as formless chaos. As Coleridge put it in a notebook entry, "For pure Evil what is it but Will that would manifest itself as Will, not in Being (…), not in Intelligence (therefore *form*less) not in Union or Communion, the contrary therefore of Life, even eternal Death."[108] And since it lacks actuality, it is in this sense merely a critical entity. But it nonetheless is important because it introduces polarity into Coleridge's system. For where the relations

---

[105] Quoted in Perkins, *Coleridge's Philosophy*, 48.

[106] *Op Max*, 164, 194, 199; see Reid, "Coleridge and Schelling" (473–75) and Reid, "The Satanic Principle" for a more detailed explanation of the finite creation.

[107] *Op Max*, 233, 237, 326.

[108] *CN*, IV, 5076 (December 1823); Perkins, *Coleridge's Philosophy*, 194; see also, 214, 218–29.

between the members of the Trinity are characterized by a triune logic, which acknowledges their essential and underlying unity, the Satanic impulse is towards categorical distinction, the setting up of a will that is autonomous and acknowledges no underlying unity. This logic of opposition, or of complete distinction, is a polarizing logic, and it is the origin of the reificatory Understanding.[109]

Before we explore the implications of this opposition, however, we need to consider another dimension of will, the distinction between the infinite and the finite. Coleridge argues that the idea of distinct individuals (that is, the archetypal origins of us, as distinct beings) is consistent with that of the Divine unity so long as the distinct wills will themselves as *forms* of the Divine Will.[110] Distinctness here is a relative term: the distinct wills are nonetheless *actual* (i.e. part of the Divine unity) so long as (and only so long as) they will themselves as forms of the Divine Will. And the Logos again enters the picture here, for as Coleridge's "On the Divine Ideas" ("Fragment 3") argues, the finite beings are part of the Divine intelligence, the pleroma which has its location in the Logos.[111]

I spoke above of a polar opposition between God and the Satanic principle, a polarity that was merely critical (merely a notion), since it entirely lacked actuality. Here again the Logos steps in, and in an act of grace offers the gift of actuality, or the gift of form, to the fallen spirits.[112] This gift is what first actualizes polarity. It is also what allows us, as finite beings, to live our lives and what allows the cycle of history, from fall to redemption, to progress. While it may seem odd to offer the gift of actuality to the Satanic principle, it is a gift that evil, being entirely self-frustrative, immediately undoes. While the polarity becomes actual, the Satanic pole remains purely critical, and Coleridge at least in places doubted the personal existence of Satan.[113] Finite beings, on the other hand, belong within the continuum established by the polarity, for while they do not go as far as a Satanic renunciation of God, they do not fully recognize their true origins within the pleroma. The Christian drama of

---

[109] Reid, "Coleridge and Schelling," 469, 474.

[110] Coleridge describes the origins of the finite selves in the following terms: "The Logos — or coeternal idea — feeling himself infinitely representative of God & infinitely happy in contemplation of himself as the absolutely infinite & perfect likeness of God was impelled by *infinite Love* to multiply finite images of Deity each happy in contemplating itself & the images around it — as being representative of Deity" (Coleridge, British Library MS Egerton 2801, *f*.113).

[111] *Op Max*, 223n, 231, 235; *CN*, IV, 5233 (1825); *CN*, V, 5523 (June 1827).

[112] *Op Max*, 326; Reid, "Coleridge and Schelling," 474.

[113] *CN*, IV, 5078 (*f*.37).

redemption (through the original gift of actuality, and through the influence of the Word within the human world) offers them the chance to recognize their true origins and achieve salvation.

Schelling's Metaphysics

We need to say more about how individuals come into existence within this world, and this is where Schelling enters the story. Finite beings belong within the world of polarity, which is the origin of the human Understanding. Schelling has two basic premises, the first being the correspondence theory of knowledge.[114] This is the view that truth implies a correspondence between ideas and the realities they represent. It follows that all knowledge requires a relation between a subject (the knowing mind) and an object (the object of knowledge). The second premise is that selfhood is essentially a form of limitation, since selfhood implies a limitation that excludes everything outside the self.[115] It should be noted that in the *Opus Maximum* Coleridge's communal definition of self, within the Trinity, does not involve this kind of limitation, although until September of 1818 Coleridge's views were Schellingian.

We thus have a self as subject that seeks to know itself as object, and the requirement for an underlying relation between those two. Schelling argues that this underlying relation cannot be an object, since it is prior to objectness, and cannot be described in terms of any of the Kantian categories of knowledge. It must therefore be an act, and an act that is without limitation, since limitation is a categorical term. In order for selfhood to emerge, however, we required limitation, and so a second limiting act is required. We now have an opposition of two infinite activities, identical except in their directions. From the dialectical interplay of these activities, Schelling derives the Kantian understanding, the finite imagination, and the illusion of finite selfhood.[116] But since in Schelling there is not actually a final identity of subject and object, it is worth noting that what really runs his system is the will, a blind drive towards self instantiation that belongs within Kant's noumenal sphere, and about which accordingly nothing further can be said.[117]

---

[114] Reid, "Coleridge and Schelling," 456–57.
[115] Reid, "Coleridge and Schelling," 458.
[116] Reid, "Coleridge and Schelling," 458–66.
[117] Reid, "Coleridge and Schelling," 454, 464.

It seems probable that in the *Biographia* Coleridge intended to use the deduction outlined above to derive the three persons of the Trinity, and thus to place a conscious God in the place of Schelling's blind, driving will, and its first product, an unconscious Absolute which is quasi-pantheistic.[118] I do not intend here to describe the details of that attempt. It is enough to note that since even Schelling acknowledges that the self is not ultimately an object, such an argument would have produced an illusory Trinity, and would have been prey to all of the logical problems that follow from a system in which no final synthesis is possible.[119] In his mature philosophy, from September 1818 onward, however, Coleridge was happy to adopt Schelling's dialectic of illusion to describe the misguided attempts of the finite selves to discover their putatively objective natures. It is a dialectic that depends for its actuality entirely on the gift of the Logos, a fact that accounts for the immanence of God within our natures, as demanded by theology. And where Schelling's system "explains" the objectivity of the world, the Divine gift, as a gift of form to a potential that is mere formless chaos, explains the manifold *forms* that nature takes.

It is worth adding that where the Logos grounds the dialectic that forms the finite and fallen self, the Logos also plays a technical role in its redemption. For the human soul depends, in its fallen state, on the existence of the body, but "[t]his in the present life is to be continually loosening till finally it is transferred to a new ground — from that of Hades or Nature to Christ… What nature is to the Natural Man, in all it's particulars…, that Christ is to the Souls of the Redeemed."[120]

Conclusion

In this essay, I have tried to reveal something of the all-encompassing role of the Logos in Coleridge's philosophy — the Logos that "seems so puzzlingly to be at the same time the word he utters, the truth which it contains, and the external reality which he conceives himself to be

[118] In Reid, "Coleridge and Schelling" (476), I discuss the ways in which Coleridge seems in the *Biographia* to have been trying to privilege the subject within an analysis which was broadly Schellingian.

[119] See Joan Steigerwald, "Epistemologies of Rupture: The Problem of Nature in Schelling's Philosophy," *Studies in Romanticism* 41 (2002): 545–84.

[120] *CN*, V, 6034 (*f*.27); Perkins, *Coleridge's Philosophy*, 224.

describing."[121] I have naturally been heavily dependent on Perkins's work (it could not be otherwise), but I hope to have offered a relatively synthetic account while placing more emphasis on the role of Schelling in the later Coleridge's thought, qualifying the role of human language in Coleridge, and most importantly bringing the role of form much more centrally into focus. Indeed, I cannot place too much emphasis on the importance of form in Coleridge's thought, for it lies at the heart of the primal moment in Coleridge's metaphysics, the moment in which the Father recognizes himself in the *form* of the Son and so brings the whole cosmonogy into existence. Much follows from that first *formal* act of embodiment, for it provides the archetypes for Nature in Coleridge's world, along with the foundation for an aesthetic based on Imagination and (formed) symbol. But more importantly, from a twenty-first century, secular point of view, Coleridge's view of form is based in a phenomenology that, in the work of Damasio, Lakoff, Ellis, Humphrey, and others, is re-emerging as the best contemporary paradigm for the workings of the human mind. The structuralist view, that all is language, has shown us much that we did not formerly appreciate, but it is time to readmit an aesthetic of form into our view of art: to acknowledge (*contra* Barthes) that art does things that go beyond conventional language.

Since I have written on these matters elsewhere, I want to end here by returning to Coleridge.[122] In this essay, I have explored the Logos in Coleridge's thought, with emphasis on the *Opus Maximum* but with an eye on the broader context of Coleridge's long-fabled "Logosophia." What impresses me is just how much of the "Logosophia" is extant, not admittedly in the finished form one expects of a universal encyclopaedia, but in the more characteristically Coleridgean form of the fragment.

The Logosophia, at least in its most detailed projection, was to fall into six parts:

I.   The first part was to deal with "Absolute Actuality," or the nature of God. It thus was to discuss the Tetractys, and the role of the Logos therein — matter dealt with in the *Opus Maximum*.

II. The second part was to deal with polarity, and the birth of the finite, or fallen world — and the role of the Logos in communicating the gift of form and actuality. This would have included

[121] Perkins, *Coleridge's Philosophy*, 11, quoting Guthrie on the Logos idea of Heraclitus.
[122] See Reid, "Form in Coleridge."

Coleridge's *naturphilosophie*, or attempt at an *a priori* science. It was discussed in the *Opus Maximum* and refined in later notebook entries.

III. The third part was to deal with revelation, the relation of the Logos to the Bible, and "[t]he superior Authority and Historical Reliability of the Hebrew Origines Gentium, or earliest History contained in the Mosaic Writings." In other words, it was to deal with the same material as the second part, the origins of the Creation, but from the perspective of the Mosaic account in *Genesis*. Much of this material is to be found in Volume V of the *Notebooks*.

IV. The fourth part was to take the story forward into the developing history of the Creation. It was to reveal the salvatory influence of the Logos, and the influence of the Logos on the later history of the world up to his incarnation in Jesus. Again, there is much discussion of this in the later *Notebooks* and in Coleridge's published writings.

V. The fifth part was to deal with the historicity of the Bible, and a higher-critical reading thereof. This was to be based on the *Confessions of an Inquiring Spirit*, but would presumably have taken in the hundreds of relevant marginal and other notes scattered through Coleridge's writings. It was to reveal the Coleridgean approach "as a Substitute for the German." Presumably its placement after the third and fourth sections is to some extent arbitrary, but since the historical understanding of the Bible only occurred in Coleridge's own time, its placement in the fifth section ties in with the chronological structure that Coleridge is developing.

VI. The sixth and final section was to follow the chronology forward into the Christian era. It was to consist of a history of the Church, "from the Apostles to the present times... with a View of the Church of England as an Estate of the Realm." This would presumably have drawn heavily on his *On the Constitution of the Church and State*, but would also have drawn on the historical understanding of the Church revealed in the fifth section: the Church as a developing hermeneutical agent.[123]

Coleridge's "Logosophia" lies before us, if only we can recognize the underlying links between fields of Coleridgean concern that have seemed altogether unconnected.

---

[123] *CN*, V, 5868; *Op Max*, c–civ.

COLERIDGE'S *MAGNUM OPUS* AND HIS *OPUS MAXIMUM*

By JOHN BEER

The appearance of the *Opus Maximum* as one of the final volumes in the *Collected Works* marks the conclusion of a long saga in which I have had the pleasure of playing a small part. Indeed, I am a survivor from the initial inception, being one of the few who attended the early lunch in London at which the first projections were announced to the potential participants. I have long enjoyed recalling how at that meeting our first publisher, the late Rupert Hart-Davis, ebulliently told us that the plan was to have all the volumes finally edited, printed, and published, together with a complete index, in time for the Bicentenary celebrations of 1972.

Considering that at that time it was extremely difficult even to have anything photocopied, and that completion of both the *Letters* and the *Notebooks* was still a long way off (the latter would be completed only very recently) such projections now seem to have been hopelessly blithe; and indeed there have been times in the intervening years when it seemed optimistic to believe that the project would ever be completed at all. Yet technology has also been on our side: some parts of the production could actually have been carried out much faster had recently developed methods of word processing been available earlier. In any case that is all water under the bridge now, when it becomes possible to cast a backward look over the whole series and ask what gives most cause for pride and what lessons might be learned for the future.

It has increasingly come to be recognized, first, that in addition to the *Works*, the bulk of Coleridge's writings as a whole must be considered — which means taking in the six volumes of *Letters* and the ten of *Notebooks*, in addition to the thirty-four of the published edition. As things turned out the main event to mark the 1972 Bicentenary was not the, now much to be postponed, concluding of the edition but the publication of Norman Fruman's *Coleridge the Damaged Archangel*, a survey of his unacknowledged borrowings that convinced some reviewers that he was simply a thief and a charlatan whose achievements, apart from a few acknowledged masterly poems, could henceforward be safely disregarded. Those of us already familiar with the fuller extent of his writings knew the truth to be very different, but Fruman's clever polemic meant that the

full case would need to go on being argued for many years. The fifty volumes now available, however, scotch one legend — fostered by himself,
among others — that he was an unproductive addict who wasted most of
his time. In view of them that view is now no longer sustainable.

The second and most obvious point to be made about the *Collected
Works* as a whole is that in this fuller form they present an array of his
achievements which is now normally — and usually to his advantage —
chronologically arranged. Within that acceptance, however, some caveats
must be entered: while it is most useful to see the notebook entries in the
chronological order in which they were made, closer consideration of the
texts involved shows that he sometimes reserved various notebooks for
differing subjects — a habit which grew with the years. It can sometimes
be equally profitable, therefore, to look at the contents of a particular
notebook together and see what the entries in it have in common. With
the letters, similarly, while it is a major advantage to be able to put
together all those that were written on a particular day, it is also important to remember that he tended to write variously, and often on varying
subjects, to different correspondents. To isolate the surviving letters to
Poole, say, or to Humphry Davy, and read them in sequence, may be illuminating in a new way.

In the case of the various volumes of the *Works* the problem is less
pressing, since in each case there has already been further organization.
Here again the chronological principle is valuable; and on further consideration, perhaps, it might have been invoked even more often: it might
have been better to present the 1809 *Friend* first, in its own right, and then
the 1818 rifacciamento later in the sequence. The main point where
chronology becomes a difficult issue, however, is where Coleridge revises
an important text. The 1798 version of "Frost at Midnight," for example, is not quite the same poem as the versions printed later, when he
loses the lines about the child's anticipated delight next day in favor of
preserving the "rondo" of the poem by confining his conclusion to lines
that go back to the opening. The 1797 version of *Kubla Khan*, also, is not
the same as the 1816 one, with its psychological preface and its small
changes of wording; certainly the 1798 "Ancient Mariner" differs crucially from the 1817 version, with its added marginal glosses. In each
case the editor has been faced with difficult choices as to which text
should be given precedence. When I produced my Everyman collection
I sometimes solved the problem by presenting both major versions side
by side; in the same spirit I found that to go to the collection of 1796 and
present that as a separate section revealed important things about

Coleridge as a young poet. Given the lowly status of the volume, I could afford to be a little cavalier in such matters and hope to assist the general reader by doing so; Jim Mays, the editor of the Princeton volume, found that there, on the larger scale involved, hundreds of small revisions needed to be dealt with: he therefore had to adopt a more thorough and painstaking method.

How do such matters relate to the *Opus Maximum* volume? The exact responsibility for a great deal in it is unclear, since McFarland himself has been very ill for some years, but it is clear that the role of his "assistant," as he is called in the volume, Nicholas Halmi, was larger than his own rather modest preface might suggest: he certainly deserves more credit for his part than he is given in the actual volume, where his name does not even appear on the dust-jacket or the advertising. At the same time, there are indications that the final stages of the final publication were carried out rather hastily. Some of the quotations had not been properly checked, for example. I was surprised, similarly, to find the anecdote of Lieutenant Bowling and the Roman Catholic priest on page 1 without any note at all, though only a little research is needed to discover that Coleridge is quoting very exactly from Smollett's *Roderick Random* (chapter 14).[1]

McFarland shows his particular strengths as a scholar, on the other hand, when he deals with some of the figures who came immediately after Coleridge and who tried, often rather unsuccessfully, to sustain his reputation. I am thinking here particularly of his follower Joseph Henry Green, who was entrusted with the *Opus Maximum* manuscripts after Coleridge's death, but who, instead of simply presenting them to the world, with all their imperfections, resolved instead to present his own book, *Spiritual Philosophy: Founded on the Teaching of the Late Samuel Taylor Coleridge.*[2] A chief opponent at the time, Clement Mansfield Ingleby, complained of the book's "inertness," commenting that it had not even "the evidences of a past vitality": "in comparison with the veriest fragment of Coleridge's, how barren is that creation."[3] McFarland concurs with that judgment, and perceptively traces the sense of "inertness"

---

[1] *Op Max*, 3. I also notice, incidentally, that not only are all the quotations from *Aids to Reflection* cited from the 1825 edition rather than my Princeton volume, which is perhaps understandable in view of the fact that I used the 1831 edition as my copy-text (though significant differences between the two texts are in fact rare), but that my volume was only occasionally cited in terms of the annotations it contained.

[2] Joseph Henry Green, *Spiritual Philosophy: Founded on the Teaching of the Late Samuel Taylor Coleridge* (London: Macmillan, 1865).

[3] Quoted in *Op Max*, ccxxxvi.

to the lack of what he most values in Coleridge: "… it lacks the vitalis-
ing contexts of Coleridge's lived-through intellectual experience."[4] What
he finds most valuable in it evidently, is the constant sense of a mind at
work — and sometimes coping with its own contradictions. Green, by
contrast, worked mainly through reformulation and repetitions of assertions by Coleridge which, however well done, could not hope to reproduce the sense of engagement to be sensed everywhere in the original.

The manuscripts for the *Opus Maximum* volume present certain differences from what has gone before — notably by reason of the fact that
much of what is presented is a dictated text and cannot therefore be
assumed to have had Coleridge's final *imprimatur*.[5] Chronology is again
important, also, since it affects the matter of the order in which the fragments should be presented. There is now general agreement that "Fragment
4" was in fact the earliest to be composed; as a result it might be best that
it should be dealt with first, though then it would be misleading to renum-
ber it as "Fragment 1," since its status makes it rather a separable part of
the enterprise. For whatever relation to the *magnum opus* Coleridge may
have conceived for it, it must I think be linked less to the form that he was
projecting in the early 1820s than to the intellectual excitement that had
overtaken him in the years before, when he had been impressed by
Schelling's philosophy and captivated for a time by the work of the *natur-
philosophen*, particularly Heinrich Steffens. It is to be supposed that he
saw the possibility that this range of scientific speculation might in the
course of things emerge as providing an intellectual key to all things; in
the absence of such a further development, however, it was better left to
one side, while he concentrated on what lay closer to his religious concerns.

Daniel Hardy's essay builds particularly on "Fragment 4," drawing on
other statements from Coleridge's work as a whole — particularly the
"Essay on Method" — to support a reading of his culminating achievement in terms of an effort to harmonize all knowledges. Hardy's insight
into his stress on the role of *relatedness* is perhaps his major contribution to an understanding of the thought: Coleridge's view of knowledge,
he argues, differs from most conventional versions once one attends to the
inter-relatednesses in it, which result in a process of constant mutual modifications. An acute reader needs to develop a correspondingly gymnastic

---

[4] *Op Max*, ccxxxvii.

[5] Dictation played a part in the production of texts for the 1809 *Friend* and for
Biographia Literaria, of course. But in these cases there is more evidence of the author's
having carefully approved the text produced by his amanuenses.

ability, therefore, an ability to attend at one and the same time to several facets of any one of his statements, while keeping the whole in play.

If we accept the persuasive thesis in Luke Wright's essay, where it is argued that "Fragment 3," "On the Divine Ideas," should be regarded as the first, and that when in "Fragment 1" reference is made to preceding chapters it is in fact that fragment that is being referred to, the likely ordering of the subsequent work in Coleridge's mind ("Fragment 4" being set to one side) becomes clearer. Wright's thesis, as will be recalled, is that if one reads fragments "1," "2," and "3" in the order "3," "1," "2" they make sense as an extended treatise, setting out a view of religion over which God presides as Absolute Will — again a persuasive argument.

Certain difficulties against taking the view that these fragments, in this order, actually constitute Coleridge's *magnum opus*, remain, nevertheless. Most notably, whereas the successive chapters in "Fragment 1" were each firmly numbered, those in "Fragment 2" were left unnumbered — even though each was given a title that suggests the place they might have occupied in the final series. It would be strange if, having reached an ordering clear enough for him to give each chapter a descriptive title, he should have shrunk from committing himself to a final numbering — unless he envisaged that these chapters, with their subjects, might still need to be enrolled in a different arrangement. It is hard, in other words, to interpret the absence of numbers from these chapters as signs of anything other than a lack of certainty concerning his final organization.

It seems likely, therefore, that even as he constructed the pages to be found in "Fragment 2" his conception of the overall shape of what he was doing was still in a process of development. If this was so it becomes more appropriate to see the fragments before us less as the remains of Coleridge's *magnum opus* than as constituents to the *Opus Maximum* that in one way or another he was endeavoring to fashion out of those remains. If so, it means that the fine ordering he had managed to impose on his materials so far was nevertheless giving place by now to a less fully ordered body of work — which might be less immediately satisfactory but which would more fully reflect the full range of his thinking in these years.

Such a reading is encouraged if one reads the fragments separately, in terms of the concerns that dominate them. The key to the development seems to me to lie in the word that Luke Wright uses to characterize the philosophy that Coleridge had roughed out in the main fragments: the word "vitalism." It directs us, I believe, to the philosophical position that he had been working towards earlier, during the time of his intimacy with the Wordsworths, and which had been based on the idea of the "one Life." Even at that time he was still anxious to safeguard himself from charges of pantheism, but he seems to have believed that the distinctive quality of Wordsworth's devotion to nature fell short of such a position — that his sense of "something far more deeply interfused" was compatible with a Christian view of the world. In the later years when he worked towards his "Assertion of Christianity" he wanted to retain this insight as part of his religious attitude, I would argue, though it meant that he still felt a constant need to defend himself against possible charges of heresy.

Other essays in the present volume offer profitable ways of approaching what Coleridge left in the remainder of these manuscripts (ably introduced by the editor in his opening essay). Both Murray Evans and James Vigus are attracted by the possibilities of looking at them in terms of the rhetorical questions they raise — Evans being particularly drawn to Coleridge's fondness for the forms of "transition" and "repetition," while Vigus shows how his natural tendency to draw on his reading of literary classics remains almost as active in these manuscripts as in earlier works.

A general theme that runs through all the essays is that of Coleridge's feeling for interconnectedness. This is particularly true of Graham Davidson's piece, which is notable not simply for its firm grasp of Coleridge's central philosophical and theological concerns but for his awareness of the ways in which they were as integral to his everyday life as to his writings. The man who could toil at his *magnum opus* was also the poet who could write pieces such as "Youth and Age" or "Work without Hope," where precisely the same concerns provide the dynamism for what is being expressed in a more succinct poetic form. Scott Masson's essay, similarly, is alive to the prophetic content of these passages, arguing for Coleridge's recognition of the crucial flaw in the discussions by contemporaries who failed to recognize the significance created through the rational power of their own arguments. Such thinkers tended not to perceive their crucial mistake in supposing that their own Reason must be subject similarly to the external influences to which they were drawing attention and could not therefore possess any self-originating quality of its own. His implication is that some of the horrors initiated in the aftermath of writings by men as Comte, Marx, and Nietzsche might have been avoided if Coleridge's arguments had received more acknowledgment in their time.

Masson's essay thus places the basic thought in the fragments at a pivotal point in the development of early Romantic thought. Jeff Barbeau's piece, "Science and the Depersonalization of the Divine," looks back, in complement, to their previous context, that of the Enlightenment and the fashion for Natural Religion in the eighteenth century. Coleridge's concern, he argues, was to establish a crucial distinction: while continuing to support the tracing of the natural in the Divine as a laudable enterprise — which his own early writings had indeed often fostered — he saw any attempt to *prove* the existence of the Divine by invoking demonstrations from nature as essentially mistaken. Since the days of his early writing and speculations the disappointments and failures of his own personal life had led him to an opposite belief: that the relation of the Divine to the human must ultimately be different, involving human beings in necessary acknowledgment of their sin and need for redemption.

This growing conviction, and Coleridge's investigation — perhaps as a consequence — into the nature of the human self and its development, were to provide the most original elements in the thinking evidenced in the *Opus Maximum* documents. Alan Gregory's essay, in particular, conveys something of the insight shown in "Fragment 2" by his tracing of the sense of self as it emerges from the child's initial inability to distinguish its own from its mother's body, and the subsequent process by which, in over-emphasizing the necessary difference, the adult loses the ability to respect the qualities of other human selves.

The remaining essays in the volume explore further the thinking to be associated with such central insights, extending into other spheres. Douglas Hedley and Karen McLean offer varying explorations into the role of Neoplatonism in Coleridge's thought: McLean extends the argument concerning self and its alienation by giving special attention to the role of alterity in Plotinus' philosophy, while Hedley argues that his Neoplatonic strain needs to be distinguished carefully from pantheism, since in the writings of the Neoplatonist philosophers the element of personality in the Divine is always afforded a prominence that the pantheists cannot concede.

Nicholas Reid, finally, tries to tease out the relation of the natural to the Divine as it participates in the idea of the Logos that was one of Coleridge's most central themes. In the Logos, it can be argued, the natural, the personal, and the Divine finally come together in a manner that respects the essential qualities of each.

The various contributions to the present volume can be said to continue the work of Coleridge in his *Opus Maximum* manuscripts in a way that Green could not: instead of simply endeavoring to expound a body of doctrine that was thought to have been incompletely rendered in

Coleridge's writings, they are trying rather to engage further with the issues that engaged him — and in something of the same spirit. As in doing so they illuminate further the problems that engaged him, the fragments, supplemented by their essays, become in their own right a further *opus maximum*, in which Coleridge and his successors can be seen joining together in a series, traced in these volumes, of investigations to which might be applied his favorite classical tag, "hoc opus, hic labor est."[6]

The problem of the relation between the two enterprises to be traced in these manuscripts persists, nevertheless, bearing some relevance to one that I found when I first read the preface to the original draft version in the original form in which Thomas McFarland submitted it for publication. At that stage the "Prolegomena" ran to 660 pages of generously typed script as opposed to the two hundred pages of print that survived into the published version. It seemed to me that there was a difficulty for the general reader in this "Prolegomena" as a whole, which arose from an ambiguity involved in the concept of the projected volume itself: that is, the editor's only partial acceptance of the fact that the *magnum opus* was not to be identified with the *Opus Maximum*. The most prominent idea in the original "Prolegomena" was associated with the roots of the idea of the *magnum opus* in Western culture, Coleridge's fascination with it as a concept, and his desire to complete one of his own. Yet to an intelligent reader of the texts themselves it soon becomes clear that what is presented here — as McFarland himself recognizes and states in various places — is not his *magnum opus* but a series of manuscripts associated with that dream. The problem to my mind was that by concentrating so heavily on the traditional concept the ultimate achievement of McFarland's massive scholarship was to give Coleridge's actual writing in this edition a quality of inevitable anti-climax, since if I understood his attitude correctly, he had come to believe that the *Opus Maximum* might be thought of as the "greatest work" that Coleridge found himself able to achieve towards a whole, but not as the "Great Work" he was earlier hoping for. I thought that a better solution might be for McFarland to produce a separate book devoted to the idea of the *magnum opus* and Coleridge's place in its history, and to devote this volume to the actual material, the manuscripts themselves, together with the history of their transmission and the problems associated with them. In this way, I thought, McFarland's fine feat of scholarship would receive its

---

[6] "This is the task, this the labour" (Virgil, *Aeneid*, vi, 126).

recognition without danger of his presentation of the *Opus Maximum* manuscripts losing its effect.

In the event this suggestion did not find favor. Instead, a heavily pruned version of the "Prolegomena" was commissioned. I gather that the person who was responsible for this new version was a fresh editor,[7] who deserves considerable credit for managing to produce a version from which an immense amount of material that was interesting but not very relevant to the immediate questions had been cut away. Meanwhile, however, the larger problem still survives — though I should immediately go on to say that in other respects McFarland has always shown himself thoroughly alive to the issues involved, which is not surprising, since one of his most important books was a series of studies entitled *Romanticism and the Forms of Ruin*,[8] in which a constant theme was the difficulty that Romantic writers had in achieving great and fully satisfying wholes, the fragment thus becoming the most characteristic Romantic form. What we have in this volume are of course labeled, precisely, as "Fragments"; but I think that the treatment as a whole has still allowed some of the ambiguities to remain unresolved.

Insofar as these ambiguities can be tackled in a volume such as the present one, Jeff Barbeau's initial essay on Coleridge's "Quest for System" offers some excellent leads, returning constantly to the question, how far can what Coleridge left in his writings, whatever the fragmentariness of its forms, still be thought to amount to a "great work" in its own right? McFarland, to whom he naturally turns, has always been a strong contender for the unity of Coleridge's thought: over and again he has stressed the ways in which his various statements link with each other across time. This is a valuable service; even if recent scholarship, notably that of Seamus Perry,[9] has come to dwell equally on his failures of unity, and how his thought sometimes developed in ways that makes it hard not to trace contradictions. In particular, as McFarland shows, he is drawn to the idea of duality, and indeed of polarity, and at times these dominate his thought. He is also clearly anxious to establish a Trinitarianism of thought, which encourages him to think in terms of triads, sometimes making a threefold pattern of thesis, antithesis, and synthesis like that

[7] Allison May, a history Ph.D. and free-lance copyeditor in Toronto.

[8] Thomas McFarland, *Romanticism and the Forms of Ruin: Wordsworth, Coleridge, and Modalities of Fragmentation* (Princeton: Princeton University Press, 1981).

[9] Seamus Perry, *Coleridge and the Uses of Division*, Oxford English Monographs (Oxford: Clarendon Press, 1999).

associated with Hegel. Yet even this does not seem to be enough, for we also find him thinking in terms of a tetractys, or fourfold design, which he traces to Richard Baxter; and in the end he is even drawn to a kind of fivefold thought, so that we find him writing of the Divine "Pentad."

There are other cases of this kind, where an apparent unity of thought masks apparent contradictions; and this feature also embraces his personal career. One of the major points in the fragments, as elsewhere in Coleridge's work, is the very high valuation given to the Will in human beings, which is seen as crucial in establishing our moral responsibility; yet as McFarland also emphases, he was also painfully aware of his own deficiencies in this very respect, so that a friend such as Southey was able to speak of his "disease of the volition" and Wordsworth to assert that he had "no voluntary power of mind whatsoever."[10] His awareness of failings in this regard led to extraordinary shifts of mood and to a deep sympathy with St. Paul's confession of inability to perform the good that he wished to achieve. That awareness also preserved him, however, from falling into the trap of over-optimism about the Will that seems to have lain in wait for some German thinkers later in the century and beyond.

One contradiction of the kind that I have mentioned deserves particular notice. As has already been pointed out, some of the most interesting and original writing Coleridge ever produced is in "Fragment 2," where he discusses the relationship between mother and child and the creation of personal identity for a child after its experiences of primal unity with its mother while at her breast. In this case one is forced to ask how far what Coleridge has to say may be drawing on his own experiences, whether as child, as parent, or simply as acute observer. Some psychoanalytic writers have drawn attention to what they see as a coldness in his relationship with his own mother. It should also be said, however, that he himself spoke of having been his "mother's darling"[11] and of how his treatment by brothers led him to sit constantly by her side and read excessively.[12] What may or may not have happened during the early days of his life we cannot fully judge, of course, but I would personally be inclined to ascribe much that went wrong with his subsequent life (if a cause is to be sought at all) less to a coldness on his mother's part than

[10] *The New Letters of Robert Southey*, ed. Kenneth Curry (New York: Columbia University Press, 1965), II, 117–18; *The Letters of William and Dorothy Wordsworth: The Early Years, 1787-1805*, ed. Ernest de Selincourt (Oxford: Clarendon Press, 1967), 352; cf. *Op Max*, cxxii.
[11] *CL*, I, 347.
[12] *CN*, V, 6675.

to the effects of her decision to send him off to a London boarding school immediately after the sudden death of his father.

Just as we cannot fully know the intimate details of his earliest childhood we cannot be sure whether what he has to say about the mother-child relationship in this fragment reflects observations of his own family. His reminiscence of a child feeling that it has no identity unless it can touch its mother does sound as if it might have come from recollection of a cry from one of his own offspring — or another's; though I would also join McFarland in detecting a possible linkage with the passage in Wordsworth's "Immortality Ode" on the child

> Fretted by sallies of his mother's kisses
> With light upon him from his father's eyes...[13]

This leads me to develop another point made by McFarland: the extent to which Coleridge's study of relationship involves his sense of the degree to which Christian thought must necessarily reflect a sense of a Father-Son relationship within the very Godhead. A point that McFarland does not make, however, is that just as Coleridge's elevation of the human Will must always have been undermined by awareness of his own failings, so any reflections on the father-son relationship would be likely to reflect some consciousness of the way in which his relation to his son Hartley, with an evident hope that he might carry on his father's thought, had been an almost total disappointment. Few events in his life are more heart-rending than his growing realization that he could not depend on his own son to do anything that might help to fulfill any of his dreams for him (and so, vicariously, dreams of his own). Here again, his disappointment was likely to be undercut by his awareness that he could not look to his own experience to support it, for while he had reveled for a time in Hartley's election to a fellowship at Oriel College, Oxford, his own attempts to pass on his own knowledge and intellectual aspiration to his son had been unsuccessful: Hartley had been expelled from his fellowship for misconduct and had continued to be a disappointment at the personal level. In other words, awareness of his own deficiencies as far as the Will was concerned seemed to be reinforced by the need to recognize even more evident shortcomings on the part of his own son. The gap between that which he valued so centrally in his own doctrine of the Divine and his own human experience was in other words made more

---

[13] William Wordsworth, "Ode: Intimations of Immortality from Recollections of Early Childhood" (lines 88–89).

abysmal by the failure of one of his own most intimate relationships. When it is remembered how his philosophy of love had in earlier life been undermined by the failure of his love for Sara Hutchinson to provide an adequate substitution for the deficiencies of his own marriage, his growing tendency to abandon his earlier delight in creativity, whether human or Divine, in favor of an emphasis on the staggering incompatibility between the moral perfection of God and the inadequacy of human creatures becomes more readily comprehensible.

The consideration of such questions helps to bring out one of the most revealing features of Coleridge's whole enterprise: his readiness to indulge in the most expansive of speculations while at the same time acknowledging the extent of his own personal vulnerability. This contrary nature of his becomes steadily more evident as one comes to see the full extent of what is on offer across the range of his letters, notebooks, and published works. And one of its most significant aspects is to be found in the very tension that we have been exploring: the implicit contrast between his systematizing capabilities and the sense he can so successfully convey of an ongoing, still incomplete development. In this double sense of Coleridge we find most fully explained the struggle in his mind between *magnum opus* and *Opus Maximum*. It is in such areas of the *Collected Works* and his other collected writings, also, that future work on Coleridge's great project may be expected to concentrate and that scholars and critics alike may hope to look for particular shafts of new illumination: here, if anywhere, it will be proper to conclude, "hoc opus, hic labor est."

SELECT BIBLIOGRAPHY

The following is a select list of works that devote substantial attention to either Coleridge's magnum opus or the manuscripts that form the published <u>Opus Maximum</u>:

BARTH, J. Robert. *Coleridge and Christian Doctrine*. Cambridge: Harvard University Press, 1969.

BATE, Walter Jackson. *Coleridge*. Masters of World Literature Series. London: Weidenfeld and Nicolson, 1968.

BOULGER, James D. *Coleridge as Religious Thinker*. Yale Studies in English, 151. New Haven: Yale University Press, 1961.

CHINOL, Elio. *Il pensiero di S. T. Coleridge*. Collezione di varia critica, 10. Venezia: N. Pozza, 1953.

EVANS, Murray J. *Coleridge's Sublime Rhetoric in the <u>Opus Maximum</u>*. Forthcoming.

—. "The Divine Ideas in Coleridge's *Opus Maximum*." *The Coleridge Bulletin* n.s. 22 (2003): 39–47.

GREEN, Joseph Henry. *Spiritual Philosophy: Founded on the Teaching of the Late Samuel Taylor Coleridge*. London: Macmillan, 1865.

HAPPEL, Stephen. *Coleridge's Religious Imagination*. 3 vols. Salzburg Studies in English Literature. Salzburg: Institut für Anglistik und Americanistik, 1983.

Hardy, Daniel W. "Coleridge on the Trinity." *Anglican Theological Review* 69 (1987): 145–55.

LEVERE, Trevor H. *Poetry Realized in Nature: Samuel Taylor Coleridge and Early Nineteenth-Century Science*. Cambridge: Cambridge University Press, 1981.

LOCKRIDGE, Laurence S. *Coleridge the Moralist*. Ithaca: Cornell University Press, 1977.

MCFARLAND, Thomas. *Coleridge and the Pantheist Tradition*. Oxford: Clarendon Press, 1969.

—. "Prolegomena" to *Opus Maximum*. Vol. 15 of *The Collected Works of Samuel Taylor Coleridge*. Bollingen Series 75. Princeton: Princeton University Press, 2002.

—. *Romanticism and the Forms of Ruin: Wordsworth, Coleridge, and Modalities of Fragmentation*. Princeton: Princeton University Press, 1981.

MUIRHEAD, John H. *Coleridge as Philosopher*. London: G. Allen & Unwin Ltd., 1930.

PERKINS, Mary Anne. *Coleridge's Philosophy: The Logos as Unifying Principle*. Oxford: Clarendon Press, 1994.

REID, Nicholas. *Coleridge, Form and Symbol*. Aldershot: Ashgate, 2006.

—. "Coleridge and Schelling: The Missing Transcendental Deduction." *Studies in Romanticism* 33 (1994): 451–79.

RULE, Philip C. *Coleridge and Newman: The Centrality of Conscience*. Studies in Religion and Literature, 8. New York: Fordham University Press, 2004.

SHAFFER, Elinor. "Iago's Malignity Motivated: Coleridge's Unpublished 'Opus Magnum.'" *Shakespeare Quarterly* 19 (1968): 195–203.

SNYDER, Alice D. *Coleridge on Logic and Learning.* New Haven: Yale University Press, 1929.

TAYLOR, Anya. *Coleridge's Defense of the Human.* Columbus: Ohio State University Press, 1986.

TOMLINSON, Richard S. "An Edition of Coleridge's Opus Maximum." D.Phil. thesis, University of Oxford, 2004.

CONTRIBUTORS

Jeffrey W. Barbeau is Assistant Professor of Theology at Oral Roberts University, Tulsa, Oklahoma. His research interests include historical theology, contemporary hermeneutics, and systematic theology. He has recently completed a monograph on Coleridge's late notebook commentaries on the Bible. Currently, he is working on projects related to John Wesley and the reception of Methodism in the nineteenth century.

John Beer is Emeritus Professor of English Literature at the University of Cambridge and Fellow of Peterhouse. His research interests include English Romantic literature and the history of thought. Recent publications include the Princeton *Collected Works* edition of Coleridge's *Aids to Reflection* (1993); *Romantic Consciousness: Blake to Mary Shelley* (Palgrave, 2003); *Post-Romantic Consciousness: Dickens to Plath* (Palgrave, 2003); and *William Blake: A Literary Life* (Palgrave, 2005). He is currently working on the intellectual and literary implications of events at the turn of the eighteenth into the nineteenth century.

Graham Davidson is a freelance writer who works and lives in Bristol, England. He is the editor of *The Coleridge Bulletin* and Secretary to the Coleridge Summer Conference. His research interests include the study of non-conformist writings in England and their influence on Romantic poetry. His publications include a book on Coleridge's intellectual development, *Coleridge's Career* (Macmillan, 1990). He is currently working on a biography of the last fifteen years of Coleridge's life.

Murray J. Evans is a Professor in the English Department at the University of Winnipeg, Canada. His research interests include medieval literature and manuscript studies, Coleridge, and sublime studies. His recent publications include *Rereading Middle English Romance: Physical Layout, Decoration and the Rhetoric of Composite Structure in Some Late Medieval Manuscript Collections* (McGill-Queen's, 1995), and essays on Piers Plowman and the sublime, and on Coleridge's *Opus Maximum*. He is currently revising a completed book manuscript on the *Opus Maximum*.

Alan P. R. Gregory is Associate Dean and Associate Professor of Church History at the Episcopal Theological Seminary of the Southwest, Austin, Texas. His research interests include seventeenth and eighteenth-century theology and mysticism, Romanticism, literature and theology, and critical theory. His recent publications include *Coleridge and the Conservative Imagination* (Mercer University Press, 2003) and the chapter "Religion and Philosophy" for *Romanticism: An Oxford Guide* (Oxford, 2005). He is currently working on *Quenching Hell*, a study of the eighteenth-century mystic William Law.

Daniel W. Hardy is a Senior Member of the Faculty of Divinity and a Life Member of Clare Hall in the University of Cambridge. His research interests include contemporary theology, the history of modern theology, and ecclesiology. His recent publications include *God's Ways with the World* (T & T Clark, 1996), *Finding the Church* (SCM Press, 2001) and *Living in Praise* (with David Ford, DLT/Baker Books, 2005). He is currently working on a book on the theory and practice of the church.

Douglas Hedley is University Senior Lecturer in the Faculty of Divinity and Fellow of Clare College, University of Cambridge. His research interests include contemporary philosophy of religion, history of philosophy, and systematic theology. His recent publications include *Coleridge, Philosophy and Religion: Aids to Reflection and the Mirror of the Spirit* (Cambridge, 2000) and, as co-editor, *Deconstructing Radical Orthodoxy: Postmodern Theology, Rhetoric and Truth* (Ashgate, 2005). He is currently working on a monograph on Imagination.

Scott Masson is Assistant Professor of English Literature at Tyndale University College, Toronto, Canada. His research interests include the fields of Romanticism and hermeneutics. His recent publications include *Romanticism, Hermeneutics and the Crisis of the Human Sciences* (Ashgate, 2004) and a chapter in a book he also co-edited, *Silence, Sublimity and Suppression in the Romantic Period* (Edwin Mellen, 2002). His entry on "Romanticism" will appear in the forthcoming *Oxford Handbook to English Literature and Theology* (Oxford University Press, 2006).

Karen McLean is a Teaching Fellow in the Department of English at the University of Otago, New Zealand. Her research interests include early, classical, and late Greek philosophy; recent developments in cosmology; and Romantic theories of perception. She has recently completed her doctoral thesis, *Samuel Taylor Coleridge's use of Platonic and Neoplatonic theories of evil and creation*, and is currently working within the nexus between Coleridge, Neoplatonism, and modern cosmological accounts of the Big Bang.

Nicholas Reid was a senior lecturer at the University of Otago in New Zealand, where he taught in the English Department for twelve years before returning to Australia. His interests range from Coleridgean philosophy to contemporary theory of mind, and he also takes an interest in a range of poets from the eighteenth century to the present. His most recent publication is *Coleridge, Form and Symbol* (Ashgate, 2006), a volume in which he attempts to give a positive theoretical account of the relation between form and content. He is currently building a house.

James Vigus is a doctoral student at Clare College, University of Cambridge, writing a thesis entitled *Platonic Coleridge*. He is co-editor of a forthcoming collection of essays, *Coleridge's Afterlives: 1834–1934*. Other research interests include the British reception of German writing in the early nineteenth century, with particular focus on Henry Crabb Robinson.

Luke S. H. Wright is a lecturer at the University of Winchester, England. His research interests, other than Coleridge, include the history of the Tory party and its influence on the Church of England from Queen Anne through Gladstone. Wright's recent papers have considered the relationship between politics and theology in Jeremy Taylor, Bolingbroke, and Warburton. He is currently working on the influence of Jeremy Taylor's early writings on the polity and theology of the Church of England.

INDEX

abduction, 45, 50-52

absurdity, 75-76, 123

Addinall, Peter, 166-67n, 169n

Aders, Mrs. Charles, 136n, 138-40

aesthetic(s), 37, 75, 106, 147, 150, 273, 279

affection(s), 46-47

agnosticism, 33

Agrippa, Heinrich Cornelius, 67

Akenside, Mark, 272n

allegory, 91-92, 181, 245, 274

Allsop, Thomas, 11

alterity, 24, 92, 207, 227, 250-52, 256-60, 274, 287. *See also* otherness; Trinity

ambition, 110, 192

Anderson, Wayne C., 105n

animals/beasts: consciousness of, 94, 115-16, 191; design of, 165, 168, 169n, 172; and life, 46-47; love of, 39; and nature, 16; and personality, 69; Reason distinguishes humans from, 122-24, 126-28, 130, 154, 155n, 203; worship of, 179

anthropology, 8, 13, 34, 55, 63, 145-62, 191-92, 194, 208. *See also* human(s)

apologetics. *See* Christianity

apophatic theology, 64-65, 112

apostasy, 49-50

appetite: of child, 133-35; and conscience, 128; and instinct, 46-47, 81; of public readers, 14, 102, 104; and will, 121, 124, 192

Aquinas, Thomas, 4, 14, 223, 225

Arianism, 113

Aristophanes, 82, 107

Aristotle, 10, 20, 82, 102-3, 226

Armstrong, A. Hilary, 224, 237-38, 240n, 241-42, 253

art(s), 37, 41, 44, 46, 75, 94, 150, 158n

Ashton, Rosemary, 180n

associationism, 156, 189

atheism: 154, 198; and Cudworth, 4; humanistic, 145; and pantheism, 111, 176-77, 179, 181-82, 184; and the self, 129-30; and natural theology, 163, 165-71, 205n

atonement, 64n, 252

audience, 99-104, 110n, 118

Augustine, 202-8, 215-16, 223, 234, 248n, 257, 265-66

Baader, Franz von, 221

Bacon, Francis, 100

Bacon, Roger, 10

Barbeau, Jeffrey W., 170n, 234-35, 253n, 269n, 286, 289

Barker, Juliet, 97n

Barth, J. Robert, 79n, 103n, 206n, 258n

Barth, Karl, 48

Bate, Walter Jackson, 1, 179n

Baxter, Richard, 290

beauty, 224

Beer, John, 141n, 143, 184n

Beierwaltes, W., 226n

Benz, Ernst, 221n

Berkeley, George, 255, 258-59n

Bhagavad-Gita, 111-12

Bible: apologetic use, 154, 167; and authority, 99, 103, 108, 118, 189; commentary on by Coleridge, 12, 48-50; conception of sin, 171; criticism of, 72, 155, 256, 267-68, 280; and evil, 136; and history, 17, 65,

143; marriage of, 181; and method, 45-48; and nature, 163; opium addiction, 40, 181, 235, 282; plagiarism, 3, 148, 153, 281; plan to form a school, 5; and poetry/as poet, 7, 97-119, 282-83; preaching, 4-5, 7; relationship with Ann Gillman, 137-40, 142; relationship with his children, 291; relationship with his parents, 179-80, 187, 290; relationship with Mrs. Charles Aders, 137-40; and system, 286, 292; theater and, 9; and Unitarianism, 4, 170, 178-85, 256, 261; writing habits of, 282, 284; Works: *Aids to Reflection*, 12-14, 23, 26, 30, 51, 54, 153, 163, 169, 172, 174-75, 177-78, 182, 185, 235, 238n, 265n, 270n, 283n; *Biographia Literaria*, 3, 9, 12-13, 23-24, 26, 30, 67, 74-75, 98, 102, 106, 110, 113, 118, 127, 128n, 134, 148-55, 158, 160, 162, 198n, 199n, 216, 227, 229, 235, 256, 261n, 265n, 271, 278, 284n; *Christabel*, 7; *Confessions of an Inquiring Spirit*, 13, 16n, 17, 30, 58-59, 103, 157, 268-69, 280; *On the Constitution of the Church and State*, 12, 17-18, 25, 37, 51, 54, 59, 67, 100, 271n, 280; "The Day Dream," 133n; "Dejection: An Ode," 259; "Duty, Surviving Self-love," 139-42; "Encyclopaedia Metropolitana," 37, 41-43, 284; *Essay on Faith*, 26n, 27, 79, 84, 91, 129n, 153, 170, 193n, 252n; "Formula Fidei," 262n; *The Friend*, 13, 27, 27n, 30, 67, 83-84, 97-107, 110, 117-18, 125n, 228, 262n, 282, 284n; "Frost at Midnight," 258n, 282; "The Garden of Boccaccio," 142; *Kubla Khan*, 282; *Lectures on the History of Philosophy*, 3, 12, 17, 23, 26, 214, 265, 267; *A Lay Sermon*, 187-88; *Lay Sermons*, 13, 37, 59,

67, 112n; *Logic*, 8, 8n, 11-12, 14, 19-21, 23, 29, 54, 256
magnum opus: as "Assertion of Religion," 11, 11n, 27, 286; attempts to edit and publish, 27-32; and biblical commentary, 12, 15, 17, 24; dating/ordering manuscript remains of for *Opus Maximum*, 41, 53-73, 78n, 284-85; as defense of Christianity, 1, 13, 16, 154; as "On the Divine Ideas," 29, 54, 56, 62; fields of study towards, 5-6; fragmentary state, 1-2, 12, 28, 40, 145, 147, 149, 279, 288; and history of philosophy, 9, 21-23, 72n; as "Logosophia," 8, 41, 182, 255-80; names, alternate, 1, 11; not the *Opus Maximum*, 288; parallels with *Paradise Lost*, 114; planned, 1-32, 40-43; and religion, 12, 98; and system, 2-3, 18-19, 27-29, 54-55, 61, 98, 119, 230, 255, 284. *See also* McFarland, Thomas
"To Mary S. Pridham," 139n; "The Pang More Sharp than All," 133n; "Phantom," 141n; "On the Prometheus of Aeschylus," 123, 136; *Remorse*, 107; *Rime of the Ancient Mariner*, 33, 38-40, 47-48, 282; *Sibylline Leaves*, 9; *The Statesman's Manual*, 27n, 173, 260n, 271n, 273-74; *Table Talk*, 230; *Theory of Life*, 26; "Travels in Body and Mind," 14, 21; "The Two Founts," 138; *Watchman*, 4-6, 4n, 67; "Work without Hope," 137-38, 141, 286; "Youth and Age," 136-37, 140, 142-44, 286; *Zapolya*, 9
Coleridge, Sara (*daughter*), 53-54, 59
Collected Coleridge, Princeton edition, 30-31, 54, 73, 119, 170, 281, 283. *See also* McFarland, Thomas; Halmi, Nicholas
Collins, Randall, 37n
commercialism, 104

life, theory of, 15, 17, 22, 69, 136-37, 142-43, 286. *See also* Coleridge, Samuel Taylor, Works
light: 83, 108, 200; lucific act, 48-51, 249. *See also* revelation
Liverpool, Lord, 13
Locke, John, 5, 7, 10, 20, 45, 159, 189
logic: *a priori*, 98, 118; and being, 253; and Christianity, 155, 161; and distinctions, 266; and human nature, 230; and language, 107; and nature, 172; Pythagorean, 85-86; study of connected to *magnum opus*, 10, 24, 41-42; and Trinitarian language, 190, 200, 261, 276; and truth, 122. *See also* Coleridge, Samuel Taylor, Works, *Logic*
Logos: and Cabbala, 218-19; as central theme in Coleridge's writings, 43, 287; and moral conscience, 170; as "Idea of Man," 271; incarnation of in Christ, 17; as name of God, 269-70; and planned *magnum opus*, 8-9, 24, 41, 182, 255-80; and Christian Neoplatonism, 214, 221, 231; and the unreasonable, 177n; relation of all things to, 48, 50-52; and Reason as a revelation, 155, 199, 251; and Son, 252; as wisdom, 41. *See also* Christ (Jesus); Coleridge, Samuel Taylor, Works, *magnum opus*
love: between the sexes, 272-73n; of all creatures, 38-40, 46-48, 129; and faith, 196; and family, 130n, 132-44, 197-98; and God's unity, 204, 207-8, 272-73, 275; and hunger, 134-35, 197; and lust, 129; and neighbor, 194; Coleridge's philosophy of, 291-92; of self, 63, 121, 127, 129-30, 141-42, 245, 262-63n; as true center, 51-52. *See also* mother and child; marriage; self
Lubac, Henri de, 145n
lusts, 129, 106, 112, 118. *See also* love

Luther, Martin, 82, 107, 127n, 155, 158, 171, 266, 269, 271

magnetism, 37, 42
marriage: 127, 130-31, 131n, 135; and poetry, 139
Marsh, James, 37
Marx, Karl, 145, 286
Masson, Scott, 151n, 286
Mattenklott, Gert, 217n
May, Allison, 289n
May, John, 9
Mays, J. C. C., 7n, 9n, 283
McFarland, Thomas: and Coleridge's anxiety, 101n; and editing of *Opus Maximum*, 30-31, 54-59, 67n, 73-74, 109, 110n, 283; on "I" and "Thou" as "philosophical fulcrum," 159; interpretation of *magnum opus/Opus Maximum*, 4, 6n, 18n, 25-27, 74, 175n, 255, 283-84, 290-91; and interpretation of Neoplatonism, 213-14, 216, 220-24, 230-31; and interpretation of Romanticism, 121n; and unity of Coleridge's thought, 28n, 97, 289; *Coleridge and the Pantheist Tradition*, 89n, 148n, 189n, 213-14; "Prolegomena" of *Opus Maximum*, 74n, 145, 147, 161, 288-89
McKusick, James C., 263n
McLean, Karen, 236n, 239n, 243n, 258n, 261n, 287
memory, 69, 208
Mendelssohn, Moses, 213
metaphor, 85, 108n, 177
metaphysics: Coleridge's turn to, 7, 53-54, 97, 182; debates over, 100; and Logos, 267, 279; and mechanistic philosophy, 60; of mind, 229-30; plans history of, 20; Plotinus and, 224; and reading public, 102; Spinoza and, 218-19
method: 131; Greek meaning, 46; scientific, 56, 103. *See also* rhetoric

STUDIES IN PHILOSOPHICAL THEOLOGY, 33

Series editors:
Lieven Boeve (Leuven), Willem B. Drees (Leiden), Douglas Hedley (Cambridge)
Advisory Board: H.J. Adriaanse (Leiden), V. Brümmer (Utrecht), P. Byrne
(London), I.U. Dalferth (Zürich), J. Greisch (Paris), E. Herrmann (Uppsala),
M.M. Olivetti (Rome), C. Schwöbel (Heidelberg), J. Soskice (Cambridge),
C. Stenqvist (Lund).

Editorial Profile:
Philosophical theology is the study of philosophical problems which arise in
reflection upon religion, religious beliefs and theological doctrines.

1   H. de Vries, *Theologie im Pianissimo & zwischen Rationalität und Dekon-
    struktion*, Kampen, 1989
2   S. Breton, *La pensée du rien*, Kampen, 1992
3   Ch. Schwöbel, *God: Action and Revelation*, Kampen, 1992
4   V. Brümmer (ed.), *Interpreting the Universe as Creation*, Kampen, 1991
5   L.J. van den Brom, *Divine Presence in the World*, Kampen, 1993
6   M. Sarot, *God, Passibility and Corporeality*, Kampen, 1992
7   G. van den Brink, *Almighty God*, Kampen 1993
8   P.-C. Lai, *Towards a Trinitarian Theology of Religions: A Study of Paul
    Tillich's Thought*, Kampen, 1994
9   L. Velecky, *Aquinas' Five Arguments in the* Summa Theologiae *Ia 2, 3*, Kampen,
    1994
10 W. Dupré, *Patterns in Meaning. Reflections on Meaning and Truth in Cultural
    Reality, Religious Traditions, and Dialogical Encounters*, Kampen, 1994
11 P.T. Erne, *Lebenskunst. Aneignung ästhetischer Erfahrung*, Kampen, 1994
12 U. Perone, *Trotz/dem Subjekt*, Leuven, 1998
13 H.J. Adriaanse, *Vom Christentum aus: Aufsätze und Vorträge zur Religions-
    philosophie*, Kampen, 1995
14 D.A. Pailin, *Probing the Foundations: A Study in Theistic Reconstruction*,
    Kampen, 1994
15 M. Potepa, *Schleiermachers hermeneutische Dialektik*, Kampen, 1996
16 E. Herrmann, *Scientific Theory and Religious Belief. An Essay on the
    Rationality of Views of Life*, Kampen, 1995
17 V. Brümmer & M. Sarot (eds.), *Happiness, Well-Being and the Meaning of Life.
    A Dialogue of Social Science and Religion*, Kampen, 1996
18 T.L. Hettema, *Reading for Good. Narrative Theology and Ethics in the Joseph
    Story from the Perspective of Ricoeur's Hermeneutics*, Kampen, 1996
19 H. Düringer, *Universale Vernunft und partikularer Glaube. Eine theologische
    Auswertung des Werkes von Jürgen Habermas*, Leuven, 1999
20 E. Dekker, *Middle Knowledge*, Leuven, 2000
21 T. Ekstrand, *Max Weber in a Theological Perspective*, Leuven, 2000
22 C. Helmer & K. De Troyer (eds.), *Truth: Interdisciplinary Dialogues in a
    Pluralist Age*, Leuven, 2003
23 L. Boeve & L.P. Hemming (eds.), *Divinising Experience. Essays in the History
    of Religious Experience from Origen to Ricœur*, Leuven, 2004
24 P.D. Murray, *Reason, Truth and Theology in Pragmatist Perspective*, Leuven, 2004
25 S. van Erp, *The Art of Theology. Hans Urs von Balthasar's Theological Aesthet-
    ics and the Foundations of Faith*, Leuven, 2004

26 T.A. Smedes, *Chaos, Complexity, and God. Divine Action and Scientism*, Leuven, 2004
27 R. Re Manning, *Theology at the End of Culture. Paul Tillich's Theology of Culture and Art*, Leuven, 2004
28 P. Jonkers & R. Welten (eds.), *God in France. Eight Contemporary French Thinkers on God*, Leuven, 2005
29 D. Grumett, *Teilhard de Chardin: Theology, Humanity and Cosmos*, Leuven, 2005
30 I.U. Dalferth, *Becoming Present. An Inquiry into the Christian Sense of the Presence of God*, Leuven, 2006
31 P.F. Bloemendaal, *Grammars of Faith. A Critical Evaluation of D.Z. Phillips's Philosophy of Religion*, Leuven, 2006
32 J.-M. Narbonne & W.J. Hankey, *Levinas and the Greek Heritage followed by One Hundred Years of Neoplatonism in France: a Brief Philosophical History*

PRINTED ON PERMANENT PAPER • IMPRIME SUR PAPIER PERMANENT • GEDRUKT OP DUURZAAM PAPIER - ISO 9706

N.V. PEETERS S.A., WAROTSTRAAT 50, B-3020 HERENT